Today, Crac des Chevaliers is a beautiful fortress that you can visit as a tourist. If the howling wind drops for a moment, listen hard. You might just hear the ghostly echo of horses' hooves on the cobbles, and orders shouted in medieval French!

Many castles elsewhere in the world are older or bigger than Crac des Chevaliers. Modern castles are much stronger. But none has aroused more fear, anger, and envy. No wonder an Arab writer called it "a bone in the throat of the Muslims."

The castle was a stronghold of the European Christians who ruled the Holy Land for nearly two centuries. Its warrior monks divided their time between battle and prayer. Their defence of the castle is an exciting story of faith, blood, and glory.

On a windswept hill-top in Syria stands one of the world's mightiest and most amazing castles – Crac des Chevaliers. Despite earthquakes, torrential rains, and scorching heat, its 900-year old walls and beautifully carved arches still stand firm.

experience

CASTLE

written by
RICHARD PLATT

CASTLES AND KNIGHTS

CASTLES IN HISTORY

Towering high above the land around, the solid walls of castles are impressive reminders of power and wealth from the past. For castles were once the massive (and costly) stone strongholds of proud rulers, and bases for the warriors at their command.

First castles

Fortresses and protected camps have a long history – they were first built in Mesopotamia (now Iraq) more than 5,000 years ago. The most famous European castles date from the Middle Ages (roughly the 5th to the 16th centuries). From the safety of their walls, lords and monarchs controlled their lands with help from armies of knights. These horse-back warriors rode into battle dressed in iron armour. Their swords and long lances made them dangerous and frightening foes. At first knights fought out of duty. In exchange for their service on the battlefield, they received lands and homes from their more powerful masters.

Castle armies

Knights were the glittering, colourful officers of much larger armies. These also included many humbler soldiers who fought on foot. Known as infantry, they owed a debt of duty to their knight masters – just as the knights served more powerful lords. In time, though, debts of duty changed to money payments. Then gold, not promises, guaranteed a battlefield lined with armoured warriors and archers.

> "They cruelly oppressed the wretched men of the land with castle-works; and when the castles were made, they filled them with devils and evil men."
>
> *The Anglo-Saxon Chronicle, 1137*

In peacetime, castles hosted great banquets, like this one in 15th-century France. Guests judged their host's wealth by the number of dishes served and the rarity of the ingredients.

Chaotic lands

With their masters and foot-soldiers, knights fought to control a restless world. For in the Middle Ages Europe was not divided up into large, peaceful countries with neat borders as it is today. Monarchs struggled to keep hold of power in lands that were often torn apart by violent and chaotic feuds. They could rule over large regions only by making alliances with other powerful people. Each of these lords controlled a small area – and castles played a vital part in their schemes.

Built to last

Designed from the ground up for defence, castles used ingenious plans and clever features to keep attackers out. Solid foundations discouraged undermining (tunnelling into the castle). The height of the walls aimed to protect them from attackers on ladders. Their thickness helped them resist stone missiles thrown from giant catapults. The weakest points, the gates, were defended with cunning and murderous traps.

Through jousting – mock charges with lances – knights kept their fighting skills sharp. In this 13th-century illustration, the king of Sicily defeats his rival.

...astles relied on manor farms, like this one outside the ...stle walls, to provide the food they needed for the soldiers ...side. Sale of farm produce also provided income for castles.

...hat castles were for

...s strongholds, castles provided their owners with ...fe homes in unsafe times. However, they were ...uch more than houses with thick walls. The most ...portant job of a castle was to control a region – ... protect it from attack and conquest by a warlike ...eighbour. So castles were built at carefully chosen ...laces. They guarded river-crossings such as bridges ...d fords. They loomed above important roads or ...ear passes in high mountain ranges. Or they clung ... hard-to-reach (but strategic) hill-tops.

...astle supplies

...ar wasn't the only reason for a castle's ...osition, though. A castle garrison (guard-...orce) needed food and drink to survive ...ttack. So a castle site had a deep well, a

spring, or a river that provided water for the troops and their animals. Food supplies came from the farms that surrounded most castles. Cool, dark rooms within the castle walls were warehouses for surplus crops. These stores could feed the garrison in a long siege (an encircling attack that cut off supplies from outside).

Luxurious home

Though military might was a castle's main purpose, it was usually also a home – and sometimes a luxurious one. Many had grand halls where the owner might entertain important guests, with great kitchens and wine-cellars to match. Living rooms and bedrooms, heated by roaring fires and hung with tapestries, provided the castle's owner and his family with privacy that few others enjoyed.

Building a better castle

No two medieval castles are exactly alike, because ideas about warfare and defence changed all the time. The masons who constructed castles aimed to make each one better and stronger than those that had gone before. Their employers exchanged ideas for new defences, and copied the best features from their enemies' castles. Wars in distant lands introduced castle-builders to new defensive architecture. And some of the most radical ideas about castle defences came from the most distant wars of all – the crusades in the Holy Land.

Building a castle on a towering crag, like this one on the river Var in France, made it easy to defend – but almost impossible to supply with food during a siege.

Through these holes atop the walls, the castle guard dropped rocks on attackers below. European masons probably copied the idea from Muslim castles.

When England's King Edward I began building Harlech Castle in Wales in 1283, he included in it design features he had seen on castles in the Holy Land 12 years earlier.

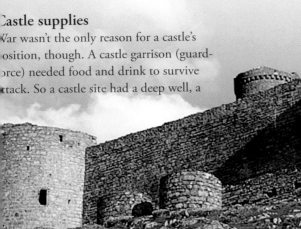

THE BATTLEGROUND

In the most destructive wars of the Middle Ages, Christians and Muslims struggled for control of the lands to the east of the Mediterranean Sea, where Lebanon, Syria, Israel, and Palestine are today. To Christians, this was the Holy Land because Jesus Christ had lived and died here. But by the 11th century much of the Holy Land was ruled by Muslims. This led the kingdoms of Europe to send knights to protect the Christian shrines they believed were threatened. The religious wars they fought were called crusades. Brutal and bloody, the crusades divided Christians and Muslims with a bitter rivalry that has never been forgotten.

AMERICA

ASIA

EUROPE

AFRICA

CYPRUS

Since the time of Jesus, Christian **pilgrims** had been visiting holy sites in Palestine. The conquest of the region by Muslim Arabs in the 7th century made these religious journeys, called pilgrimages, more difficult and dangerous.

Just 150 km (100 miles) from the coast of the Holy Land, Cyprus was in a strategic location. English king Richard I captured the island in 1191. It became a major stronghold for the crusades, and a supply base secure from Muslim attack.

Though some **crusaders** marched to the Holy Land, many travelled by sea. Once Christians captured the port of Tyre in 1124, Egyptian Muslim sailors had nowhere on the coast to get fresh water. This limited the range of their war fleet, making the Mediterranean safer for Christian shipping.

THREE FAITHS

For Jews, the land at the Mediterranean's eastern end was a homeland, but they had been persecuted and driven from it since Roman times. Christians also claimed it as their own, because it was where the stories of the Bible took place. Muslims, too, believed they had a right to Jerusalem, the place from which they believed the Prophet Muhammad rose to heaven.

THE STAR OF DAVID, SYMBOL OF THE JEWISH FAITH

A CERAMIC DECORATED WITH MUSLIM HOLY WORDS

A CRUSADER TOMBSTONE AT TYRE

pilgrims People who journey to a sacred place to pray and to show their religious faith.

crusaders Men who answered the church's call to fight in the Holy Land in return for the forgiveness of their sins.

crusader states The new Christian states, such as the Kingdom of Jerusalem, set up by the crusaders in the Holy Land.

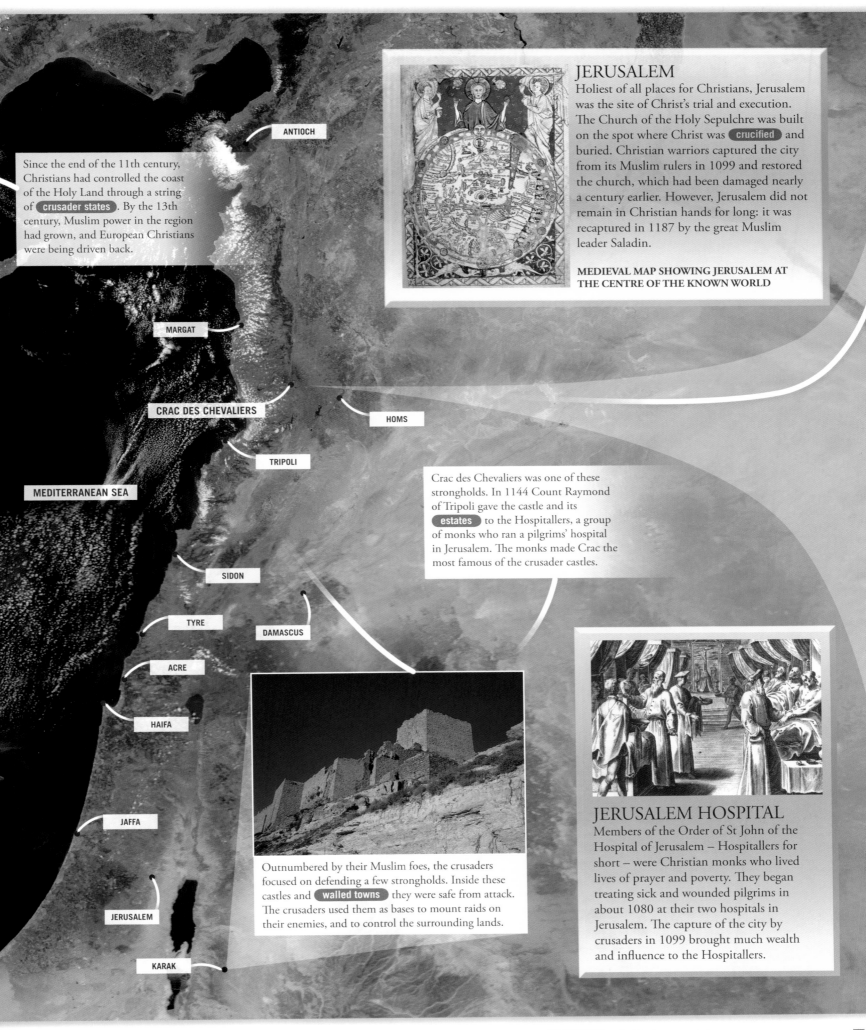

JERUSALEM

Holiest of all places for Christians, Jerusalem was the site of Christ's trial and execution. The Church of the Holy Sepulchre was built on the spot where Christ was **crucified** and buried. Christian warriors captured the city from its Muslim rulers in 1099 and restored the church, which had been damaged nearly a century earlier. However, Jerusalem did not remain in Christian hands for long: it was recaptured in 1187 by the great Muslim leader Saladin.

MEDIEVAL MAP SHOWING JERUSALEM AT THE CENTRE OF THE KNOWN WORLD

ANTIOCH

Since the end of the 11th century, Christians had controlled the coast of the Holy Land through a string of **crusader states**. By the 13th century, Muslim power in the region had grown, and European Christians were being driven back.

MARGAT

CRAC DES CHEVALIERS

HOMS

TRIPOLI

Crac des Chevaliers was one of these strongholds. In 1144 Count Raymond of Tripoli gave the castle and its **estates** to the Hospitallers, a group of monks who ran a pilgrims' hospital in Jerusalem. The monks made Crac the most famous of the crusader castles.

MEDITERRANEAN SEA

SIDON

TYRE

DAMASCUS

ACRE

HAIFA

JERUSALEM HOSPITAL

Members of the Order of St John of the Hospital of Jerusalem – Hospitallers for short – were Christian monks who lived lives of prayer and poverty. They began treating sick and wounded pilgrims in about 1080 at their two hospitals in Jerusalem. The capture of the city by crusaders in 1099 brought much wealth and influence to the Hospitallers.

JAFFA

Outnumbered by their Muslim foes, the crusaders focused on defending a few strongholds. Inside these castles and **walled towns** they were safe from attack. The crusaders used them as bases to mount raids on their enemies, and to control the surrounding lands.

JERUSALEM

KARAK

walled towns Towns that could be defended against attacking armies. Many ancient towns had defensive walls.

estates The lands that belong to a castle and which supply it with income and food.

crucified Killed by being nailed to a wooden cross. This was a common form of execution in Roman times.

7

CRAC'S CRUCIAL POSITION

In the region surrounding Crac, the Hospitallers have their own mini-state. They are already important in the Holy Land through their hospital work in Jerusalem and elsewhere, but by the middle of the 12th century, caring for the sick and wounded is no longer their only mission. They also have a military purpose, fighting as the **shock troops** in crusader battles. The gift of the castle means that the Hospitallers have a military base. Its position makes it immensely valuable. They have strengthened it to protect the eastern frontier of the Christian domain, and it has become a centre for the administration of their little state.

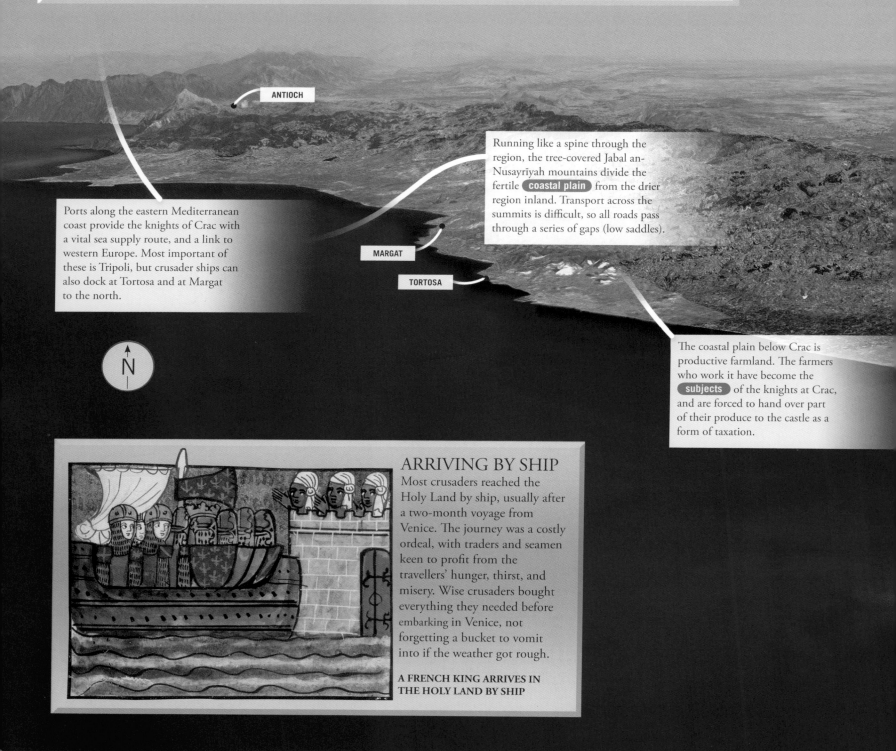

ANTIOCH

Ports along the eastern Mediterranean coast provide the knights of Crac with a vital sea supply route, and a link to western Europe. Most important of these is Tripoli, but crusader ships can also dock at Tortosa and at Margat to the north.

Running like a spine through the region, the tree-covered Jabal an-Nusayrīyah mountains divide the fertile **coastal plain** from the drier region inland. Transport across the summits is difficult, so all roads pass through a series of gaps (low saddles).

MARGAT

TORTOSA

N

The coastal plain below Crac is productive farmland. The farmers who work it have become the **subjects** of the knights at Crac, and are forced to hand over part of their produce to the castle as a form of taxation.

ARRIVING BY SHIP

Most crusaders reached the Holy Land by ship, usually after a two-month voyage from Venice. The journey was a costly ordeal, with traders and seamen keen to profit from the travellers' hunger, thirst, and misery. Wise crusaders bought everything they needed before embarking in Venice, not forgetting a bucket to vomit into if the weather got rough.

A FRENCH KING ARRIVES IN THE HOLY LAND BY SHIP

shock troops Soldiers specially trained and equipped to carry out an assault.

coastal plain A flat area of land in between the sea and higher ground where the Earth's crust folds into mountain ranges.

subjects People who are under the power of a ruler.

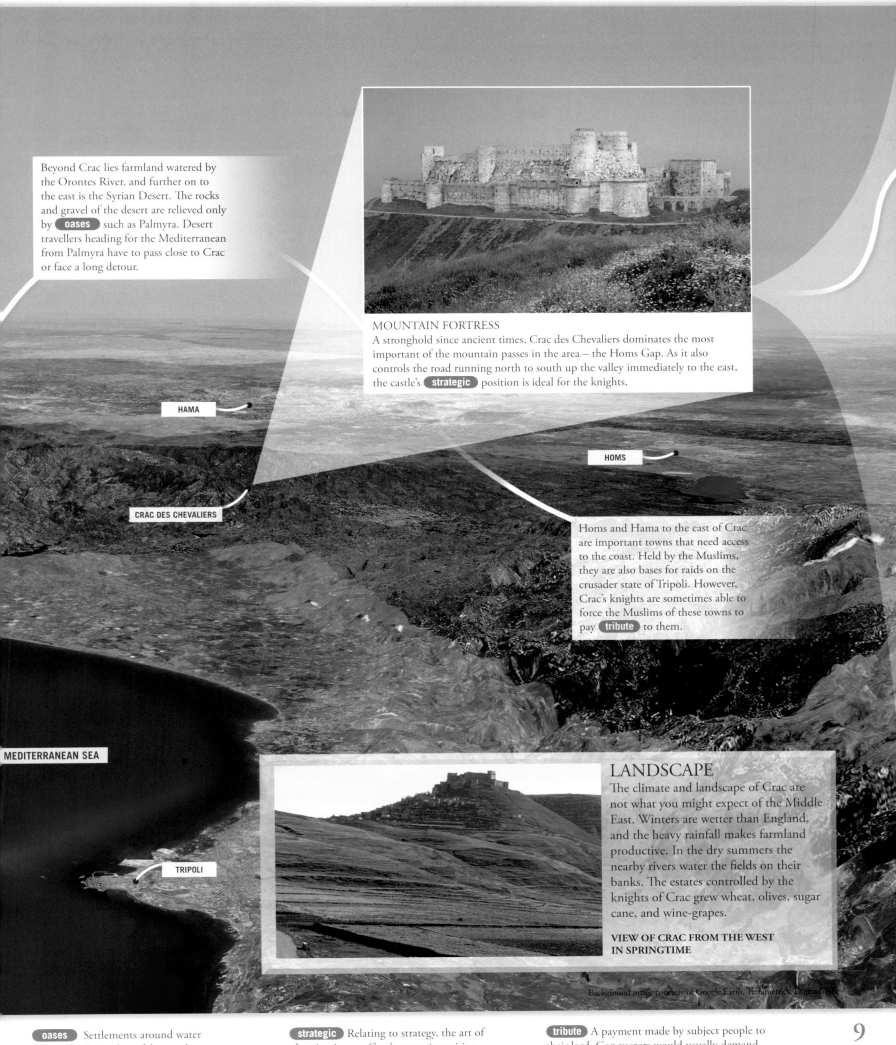

Beyond Crac lies farmland watered by the Orontes River, and further on to the east is the Syrian Desert. The rocks and gravel of the desert are relieved only by **oases** such as Palmyra. Desert travellers heading for the Mediterranean from Palmyra have to pass close to Crac or face a long detour.

MOUNTAIN FORTRESS

A stronghold since ancient times, Crac des Chevaliers dominates the most important of the mountain passes in the area – the Homs Gap. As it also controls the road running north to south up the valley immediately to the east, the castle's **strategic** position is ideal for the knights.

HAMA

HOMS

CRAC DES CHEVALIERS

Homs and Hama to the east of Crac are important towns that need access to the coast. Held by the Muslims, they are also bases for raids on the crusader state of Tripoli. However, Crac's knights are sometimes able to force the Muslims of these towns to pay **tribute** to them.

MEDITERRANEAN SEA

TRIPOLI

LANDSCAPE

The climate and landscape of Crac are not what you might expect of the Middle East. Winters are wetter than England, and the heavy rainfall makes farmland productive. In the dry summers the nearby rivers water the fields on their banks. The estates controlled by the knights of Crac grew wheat, olives, sugar cane, and wine-grapes.

VIEW OF CRAC FROM THE WEST IN SPRINGTIME

Background image courtesy of Google Earth, Terrametrics, DigitalGlobe

oases Settlements around water holes – fertile patches of desert where ground water reaches the surface.

strategic Relating to strategy, the art of planning in war. Crac's strategic position gave it a military advantage.

tribute A payment made by subject people to their lord. Conquerors would usually demand tribute from those conquered.

9

HOW CRAC DES CHEVALIERS GREW

The castle given to the Hospitallers was known as the castle of the Kurds, because it had once been guarded by Kurdish soldiers. The Hospitallers saw that the castle's position made it strong, and they set to work to make sure it could withstand attack from any direction. In two main phases of building, they created an inner ring of walls and towers, then surrounded this with an outer wall. The result was one of the finest medieval castles anywhere in the Christian world. From this hill-top they could control vast areas of surrounding countryside. Even if threatened, they could return to the safety of the place that became known simply as Crac des Chevaliers – Castle of the Knights.

1142
Since all signs of it have disappeared, we can only guess at the size of the castle that the Hospitallers inherited. It may have been a simple stone wall enclosing the summit on which the present castle stands.

Little remains of the defences that once protected the south side. Probably built in the first, **Frankish**, period of construction, they may have been just a series of ditches or timber walls aimed at stopping invaders from bringing **siege engines** too close.

1169
The knights probably began rebuilding Crac as soon as they took over. By 1169 they had completed a ring of strong walls, reinforced by square towers. This enclosure hid a chapel, **vaulted** rooms, and possibly a hall. Over the next half century earthquakes twice damaged Crac. In the repairs that followed, the knights added first an outer ring of walls, then extra defences to the tops of the walls (main picture).

Even today, different phases of construction are plain to see in the walls of Crac. The southeast corner, probably among the last of the Hospitallers' building works, is made from badly fitting rubble blocks. The carved stonework on top is a recent restoration.

vaulted A structure with a roof or ceiling that is arched. The stone-vaulted roof was a medieval invention unknown to the Romans.

Frankish The name given by medieval Muslims to anything western European.

siege engines Heavy wooden constructions used to attack a castle by battering its defences or scaling its walls.

In the 1230s the knights added an arched **cloister** to their great hall in Crac's main courtyard. Its decorative stonework is as fine as that found in the cathedrals of Europe. The cloister reminded visitors that the knights belonged to a wealthy monastic order.

Crac had always had a back door – a **postern** gate in the north wall. In the final phase of building, after 1250, the knights built extra towers on either side of the postern in the outer wall, and strengthened the tall northwest tower where a second postern pierced the inner wall.

The Hospitallers were wealthy in the early 13th century and spent lavishly on building the outer enclosing walls. Rising to an imposing 9 m (30 ft) in places, they are strengthened with six major towers and several smaller ones. However, after 1250 the money ran out so new building work was limited.

After 1250 the knights strengthened the entrance, making the approach to Crac more elaborate. Leading into the courtyard was a gatehouse that would not be out of place in any castle of the period. But to reach its fortified doorway, an attacker had to climb a zig-zag slope under fire from the castle.

Beyond the walls of Crac clustered the burgus – a suburb. Long since destroyed, it may have been a mix of houses belonging to the knights' local allies, craft workshops, offices squeezed out of the castle's cramped interior, and extra stabling for the knights' many horses.

BUILDERS

Castles like Crac employed huge numbers of labourers and skilled **masons**. At Harlech Castle (see page 5), which was a similar size to Crac, 227 masons cut stone on the site. They were supplied with the stone by 115 quarriers. At Crac, the master mason who controlled a crew of similar size would have come from France, where he might have learned his trade building cathedrals. Labourers would have been recruited locally – by force if necessary.

MEDIEVAL BUILDERS WITH THEIR TOOLS

cloister A covered walkway usually around a square, having open arches on the inside and a wall on the outside.

masons People skilled at building with stone. Medieval masons were important people.

postern A small back door or gate, especially one for private use.

THE CRUSADES

KILLING FOR GOD

Christian crosses stitched onto their clothes earned the crusaders their name: "crusaders" means "the crossed ones" or "those who have taken the cross".

By calling for the First Crusade, Pope Urban II (1035–1099), shown here preaching, started a series of religious wars that continued for 200 years.

With a cry of "God wills it!" Christians from all over medieval Europe gave up their families and their livelihoods to go and fight in a distant land. They knew they might never return home. But burning religious faith – and the promise of a fast-track to heaven – inspired them to "take the cross" and fight in the crusades. These religious wars aimed to reclaim the Holy Land from the Muslims who lived there.

The pope's call to arms

The crusades began with the preaching of Urban II, the pope (holy leader) of the Catholic Church. In the spring of 1095 he toured France, speaking to huge meetings. He told of the sufferings of pilgrims in the Holy Land. He warned of the threat to Christians in the east from the Seljuqs – Muslim Turks from central Asia. And he reminded the crowds that Muslims had destroyed Jerusalem's most holy church less than a century earlier. The pope ended his sermon by calling for a holy war, a crusade to recapture Jerusalem.

Rapid reaction force

The crowds' reaction to the pope's sermons was far better than he expected. Within a few months, a ragged and disorganized army of poor but devout Christians had gathered. They had stitched crosses to their clothes and were heading for the Holy Land. The following year wealthy and well-armed Christian knights from all over Europe followed them. By 1097 the crusaders had encircled the ancient city of Antioch.

Sieges and success

After an exhausting and desperate siege, Antioch fell to the crusaders in June 1098. A year later so, too, did Jerusalem. At both cities, the crusaders slaughtered every Muslim and Jew they found until the buildings were full of corpses and the streets running with blood. Today, these massacres of innocent people seem cruel and barbaric. But to the crusaders they were vital. They believed their victims were "godless" heathens. Killing them was a religious duty. The murders provoked in Muslims a bitter hatred for the crusaders.

> "Let this one cry be raised by all the soldiers of God: It is the will of God!"
>
> *Robert the Monk, reporting on Urban II's sermon at Clermont, 1095*

Crusaders made the sea journey to the Holy Land in stinking galleys (rowed ships) like these. All but the wealthiest passengers slept head-to-foot on deck.

Two centuries later they would avenge the Antioch massacre when they recaptured the city.

Crusader kingdoms

The First Crusade was a spectacular and unexpected success. The crusaders were able to push back the Seljuqs and set up kingdoms along the Mediterranean shore. Devout Christians hailed the victory as a miracle, and claimed that God had helped them in their campaign. However, Christian Europe found that winning the Holy Land was easier than keeping it. Over the next two centuries, there were many more crusades to defend the first victory. None had the same success, and some of the campaigns were disasters. As well as being slaughtered in bitter battles, crusaders died of hunger and disease.

Saladin's revenge

A turning point came in 1187 when the sultan (ruler) of Egypt and Syria, Saladin (1137–1193), recaptured Jerusalem. The Third Crusade to recover the city was only a partial victory, and Christians would never again rule Jerusalem for longer than ten years. The crusader kingdoms held out for longer. Saladin's attacks had reduced them to three small regions around Antioch, Tripoli, and north of Acre. However, by 1197 the crusaders had recovered most of the coast. For the next 50 years or so Christians thrived in the Holy Land and even traded peacefully with their Muslim neighbours.

Key

- Catholic Christian c.1100
- Orthodox Christian c.1100
- Muslim territory c.1100
- → First Crusade 1096–1099
- → Second Crusade 1147–1149
- → Third Crusade 1189–1192
- — Border of crusader states

SWEDEN
IRELAND
North Sea
Baltic Sea
ENGLAND London
Hamburg
GERMANY
POLAND
Paris
FRANCE
HOLY ROMAN EMPIRE
Regensburg
Cracow
MOLDAVIA
Kiev
Carpathians
Alps
PORTUGAL Lisbon
ARAGON Saragossa
CASTILE
Córdoba
GRANADA
Genoa
Venice
Pyrenees
Corsica
ITALY
Rome
Sardinia
Balearic Islands
BALKANS
BYZANTINE EMPIRE
Black Sea
Kherson
Constantinople
MOROCCO Tunis
Sicily
ARMENIA
Crete
Cyprus
Antioch
Mediterranean Sea
Tyre
Acre
Jerusalem

> "Piles of heads, hands, and feet were to be seen in the streets of the city. It was necessary to pick one's way over the bodies of men and horses... Indeed, it was a just and splendid judgment of God..."

Raymond d'Aguilliers describes the capture of Jerusalem in his History of the Franks

Baybars

But then, a new threat grew in Egypt. The Mamluks, once a class of Turkish-born warrior-slaves, had seized power there. By 1260, they had won control of all the land around the crusader kingdoms. Year by year, they raided and captured more and more of the Christian lands. Under the command of Sultan Baybars I, the Mamluks became more ambitious. They saw a chance to drive the hated Westerners out of the Holy Land for good. By 1268, Baybars had captured Caesarea, Arsur, Saphet, and Antioch. Though the crusader states were fatally weakened and isolated, some Christian strongholds still defied the Muslim onslaught. The mightiest of these was Crac des Chevaliers.

The Latin states in the Holy Land 1099–1229

- Muslim territory
- Muslim territory
- Latin Christian states 1144
- Latin Christian states 1229
- Byzantine Empire 1144
- lands recaptured by Saladin by 1190
- Muslim victory
- Christian victory
- Crusader castle
- 1191 date captured by Crusaders

ARMENIA
Tarsus
COUNTY OF EDESSA 1098–1144 Edessa
Alexandretta
Antioch 1098
Aleppo
Battle of the Field of Blood 1119
PRINCIPALITY OF ANTIOCH 1098–1268
KINGDOM OF CYPRUS
Crac des Chevaliers
Tripoli 1109
Homs
Euphrates
Mediterranean Sea
Beirut
Sidon 1110
Tyre 1124
Saphet
Acre 1104
Haifa
Damascus
Hattin 1187
Caesarea 1101
Arsur 1191
Belvoir
Lake Tiberias
Jaffa 1099
Ascalon 1191
Jerusalem 1099–1187
Karak
Mansurah 1250
Dead Sea
Cairo
KINGDOM OF JERUSALEM 1099–1187
Nile
Sinai
Red Sea

THE CHAPEL

The centre of life in Crac des Chevaliers is the chapel, for in many ways the whole castle is a fortified monastery. The "brother knights" who live, work, and train here are monks first, and soldiers second. Their daily routine revolves around a regular timetable of prayer and religious ritual within the chapel's walls. Each day in the early morning most of the brother knights file into the chapel to celebrate Mass – the most important service of their Catholic religion. So when a messenger reaches Crac bringing news of danger it is natural that he heads straight for the place where most of the brothers are assembled.

When not praying on their knees, the brother knights sit on hard benches. A monk's life was not supposed to be easy. The Hospitallers' second Master, Raymond de Puy, set rules for the order that demanded "...poverty (having few possessions), chastity (purity), and obedience."

Standing at the northeast corner of the inner stronghold, Crac's chapel was probably built in about 1170 following an earthquake. Its solid construction ensures that later tremors would do no further damage. The chapel's priest leads the service from the altar at the northeast end.

As the most sacred and precious part of the castle, the chapel is beautifully decorated with religious scenes. A Syrian Christian artist has painted the pictures over plaster covering the arched north walls. Some fragments of his work survive there today.

Crac's brothers follow the same timetable of prayer, called the hours, as other monks. It begins with Matins at midnight. Prime follows at 6am, with Mass at 9am and 11am. In the afternoon and evening there are three more services: Nones, Vespers, and Compline. Each lasts 30–60 minutes.

CRUSADING MONASTIC ORDERS

The idea of warrior monks might seem surprising today, but it was not odd in the Middle Ages. Christians believed that their religion was under attack, and warfare was the natural way for devout people to defend it. The first of the crusading monks were the Knights Templar. Their order was set up in 1118 to protect pilgrims after the First Crusade. Their rivals, the Hospitallers, became fighting monks some 40 years later. Both orders grew rich on gifts of money and land in Europe, which supported their work in the Holy land.

SIMON DE MONTFORT, AN ENGLISH TEMPLAR, WITH A SHIELD DISPLAYING THE CRUSADER CROSS

Mass The most important service of the day, in which Christ's Last Supper is remembered by sharing bread and wine.

order A society of people who have taken holy vows so that they can devote themselves to a religious cause.

devout Deeply religious. Joining the crusades was one of the highest expressions of faith during the Middle Ages.

THE HOSPITALLERS

The order of the Hospital of St John was the most successful, and most famous, of the crusading monastic orders. Their work caring for the sick and fighting for Christianity made them immensely wealthy and powerful, and they obeyed nobody except the pope – the head of the Catholic church.

POPE PASCAL II BLESSES THE HOSPITALLERS' RULES IN 1113

Morning sunbeams light the painted walls of the chapel. The window in the northeast wall is small, but afternoon sunlight floods through the window at the other end. The windows are just openings – there is no glass to keep out the cold winter's winds.

Setting parts of the service to music makes it easier to remember. The chapel walls echo to the sound of **plainsong**. However, the monks may have accompanied the singing on a shawm, an instrument similar to a modern bassoon.

Knights normally wear on their heads large skull-caps, turbans, or wide-brimmed hats. At prayer they take these off, but they keep on their **coifs** that they wear underneath. All the knights wear **habits**. The wearing of mail coats and other armour is banned in the chapel.

plainsong Holy verses sung in unison and without a musical accompaniment. Plainsong is a medieval monastic tradition.

coifs Small white caps worn beneath another hat. Coifs were also worn beneath mail coats.

habits Coarse, loose-fitting robes worn by monks, as befitted people who had taken a vow of poverty.

15

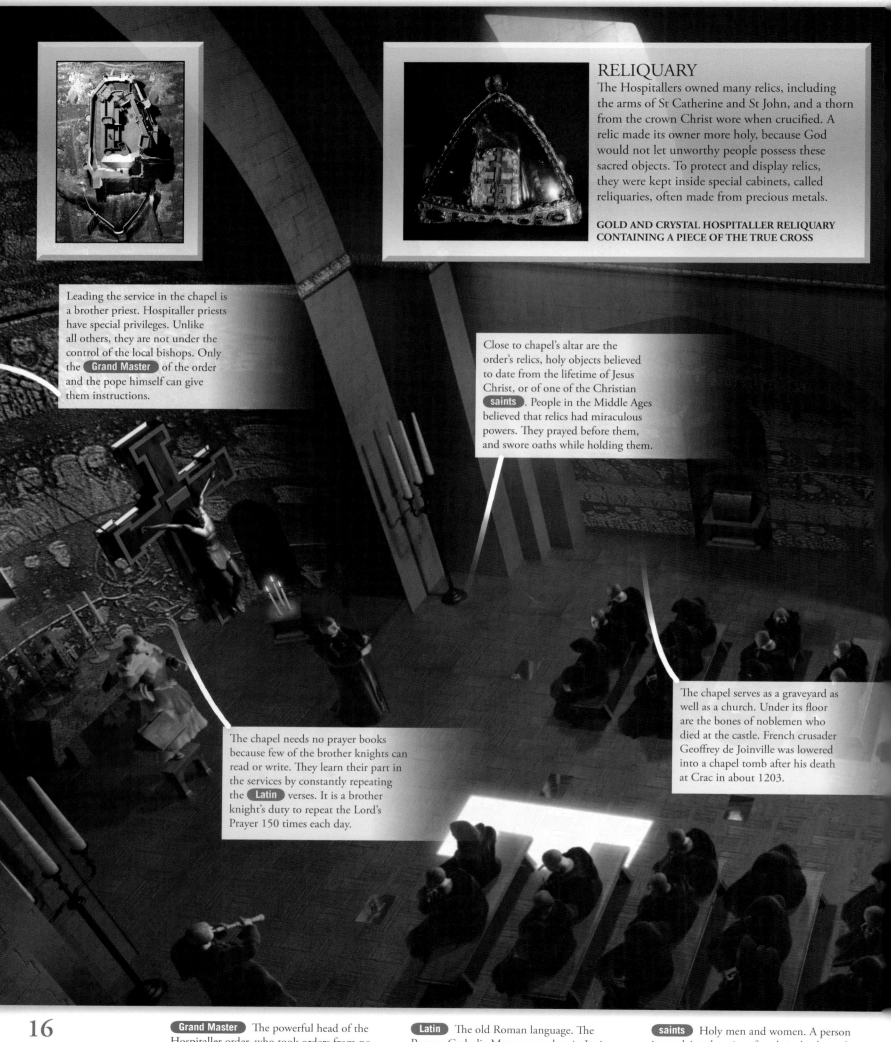

RELIQUARY

The Hospitallers owned many relics, including the arms of St Catherine and St John, and a thorn from the crown Christ wore when crucified. A relic made its owner more holy, because God would not let unworthy people possess these sacred objects. To protect and display relics, they were kept inside special cabinets, called reliquaries, often made from precious metals.

GOLD AND CRYSTAL HOSPITALLER RELIQUARY CONTAINING A PIECE OF THE TRUE CROSS

Leading the service in the chapel is a brother priest. Hospitaller priests have special privileges. Unlike all others, they are not under the control of the local bishops. Only the **Grand Master** of the order and the pope himself can give them instructions.

Close to chapel's altar are the order's relics, holy objects believed to date from the lifetime of Jesus Christ, or of one of the Christian **saints**. People in the Middle Ages believed that relics had miraculous powers. They prayed before them, and swore oaths while holding them.

The chapel needs no prayer books because few of the brother knights can read or write. They learn their part in the services by constantly repeating the **Latin** verses. It is a brother knight's duty to repeat the Lord's Prayer 150 times each day.

The chapel serves as a graveyard as well as a church. Under its floor are the bones of noblemen who died at the castle. French crusader Geoffrey de Joinville was lowered into a chapel tomb after his death at Crac in about 1203.

Grand Master The powerful head of the Hospitaller order, who took orders from no one but the pope.

Latin The old Roman language. The Roman Catholic Mass was spoken in Latin until 1965.

saints Holy men and women. A person is proclaimed a saint after their death on the evidence of miracles and saintly acts.

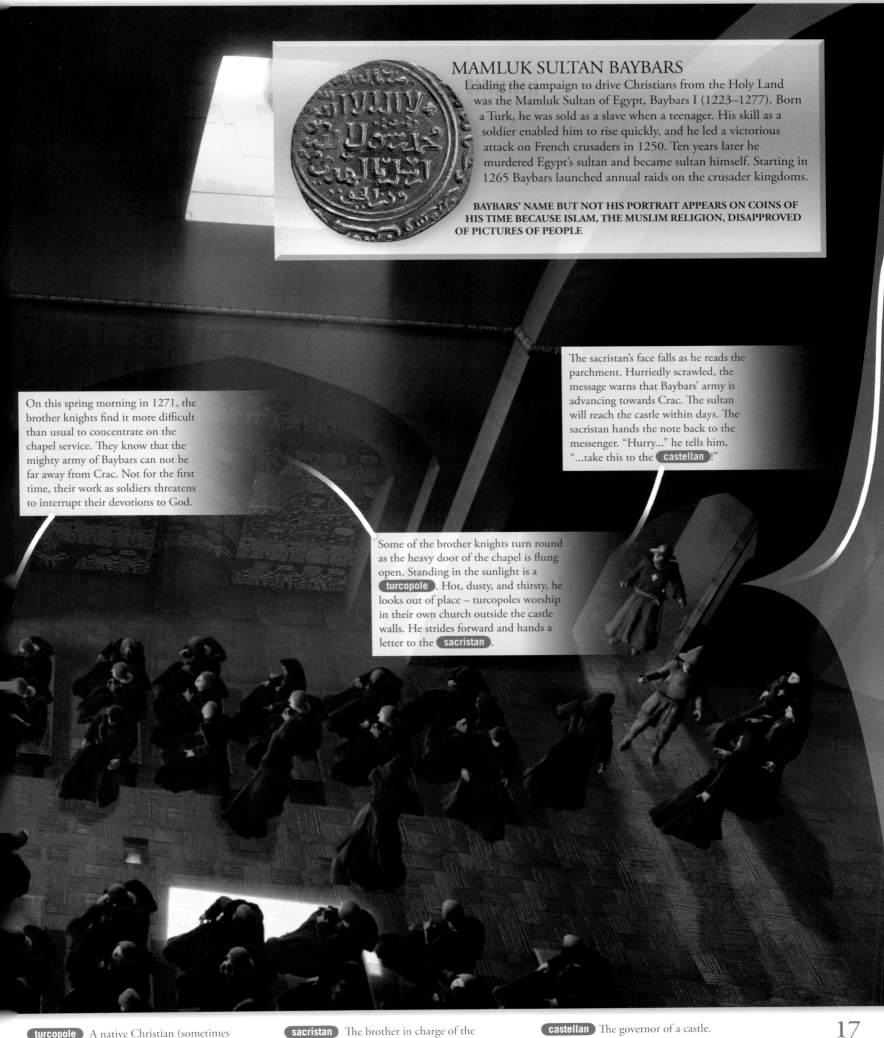

MAMLUK SULTAN BAYBARS

Leading the campaign to drive Christians from the Holy Land was the Mamluk Sultan of Egypt, Baybars I (1223–1277). Born a Turk, he was sold as a slave when a teenager. His skill as a soldier enabled him to rise quickly, and he led a victorious attack on French crusaders in 1250. Ten years later he murdered Egypt's sultan and became sultan himself. Starting in 1265 Baybars launched annual raids on the crusader kingdoms.

BAYBARS' NAME BUT NOT HIS PORTRAIT APPEARS ON COINS OF HIS TIME BECAUSE ISLAM, THE MUSLIM RELIGION, DISAPPROVED OF PICTURES OF PEOPLE

On this spring morning in 1271, the brother knights find it more difficult than usual to concentrate on the chapel service. They know that the mighty army of Baybars can not be far away from Crac. Not for the first time, their work as soldiers threatens to interrupt their devotions to God.

The sacristan's face falls as he reads the parchment. Hurriedly scrawled, the message warns that Baybars' army is advancing towards Crac. The sultan will reach the castle within days. The sacristan hands the note back to the messenger. "Hurry..." he tells him, "...take this to the castellan!"

Some of the brother knights turn round as the heavy door of the chapel is flung open. Standing in the sunlight is a turcopole. Hot, dusty, and thirsty, he looks out of place – turcopoles worship in their own church outside the castle walls. He strides forward and hands a letter to the sacristan.

turcopole A native Christian (sometimes a convert from Islam) who served the Hospitallers in a lightly armed cavalry unit.

sacristan The brother in charge of the chapel's relics and vestments.

castellan The governor of a castle.

17

THE COURTYARD

Circled twice round with strong walls, Crac des Chevaliers is a castle within a castle. At the very heart of this `concentric` design is the courtyard: a paved open space that leads to all the main buildings. The courtyard guards access to the chapel – the most sacred part of the castle. It also leads to the Great Hall, the castle's administrative centre. In peacetime the courtyard bustles with activity. As well as knights, there are merchants, servants, pilgrims, and local Syrian Christians to be seen here. But when danger threatens, the courtyard becomes a controlling hub. Commands echo around the walls as soldiers rush to their posts.

The walls that enclose the courtyard are thick and solid. This is not just for defence. In summer, shade temperatures soar to 40°C (104°F) and the flagstones burn bare feet. The heavy masonry keeps the rooms cool by day, and stores heat to keep them snug in the cold nights.

Considering the size of Crac des Chevaliers, the courtyard is surprisingly small. A raised platform with arches beneath covers half its area. The chapel takes up more room. The space that's left feels cramped and crowded when the anxious knights spill out from the chapel.

Large halls surround the courtyard on three sides. The one on the east side was perhaps Crac's hospital. Sick and wounded knights and turcopoles regain their strength here. The knights may also nurse the ill and dying from beyond the castle walls: care of the sick is one of their duties as monks.

MUSLIM SLAVES

Some of the hardest, nastiest work at Crac is done by Muslim `slaves`. Slaves are captured in battle, or born of slave parents. Slavery is an accepted part of life: the crusaders' Muslim foe own Christian slaves, and starving crusaders have sometimes even sold their own children as slaves to buy food.

MEDIEVAL PAINTING OF MUSLIM CAPTIVES REQUESTING BAPTISM

`concentric` A circle that has the same centre as another a circle. The courtyard is at the centre of both encircling walls.

`slaves` Prisoner workers bought and sold as possessions. Slavery was not generally made illegal until the 1800s.

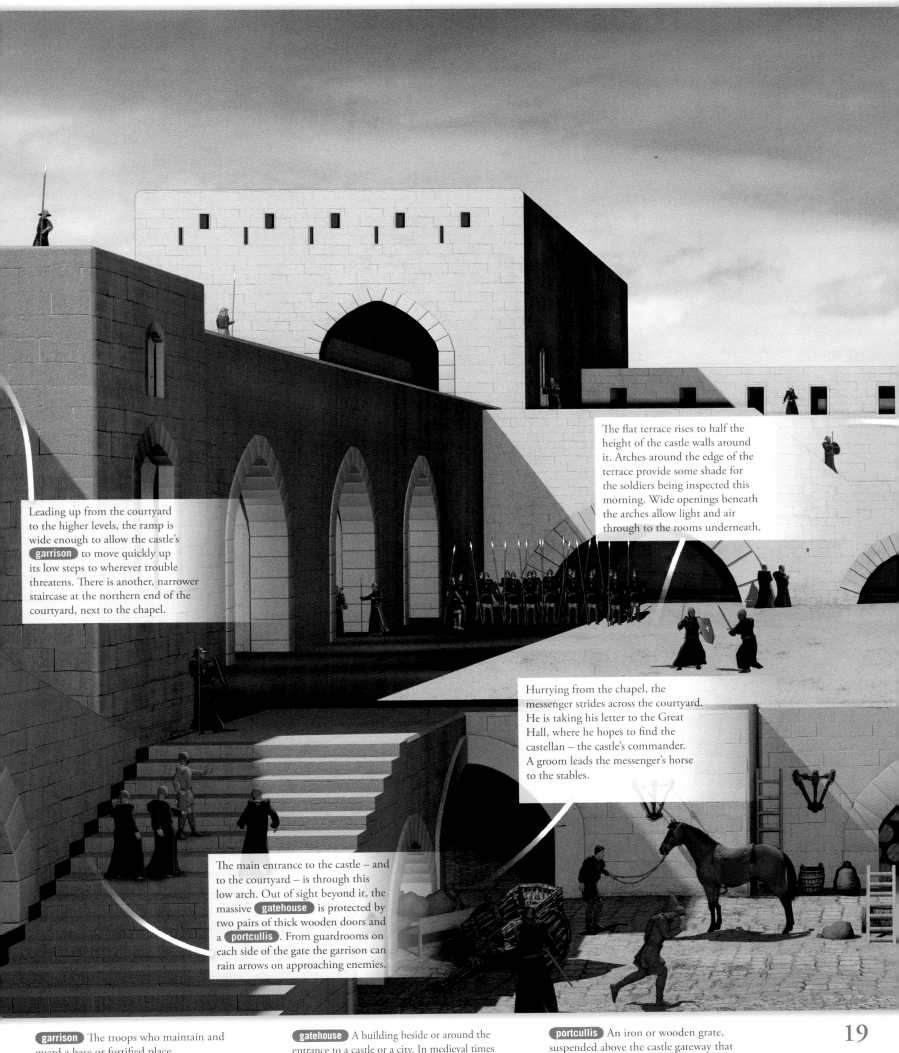

Leading up from the courtyard to the higher levels, the ramp is wide enough to allow the castle's **garrison** to move quickly up its low steps to wherever trouble threatens. There is another, narrower staircase at the northern end of the courtyard, next to the chapel.

The flat terrace rises to half the height of the castle walls around it. Arches around the edge of the terrace provide some shade for the soldiers being inspected this morning. Wide openings beneath the arches allow light and air through to the rooms underneath.

Hurrying from the chapel, the messenger strides across the courtyard. He is taking his letter to the Great Hall, where he hopes to find the castellan – the castle's commander. A groom leads the messenger's horse to the stables.

The main entrance to the castle – and to the courtyard – is through this low arch. Out of sight beyond it, the massive **gatehouse** is protected by two pairs of thick wooden doors and a **portcullis**. From guardrooms on each side of the gate the garrison can rain arrows on approaching enemies.

---

garrison The troops who maintain and guard a base or fortified place.

gatehouse A building beside or around the entrance to a castle or a city. In medieval times the gatehouse was usually fortified.

portcullis An iron or wooden grate, suspended above the castle gateway that could be lowered to bar the entrance.

19

The wide surface of the terrace has enough space for the whole garrison to assemble. Here there's also room for troops to train, or for the staging of **mystery plays** on festival days. This morning, some knights are demonstrating their swords skills for the benefit of a visiting commander.

Beneath the terrace, wide columns support the low, arched roof of the armoury (see pages 32–33). The thick masonry ensures that this vital building is safe even in a siege – unlike a timber roof, it's fireproof and can withstand the heaviest of stone missiles.

The courtyard's flagstone floor has a vital function – it collects rainwater. Though little rain falls between May and September, winters are very wet. Rainwater draining from the dripping slabs runs along special channels into vast, rock-cut **cisterns** below the castle.

mystery plays Types of medieval drama that were based upon the life of Christ and performed on holy days.

cisterns Underground reservoirs for storing water. The word comes from the Latin "cisterna", meaning "underground tank".

Every part of the castle has to help in its defence, and the castellan's tower is no exception. From the round upper room a narrow **spiral staircase** rises to a **turret** on the roof. From here, the highest point in the castle, watchmen have a commanding view over the landscape to the south and west.

The castellan's apartment is spread across two floors of the southwest tower of the castle. In keeping with his high status, the rooms are comfortable, and finely decorated – there's even a private lavatory. On the shady north side, a big window looks out across the courtyard.

WISE WORDS
Within the cloisters is an inscription carved upon the wall: "Have richness, have wisdom, have beauty, but beware of pride, which spoils all that it touches." The message reminds brothers that as followers of Christ they must be humble – but not necessarily poor!

Just like a monastery in the knights' French homeland, the castle has a cloister leading into the Great Hall. The cloister's open stone windows are carved as beautifully as those of a cathedral. Under the cloister's roof, brother knights can spend time outdoors, even during torrential winter rain.

spiral staircase A type of narrow, winding stone staircase found inside the towers and turrets of medieval castles.

turret A small, usually rounded tower that projects out from the wall of a castle.

CASTLE ESTATES

The castle estates contolled from the Great Hall are worked by local Christian and Muslim farmers. The knights could be generous landlords. The Muslim traveller Ibn Jubayr (1145–1217) noticed with surprise that the Franks allowed their farmers to keep half the harvest, and charged them less tax than Christians farmers paid to Muslim masters.

A simple cross decorates the shields that the brother knights use in battle, but the shields of visiting crusaders that line the walls are not nearly as plain. Painted with **heraldic achievements** the shields tell the story of a knight's ancestry.

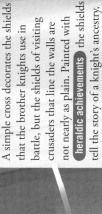

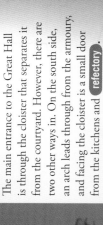

The main entrance to the Great Hall is through the cloister that separates it from the courtyard. However, there are two other ways in. On the south side, an arch leads through from the armoury, and facing the cloister is a small door from the kitchens and **refectory** .

THE GREAT HALL

Spacious, high, and beautifully decorated, the Great Hall is the castle's finest room. On special occasions this is where the knights gather to celebrate, or perhaps to share a feast. Here, too, the castellan greets important visitors from Europe. However, the hall is also a working space. It serves as a courtroom, where the knights deliver justice to the local people under their rule. When danger threatens Crac des Chevaliers, it is a centre for command and control. The messenger now brings his news of the impending attack to the Great Hall, as it's here that he will most likely find the castellan, the commander of the knights.

ORNATE STONEWORK

Pointed arches support the heavy stone-vaulted ceilings of the castle. It is a tribute to the skill of the medieval masons and engineers that these buildings still stand robustly even though they were erected in the 13th century. Arches allowed ceilings to be high without supporting columns. The heavier the weight pressing down upon the arch, the more secure the building.

heraldic achievements Patterns of mythical beasts and special signs unique to a knight's family.

refectory A communal dining room in a religious or academic institution.

papal legates Visiting officials bringing instructions from the pope.

As lords of the estates around the castle, the knights are in charge of law and order. At the courts held in the Great Hall, the knights respect the religion of their Muslim and Oriental Christian subjects. To ensure fairness, when a Christian accuses a Muslim of a crime, only Muslims can be witnesses.

Hunting game with dogs and **falconry** are popular pastimes for wealthy knights in Europe, but for brother knights in the Holy Land these are forbidden. When the castle is not in danger some hunt gazelle anyway, forcing the order's Grand Master to remind them of the rules.

When pilgrims, kings, and **papal legates** visit Crac des Chevaliers, the Hospitallers entertain them in grand style, for the generosity of the wealthy helps them to continue their work. After visiting the castle in the Fifth Crusade, Hungary's King Andrew II (c. 1175–1235) paid for the walls to be strengthened.

As the brother knights talk about the battle to come, two of the castle's guests seated at the table strain to pick some hard facts out of the conversation. In the excitement they forget their thirst and hunger and a servant removes the dishes of food and the wine brought for him.

Bad news travels fast. When the messenger reaches the Great Hall he finds that a brother has raced ahead of him. Already the knights are gathering to discuss how to defend Crac. But the one person he is seeking – the castellan – is not here. The messenger will have to look further before he can deliver his message.

falconry The art of training falcons to return from flight to their trainer and to hunt prey.

THE KITCHEN

In a cavernous and bustling room, a small army of cooks works to feed the castle's hundreds of hungry mouths. The kitchens fill about a quarter of this household part of the castle, which wraps around the west and north sides just beneath the inner walls. The rest of the space is mostly taken up by the refectory – Crac's huge dining room – and by storage rooms. Normally piled to the roof with provisions, the store-rooms are now almost empty. Their contents were used up last year, when Baybars' army overran Crac's estates and took the harvest. The shortage that followed has seriously weakened Crac's power to withstand a siege.

A PLACE TO SIT

The castle's `latrines` have no doors. The holes below the seats open onto the castle's outside wall. The science of germs and hygiene is still many centuries in the future, and for the flies that swarm around the stinking cubicles it's only a short flight to the kitchens next door.

In these rambling kitchens, the cooks prepare a menu that is nourishing and varied by medieval standards. The knights eat fresh pork, lamb, chicken, pigeon, and partridge. On the many days when their religion forbids them to eat meat, they have bread, fish, eggs, beans, and a wide choice of vegetables and fruit.

The servant who returns from the Great Hall next door brings the first news of Baybars' expected attack. The warning has a special importance for the cooks. They must now try to figure out how to make the castle's limited food supplies last through what could be a lengthy siege.

As well as the pots and pans found in every kitchen, the castle has many `pestles and mortars`. Medieval cutlery does not include forks, and to make eating easier food is pounded until it has the texture of porridge. Knights use a slice of bread called a trencher to mop the delicious paste from their plates.

The brother in charge of the kitchen is also responsible for enforcing the order's rules at meal times. It isn't always easy. Brother knights are supposed to eat politely and silently, but not all do. At times, they have beaten the servants waiting on them and pelted them with bread and wine.

`pestles and mortars` A pestle is a club-shaped tool for grinding and pounding food in a mortar, a type of heavy bowl.

`latrines` Toilets in castles, camps, or barracks. The word comes from the Latin *lavatrina*, meaning a bath.

`spices` Aromatic substances, such as ginger, cinnamon, nutmeg, and chilli used to season and flavour food.

MEDIEVAL COOKING

Without refrigeration, fresh food spoiled quickly in the Syrian summer. Butchers slaughtered food animals just before they were needed. They made surplus meat last longer by covering it in salt, or by smoking. Fish was preserved in the same way. Plant crops such as beans and fruit kept well when dried in the sun or pickled.

A SKILLED BUTCHER SLAUGHTERS A PIG WITH SINGLE BLOW

Boiling, roasting, and baking are the main cooking methods. Fresh meat is roasted on a (spit) in front an open fire. Keeping the meat rotating is the job of a turnspit – a small boy – or a dog running in a cage. Salted fish boils in a huge pot, and the baker uses the bread oven to cook pies and pastries.

The baker uses a vast stone oven to bake the loaves once they have risen. To heat it, he lights a fire inside the oven. When the stones are glowing, he rakes out the ashes, then sets the loaves inside using a long-handled wooden shovel. Heating the oven uses a lot of fuel, so there's fresh bread only once or twice a week.

Under the Hospitaller's rules, the knights must be given bread to eat. Though they also eat many other foods, bread still makes up a large part of their diet. Made from (rye) and wheat flour, it's like modern brown bread. The baker (kneads) the dough in a giant trough made from a hollowed-out tree-trunk.

The knights are used to eating spicy food. In their native France, (spices) are costly, so cooking with them shows off wealth. In the Holy Land, the knights' food is highly spiced for other reasons. Spices are cheap here, and the Syrian cooks who staff the kitchens use them in traditional recipes.

(spit) A pointed rod on which meat is roasted before an open fire. The castle kitchen could roast a whole carcass on its spit.

(rye) The grain of the rye cereal, used for making flour for bread, and as food for livestock.

(kneads) To work and press the dough with the hands so that it is thoroughly mixed. The dough is then left to rise.

THE BATTLE OF HATTIN

4 JULY 1187

Saladin

The bravery and fighting skills of the Hospitallers were famous in the Holy Land, but sometimes even these qualities were not enough to make them victorious. The knights' worst defeat came in 1187 when they fought a Muslim army close to the Sea of Galilee.

Saladin in command

Commanding it was Saladin (see page 13). As sultan of Egypt, he had gradually increased his power until he ruled all the land around the Kingdom of Jerusalem. In 1185, Saladin had made a truce (an agreement not to attack) with Jerusalem, so the people of the kingdom hoped for a lasting peace with their Muslim neighbours. But after only a year, a reckless knight, Reynald of Châtillon, broke the truce. He attacked Muslim travellers passing through his land and stole their belongings.

This was enough to provoke Saladin, and he invaded the kingdom to take his revenge. The king of Jerusalem, Guy of Lusignan, raised a huge army to stop Saladin's advance. The Hospitallers joined him at the beginning of July at Sephorie, where springs supplied fresh water. In the searing heat the water was as vital as arrows and armour: without it the soldiers and their horses would soon die.

Guy of Lusignan was crowned king of Jerusalem in 1186 on the death of King Baldwin. Guy was weak and vain: everyone agreed when a knight snorted "...he won't be king for a year!"

Saladin's army was camped to the east, between the Christians and the Sea of Galilee. They, too, had water, and more troops. However, Saladin knew that the crusaders' numbers included the Hospitaller and Templar knights, who were fierce fighters, and he was concerned that he might be defeated in a direct attack.

Water weapon

Saladin guessed that thirst was his best weapon. If he could separate the Christians from their water supply, they would soon be begging for mercy – and for water. So he attacked the town of Tiberias on the Sea of Galilee. Some of the crusaders' families were trapped inside, and he believed that the Christians would race across the waterless desert to rescue their wives and children.

When news of Saladin's attack reached Sephorie, it divided the crusaders. Some wanted to relieve the siege. But more experienced leaders saw that Saladin was laying a trap. "Let him take the town," they told King Guy. "We can always ransom the prisoners afterwards."

At first Guy agreed, but Reynald of Châtillon tried to make him change his mind. Reynald argued that failing to rescue Tiberias looked like cowardice. Finally, and fatally, Guy was persuaded. On 3 July, he led his army from their green camp across the parched land. The Hospitaller knights were among the last to leave, protecting the rear of the long line of soldiers.

The Hospitallers attacked

It was the worst place to be exposed to their enemy. Almost as soon as the army had set off, Muslim cavalry began attacking the column. The Hospitallers and Templars had to stop to defend themselves. To

> "A year later I crossed the battlefield, and saw the land all covered with their bones."
>
> *Ibn Al-Athīr, Muslim chronicler of the crusades, on the Hattin battlefield*

he Horns of Hattin are twin volcanic peaks. The green ...lds around turn to dust in the summer.

...oid leaving them behind, the army ahead of ...em halted, too. Unable to advance or retreat, the ...hristians had no choice but to camp for the night ... a waterless plain.

Their situation was desperate, and in the ...orning it got worse. Saladin's soldiers set fire to ...e grass around the camp – then attacked through

...aladin's cavalry picked off the knights easily when their ...fantry deserted them. Their horses killed, they were forced ... fight on foot. Hot, heavy armour weighed them down.

...he smokescreen. A Muslim writer describes how ...rchers shot "clouds of arrows like thick swarms ...f locusts" at the knights. Exhausted, scorched by ...he sun, and gasping with thirst, the Christians ...ade a panic-stricken charge towards the springs ...f Hattin – the nearest water. However, Saladin's ...rmy was waiting for them. Worn out and

frightened, the crusaders' infantry (foot soldiers) deserted. They fled up the slopes of twin hills called the Horns of Hattin. Before long the rest of the army followed them, and was quickly surrounded by Muslim troops.

Loss of the cross

The knights tried three times to escape, but most were driven back each time. They knew they had lost the battle when their foes captured the True Cross (see page 16). The knights believed that their most precious relic would protect them. Its loss seemed like the complete defeat of Christianity by Islam. Soon after, the Christians surrendered.

Saladin had King Guy and Reynald of Châtillon brought to his tent. To show his mercy, he offered Guy a cup of iced water: it was an Islamic custom to spare the lives of prisoners who had shared food or water with their captor. Guy drank, then handed the cup to Reynald. Gasping with thirst, he gulped it down. Saladin told him "Remember it was King Guy who shared his water with you. I did

The Sea of Galilea provided ample water for Saladin's army, which was camped close to the banks. It gave his troops a crucial advantage in the battle of Hattin.

not give it to you." Saladin then listed Reynald's crimes and treachery, including his breaking of the truce. "Kings have always acted as I have" replied Reynald, swaggering and defiant. So Saladin picked up his sword and personally beheaded Reynald.

The battle of Hattin was a catastrophe for the Christians. In their bid to defeat Saladin, they had sent almost all their military forces onto the battlefield. Only a handful had escaped death or capture. Though Saladin had lost many soldiers too, he still had a large army. With it, he recaptured Jerusalem and drove the crusaders back into a few tiny regions. It was a terrible blow, not only for the Hospitallers, but for all of western Christianity. When news reached Pope Urban III, the shock killed him.

Muslim cavalry (right in the picture) attack the column. They stood a better chance of defeating the crusaders on the battlefield than in a siege. Knowing this, Saladin lured the crusaders out of their walled cities to Hattin.

THE TOWERS

The tallest, strongest towers of Crac des Chevaliers look out to the south: the direction from which an attack is most likely to come. Towers have an important military purpose. From their  archers can pick off attackers who are out of reach of arrows shot from the walls. The towers are not just for warfare, though. Their upper chambers provide the castellan and other senior knights with private rooms where they sleep, work, receive visitors, and take meals. It's in his apartment in the southeast tower that the castellan learns of the threat to Crac. He rushes to the window and scans the horizon for signs of Baybars' advance.

The grandest apartment is in the southwest tower. Here the castellan has an apartment, and it's here that the Hospitallers' Grand Master stays when he visits. The tower's upper floor has a soaring vaulted ceiling. A large window faces the courtyard, but only a narrow arrow-slit looks out of the castle to the south.

The castellans of Crac don't sit in their rooms while the other knights fight. When Muslim soldiers ambushed a troop of 300 knights in 1170, one of the dead was Crac's castellan. Syria's prince Nur-ad-din recognized the castellan's face among the piles of severed heads.

Guards on the tower tops are the first to spot the approaching Muslim army. Baybars has taken Castel Blanc (White Castle) of Safita, so vigilant sentries have been gazing in that direction. Now tell-tale flashes of light to the west provide the first sign of the army's approach, as sunlight glints on weapons and armour.

From the tops of the tallest towers, guards can look right across to the Homs Gap in the south (see page 9). Less than 8 km (5 miles) away to the northeast is the crusader castle of Montferrand. It's close enough for the garrisons to exchange messages using a flaming beacon on the tower top.

HOSPITALLER SEAL

As well as signing his name on important documents, the castellan marks them with wax into which he presses the Hospitaller seal. This shows an "oriflamme" (a sacred banner given to the early kings of France) and a hospital bed, a sign of the knights' original mission.

A private room is a privilege in the castle: most knights share dormitories. Of greater advantage to the castellan, though, is the promotion he can expect. Crac is among the crusaders' most important castles, and castellans have risen from here to the highest positions, as Masters, Marshals, or Grand Commanders of the Hospitallers.

bow-loops Slit-like openings in walls that are wide on the inside to allow an archer to use a bow, and narrow on the outside to protect him.

PREPARING FOR SIEGE

Those who defended medieval castles feared sieges, for they always brought hunger and disease. To make supplies last longer defenders threw out "useless mouths" – women and children who ate but did not fight. Then they stockpiled as much food as they could find. Crac's supplies are low when the siege begins: the castle's soldiers and horses usually eat food not from the stores but brought from the surrounding estates.

A 14TH-CENTURY FRENCH MANUSCRIPT SHOWS SUPPLIES BEING DELIVERED TO A CASTLE

Some towers are reinforced to bear the weight of siege engines (see pages 48–49). These are used for defence as they are for attack, but only smaller machines can be mounted on the tower tops. The larger catapults need solid ground. On a tower they might shake the masonry apart.

Like gappy teeth or rows of tombstones, the battlements that top the castle's walls provide vital protection for the soldiers on the **allure**. Archers shoot through the **crenels** between the high **merlons**. Wooden shutters closing off the crenels provide extra shelter during very fierce fighting.

Rooms within towers serve purposes besides defence. Some are offices for the order's scribes. Documents, weapons, and supplies fill others. The few that are used as prisons are surprisingly comfortable. When the Hospitallers hold noble captives for **ransom** they treat them more like house guests than criminals.

Most of the slits that pierce the castle walls are bow-loops. The loops are not always as safe as they look. Skilled archers can occasionally shoot a well-aimed arrow clean through a loop to hit an unwary guard inside.

ransom The money demanded by a prisoner's captors in return for his release.

allure A wall-walk. The passage behind the battlement wall of a castle.

crenels The low rectangular openings in a battlement wall or parapet that may sometimes be closed with shutters.

merlons The solid rectangular upright sections in a battlement wall or parapet.

THE BARRACKS

Crac's brother knights may be warriors on the battlefield, but when they are resting there's no mistaking them for anything but monks. Their sleeping quarters are plain and shared. There are no signs of luxury in the rows of straw mattresses that line the walls. And the small chests that hold their few possessions are a reminder that all have taken vows of poverty. The brothers' **dorter** is in the heart of the castle, close to the main gate. When news of the expected attack reaches the barracks, only the sick and those who were standing guard all night are still in bed. The message, shouted by a page, shakes them awake, and they rush to wash and dress.

SERGEANTS

Not all of the castle's soldiers are brother knights. Those who were not born of noble families are called brother sergeants-at-arms. Though they do almost the same jobs as brother knights, they have lower status and the two groups eat and sleep apart. Brother sergeants-at-arms wear cheaper armour, and are each allowed only two horses to the knights' four, and one **esquire** (knights each have two). Sergeants-at-service are lower still. Though they are little better off than servants, they do important work as the castle's administrators.

There's no time for sleepy-heads in Crac. The brothers' schedule of worship makes them rise early and stay up late. By day, the brothers are forbidden from returning to the dorter except to change their sheets. The sick may rest in bed, but if their illness lasts more than three days their beds are moved to the hospital.

Beds are uncomfortable by modern standards. Brother knights sleep on wooden **pallets** covered with straw-filled mattresses. Emptying them each year and burning the straw keeps down the numbers of bed-bugs. Knights sleep in wool or linen bed clothes, and are allowed three sheets.

Except when sunlight floods through the narrow loops, the dorter is a gloomy place. When night falls the only light comes from shared lanterns. In a monastery, personal candles are forbidden luxuries, and often monks are not even allowed to sit reading near a lantern.

   dorter A dormitory, or communal sleeping area.   **pallets** Simple low beds.   **esquire** The young servant and shield-bearer of a knight. Esquires often became knights themselves.

TURCOPOLES

About half of the soldiers based at Crac are locally born Christian men. Known as turcopoles, they fight as cavalry – horseback warriors armed with bows – but are less heavily armoured than the knights they serve. The knights rely on turcopoles to boost their numbers in battle. They also use them for many other battlefield tasks – as messengers, scouts, and spies. Turcopoles ride smaller, more nimble horses than the knights, so they can attack and retreat swiftly. They make up raiding parties, carry out ambushes, and protect columns of knights on the march.

Some monasteries permitted monks a little privacy, with beds in **cells**. The Hospitaller order specifically requires communal sleeping, which is not very popular with the brothers. However, Crac is close to the frontier with the Muslim world, and here the dorter is more barracks than bedroom.

Corridors lead from the dorter to the chambers of the castellan, who sometimes checks on the brothers to make sure that they are observing the rules. When it's time for services in the night, a brother sergeant comes through the corridor to wake the knights with a loud bell or a clapper.

Keeping clean is less important to the monks than prayer and castle defence. Servants bring buckets of water to the knights for washing, but baths are rare. Most monasteries follow the advice of Pope Gregory, who permitted regular baths only if they did not become "time-wasting luxury".

Knights are each issued with three pairs of trousers, three shirts, a tunic, a gown, an overcoat with a hood, two cloaks – one lined with fur – and stockings of wool and linen. Though they are hardly enough to fill a drawer, the clothes make the knights well-dressed by the standards of the time.

cells Small, sparsely furnished single bedrooms for a monk or a nun in a monastery.

THE ARMOURY

In the darkness of Crac's armoury, an ear-splitting hammering noise rattles around the walls. For it's here, in a small forge, that the castle's armourers repair the knights' helms and weapons. They clean and maintain coats of mail, too, but they don't make armour here. The Hospitallers import most of their armour and weapons from Europe, where it's made in specialist workshops. Though helms and mail coats line the walls, there's only just enough for all the knights, and there's constant work for the armourers, bashing out dents and riveting damaged plates. It's not all metalwork, though. Protection also comes from leather and quilted fabric.

LAYERS OF ARMOUR

The four layers of protective clothing that a knight wears in battle give him almost as much protection against arrows and sword cuts as plate armour. Over his underclothes he wears a long-sleeved, quilted tunic. A thigh-length coat of mail with built-in mittens covers this. Next comes another sleeveless tunic, also quilted. And on top of it all the knight wears his hooded cape.

QUILTED TUNIC

TUNIC

HELMETS

MAIL COAT

CAPE

Knights begin arriving at the armoury as news of the impending siege spreads. The armoury is close to the heart of Crac, at the side of the central courtyard. Heavy stone columns support an immensely thick ceiling, protecting this essential room from attack. The stone is flameproof, too, so the armourer's forge is not a fire hazard.

Armour is costly and easily damaged by damp. To protect it, and prolong its life, armour that is not needed immediately is wrapped in greasy rags and stored in baskets or sacks in the driest part of the armoury. It only needs to be cleaned and polished before use.

Barrels of sand moistened with vinegar clean mail coats. Armourers half fill the barrels with mail coats, then roll them around. The sand removes rust from the wire links of the mail. Mail needs frequent cleaning – it rusts in winter because of rain, and in summer because the knights sweat heavily in the heat.

The Hospitallers don't wear shiny armour over the whole body. Only their heads are completely protected – by helmets made from sheet metal. The knights use wooden shields covered in leather to protect their bodies. Long straps on the back allow them to carry the shields over their shoulders when on the march.

forge A place in which metal is worked by heating and hammering, or the furnace used for heating the metal.

riveting The process of fastening pieces of metal together using short metal pins that are hammered into place.

THE BLACKSMITH

The forge at Crac is quite small, since the armourer does not actually make any weapons or armour here. A large bellows pumps air into the charcoal heaped in the hearth, raising the temperature until iron held in the flames glows red hot and becomes soft enough to bend and shape. Working (bending and hammering) metal hardens it; reheating and cooling stops the metal from becoming brittle. The hearth also hardens metal: covered in hot charcoal, a weapon absorbs `carbon`, turning the outside from soft iron to tougher steel.

The armoury stores all the weapons that the knights, sergeants, and turcopoles use in battle. None of the metal parts of the weapons is made in the castle, but local craftsmen provide the wooden poles for lances, and bundles of arrows ready to be fitted with their steel tips and `feather flights`.

Cloth may not seem like much protection, but it is surprisingly effective, especially under a layer of mail. The knight's undergarments are thickly quilted, either by stuffing with rags, or by stitching together up to 30 layers of cotton or linen.

Armourers make mail coats from iron rings. They hammer each wire. These are bent into rings, which are then linked together and riveted. A single coat of mail might use 30,000 rings. Though it weighs up to 12 kg (26 lbs) the weight is spread evenly, so it does not feel this heavy.

`carbon` A non-metallic element found in coal and charcoal, among other things.

`feather flights` The feathers fixed to the end of an arrow to give it stability during flight.

CATALOGUE OF CRUSADER WEAPONS

Medieval warfare is an ugly, bloody, and personal business. Though arrows kill at a distance, much of the fighting is hand-to-hand combat. Knights' personal weapons are made from hardened steel, and are honed sharp enough to shave with. Wielded with skill, they can kill with a single blow. Even when they merely maim, they leave deadly wounds. For without modern medical care, blood loss and infection finish the job that sword, axe, and lance began.

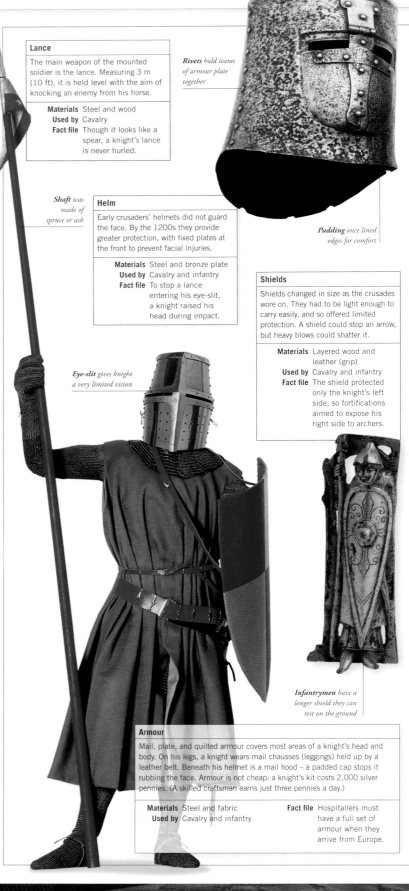

Rivets hold seams of armour plate together

Padding once lined edges for comfort

Lance
The main weapon of the mounted soldier is the lance. Measuring 3 m (10 ft), it is held level with the aim of knocking an enemy from his horse.

Materials Steel and wood
Used by Cavalry
Fact file Though it looks like a spear, a knight's lance is never hurled.

Shaft was made of spruce or ash

Helm
Early crusaders' helmets did not guard the face. By the 1200s they provide greater protection, with fixed plates at the front to prevent facial injuries.

Materials Steel and bronze plate
Used by Cavalry and infantry
Fact file To stop a lance entering his eye-slit, a knight raised his head during impact.

Eye-slit gives knight a very limited vision

Shields
Shields changed in size as the crusades wore on. They had to be light enough to carry easily, and so offered limited protection. A shield could stop an arrow, but heavy blows could shatter it.

Materials Layered wood and leather (grip)
Used by Cavalry and infantry
Fact file The shield protected only the knight's left side, so fortifications aimed to expose his right side to archers.

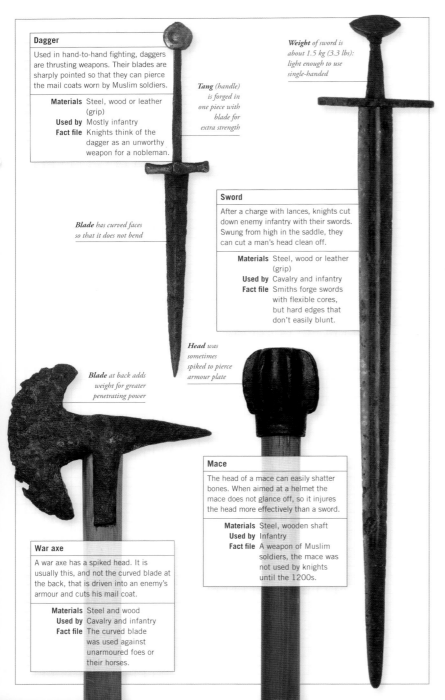

Dagger
Used in hand-to-hand fighting, daggers are thrusting weapons. Their blades are sharply pointed so that they can pierce the mail coats worn by Muslim soldiers.

Materials Steel, wood or leather (grip)
Used by Mostly infantry
Fact file Knights think of the dagger as an unworthy weapon for a nobleman.

Weight of sword is about 1.5 kg (3.3 lbs): light enough to use single-handed

Tang (handle) is forged in one piece with blade for extra strength

Blade has curved faces so that it does not bend

Sword
After a charge with lances, knights cut down enemy infantry with their swords. Swung from high in the saddle, they can cut a man's head clean off.

Materials Steel, wood or leather (grip)
Used by Cavalry and infantry
Fact file Smiths forge swords with flexible cores, but hard edges that don't easily blunt.

Head was sometimes spiked to pierce armour plate

Blade at back adds weight for greater penetrating power

Mace
The head of a mace can easily shatter bones. When aimed at a helmet the mace does not glance off, so it injures the head more effectively than a sword.

Materials Steel, wooden shaft
Used by Infantry
Fact file A weapon of Muslim soldiers, the mace was not used by knights until the 1200s.

War axe
A war axe has a spiked head. It is usually this, and not the curved blade at the back, that is driven into an enemy's armour and cuts his mail coat.

Materials Steel and wood
Used by Cavalry and infantry
Fact file The curved blade was used against unarmoured foes or their horses.

Infantrymen have a longer shield they can rest on the ground

Armour
Mail, plate, and quilted armour covers most areas of a knight's head and body. On his legs, a knight wears mail chausses (leggings) held up by a leather belt. Beneath his helmet is a mail hood – a padded cap stops it rubbing the face. Armour is not cheap: a knight's kit costs 2,000 silver pennies. (A skilled craftsman earns just three pennies a day.)

Materials Steel and fabric
Used by Cavalry and infantry
Fact file Hospitallers must have a full set of armour when they arrive from Europe.

Infantry

This 12th-century mosaic shows a knight and a Muslim in combat. Knights use their weapons skilfully in battle, but their enemy often outnumbers them. So the knights prefer to defend their kingdoms from the safety of castles, where bows are the best weapons.

Cavalry

Cavalry battles might begin with knights thundering towards each other, their lances lowered, but they quickly become messy and confused, as this image of a 13th-century clash shows. Knights cut down humble soldiers, but capture noble foe to hold ransom.

Bodkin point

Broad point

Hollow socket holds wooden shaft securely

Arrow heads and bolts

For accurate aim each arrow must have the same weight and length. The arrow's steel head is what makes it deadly. Bodkin points concentrate all the arrow's energy into a tiny area – at short range they can pierce armour. A "V"-shaped point is more effective against unprotected enemies: its backward-facing wings do immense damage to the flesh when pulled out.

Materials Steel	**Fact file** Even if they do not
Used by Infantry and	hit a vital organ,
mounted archers	arrows can cause
	fatal bleeding.

Crossbow

The crossbow is slow to load, but easy to master. Once an archer has pulled back the string he can take his time in picking a target. This makes crossbows ideal weapons for defending castles.

Materials Steel, cord, wood, and sinew
Used by Infantry
Fact file Pope Urban II banned crossbows as terror weapons in 1097 – but still permitted their use against Muslims.

Longbow

Trained archers can shoot longbows more quickly than crossbows, but learning to use the weapon takes years. Inside Crac, the bow's size makes it difficult to use in the cramped spaces.

Materials Wood and cord
Uses Infantry and cavalry
Fact file Armed with a longbow, an archer can aim and shoot six arrows in a minute.

THE OUTER BAILEY

Between Crac's towering (bastion) and its protective outer walls lies a narrow circle of land. Though more vulnerable than the inner castle, it's still secure from casual attack. Here in the outer (bailey) the knights can train their troops, and easily reach the ramparts on the outer walls. Here, too, there's enough space to move building stone for repairs in peacetime, or the massive timbers of siege engines when danger threatens. And it's here that news of Baybars' approaching army spreads as fast as the wind that whips around the Hospitaller banners flying defiantly from the bailey walls.

When the knights took over the castle there was no outer bailey. They began building the walls that enclose it at the beginning of the 13th century. At this time the inner fortifications were already very strong. By constructing the outer ring the knights aimed to make Crac (impregnable).

The towers spaced out around the walls of Crac make it possible for the defending archers to shoot at attackers wherever they are. From the towers, the areas covered by each bow-loop overlap, so that nowhere surrounding the outer bailey is safe from archery.

Twin towers on either side of the postern defend the gate against attack. Solidly built, they turn the gate into a barbican. The Franks borrowed this word from the Persian *barbār khanāh* ("house on a wall") to describe any specially strong tower.

The northern postern, or sally-port, provides a back door in the outer walls. It was probably completed in the 1250s under the command of castellan Nicolas Lorgne. It's protected by (machicolation) and a heavy wooden portcullis slides down to block the entrance.

(bastion) A fortified place.

(bailey) The outer wall of a castle. The word comes from the Old French word *baille*, meaning to enclose.

(impregnable) Something that is impossible to break into or capture by force.

(machicolation) A projecting platform at the top of a castle wall with holes through which missiles can be dropped.

The northern part of the inner castle clings to a rocky **crag** . Its hard stone foundations provide the perfect protection against **undermining** . Though tunnelling through rock to destroy the wall above is not impossible, it is very slow.

Another postern gate allows the knights to move freely between the inner castle and the outer bailey. Since any gate is a weak point in a wall, the postern is heavily defended. Huge machicolation overlooks it, and the steep slope leading up to it makes the postern extremely difficult to attack.

On top of one outer tower there is a windmill. It can be turned so that its sails face into the wind. The knights use it to grind grain into bread-flour and to mill food for horses. Windmills are a new invention adopted by the Europeans from the Middle East.

The open space within the outer bailey isn't really big enough for training cavalry, but there is enough space here to set up **butts** . The longbow, in particular, is difficult to master, but once trained, archers can hit a target up to 250 m (820 ft) away.

butts Archery targets

crag A steep rugged rock or peak. Crags were strategic places to build castles.

undermining Digging beneath a wall to loosen its foundations so that the wall falls down.

BUILDING METHODS

The masons who built Crac's walls had widely varied skills. Those employed at the quarries roughly trimmed the blocks to the correct size to reduce their weight. (Moving the stone was hard work.) Once the blocks had been hauled to Crac, rough masons shaped and placed most of the stone. **Freemasons** were the most skilled: they carved the fine details around windows, and chiselled decorations such as those in the Great Hall.

MEDIEVAL STONEMASON c. 1507

The northwest corner tower is both the oldest and the newest in the castle. A tower stood here when Crac was still the "Castle of the Kurds". Yet this was one of the last features to be completed by the knights: in the 1250s they strengthened its gate and added massive machicolation.

The western wall slopes steeply down, forming a **talus**. This makes the wall thicker at its base, forcing attackers further out from the wall top so that they are more exposed to fire. It also provides extra protection against undermining should the enemy succeed in draining the moat.

Masons are always at work on Crac's walls. When the walls are not being damaged in warfare, heavy winter rains wash away stonework. Less often, earthquakes shatter the foundations. Masons cut **ashlar** for the outsides. They fill the space in between the walls with rubble.

Sections of the wall that do not stand directly on rock need extra protection against undermining. The moat behind the west wall provides this: its waters would flood any tunnel. Digging the trench for the moat was an enormous task. All the work had to be done by hand, and the spoil removed in baskets.

ashlar A block of trimmed stone with straight edges for use in building.

Freemasons Members of a society of skilled stonemasons who recognized each other with secret signs and passwords.

talus A castle wall that slopes outwards as part of the castle's fortifications.

The south side is the most heavily defended in Crac, for this is the only place where the land does not drop away in a hill. Here the wall is especially wide. Within its thickness there is a corridor pierced with bow-loops and three strong towers.

In many castles towers interrupt the wall-walk, so that defenders can retreat in stages without surrendering the whole wall. At Crac, though, the wall-walk is continuous, because it is overlooked by the high towers of the inner castle. From there, the retreating troops can train fire on any attackers.

Overhanging, machicolated portions of the wall-walk allow defenders to direct arrows and other missiles onto attackers directly below. They never pour boiling oil, which is much too expensive. Instead they pour furnace-hot sand or boiling water, which penetrates armour and causes horrible burns.

The ground on the western side of the castle slopes steeply into the valley, offering a natural defence. However, the knights dare not risk an attack on this side, and the walls are a massive 9 m (30 ft) high. The wall's towers are rounded to deter undermining, which is always aimed at vulnerable corners.

Crossing the wall on arches, an aqueduct brings water to the castle. The channel, which runs from a spring on a distant hill, could be cut in a siege, but wells in the castle provide enough to drink for many months.

THE STABLES

Behind the massive stonework of the castle's southern wall, the dimly lit stables are home to 60 of the knight's finest horses. When a turcopole dashes in, he blinks for a moment in the gloom before passing on his message to mobilize. Now the **grooms** must stop their routine chores, put saddles and **bridles** on all the horses, and make them ready for action. Despite the urgency, the grooms work carefully, for horses are valuable and scarce. Most are brought from Europe, and any fighting leads to heavy losses. Unprotected horses make easier, bigger, and softer targets for Muslim archers than the armoured knights who ride them.

The stables form a vast vault that echoes with the whinnies of its occupants. Built from the same stone as the castle walls, the stables' arched construction gives them great strength. The few windows face out to the south. During a siege, archers will use them as bow-loops. Openings in the roof help air to circulate.

The horses stand side-by-side in stalls that line both sides of the room. Though the stables are 60 m (200 ft) long, there is only room for stalls for some 60 horses. Knights have four horses each, and turcopoles and sergeants two, so about four times as many horses are kept in the burgus and on surrounding estates.

The knights' horses are cared for by a team of grooms and veterinarians. To ensure the health of the valuable mounts, there are strict rules governing their work. Grooms must clip horses in a standard pattern. Vets nurse wounded or sick horses for six weeks, and put out to grass those that don't recover.

grooms People who clean and look after horses.

bridles The straps put around the head of a horse, which the rider uses to control the animal through the reins.

BREEDS OF HORSE

The Hospitallers use many different breeds of horses, ranging from small pack-animals to large warhorses. The knights themselves ride the biggest beasts, which are usually reared in Europe. These are muscular horses bred specifically to stand up to a cavalry charge, which jolts the rider in his rigid saddle. Though smaller than a modern cart-horse, they are nevertheless up to 15 hands high – 1.5 m (5 ft) at the shoulder. Turcopoles, who rarely charge with couched lances, do not need such big horses. Instead they ride faster, more agile Arab horses. The Hospitallers run stud farms on their estates, and sometimes cross the larger war horses with local Arab stock.

ARAB HORSE

FRIESIAN HORSE

MULE

Horses are very particular about their food. They need to be fed grain, usually oats. They eat up to 18 litres (half a bushel) a day. When the knights collect the taxes and **tithes** from farms they control, they expect some payment in oats. Horses also graze on the pastures near the castle.

Stable lads do one of the most unpleasant tasks in the castle – mucking out. Every horse in the stable produces more than 20 kg (45 lbs) of dung each day – that's more than a ton to shift every morning. It's shovelled from the stables and carted out to the fields around. There it's used as fertilizer to enrich the poor soil.

tithes Payments of one tenth of a farmer's produce, paid to the church to support its charitable work.

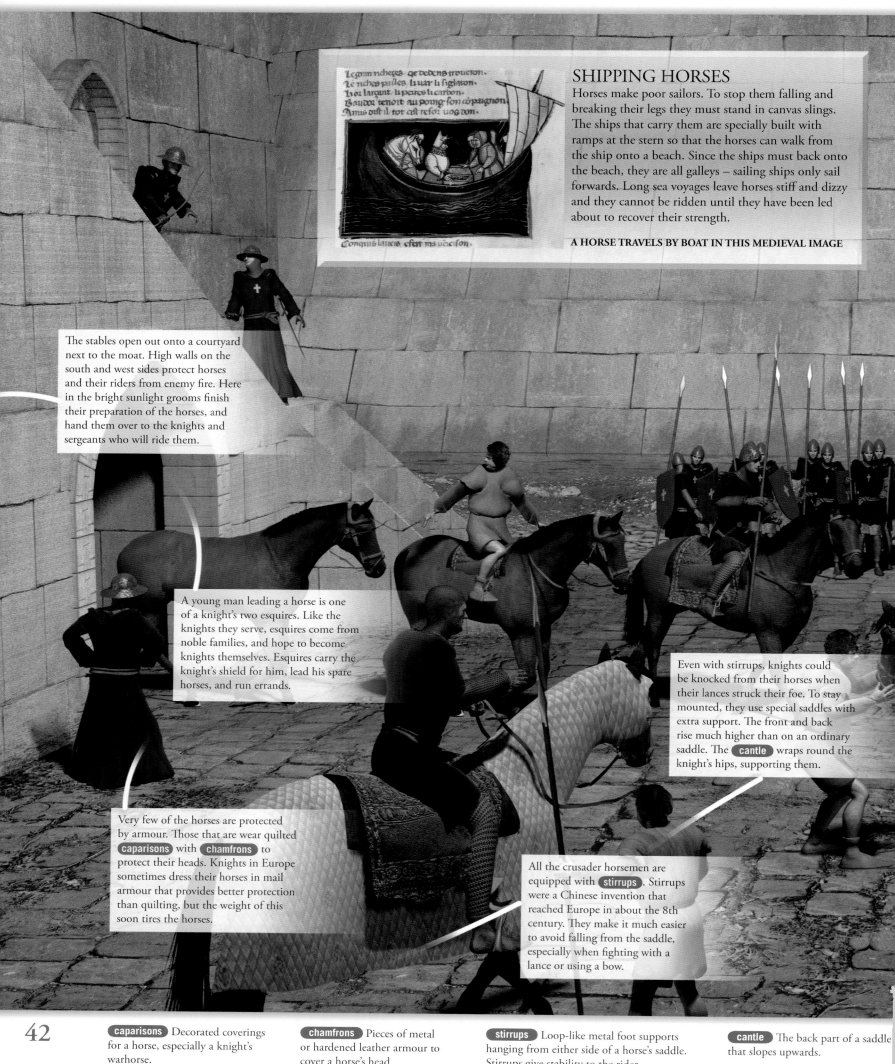

SHIPPING HORSES

Horses make poor sailors. To stop them falling and breaking their legs they must stand in canvas slings. The ships that carry them are specially built with ramps at the stern so that the horses can walk from the ship onto a beach. Since the ships must back onto the beach, they are all galleys – sailing ships only sail forwards. Long sea voyages leave horses stiff and dizzy and they cannot be ridden until they have been led about to recover their strength.

A HORSE TRAVELS BY BOAT IN THIS MEDIEVAL IMAGE

The stables open out onto a courtyard next to the moat. High walls on the south and west sides protect horses and their riders from enemy fire. Here in the bright sunlight grooms finish their preparation of the horses, and hand them over to the knights and sergeants who will ride them.

A young man leading a horse is one of a knight's two esquires. Like the knights they serve, esquires come from noble families, and hope to become knights themselves. Esquires carry the knight's shield for him, lead his spare horses, and run errands.

Even with stirrups, knights could be knocked from their horses when their lances struck their foe. To stay mounted, they use special saddles with extra support. The front and back rise much higher than on an ordinary saddle. The **cantle** wraps round the knight's hips, supporting them.

Very few of the horses are protected by armour. Those that are wear quilted **caparisons** with **chamfrons** to protect their heads. Knights in Europe sometimes dress their horses in mail armour that provides better protection than quilting, but the weight of this soon tires the horses.

All the crusader horsemen are equipped with **stirrups** . Stirrups were a Chinese invention that reached Europe in about the 8th century. They make it much easier to avoid falling from the saddle, especially when fighting with a lance or using a bow.

42 **caparisons** Decorated coverings for a horse, especially a knight's warhorse.

chamfrons Pieces of metal or hardened leather armour to cover a horse's head.

stirrups Loop-like metal foot supports hanging from either side of a horse's saddle. Stirrups give stability to the rider.

cantle The back part of a saddle that slopes upwards.

On all but the shortest trips, pack animals such as mules accompany the troops. They carry weapons, food, water, and everything the men need to set up camp. Some are loaded with grain and hay to feed the horses. The pack animals will form a **caravan** that follows the expedition.

Mounted and armoured, the cavalry urge their horses out of the courtyard towards the castle's gate. They are riding out to face a Muslim force of unknown size. Some of them will not return, but they know that if they do not stop Baybars now, there will be no second chances.

Roughly half of the cavalrymen who are leaving the castle today are turcopoles. They wear light armour: just a quilted **aketon**, and a cone-shaped helmet. Though this affords less protection than heavy mail, it enables them to ride faster and further as they **skirmish** with the enemy.

Between them, Crac's knights and sergeants have more then 500 horses, each of which needs a new set of shoes every fortnight or so. Making the shoes keeps three blacksmiths busy, and the same number of **farriers** fit them to the horses.

caravan A group of pack-animals or wagons travelling in single file.

aketon A type of padded jacket worn for protection.

skirmish A brief clash between soldiers.

farriers People who nail shoes to horses.

43

THE RAMP

As the knights ride out, they pass through Crac's most ingenious defence – its sloping ramp. Gatehouses are the weakest point of any castle wall, so the Hospitallers have lavished special attention on this, the castle's main entrance. Completed less than 20 years ago, the ramp is cunningly designed to make a successful assault impossible. Before they even reach the ramp attackers must cross a moat, and fight their way through the outermost gatehouse. The ramp's gradient gives the advantage to the defenders, and four gates and a portcullis bar the way in. Little wonder that no Muslim army has tried to enter Crac by the front door!

Both sections of the ramp are built on a massive scale. They are wide and high enough for knights to ride two abreast. This means that the knights can leave the castle very quickly to deal with a threat – and retreat just as fast if they are outnumbered!

Through an arch facing the departing knights, infantrymen rush to join the expedition. The corridor down which they hurry leads from Crac's main gate. Like the lower part of the ramp, it slopes downwards, and is overlooked by bow-loops.

Heavy doors block the route into the castle at intervals. When danger threatens, guards strengthen them with thick timbers that slide into slots in the stone door-frames. Metal studs on doors aim to blunt attacking axes, and machicolation above allows the defenders to quench fires.

PORTCULLIS

Grid-shaped drop-gates like these were first used by the Romans in the 3rd century BC. The Franks call them "harrows" after the farmers' clod breakers that are a similar shape. Generally made in heavy wood, all have spiked iron tips; some are also iron-clad to protect against fire. They were raised by a **winch** in a room above, where there is a quick release device. Knocking this out allows the portcullis to drop down instantly.

PORTCULLIS AT BODIAM CASTLE, ENGLAND

 winch A pulley, or winding device, used to lift something up by a rope.

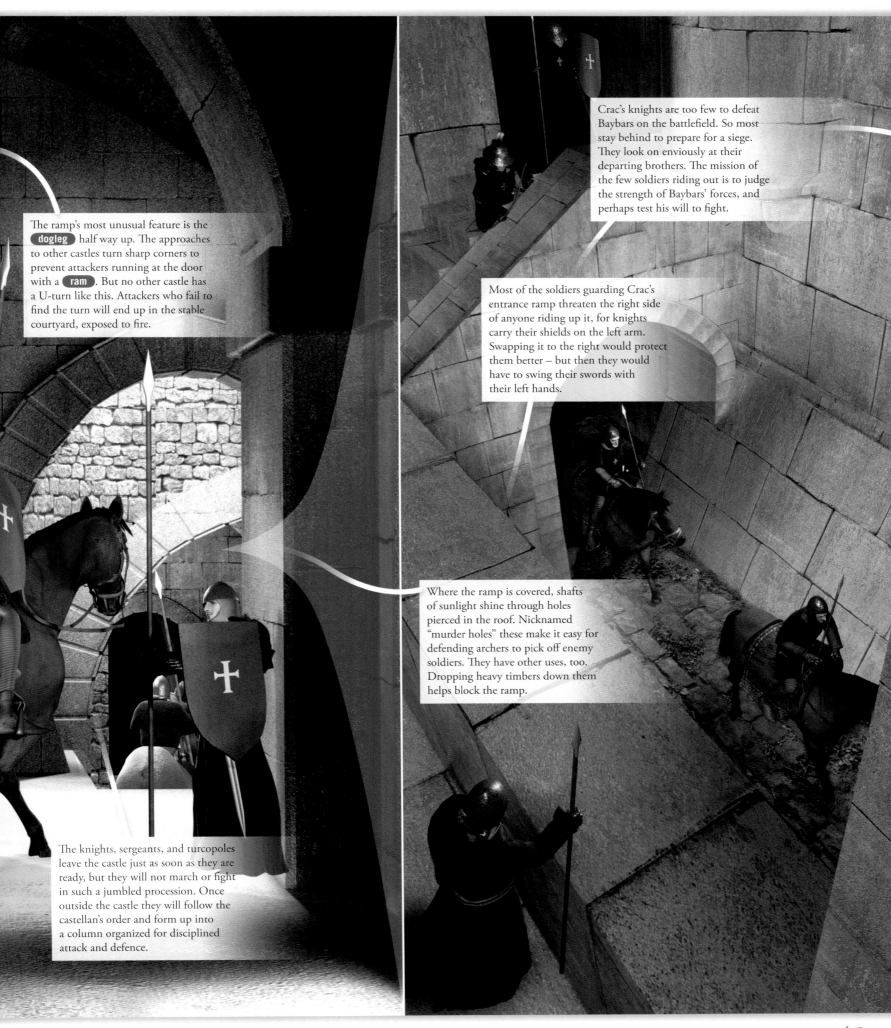

The ramp's most unusual feature is the dogleg half way up. The approaches to other castles turn sharp corners to prevent attackers running at the door with a ram . But no other castle has a U-turn like this. Attackers who fail to find the turn will end up in the stable courtyard, exposed to fire.

Crac's knights are too few to defeat Baybars on the battlefield. So most stay behind to prepare for a siege. They look on enviously at their departing brothers. The mission of the few soldiers riding out is to judge the strength of Baybars' forces, and perhaps test his will to fight.

Most of the soldiers guarding Crac's entrance ramp threaten the right side of anyone riding up it, for knights carry their shields on the left arm. Swapping it to the right would protect them better – but then they would have to swing their swords with their left hands.

Where the ramp is covered, shafts of sunlight shine through holes pierced in the roof. Nicknamed "murder holes" these make it easy for defending archers to pick off enemy soldiers. They have other uses, too. Dropping heavy timbers down them helps block the ramp.

The knights, sergeants, and turcopoles leave the castle just as soon as they are ready, but they will not march or fight in such a jumbled procession. Once outside the castle they will follow the castellan's order and form up into a column organized for disciplined attack and defence.

dogleg A sharp bend, or angle, in the shape of a dog's leg.

ram Short for battering ram. A large wooden beam used for battering down the doors of castles.

45

LEAVING THE CASTLE

The knights are used to assembling swift, efficient raiding parties to attack points nearby. Indeed, this is their tactic for controlling the surrounding area and occasionally exacting tribute from villages and towns in Muslim hands. Crac is perfectly placed for this function – the knights can return to its protection, and simply ignore threats of retaliation. But now there is a threat they can not afford to ignore. The Hospitallers and their allies do not expect to defeat the much larger Mamluk army in the field, but a small scouting force can at least see their foes at first hand, so that the garrison at Crac can plan its defence.

Surrounding the castle are estates allied to the Hospitallers. Knights who manage Hospitaller estates have a duty to defend the castle in times of danger. The Hospitallers employ **mercenaries** from villages on the estates, which also supply food and horses.

Even on short journeys, the knights can't travel light. They carry their own food, supplies of weapons and armour, and take extra horses. Pack animals carry fodder for the horses. Even when there is enough grass growing to feed them, grazing is too time-consuming.

The width of the ramp and the main gate beyond means that the knights can move men and war materials out of the castle quickly. Guards on the walls above them have a panoramic view over the surrounding landscape, so they can quickly spot any threat to the knights forming up outside.

The core of the expedition is the cavalry – the soldiers on horseback. To avoid riding in their uncomfortable body-armour, the knights can tie it to the saddle behind them when not actually fighting. However, they always wear their helmets and leg armour.

The knights are disciplined about the formation of raiding parties. Everyone has their place in the column: the knights lead the way, followed by sergeants. Turcopoles follow at the rear. Knights always pass around the column downwind, to avoid blowing dust in their companions' faces.

SKIRMISHING

To take advantage of the greater speed and mobility of the turcopoles, the knights usually send them on ahead in a skirmish. By raining their arrows on an enemy column, the turcopole archers can force it to come to a halt, or split it up. Then the more heavily armed knights can mount a deadly attack.

TURCOPOLES ATTACK TURKISH CAVALRY

mercenaries Hired soldiers who fight for money rather than out of loyalty or belief in a cause.

CARRIER PIGEONS

The knights probably took with them pigeons. Released with a message tied to their legs, they could fly back to Crac much faster than a messenger could ride. The knights' foe, Baybars, had an elaborate pigeon-post service: his people called the winged messengers "angels of the kings".

MEDIEVAL PIGEON MESSENGERS

We can only guess at what Crac's walled burgus (suburb) looked like because all trace of it is now hidden beneath a village. This area of housing, workshops, and offices may have been separate from the castle. But possibly its walls joined up with those of Crac.

As news of the imminent attack spreads through the burgus, local people flock past the knights' column towards the gates of Crac. Its solid walls offer a safe haven, and they fear that their sympathy for the knights will make them targets for Baybars.

Some of the turcopoles waiting to join the column will fight on foot and some on horseback. Sergeants within the knights' column will also provide infantry backup, often outnumbering cavalry. In 1233, an expedition numbered 400 cavalry to 500 infantry.

CATALOGUE OF MEDIEVAL SIEGE WEAPONS

Huge, powerful war machines pound the walls of medieval fortresses. Hurling rocks, flaming arrows the size of broomsticks, or even human heads, these weapons can turn a siege from a tedious waiting game into a terrifying ordeal. Called siege engines, most get their power from gravity, or from energy stored in twisted fibres. Carefully aimed, they can hit the same spot on a castle wall time after time – until it falls.

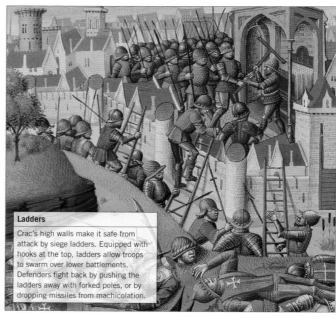

Ladders

Crac's high walls make it safe from attack by siege ladders. Equipped with hooks at the top, ladders allow troops to swarm over lower battlements. Defenders fight back by pushing the ladders away with forked poles, or by dropping missiles from machicolation.

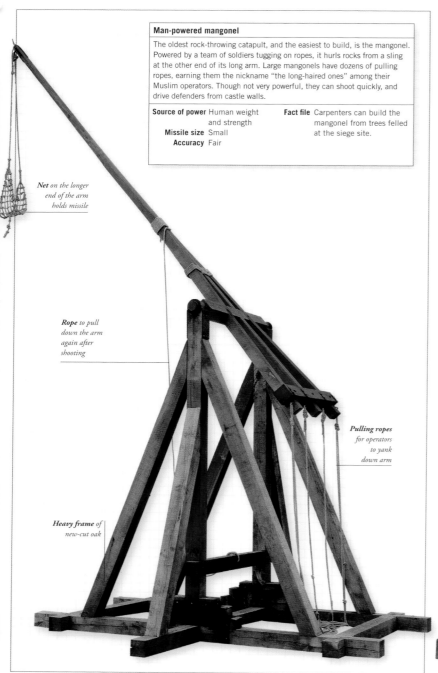

Man-powered mangonel

The oldest rock-throwing catapult, and the easiest to build, is the mangonel. Powered by a team of soldiers tugging on ropes, it hurls rocks from a sling at the other end of its long arm. Large mangonels have dozens of pulling ropes, earning them the nickname "the long-haired ones" among their Muslim operators. Though not very powerful, they can shoot quickly, and drive defenders from castle walls.

Source of power	Human weight and strength	**Fact file**	Carpenters can build the mangonel from trees felled at the siege site.
Missile size	Small		
Accuracy	Fair		

Net on the longer end of the arm holds missile

Rope to pull down the arm again after shooting

Pulling ropes for operators to yank down arm

Heavy frame of new-cut oak

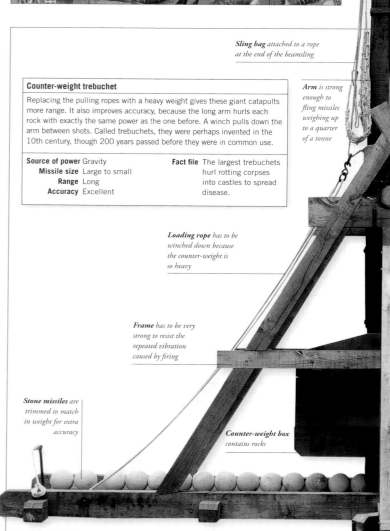

Sling bag attached to a rope at the end of the beamsling

Arm is strong enough to fling missiles weighing up to a quarter of a tonne

Counter-weight trebuchet

Replacing the pulling ropes with a heavy weight gives these giant catapults more range. It also improves accuracy, because the long arm hurls each rock with exactly the same power as the one before. A winch pulls down the arm between shots. Called trebuchets, they were perhaps invented in the 10th century, though 200 years passed before they were in common use.

Source of power	Gravity	**Fact file**	The largest trebuchets hurl rotting corpses into castles to spread disease.
Missile size	Large to small		
Range	Long		
Accuracy	Excellent		

Loading rope has to be winched down because the counter-weight is so heavy

Frame has to be very strong to resist the repeated vibration caused by firing

Stone missiles are trimmed to match in weight for extra accuracy

Counter-weight box contains rocks

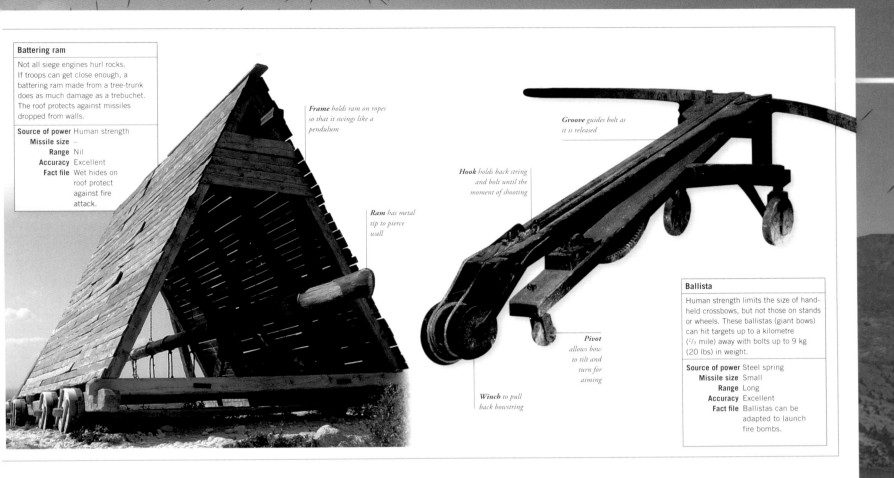

Battering ram

Not all siege engines hurl rocks. If troops can get close enough, a battering ram made from a tree-trunk does as much damage as a trebuchet. The roof protects against missiles dropped from walls.

Source of power	Human strength
Missile size	–
Range	Nil
Accuracy	Excellent
Fact file	Wet hides on roof protect against fire attack.

Frame holds ram on ropes so that it swings like a pendulum

Ram has metal tip to pierce wall

Hook holds back string and bolt until the moment of shooting

Groove guides bolt as it is released

Pivot allows bow to tilt and turn for aiming

Winch to pull back bowstring

Ballista

Human strength limits the size of hand-held crossbows, but not those on stands or wheels. These ballistas (giant bows) can hit targets up to a kilometre ($^2/_3$ mile) away with bolts up to 9 kg (20 lbs) in weight.

Source of power	Steel spring
Missile size	Small
Range	Long
Accuracy	Excellent
Fact file	Ballistas can be adapted to launch fire bombs.

Torsion-powered onager

Based on a Roman weapon, the onager is named after a wild mule because of the way it kicks as it's fired. Winching down the short arm tightens up the animal-sinew spring that provides the weapon's power.

Source of power	Twisted animal sinew
Missile size	Small
Range	Moderate
Fact file	Water softened the onager's sinews, making it useless in rain.

Crossbar stops the arm, releasing missile

Priming rope pulls down arm when wound in by winch

Arm pivots around its lower end when hurling upwards

Siege towers

To protect soldiers scaling castle walls, some besieging armies enclose ladders inside wooden towers. A wet-hide cover protects against fire. Due to their great weight, the towers are moved on rollers, so they are useless on steeply sloping ground.

THE SIEGE

It is March 1271. The scouting party has returned to Crac with bad news. Baybars' army is vast, and is carrying the parts of many siege engines. Though these enormous timbers have slowed the army's progress, it has now reached the castle gates. The castellan knows that Baybars has besieged the crusader fortress of Castel Blanc (White Castle) at Safita. The town is within sight of Crac's towers, though too far away for the knights to see its defeat clearly. Fresh from this victory, Baybars' troops are clearly hoping for another. The knights are determined to disappoint them, and have doubled their efforts to make their own castle secure.

Behind the barred gates of Crac, the knights received early warnings of Baybars' advance. Supplies of food from the estates to the west dried up as they fell one by one to the Muslim army. In the distance, Baybars' scouts appeared, watching Crac and counting the men on its walls.

Protected only by earth ditches and timber walls, the triangular **outwork** to the south of the castle is easily captured. This gives Baybars a high vantage point on which to set his siege engines and crossbowmen. From here, they can bombard the south wall.

Heavy rain following the capture of the burgus allows the knights a brief rest. But when the storms turn to showers, Baybars' engineers can be seen building mangonels behind **palisades** on the plateau to the south. By 21 March they are complete.

On Monday 3 March the waiting game ends as the Mamluk army moves into position before the castle. Baybars wastes no time. His troops immediately attack the burgus outside the castle walls. Though the knights fight hard to defend it, the burgus falls within two days.

50

palisades Strong fences supported by wooden stakes driven into the ground for defence.

outwork A defence that lies outside the main defensive works, or outside the castle.

SIEGE WARFARE

The aim of a siege was to cut the castle off from all supplies of food, water, and arms. The idea was that the garrison inside would surrender or starve. In practice, a siege wasn't quite that easy. Castles hoarded food in preparation for a siege, and had their own supplies of water. At Crac there was a deep well that could not be poisoned by the enemy, and nine cisterns to collect rainwater. Hunger also affected attackers: a large besieging army had to eat, too. If a siege continued for a long time the attackers had to travel further and further to find food. To make a siege shorter, the attackers did more than just wait. They also used siege engines to pound the walls, and dug **saps** towards the walls to that their miners could attack the foundations.

MEDIEVAL ILLUSTRATION OF SALADIN BESIEGING JERUSALEM, 1187

Baybars' position has disadvantages, too. It brings his troops within range of Crac's own siege engines. Set high on the towers, they pound the Mamluk lines. There's no shortage of missiles: the garrison collect the rocks hurled across the walls, and hurl them back.

From behind their defences, Muslim crossbowmen rain arrows on Crac's walls. Muslim archers usually use bows for attacks in the field because they can shoot them quickly while riding. For sieges they sometimes prefer crossbows, which have greater range.

saps Deep, narrow trenches dug to approach an enemy position so that it can be undermined.

51

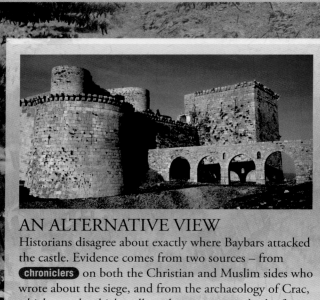

AN ALTERNATIVE VIEW

Historians disagree about exactly where Baybars attacked the castle. Evidence comes from two sources – from **chroniclers** on both the Christian and Muslim sides who wrote about the siege, and from the archaeology of Crac, which reveals which walls and towers were rebuilt after the siege. Unfortunately there are several different ways of looking at these clues, and some experts believe that the attack came not on the east side, but here, on the castle's southwest tower.

One of Baybars' first steps when he arrived at Crac was to destroy the aqueduct that channels water into the moat from springs on the hills nearby. Though the knights don't drink from the moat – it is thick with algae – it's a valuable defence. Already the water level in the moat has fallen.

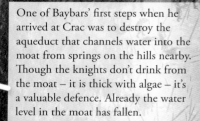

SAPS

To make a castle wall collapse, the attackers tried to undermine it – by digging a mine or a sap through the ground beneath it. Arab military engineers were expert miners. They began their tunnel as close to the castle wall as they dared. As the tunnel advanced, they held up the roof with dry timber props. Once the tunnel had reached a point directly beneath the target wall or tower, they enlarged it, and filled the chamber with **tinder-dry** brushwood and often with other materials that burn well, such as animal fat. Setting this on fire burned away the wooden props, and the mine collapsed, bringing down the great weight of masonry above it.

MEDIEVAL SAPPERS USING A CAT ON WHEELS

With control of the outworks to the south, Baybars moves to the next phase of his attack: breaking through the outer walls. While his sappers are at work, they will be under constant attack from Crac's walls. So Baybars' archers now aim to clear the walls of defenders above the site of the tunnel.

chroniclers People who write down records of events.

tinder-dry Something that's as dry as tinder – the wood or grass used for lighting a fire.

When medieval writers describe "arrows raining down", they are telling the truth. When huge armies meet on the battlefield their archers just shoot as fast as they can. Arrows travelling in opposite directions darken the sky and sometimes collide in mid-air.

Some of the archers' crossbows are slow to load. The bow is so strong that archers must use a winch to pull back the string. To shoot more quickly, archers work in threes. While two take aim, the third winches back the string on an extra bow, and loads a bolt.

From Crac's high towers, Hospitaller archers harass the Mamluk soldiers with a barrage of arrows. The castle's construction ensures that a bow-loop overlooks every part of the land around. However, some parts of the wall are more exposed than others.

To protect the sappers while they dig, the Mamluk engineers have built a "sow" or "cat" of heavy timbers. This movable tunnel has a covering of wet hides to protect it against flaming debris. Under its sturdy **canopy** sappers can approach their tunnel entrance in safety.

canopy A roof-like structure that acts as a sheltered passageway.

53

Mining is slow and dangerous work, but Baybars' sappers are determined men. They work day and night to extend the tunnel. On 29 March it's complete. They set fire to the timber stacked inside the mine. Soon the wall above collapses into the tunnel, creating a wide gap in Crac's defences.

Breaching the outer wall is a great achievement, but Crac's inner castle is yet undamaged. It may prove difficult to mine – the moat protects those walls that do not stand on rock. Worse, in the outer bailey the Mamluk soldiers are at the mercy of the castle's archers, who are now much closer than before.

Sensing victory, Mamluk soldiers storm through the gap with a tremendous roar – to discover that the outer bailey is filled with terrified peasants from the Hospitallers' estates. The soldiers send them back to their fields, but slaughter the few Christian soldiers they come across.

To threaten the garrison, Baybars sets up mangonels within the outer bailey. His engineers take the machines apart to carry them through the gap in the outer wall. Rebuilt inside, the engines are just metres from Crac's inner walls. At such short range, their destructive power is enormous.

After another week of siege, Baybars' assault on Crac strengthens. The knights inside are worn down by the impact of rocks hurled against the same point on the wall. Their supplies are dwindling daily. On 8 April, after the wall has collapsed, they admit defeat, and offer to surrender their beloved castle.

The Hospitallers strike a deal with Baybars. In exchange for surrendering the castle, the Mamluk leader allows the knights to join their comrades in Tripoli on the coast without fear of attack. Baybars also agrees to spare the lives of the Syrian Christian mercenaries who have fought alongside the knights.

THE FORGED LETTER

The pounding from Baybars' siege engines may have been enough to force the surrender of Crac. But according to legend, there was another reason why the knights surrendered. Baybars forged a letter to the castellan. Apparently from Hugues de Revel, the Grand Master of the Hospitaller order, it gave the knights of Crac permission to give up the castle and save their own lives.

GRAND MASTER HUGUES DE REVEL

With the knights gone, Baybars takes possession of the mightiest of the crusader castles, and one that had shrugged off attacks for more than 160 years. The siege has done much damage to Crac's defences, but in the years that follow, Baybars will repair the walls and make Crac stronger still.

THE MUSLIM VIEW
FIGHTING THE FRANKS

When tall, pale-skinned knights first appeared on the borders of what is now Turkey in 1096, the Muslims who lived there had no reason to fear them. They were only a few hundred armoured men, followed by a ragged army of ordinary people. Cavalry from Nicaea attacked the column of "Franks", as local people called all those from northern Europe. Those who survived the attack were enslaved.

More knights arrive

But this first disorganized column was not the last. Soon, Franks were arriving in the Holy Land in great numbers. The Muslim princes were puzzled. They were used to pilgrims visiting their lands to pray at Christian shrines, and much of the local population was Christian. On the whole, they tolerated them. But these Franks were different. They were also filled with a religious enthusiasm that was warlike in its strength. Muslim leaders were too busy fighting each other to worry about the Franks. No one ruler was strong enough to control the whole region, and each kingdom jostled to control more territory. Battles, assassinations, and plots were a way of life.

The Church of the Holy Sepulchre was the most sacred place in Jerusalem for Christians. When Saladin recaptured the city in 1187, he placed guards at its doors to make sure that none of his troops could plunder it.

Cannibals!

But by 1098, news was spreading of how the Franks had attacked Muslim-controlled towns as they advanced. Then they captured Antioch. It was bad news indeed, but it was followed by a story that horrified the whole Muslim world. At the town of Ma'arra, in what is today Syria, the Franks had cooked and eaten the bodies of those they killed! Of course, stories of horrible war crimes are often invented, but not this one. Even the Franks themselves admitted it was true. The cannibalism of Ma'arra was not

> "In Ma'arra our troops boiled pagan adults in cooking pots; they spiked children on spits and devoured them."
>
> *Frankish chronicler Radulph of Caen writing on the massacre of 1098*

The capture of Jerusalem in 1099 led Christians to rejoice. One writer called the slaughter of the city's people "a splendid judgement of God."

The massacre of 30,000 Muslim men, women, and children in Jerusalem was seen by the Franks as fair punishment because they believed that these Muslims had insulted their God.

...nough to unite the Muslim people against the Franks. Facing only small local pockets of resistance, their advance seemed unstoppable. Gradually it became clear that they were heading south, for Jerusalem.

The Franks take Jerusalem

They came within sight of the city on 7 June 1099. The city's rulers were not concerned. They had locked all local Christians outside the gates in case they helped the Franks to capture the city. And they had poisoned all wells outside the walls, to deny the Franks water. To begin with the Christians just walked around the walls barefoot, led by chanting priests. Only later did they start to build siege towers. When the attack came in July, Frankish soldiers swarmed over the walls from one of the towers. Once they were inside the city, they took a terrible revenge on those who had dared to defend it. It took them two days to slaughter the city's inhabitants.

Slaughter in the temples

The Muslims fled to a mosque, but the Franks broke down the doors. They rode inside, cutting down everyone until their horses were wading knee-deep through blood. When the city's Jews barricaded themselves in the synagogue, the Franks burned them all. Even Christians did not escape the violence. At the Church of the Holy Sepulchre the Franks tortured the Orthodox Christians who worshipped there until they led them to the hiding place of the True Cross, which had been concealed from the invaders.

Slaughter in the temples

Amazingly, even the massacre at Jerusalem did not lead immediately to a Muslim campaign against the Franks. Because the rulers of each small state hated each other, they would not fight the Franks together. And separately they could not defeat them. They followed a local proverb: "Kiss any arm you cannot break, and pray to God to break it."

Living with the enemy

Without the power to defeat the Franks, the Muslims leaders learned to live with them. They tried to understand them, too, but found this difficult. For the Franks were not very civilized. They did not wash. They were ignorant, and knew nothing of science and mathematics. They got drunk. Their physicians killed more patients than they cured.

A new leader

Divisions between the Muslims enabled the Franks to rule the Holy Land almost unchallenged for nearly 50 years. Saladin changed all this. Rising to power in Egypt, he conquered rivals in Syria and was recognized by the Muslim world as leader of the struggle against the Franks. In 1187 he advanced on Jerusalem.

The crusaders found that Muslims had left their mark on Jerusalem with many fine examples of Islamic architecture.

Saladin's capture of the holy city was almost bloodless. He allowed the Franks to leave Jerusalem unharmed. If they wished to stay, he promised they could worship freely in their churches. Not all the Muslim leaders were so merciful. When Baybars captured Antioch from the Franks in 1268, he allowed his troops to slaughter all who lived there. To Baybars, this was a fair punishment.

> "Christians everywhere will remember the kindness we have shown them."

Saladin, as he allows Jerusalem's Frankish Christians to leave the city with their belongings in 1187

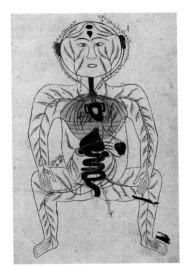

Muslim medicine was advanced. Ibn Al Nafis (1213–1288) discovered the circulation of the blood centuries before it was known in Europe.

Muslim astronomers used astrolabes like this one to calculate stars' positions. Such devices were unknown in Europe until crusaders returned with them.

CRAC UNDER THE MUSLIMS

Now the knights have gone, Crac des Chevaliers once again becomes a Muslim stronghold. Instead of the medieval French of the Hospitallers, its corridors echo with Arabic and Turkish. The fortress has been badly damaged in the siege, and Baybars sets about rebuilding it. The work moves rapidly, even though the castle is in no immediate danger. Baybars has good reasons for wanting it complete. He plans to use the castle as a military base. The Hospitallers are still in the Holy Land, so they might prove a threat in the future. And he also wants to give the castle a Muslim identity, removing all traces of the "infidels" who occupied it.

One of the most important tasks is to convert the castle's chapel into a mosque. Baybars orders the installation of a **minbar** in which the mosque's **imam** stands to preach. The minbar can still be seen today on the south side of the chapel.

Baybars wastes no time in putting right the damage the siege has caused to the castle's walls and towers. Building work is already under way in May 1271, a month or two after Crac fell. In October, Baybars visits the castle to inspect progress.

Later Mamluk building work doesn't just repair war damage. Winter rains here are torrential and some 30 years after Crac fell to Baybars, a storm will wash away this section of the inner citadel wall. The governor of the castle, emir Badr al-din Bilik al Sadidi, will organize its rebuilding.

WATER WORKS

The installation of baths at Crac is not just for luxury living. Water and washing is an important part in Islamic culture. The Prophet Muhammad taught that "cleanliness is half of faith", and all Muslims wash before prayer. Bath houses also play an important part in everyday life: they are places where people meet and relax. Beyond the bath-house, running water is central in Muslim architecture. In parched desert climates, it refreshes the spirit as well as quenching the thirst.

ENTRANCE TO THE BATH HOUSE AT CRAC

minbar The pulpit of a mosque, from which the imam speaks to the worshippers.

imam A man who leads the worshippers in prayer in a mosque

Repairs to Crac take some 18 months. In the autumn of 1275, Baybars returns to inspect the new stonework. In a symbolic gesture, he calls on the **emirs** at his side to carry into the castle ammunition for the siege engines. Then he picks up a spade and works alongside the builders.

NEW RELIGION

One of Baybars' first acts on conquering Crac is to begin public prayers in the chapel, for Crac's new Muslim owners hold religious views that are quite as devout as those of the castle's previous Christian occupants. Muslims face Mecca when praying, and Baybars adds to the chapel a **mihrab** showing the direction of the holy city.

THE MINBAR PULPIT IN THE CHAPEL

When the rebuilding work on Crac is complete, the castle is once more a powerful fortress. In 1285, the Mameluk Sultan of Egypt, Qalawun, uses Crac to launch a new attack on the Hospitallers at their stronghold in Margat. The city falls after a ferocious month-long siege.

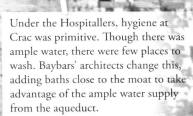

Under the Hospitallers, hygiene at Crac was primitive. Though there was ample water, there were few places to wash. Baybars' architects change this, adding baths close to the moat to take advantage of the ample water supply from the aqueduct.

Baybars' building works restore the south and east sides of Crac to their former glory. These were the parts of the castle that were most severely damaged during the siege. Muslim masons also strengthen and extend the machicolation along the western wall.

Most of the Muslim work on the castle repairs damage, but there is one imposing new structure. In 1285, Muslim masons complete a large square tower in the centre of the south wall. Its bow-loops overlook the outworks from which Baybars launched his attack 14 years earlier.

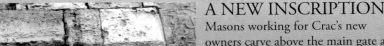

A NEW INSCRIPTION

Masons working for Crac's new owners carve above the main gate an inscription celebrating the start of the castle's restoration. "Our master Sultan Baybars and his son have ordered the restoration of this blessed fortress on Tuesday 25th Sha'ban [the 8th month]...1271".

INSCRIPTION ABOVE THE MAIN GATE

emirs Muslim military commanders or governors.

mihrab The large niche in a wall at a mosque that indicates the direction of Mecca, the holy city towards which Muslims pray.

THE END FOR THE KNIGHTS

THE SEARCH FOR A MEDITERRANEAN HOME

Losing Crac des Chevaliers was a painful defeat for the Hospitallers. But this was not the last humiliation they would suffer. In the centuries that followed, they often found themselves homeless, unwelcome, and searching for a reason to exist.

Provoking the Mamluks

At first the Hospitallers did not realize how complete their defeat had been. After withdrawing to the strongholds they had left, they broke treaties they had made with Baybars, and continued to raid

(left) A Hospitaller cross studded with jewels shows off the wealth of the knights. Such riches made others envious. In 1307, France's King Philip the Fair crushed the Templars to get his hands on their wealth. He accused them of heresy (denying that Christ was God), and killed many brothers.

their Muslim neighbours. Angered, the Mamluks attacked and swiftly took the last great remaining Hospitaller castle, Margat. The Hospitallers retreated again to the coastal town of Tripoli, but their stay there did not last long. Tripoli fell in 1289 as the Mamluk advance continued, shrinking the crusaders' kingdom little by little.

The beginning of the end

Two years later – and 20 years after the fall of Crac – the Mamluks were ready to crush the crusaders once and for all. A huge army encircled the city of Acre. The besieged town held out for two months, until Mamluk engineers undermined the inner citadel. The remaining crusader cities of Tyre, Sidon, Beirut, Tartus, and Athlit fell over the summer. The Holy Land was once again in Muslim hands. The defeated knights fled in galleys to the island of Cyprus. The once-proud and rich crusading orders suddenly found that their fortunes – and popularity – had reversed. Once the saviours of the Holy Land, they were now blamed for its loss.

The siege of Rhodes, 1522, ended after the citizens found notes on Ottoman arrows promising the safety of those who surrendered. Rhodes' people then urged the knights to leave.

Unwanted in Cyprus

The Hospitallers' time in Cyprus was not a happy one. They clashed with the island's king, Henry, over their power and wealth. They were accused of corruption and wasteful living. Finally, after a popular rebellion on the island, the knights realize that they were no longer welcome. They chose the nearby island of Rhodes as their next base. Rhodes

The siege of Acre, 1291, ended with the deaths of many of the besieging army as well as of the Christians within. Sappers had undermined the citadel walls, which collapsed. The Mamluk soldiers then swarmed over them.

Fort St Angelo still guards the entrance to Malta's massive harbour. In defending Rhodes and Malta, the knights used the knowledge they had gained of building castles in Syria.

> "With these conquests the whole of Palestine was now in Muslim hands. Praise be to God!"
>
> *Taqi ad-Din al Maqrizi (1364–1442) rejoices at the fall of Acre, Tyre, and Tortosa*

was ruled by the Byzantine empire (the Eastern Christian Church). But with help from the pope and the kings of England and France, the knights prepared a plan to capture the island. It took them two years, but by 1309 their conquest was complete. Now the Knights Hospitallers had a new name: they became the Knights of Rhodes.

Fortifying Rhodes

The knights lost no time in shaping Rhodes to meet their needs. They turned Rhodes Town into a fortress, and at the heart of the city they built a palace for the order's Grand Master. Rhodes was in the front line of the war between Christianity and Islam, and its fortifications were twice tested by Muslim attacks in the 15th century. But in 1522 Turkey's Muslim rulers, the Ottomans, sent a fleet to conquer Rhodes. Among the 200,000 men on board were 60,000 sappers, armed with explosives. Despite being outnumbered more than 25 to 1, the knights and their allies held the island for six months. Finally, though, hunger and disease wore

Lindos, Rhodes, was one of the towns that the knights turned into a fortress to resist attacks from the Ottomans.

down Rhodes' people, and the knights surrendered. On the first day of 1523 they set sail again, first to Crete, then on to Italy.

A base in Malta

The knights spent seven years in Italy, until Spain's King Charles V gave them a new home on Malta. This small island became the base from which the Christian knights could continue to wage war on Islam. Now, though, they fought their battles not on land but at sea. They built galleys, and chained Muslim slaves to the oars. With these warships they attacked the ports of the Barbary Coast – the North African shore held by the Ottoman empire. The Ottomans tried to end these attacks by besieging Malta in 1565, but the Hospitallers were ready for them. They had turned the island's capital, Valletta, into a fortress. Despite a siege lasting more than three months, they held the island. The Hospitallers stayed on Malta until 1798, when they were tricked into surrendering the island to Napoleon Bonaparte (1769– 1821), revolutionary leader of France. Napoleon also confiscated the order's estates in France.

Queen Elizabeth II is today the head of the order of the knights of St John. Here she is wearing the order's insignia.

The knights today

Napoleon weakened the Hospitallers, but he did not destroy them. The brothers would never again be warrior knights, so they changed their mission. They continued as a religious order, but instead of fighting Muslims, the knights took up charitable, social, and medical work. The order still exists today. Though it lacks land, it has its own government, laws, passports, and stamps, and even a place in the United Nations.

The St John ambulance carries on the original work of the Hospitaller knights in caring for the sick and injured. Here they provide first aid for a marathon runner.

CATALOGUE OF CASTLES

The defences of Crac des Chevaliers were perfectly suited to medieval warfare in the Holy Land, and the castle was widely copied. But elsewhere in the world, soldiers fought with different weapons, and on a variety of battlegrounds that were not at all like Syria. The strong fortresses they built had little in common with Crac's castle-in-a-castle structure. In particular, the development of guns the century after Crac fell changed castle design for ever.

Housesteads fort

Roman soldiers built this fort in about 124 CE as one of some 15 forts that lined Hadrian's Wall. This long stone barrier defended the northern limit of Rome's empire. The soldiers stationed here fought off raids by tribes from what is now Scotland.

Buhen fort

Egypt's pharaoh Senusret III built Buhen as one of a line of mud-brick forts on the river Nile. Buhen had many advanced defences, including a moat crossed by a drawbridge.

Location Nubia, southern Egypt
Date About 1860 BCE
Amazing fact Egypt's forts were the first to use machicolation for defence.

Mud-bricks of castle were destroyed in 1964 by the waters of a new reservoir.

Mycenae citadel

The early Greek people protected their cities from warlike neighbours by building them on hilltops and surrounding them by stout walls. Mycenae was their capital.

Location Peloponnese, Greece
Date 16th century BCE
Amazing fact The stone blocks of the citadel are so big that people thought it was built by giants.

Beaumaris castle, Wales

England's king Edward I saw Crac while on the Ninth Crusade in 1272. When he returned home he built a chain of castles to control his own kingdom, copying many of its features.

Location Wales, UK
Date Begun 1295
Amazing fact Beaumaris has a sea gate so that in a siege it could be supplied by ship.

Concentric design resembles Crac

Sea gate

Sacsayhuamán fortress

Built by 20,000 workers over 80 years, Sacsayhuamán towers high about the town of Cuzco – the capital of the once-mighty Inca empire. Its three rows of walls are built of blocks weighing as much as 300 tonnes.

Location Cuzco, Peru
Date 11th or 12th century
Amazing fact Cuzco's city walls formed the shape of a puma, with Sacsayhuamán forming the head.

Though huge the stone blocks fit tightly together

Backward slope helps walls resist earthquakes

Matsumoto samurai castle

Chaos and violence were tearing Japan apart when Matsumoto castle was built as a fortified palace at the end of the 16th century. Nicknamed the Crow Castle after its black walls, it was once at the centre of a much bigger complex of walls and moats.

Pepper-pot domes top Gwalior's towers

Fort is built on a ridge 3km (2 mile) long

Gwalior fortress, India

Clinging to an cliff nearly 90 m (300 ft) high, Gwalior is one of India's most famous fortresses. It protected a trade route north from the plains. Much fought over, it was captured in turn by Muslims, Hindus, and British forces.

Location	Northern India
Date	Originally built before 525 CE
Amazing fact	The castle encloses 6 palaces, 6 temples, mosque, and 8 water reservoirs.

Vauban fortified town of Neuf Brisach, France

Cannons could destroy any castle wall, so from the 16th century engineers aimed to keep attacking guns as far away as possible. Star-shaped designs, like this one built by French engineer Sébastian Vauban (1633–1707), provided the best defence. Triangular walls and trenches forced attackers into the open, where they could be picked off by the defenders' guns.

Location	French-German border near Switzerland	Amazing fact	Though described as a perfect castle, Neuf-Brisach surrendered after a heavy bombardment in 1870.
Date	1706		

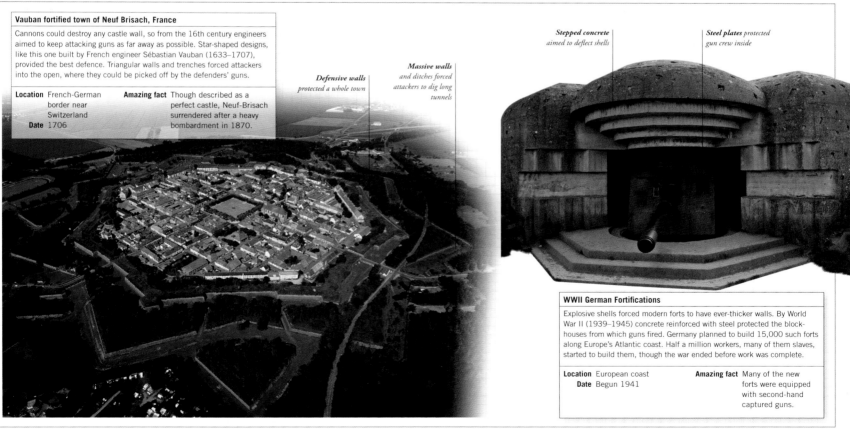

Defensive walls protected a whole town

Massive walls and ditches forced attackers to dig long tunnels

Stepped concrete aimed to deflect shells

Steel plates protected gun crew inside

WWII German Fortifications

Explosive shells forced modern forts to have ever-thicker walls. By World War II (1939–1945) concrete reinforced with steel protected the block-houses from which guns fired. Germany planned to build 15,000 such forts along Europe's Atlantic coast. Half a million workers, many of them slaves, started to build them, though the war ended before work was complete.

Location	European coast	Amazing fact	Many of the new forts were equipped with second-hand captured guns.
Date	Begun 1941		

INDEX

A page number in **bold** refers to the main entry for that subject

A

Acre 13, 60
Andrew II, King of Hungary 23
Antioch 12–13, 56, 57
aqueduct 39, 52, 59
archers 35, 37, 46, 50, 51, 52, 53, 54
architecture 22, 57
armour 4, **32**, **34**, 42, 43, 46
armoury 20, **32–33**
arrows **35**, 53
astrolabes 57
axes **34**

B

bailey, outer **36–39**, 54, 55
ballista **49**
banquets 4
barracks **30–31**
baths **58**, 59
battering ram **49**
Baybars I, Sultan 13, **17**, 24, 47, 50, 55, 57–60
Beaumaris Castle **62**
blacksmith **33**, 43
bows and arrows **35**
Buhen fort **62**
builders **11**, **38**
burgus 11, 40, 47, 50

C

cannibalism 56
carrier pigeons 47
Castel Blanc 28, 50
castellan 21, 22, 28, 45, 50, 55
Castle of the Kurds 10, 38
castles **4–5**, **62–63**
catapults 4, 29, **48–49**
cavalry 4, **35**, 43, 46
chapel 10, **14–17**, 18, 58, 59
Charles V, King of Spain 61
Christians 6, 7, 12, 13, 14, 56, 57
Church of the Holy Sepulchre 56, 57
cloister 11, 21, 22
clothes 15, 31, 32, 33
cooking 25
courts 22, 23
courtyard 18–21, 42
Crac des Chevaliers 7, **14–25**, **28–33**
    building of **10–11**, 38
    position of **8–9**, 10

siege of **50–55**
surrender of 55
under Muslims **58–59**
crossbows **35**, 50, 51, 53
crusader kingdoms 7, 13
crusaders 8, 12
crusades 5, 6, **12–13**
Cyprus 6, 60

D, E

daggers **34**
desert 9
dorter 30–31
earthquakes 10, 14, 38
Egypt 13, 17, 26, 57, 62
Elizabeth II, Queen of England 61
esquires 30, 42
estates 5, 7, 9, **22**, 23, 46, 50

F

farming 5, 8, 9, 22, 41
First Crusade 13, 14
food 5, 24, 25, 29, 46, 50, 51
Franks **56–57**

G

Galilea, Sea of 26, 27
gatehouse 11, 19, 44
gates 4, 11, 36, 37, 44, 46
Great Hall 5, 11, 18, **22–23**
Gregory, Pope 31
Guy, King of Jerusalem 26, 27
Gwalior fortress **63**

H

Harlech Castle 5, 11
Hattin, Battle of **26–27**
helmets 32, **34**, 43
Holy Land 5, **6–7**, 8, 12–13, 56, 60
Homs Gap 9, 28
horses 31, 40, **41**, 42, 43, 46
hospital 18, 30
Hospitallers 7, 8, 11, **15**, 26, 31, 58, **60–61**
    Grand Master 14, 28, 55, 61
Housesteads fort **62**
hunting 23
hygiene 31, 57, **58**, 59

I, J, K

Ibn Jubayr 22
infantry 4, 27, **35**, 44, 47
inscriptions **21**, 59

Jerusalem 6, 7, 8, 12, 13, 26, 27, 56–57
Jesus Christ 6, 7, 21
Jews 6, 12, 57
Joinville, Geoffrey de 16
jousting 4
kitchens 5, **24–25**
knights 4, 12, 41
Knights Templar 14, 26, 27

L

ladders 4, 48
lances 4, **34**, 42
landscape **9**
latrines **24**
lights 30
longbow **35**
Lorgne, Nicolas 36

M

Ma'arra 56
maces **34**
machicolation 36, 37, 38, 39, 44, 59
mail coats 32, **33**
Malta 61
Mamluks 13, 17, 46, 50, 59, 60
mangonel **48**, 50, 55
Margat 8, 59, 60
Matsumoto samurai castle **63**
medicine 57
Mesopotamia 4
moat 36, 38, 44, 52, 54
monks 14, 18, 30
Montferrand Castle 28
mosque 58, 59
Muhammad, Prophet 6, 58
murder holes 45
Muslims 6, 7, 9, 12, 18, 22, 23, **56–59**
Mycenae citadel **62**

N, O

Napoleon Bonaparte 61
Nicaea 56
Nur-ad-din, Prince 28
oases 9
onager **49**
Ottoman empire 61
outworks 50, 52

P, Q

pack animals 43, 46
pilgrims 6, 12, 14, 56
popes 12, 15, 16
portcullis 19, 36, **44**

ostern gates 11, 36, 37
risoners 29
Qalawun, Sultan 59

R

aiding parties 46
amp 19, **44–45**, 46
Raymond de Puy 14
Raymond of Tripoli, Count 7
efectory 24
elics **16**, 27
Reynald of Châtillon 26, 27
Revel, Hugues de 55
Rhodes 60–61
Richard I, King of England 6

S

addles 42
St John, knights of, *see* Hospitallers
St John's ambulance 61
aladin 7, 13, 26–27, 56, 57
aps 51, **52**, 54
cience 57
eal **28**
econd Crusade 13
eljuqs 12, 13
ephorie 26
ergeants **30**, 31, 46, 47
hields 22, 32, **34**, 45
hips 6, **8**, 12, **42**
iege 5, 12, 24, 26, 29, 45, **50–55**, 60
iege engines 29, 36, **48–49**, 50, 51
iege towers 49, 57
kirmishing 46
laves 18, 56, 61
pain 13
tables **40–43**
tirrups 42
tonemasons 11, **38**
words 4, **34**

T

Third Crusade 13
Tiberias 26
owers 10, 11, **28–29**, 36, 38, 39, 58
rebuchet **48**
Tripoli 8, 9, 13, 55, 60
True Cross 16, 27, 57
urcopoles 17, 18, **31**, 41, 43, 46, 47
Tyre 6, 60

U, V

ndermining 4, 37, 38, 51, **52**, 54, 60
Urban II, Pope 12
Urban III, Pope 27

Vauban, Sébastien 63
Venice 8
visitors 23, 28

W

walls 10–11, 18, 36, 38–39, 42, 46, 58
warfare 5, 14, 34
washing 31, 57, **58**, 59
water 5, 20, 26, 36, 39, 55, 58
weapons 32, 33, **34–35**, 46
weather 9, 18, 32, 38, 50, 58
windmill 37
World War II 63

ACKNOWLEDGEMENTS

Dorling Kindersley would like to thank Chris Bernstein
for the index.

Picture Credits
The publisher would like to thank the following for their kind
permission to reproduce their photographs:

(Abbreviations key: t=top, b=below, r=right, l=left, c=centre,
a=above)

akg-images: 15tr; British Library 18bl; Tarek Camoisson 10br,
39br, 52tl; **Alamy Images:** Kevin Lang 59br; Geoffrey Morgan
9tr; Skyscan Photolibrary 62cr; **Ancient Art & Architecture
Collection:** 49br; **The Art Archive:** 49tr; Biblioteca Capitolare,
Padua/Dagli Orti 56bc; Biblioteca Nazionale Marciana
Venice/Dagli Orti (A) 29tr, 42t; British Library, London 57bl;
Klosterneuburg Monastery Austria/Dagli Orti 38tc; Museo
Camillo Leone Vercelli/Dagli Orti 35tl; Dagli Orti 4b; Real
biblioteca de lo Escorial / Dagli Orti 25tr; **Bridgeman Art
Library:** Bibliothèque Nationale, Paris, France 7br, 14bl,
26b, 60tr; British Library, London, 11bl, 52bl, 56tl; Glasgow
University Library, Scotland 4tl; Musée Conde, Chantilly,
France/Giraudon 4tr, 5tl; Private Collection 12tr, 27cl, 56br;
British Library: 7tr, 35tr, 51tr; **CADW:** 5b; Chris Owen:
49tl; Corbis: Archivo Iconografico, S.A. 12tl, 22tl; The Art
Archive 48tc; B.S.P.I. 63tl; Fridmar Damm/Zefa 62bl; Bernd
Kohlhas/Zefa 60-61b; Horacio Villalobos 63br; Roger Wood
62tl; Adam Woolfitt 60tl; **DK Images/Courtesy of the Royal
Museum of Scotland, Edinburgh:** 57br; **Franck Lechenet/
Doublevue:** 63bl; **Getty Images:** Bridgeman Art Library 60bl;
Google Earth: 8-9; **Images and Stories:** 59tr; **Museum of the
Order of St John and St John Ambulance:** 55tr, 61bc, 61br;
NASA: 6-7; **Peter Langer/Associated Media Group:** 24tr;
Sonia Halliday Photographs: 58-59; **Stuart Whatling:** 21tr;
TopFoto.co.uk: The British Library/HIP 8bl, 17tc; HIP /ARPL
12b; **Traveladventures.org:** 58bl

Jacket images: Front: **Alamy Images:** The National Trust
Photolibrary (b/g); **Corbis:** John R. Jones/Papilio cr. Back:
Alamy Images: The National Trust Photolibrary (b/g)

All other images © Dorling Kindersley
For further information see: www.dkimages.com

London, New York, Melbourne,
Munich, and Delhi

Consultant Dr David Nicolle

For Tall Tree Ltd
Editor David John
Designer Ralph Pitchford

For DK
Senior Editor Claire Nottage
Senior Art Editor Jim Green
Managing Editor Linda Esposito
Managing Art Editor Diane Thistlethwaite
Jacket Manager Sophia M. Tampakopoulos Turner

DTP Coordinator Siu Yin Chan

Publishing Manager Andrew Macintyre
Category Publisher Laura Buller

Picture Research Sarah Hopper
Production Erica Rosen
Jacket Design Neal Cobourne
Jacket Editor Mariza O'Keeffe

Illustrators James Jordan Associates

First published in Great Britian in 2007 by
Dorling Kindersley Limited,
80 Strand, London WC2R 0RL

Copyright © 2007 Dorling Kindersley Limited, London
A Penguin Company

A CIP catalogue record for this book
is available from the British Library

ISBN 978-1-40530-836-6

Colour reproduction by Colourscan, Singapore
Printed and bound in China by Hung Hing

Discover more at
www.dk.com

WARHAMMER

THE GAME OF FANTASY BATTLES

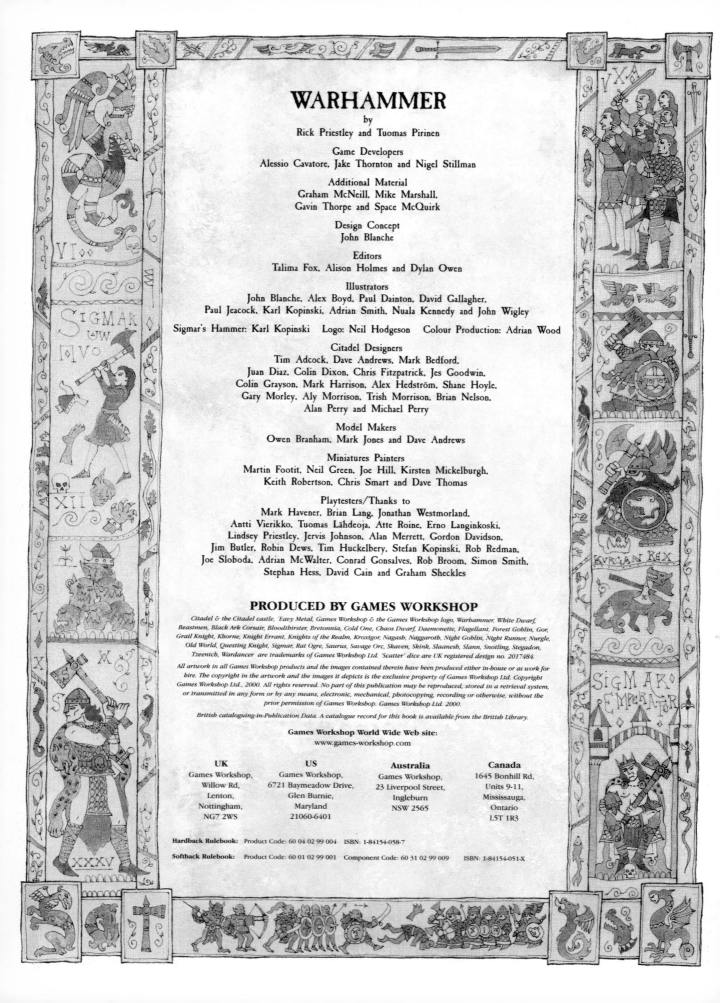

WARHAMMER

by

Rick Priestley and Tuomas Pirinen

Game Developers
Alessio Cavatore, Jake Thornton and Nigel Stillman

Additional Material
Graham McNeill, Mike Marshall,
Gavin Thorpe and Space McQuirk

Design Concept
John Blanche

Editors
Talima Fox, Alison Holmes and Dylan Owen

Illustrators
John Blanche, Alex Boyd, Paul Dainton, David Gallagher,
Paul Jeacock, Karl Kopinski, Adrian Smith, Nuala Kennedy and John Wigley

Sigmar's Hammer: Karl Kopinski   Logo: Neil Hodgeson   Colour Production: Adrian Wood

Citadel Designers
Tim Adcock, Dave Andrews, Mark Bedford,
Juan Diaz, Colin Dixon, Chris Fitzpatrick, Jes Goodwin,
Colin Grayson, Mark Harrison, Alex Hedström, Shane Hoyle,
Gary Morley, Aly Morrison, Trish Morrison, Brian Nelson,
Alan Perry and Michael Perry

Model Makers
Owen Branham, Mark Jones and Dave Andrews

Miniatures Painters
Martin Footit, Neil Green, Joe Hill, Kirsten Mickelburgh,
Keith Robertson, Chris Smart and Dave Thomas

Playtesters/Thanks to
Mark Havener, Brian Lang, Jonathan Westmorland,
Antti Vierikko, Tuomas Lähdeoja, Atte Roine, Erno Langinkoski,
Lindsey Priestley, Jervis Johnson, Alan Merrett, Gordon Davidson,
Jim Butler, Robin Dews, Tim Huckelbery, Stefan Kopinski, Rob Redman,
Joe Sloboda, Adrian McWalter, Conrad Gonsalves, Rob Broom, Simon Smith,
Stephan Hess, David Cain and Graham Sheckles

PRODUCED BY GAMES WORKSHOP

Games Workshop World Wide Web site:
www.games-workshop.com

UK	**US**	**Australia**	**Canada**
Games Workshop,	Games Workshop,	Games Workshop,	1645 Bonhill Rd,
Willow Rd,	6721 Baymeadow Drive,	23 Liverpool Street,	Units 9-11,
Lenton,	Glen Burnie,	Ingleburn	Mississauga,
Nottingham,	Maryland	NSW 2565	Ontario
NG7 2WS	21060-6401		L5T 1R3

Hardback Rulebook: Product Code: 60 04 02 99 004   ISBN: 1-84154-058-7

Softback Rulebook: Product Code: 60 01 02 99 001   Component Code: 60 31 02 99 009   ISBN: 1-84154-051-X

Welcome to this the sixth version of the renowned Warhammer game rules. Within this book you will find all the information you need to create your own armies and lead them to battle in the dark fantasy world of Warhammer.

If you are already a veteran player then you will recognise the many improvements and additions which we have made to this latest version of the game. Many of these revisions have been made at the suggestion of the growing world-wide body of Warhammer players whose influence and inspiration we gratefully acknowledge. Our aim has been to refine and improve a much-loved game rather than effect radical changes in a system which is basically sound. At the same time we have taken the opportunity to restore balance and consistency to aspects of play which had inevitably become cluttered by years of continuous development.

This book now contains not only the core Warhammer game rules but also the rules for casting spells and using magic items, fighting sieges, and playing detailed 'skirmishes' with small bands of warriors. In addition we have in preparation an entirely new series of supplementary Warhammer Armies books, each of which includes army lists, additional rules, and a collector's guide for that particular army.

Welcome to the world of Warhammer!

CONTENTS

COLLECTING AN ARMY

Collecting an Army 17
Building Regiments 22
Choosing an Army 26
Terrain 28

RULES

CHARACTERISTICS

0 Level Characteristics 39
Characteristic Profiles 39
Saves 39
Characteristic Tests 39
Leadership Test 39

UNITS

Banners, Musicians & Champions . .40
Unit Strength 40
Facing 40

THE TURN

Who Gets The First Turn 42
Improvising 43
Exceptions 43

MOVEMENT

Declare Charges 44
Charge Responses 45
Rallying 45
Compulsory Moves 45
Move Chargers 46
Flank & Rear Charges 46
Remaining Moves 46
Moving Troops 47
Manoeuvre 49
Terrain 50
Obstacles 51
Charging 52
Oddball Stuff 54
Flank and Rear Charges 54
Marching 54
Individual Models 55
Snaking 55
1" Apart 55
Magic 55

SHOOTING

Range 58
Who can Shoot & Line of Sight 59
Hills & Elevated Postions 60
Shooting & Close Combat 60
Stand & Shoot 60
Dividing Shots 60

Hitting the Target 61
To Hit Modifiers 62
7+ To Hit 63
Wounds 63
Weapon Strength 63
Saves 64
Removing Casualties 65
Panic Tests 65
Fast Dice Rolling 65

CLOSE COMBAT

Combats 67
Who Strikes First? 68
Which Models Fight 68
Hitting the Enemy 69
Cavalry 69
Defended Obstacle 69
Wounds 70
Weapons Modifiers 70
Saves 70
Removing Casualties 70
Results 71
Combat Results 72
Combat Resolution Bonuses . . .73
Losers Take a Break Test 74
Fleeing Troops 74
Rallying 75
Pursuit 75
Redress the Ranks 76
Units Taking Casualties 77
Expand Frontage 77
Lapping Round 77
Overrun Rule 78

PSYCHOLOGY

Taking Psychology Tests 79
The Order of Tests 79
Panic 80
Panicking Units 81
Voluntary Tests 81
Fear 81
Terror 81
Stupidity 82
Frenzy 84
Hatred 84
Stubborn 85

ADVANCED RULES

WEAPONS

Weapons and Units 88
Special Combat Rules 88
Special Weapon Rules 89
List of Weapons 90
Close Combat Weapons 91
Missile Weapons 92
Weapons Summary 93

CHARACTERS

Types of Characters 94
Wizards 94
Moving Characters 95
Characters & Line of Sight 95
Compulsory Moves 95
Marching 95
Characters and Units 95
Shooting at
Independent Characters 97
Close Combat 98
Challenges 98
Leadership and Psychology . . .100
Stone Throwers,
Cannons & Characters 100
Characters Riding Monsters . . .101
Special Characters 101

GENERALS & BATTLE STANDARDS

General's Leadership 102
The Battle Standard 102

MONSTERS

Monsters as Units 103
Monster Mounts 103
Close Combat 104
Slain Riders & Monsters 105
Victory Points 105

FLYERS

Flyers 106
Units of Flyers 106

STANDARDS, MUSICIANS & CHAMPIONS

Position within the Unit 108
Standards 108
Musicians 109
Champions 109

SPECIAL RULES

SKIRMISHERS

Formation 115
Moving 115
Shooting 115
Close Combat 116
Characters 116

FAST CAVALRY

Formation & Movement 117
Shooting 117
Fleeing Fast Cavalry 117
Characters & Fast Cavalry 117

WAR MACHINES
Models 118
Moving a War Machine 118
Aiming a War Machine 118
Characters 118
Combat 118
Shooting at War Machines 118
Charge Responses 119
Fleeing crew 119
Attacking a War Machine 119
Abandoned Machines 119
War Machines & Victory Points . . .119
Stone Throwers 120
Cannons 122
Bolt Throwers 124
Other War Machines 125

CHARIOTS
The Chariot Model 126
Chariot Units 127
Moving Chariots 127
Obstacles & Terrain 127
Chariot's Weapon Skill 127
Shooting at Chariots 127
Destroyed Chariots &
High Strength Hits 127
Chariot Saves 127
Characters in Chariots 127
Chariot Attack 128
Attacking Chariots
in Close Combat 128
Chariots Challenges 128
Flee and Pursuit 128
Victory Points 128
Chariot Upgrades 128

BUILDINGS
Moving Into
& Around Buildings 129
Shooting 130
Fighting Inside Buildings 130
Destruction 130

MAGIC

MAGIC
Wizards 134
Spells 134
Magic Items 134
Wizard Levels 134
Casting Spells 135
Power Dice 135
Dispel Dice 136
How to Cast a Spell 136
Miscasts & Irresistible Force . .136
Dispelling a Spell 137
Miscasts 138
Characters & Units
as Targets of Spells 139
Natural Dispels
& Magical Defences 139
Spells with Templates 139
Fleeing Wizards 139

Spells in Play 139
Dispelling Spells in Play 139

SPELL LISTS
The Eight Lores of Magic 142
Selecting Spells 142
Fire Balls and
Other Magic Missiles 142
Cancelling Spells 142

The Lore of Fire 144
The Lore of Metal 145
The Lore of Shadow 146
The Lore of Beasts 147
The Lore of the Heavens 148
The Lore of Light 149
The Lore of Life 150
The Lore of Death 151

MAGIC ITEMS
Who Can Use Magic Items 152
Types of Magic Items 152
Magic Items
Capable of Casting Spells 153
Common Magic Items 154

WORLD OF WARHAMMER

YE HISTORY OF YE OLDE WORLDE
Of the Old World 161
The Legend of
Sigmar Heldenhammer 162
Our Honoured
Land – The Empire 163
Of Bretonnia 165
Of Kislev 166
Of Tilea and Estalia 166
Of the Lands of Araby 167
Of the Southlands 167
Of the Distant
Kingdom of Cathay 167
The Land of the Dead 168
Of Dwarfs 169
Of the Elves 170
Of the Lands Across the Sea . . .172
Of the Encroachments of Dread
Chaos and the Enemy Within . .173
Of the Power of Magic 174
Of the Monstrous Beings 174
Of the Ratmen
of the Underworld 175
Of Orcs and Goblins 176

WARHAMMER ARMIES
Empire 178
Orcs and Goblins 180
Dwarfs 182
Skaven 183
High Elves 184
Wood Elves 185

Chaos Warriors 186
Daemons 187
Beastmen 188
Tomb Kings of Khemri 189
Vampire Counts 189
Bretonnians 190
Lizardmen 191
Dark Elves 192

SCENARIOS

SCENARIOS
What is a Scenario? 196
Choosing a Scenario 196
Creating Your Own Scenarios . .197
Victory Points 198

The Battle of Nebelheim 199
The Battle of the Necropolis . .201
The Battle of Swartzhafen 203
The Battle of the Burned Banner . .205
The Battle of Bogwurst 207
The Battle of Pine Crags 209
Eldreth's Last Stand 210
The Fall of Chaqua 211
The Seven Knights 213

THE BATTLEFIELD
Scenery 216
Placing Scenery 218
Dimensions of Terrain Pieces . .219

The Realms of Men 222
Wilderness Regions 223
The Chaos Wastes 224
Ulthuan & Naggaroth 225
The Dwarf Realms 226
The Deserts of Khemri and Araby . .227
Lustria and the Southlands 228

APPENDIX
Warhammer Campaigns 232
Preparing for Battle 238
Warhammer Skirmish 242
Rules of Siege 247
Accidental Charges 262
Rules Commentary 263
Special Rules 269
Sequence of Play 271
Blast Markers
& Flame Template 276
Warhammer Glossary 277
Notes on Scale
and Measurement 279
On House Rules 279
Stat Lines 280
Designer's Notes 282
Roster Sheet 284

THE SAGA OF SIGMAR

When the sun rests
And the world is dark
And the great fires are lit
And the ale is poured into flagons
Then is the time to sing sagas as Dwarfs do
And the greatest of sagas
Is the saga of Sigmar, mightiest warrior.
Harken now, hear these words.
And live in hope.

In the time before time.
Orcs roamed the land.
All was darkness.
It was a time of woes.
It was a time of doom.
It was a time of wolves.
Mankind was prey.
They looked to the sky.
Cried to the gods; deliver us.
And the gods answered them.

Into the darkness, came a light.
A torch of the gods.
A dragon with two tails.
Flying in the sky by night.
One looked to another.
What can this sign mean.
Orcs grew fearful.
Wolves slunk back into their lairs.

WARHAMMER

Warhammer is a game so it is natural that most devotees consider themselves to be gamers above all else. Fighting battles is what Warhammer is about and every player will tell you that it takes adept generalship, sound tactics and a good knowledge of your troops' capabilities to ensure victory. It is sometimes claimed that a little bit of luck helps too. Of course, before any battles can be fought it is necessary to recruit an army, and that means

choosing, assembling and painting a host of model warriors. Putting together an entire army is a challenge that requires a modicum of patience and artistic skill. Learning how to construct, paint and present models so that they look their best is one of the most rewarding aspects of the hobby. Indeed, there are those who much prefer to paint than to game, who enjoy simply collecting and painting miniatures to display.

Although it is not essential to do so, experienced Warhammer players like to indulge their modelling skills further by converting miniatures. This might involve removing the head or weapon from one model and transposing it to another to create an entirely unique piece. The most talented individuals will even go as far as to add or replace features using modelling putty, or to sculpt entire models to their own design. Just as there are those attracted to the challenge of painting, there are modellers who enjoy creating their own Warhammer miniatures.

Battles are rarely fought over featureless planes, so most Warhammer gamers create suitable scenic battlefields for their games. A selection of scenery is available to buy as part of the Citadel model range, but many players make their own from whatever materials come to hand. A battlefield can be set up on a kitchen table for an evening's play, or can be a lavish battlefield with rolling hills, tumbling streams and tangled woodlands. Only the most fortunate have the space for a permanent games room complete with scenic battlefield layout – but we can all dream!

The rapid growth in the popularity of the gaming hobby in recent years has attracted collectors who, whilst they fully appreciate the talents of expert painters and modellers, find that they do not have the amount of time or degree of skill to produce their own armies to the same standard. It is a fitting testament to the artisanship of the world's most talented painters that their works now command a high price amongst serious collectors, whilst fully completed armies painted and converted to a competent standard are highly valued and eagerly sought after.

It's reasonable to say that most games are played at home where a leisurely game can be enjoyed in relative comfort. If you are lucky enough to have an area dedicated to gaming, it is possible to leave a game in progress over several days without disrupting the battle in order to clear away.

Gaming clubs are an ideal place to meet other Warhammer players, but as they usually share their premises with other organisations it is necessary to start and complete a game over the course of an evening. There are a growing number of clubs located all over the world and more gamers are starting to organise their own in areas where they do not already exist.

Tournaments are local or world-wide events where Warhammer can be played intensely for a whole day or, more likely, an entire weekend. Tournaments involve championships, knock-out competitions, or huge campaigns in which groups of players divide into several teams. Some tournaments encompass painting and modelling competitions as well as gaming.

Games of Warhammer need not be confined only to your home or gaming clubs. Here at the Games Workshop Studio, the staff pitch the might of their armies against each other during lunch breaks and after work.

We are reliably informed that our games are played in places as diverse as schoolrooms during dinner time, in the canteen by off-duty postmen and even in the officers' mess when they're not playing at being real soldiers!

The many Games Workshop stores that are located in every corner of the world regularly run gaming events on a weekly basis. They also run tuition at all levels, from those who have never fought a battle of Warhammer before, up to advice on advanced tactics for more experienced generals.

If you are still having trouble finding an opponent then why don't you introduce a friend to the game. They'll certainly thank you for it.

There are countless generals out there, just waiting to find a worthy opponent to fight. You'd be pleasantly surprised at how many other gaming enthusiasts near by where you live or work enjoy the Warhammer hobby.

The most important part of the Warhammer game system is the rulebook that you are reading right now. This book contains all the rules you need to start playing the Warhammer game. However, rules are of no use if you don't have any models to fight your battles with. The best way to start a new army is with Games Workshop's plastic regiment boxed sets. Ideal for newcomers to Warhammer, they allow you to build up the core rank-and-file troops of your army quickly and cheaply.

In addition to this rulebook you will need the Warhammer Armies supplement for the army you are playing. Each book provides the special rules for the troops in the army, unique magic items and spells, and the army list from which the army is selected prior to play. Although you only need the book for the army you are playing, many players like to collect all of the books so that they have all the information about the game. A complete revised range of Warhammer Armies books to go with this latest version of Warhammer is in preparation along with numerous new models for each army. Check out the current range together with all the latest models on the Games Workshop website.

Regiment box sets are the easiest way to start building up your army.

The Games Workshop web site is full of useful information, news on events and new releases. There is also an online store where you can order virtually any Games Workshop product.

At the Games Workshop stores, not only will you find all the necessary models and game supplements, but also friendly staff who are eager to pass on their painting and modelling experience to you. Gamers pit their armies against each other in the weekly battles that take place in each store.

There are fourteen core armies in the Citadel Miniatures Warhammer range – in addition to these there are various mercenary forces which can be added to other armies or which can be played as a separate army in their own right. The core Warhammer armies are Empire (human), Bretonnia (human), High Elves, Wood Elves, Dark Elves, Dwarfs, Lizardmen, Tomb Lords, Vampire Counts, Orcs and Goblins, Skaven, Chaos Dwarfs, Beastmen, and Warriors of Chaos.

A comprehensive selection of models is available for each army either as plastic kits or metal miniatures. The models are packaged in either boxes or blister packs depending upon their design. Few players buy a complete army all at once. For one thing that would be very expensive. More importantly it is far more effective to buy and paint only one unit of troops at a time, building up your army over a period of weeks or months. That way you can try out your growing army in battle before deciding what units you want to buy next. If you feel that your army is lacking in long range firepower you might add a unit of bowmen or maybe some artillery, if you want to increase your army's close combat abilities you might add more heavy cavalry or maybe a large monster, and so on.

As well as the models themselves, you will also require glue, paint, brushes, and a few simple and useful tools including a modelling knife, files and clippers. We will be taking a closer look at how to go about assembling models and painting them later on in the book.

For now it is enough to know that the Warhammer game is supported by a full range of modelling and painting accessories specially designed for use with the models.

In addition you can also purchase dice, tape measures, plastic templates, and carrying cases which can be used to transport your completed armies – in fact everything you need to put together a Warhammer army.

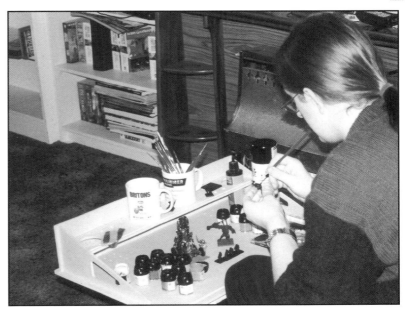

An integral aspect of the Warhammer hobby is the time you spend lovingly painting your armies.

Games Workshop supplies a full range of modelling and painting accessories, such as brushes, paints, glue, and files and clippers.

We also produce a paint station to store your paints and tools tidily, which will protect the surface of your table while you paint.

To help protect your models while being transported from battle to battle, we sell a carrying case, which can store an entire army!

THE WARHAMMER WORLD

Warhammer has grown into much more than a game. You can read about the Warhammer game every month in White Dwarf magazine where you will find news about latest releases and rules for new models. If you want to keep up with everything that is best about the Warhammer hobby then White Dwarf is a must.

The Warhammer world comes to life in a series of novels by the Black Library, a publisher dedicated to the fictional backgrounds of the Games Workshop games. These can be obtained from stores which stock Games Workshop models and also from many bookshops. There is also a comic featuring heroes and villains from the Warhammer world.

What the future might bring is impossible to say. We are always working on new projects of one kind or another. Why not check out our website (www.games-workshop.com) or, if you have a local Games Workshop store, drop in and ask our staff about latest developments.

White Dwarf is Games Workshop's monthly magazine, which includes articles on new games and models, new rules and scenarios and much more.

The Black Library publishes its regular comic, Warhammer Monthly, as well as Inferno, a compendium of short stories, and Warhammer novels.

The Journal is a fanzine written by gamers for gamers.

Forgeworld produces a range of detailed large-scale resin models for collectors.

Thousands of Games Workshop enthusiasts gather at annual Games Day events which are held in several countries across the world.

The Warhammer Museum has loads of breathtaking dioramas.

Computer games, like Dark Omen, are set in the Warhammer world.

COLLECTING AN ARMY

Over the next few pages you'll find plenty to help you get your army started and begin creating a battlefield to fight over. If you are new to wargaming, collecting and painting an army like the ones in this book can seem like a very daunting task. As you'll see, however, putting together a great looking army isn't difficult, it just requires a little patience. In this section we'll guide you through some of the decisions you'll have to make, and also provide some tips to help you. It's important to remember that there's no 'right way' of doing any of this. What we are presenting is the combined experience of many people in assembling armies for Warhammer.

Similarly, making a battlefield to fight your games over is as easy or as complicated as you want to make it. You can put together some basic terrain on pretty much any flat surface in just a few minutes. Be warned, however, because once you start painting armies and making terrain it's difficult to stop! Certain individuals have even been known to convert entire rooms of their houses for the pursuit of their hobby.

SETTING UP A PAINTING AREA

The first thing you'll need to do is sort out somewhere to do your painting and modelling. Not all of us are fortunate enough to have a dedicated area for our hobby, but any table or desk will do. Make sure that the surface is covered; newspaper will guard against paint spillages, but if you are going to be doing any cutting you'll need something more substantial, like an old tray, or a spare piece of board. A good light source is also important. Natural light is best and many painters invest in a daylight bulb to show the colours more truly. Desk lamps are a good way to ensure that you get plenty of light on the subject matter.

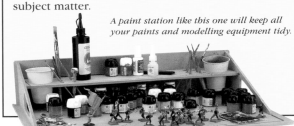

A paint station like this one will keep all your paints and modelling equipment tidy.

An Empire army in combat against an Orc horde.

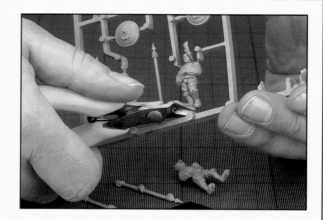

Here's a way to paint Empire Spearmen from the Imperial province of Nordland. Troops from Nordland wear a split blue and yellow uniform. Start by painting the lighter half of the split colour scheme Bad Moon Yellow. It's much easier to apply the darker colour (Enchanted Blue) over the lighter. Paint the body armour, helmet and spear tip Boltgun Metal and any straps Chaos Black. Paint the hands and the face Bronzed Flesh. Finally use Bubonic Brown on the spear staff. The Spearman is now ready for battle.

CHOOSING AN ARMY

The first thing to do is to decide which army to collect, and this in itself requires a little thought. Each army has its own distinct history and background, some of which you'll find later in this book. Every army fights in a different way on the battlefield as well; some are massive hordes of troops which are relatively weak individually, whereas others are compact elite forces. Some armies use lots of war machines and troops armed with missile weapons, whilst others favour terrifying monsters or savage hand-to-hand fighters. Most obviously, each army in Warhammer looks unique, both in terms of the miniatures used to represent it and in the way in which they are painted.

Modelling and painting is a great way to bring out the character of your army. For example, armies of the Empire are characterised by big blocks of brightly uniformed infantry, whereas Orcs fight in huge disorganised mobs of warriors, with little thought to uniformity of clothing and equipment. Some of the techniques shown in these pages are particularly appropriate to certain armies. For example, if you want to collect an army of Chaos Warriors, all you need to do is master some basic techniques for painting metal.

One way to help you decide which army to collect is to talk to someone who already plays Warhammer. Most gamers are only too happy to discuss the various merits of each army, but beware; few Warhammer players are truly impartial. You could go to a Games Workshop store where you will find plenty of gamers, and the staff will be only too happy to help you decide. You can even join in a game and see how some of the armies fight first hand.

PUTTING YOUR MODELS TOGETHER

Before you can paint your models you'll need to assemble them. Plastic miniatures usually come attached to a frame and the easiest way to remove them is with a pair of modelling clippers, being careful not to clip the model itself. Miniatures often have small pieces of unwanted metal or plastic attached to them, which is a necessary part of the moulding process (you may hear this described as 'flash'). This can easily be removed using a modelling knife or a small file. Polystyrene cement is best for sticking plastic miniatures together and comes in different forms. The liquid glue, shown right, comes with a brush to apply it, and is easiest to control. Superglue is the only practical way to stick metal miniatures (or metal to plastic), but do be careful because it really does stick to anything, especially fingers.

RACES OF THE OLD WORLD

On this page we've picked a single trooper to represent each of the races of the Old World: an Orc, a High Elf, etc. You will notice that all of these models have been painted to the highest standards by our team of expert painters (called the *'Eavy Metal team*). When you start painting your army, we recommend that you concentrate on the overall appearance of a unit or regiment, rather than each individual model. Having an army of display standard models does look great, but by just painting your units simply and neatly you can have a good-looking battle-ready force in a fraction of the time.

High Elf Spearman

Chaos Warrior

Dark Elf Spearman

Bloodletter Daemon

Bretonnian Knight of the Realm

Skeleton Warrior

Wood Elf Scout

Empire Spearman

Skaven Clanrat

Night Goblin Spearman

Orc Warrior

Beastman Gor

Dwarf Warrior

Lizardman Saurus Warrior

UNDERCOAT

Once you've assembled your models, you are ready to start painting. The first thing you need to decide is what colour undercoat to use. The undercoat is important because it gives the rest of the paint something to stick

to, and what colour you pick will determine the overall tone of your models. Generally, if you want the finished result to be bright, use a white undercoat.

If you want to get a darker feel, or the model has lots of armour, a black undercoat is best. Many people use black because it is quicker to paint over; any little recessed areas which you don't paint will be black and will seem like

White and black undercoat spray

they are in shadow. You can always try using different undercoats to see which one you prefer. Spray undercoats are a very good idea as they save lots of time.

GETTING STARTED

In order to give you a head start, we'll describe a way of painting that a lot of people use: paint the largest area of

colour on the model first and work down to the smallest. Using an Empire Spearman as an example, we'll start painting the largest area, the uniform, in Blood Red.

Here's a Top Tip: Water down your paint, preferably

SHADING AND HIGHLIGHTING

Here are some examples of easy techniques for adding more depth to your miniatures.

One of the easiest ways to paint armour is to paint metallic paint over a black undercoat. To bring out the texture of the armour try this technique: Dip your brush in the metallic paint and then wipe most of it off on a tissue. Then draw the brush across the armour and you'll see that the paint only adheres to the raised areas, leaving the recesses black. This technique is often called drybrushing and can be used on virtually any surface which has a strong texture.

Another easy way to make armour look good is to use inks. In this case we painted the armour with Boltgun Metal (shown right).

When the paint was dry we painted all over the metal area with Black Ink. As you can see from the example on the left, the ink flows into all the recesses, but leaves very little on the raised surfaces, and this brings out the detail of the model

really well. You can experiment with thinning down the ink with water, or even using thinned down paint. By trying different inks you can get different effects. In the third example we used Chestnut Ink to achieve a rusted look to the armour.

This Orc warrior was also painted using inks. First the skin was painted Goblin Green, then Green Ink was painted over the top. As you can see, it really brings out the detail.

The same technique has been used on this Empire soldier, with the face being painted first with Bronzed Flesh then the Flesh Ink applied over the top. To further bring out detail, you can try painting back over the top with either the base colour or a lighter colour. In the example on the right below, we painted just the raised parts of the face with Bleached Bone.

You could try combining drybrushing with using inks to highlight the detail of your models. Below you can see the uniform of an Empire soldier, which we first painted Enchanted Blue. When this was dry, we painted Blue Ink over the top. Inks take quite a while to dry, so try painting several models at once to give them plenty of time to dry. Better still, plan a tea break! Finally, we drybrushed Lightning Blue over the top of the uniform.

Once you've tried some of these techniques, you can start to experiment. The cloth on the Orc warrior below was first painted Bestial Brown, and then we tried two different inks. The one on the left was painted with Brown Ink, the one on the right with Chestnut Ink. As you can see, this creates very different effects; not only are they different colours, but the contrast varies depending on the ink. You can also try watering down your inks or mixing them to get different colours. Brown and orange inks over metallic surfaces can be used to create the effect of rust. With a little experience you'll

acquire a sense of which colours work best. The basic principle is simple; use lighter colours than the base colour for drybrushing and darker colours for washes.

on an old saucer or mixing palette. Several thin coats are better than one thick one as you can easily obscure the detail with thick paint. Take your time and try to be as neat as possible. You can always tidy up your models with some Skull White paint.

The next largest area is the armour, painted Boltgun Metal. Paint the hands and the face Bronzed Flesh, this is a great skin colour for humans. Then use Scorched Brown on the spear staff and finish off with Chaos Black for the beard.

An Empire Swordsmen regiment with shields, all painted in a matching colour scheme.

INSIDE OUT

Here's another way to paint your models that you may prefer – paint from the inside out. This means starting from the hands and skin of the model, then the uniform, then the armour. Just follow the natural layers of the model. Some models are easier to paint inside out, others are better painted the largest area first. With a little experience you'll soon be able to tell. You can even combine both ideas together. There are lots of ways of painting miniatures and everyone eventually settles on a way that suits them.

FINISHING OFF

Once you get a bit more confident you can add shading and highlighting to your models but this is unnecessary when you are just starting painting. Just concentrate on being neat, you can always add shading and highlighting afterwards.

To shade your models start by painting a darker colour into those areas which are naturally in shadow. Next paint a lighter colour on the highpoints of a model to make a highlight. You can do all this with ink washes and drybrushing. Another way to shade and highlight is to paint a darker colour first, then add a mid-tone colour on top. For instance, to paint Orc skin you can start with Dark Angels Green and then paint Goblin Green over the top. This creates a skin tone with really dark, dramatic shadow. Master model painter Dave Andrews, who has sculpted many of the models in the Warhammer range, uses this technique to paint all of his models.

SHIELDS

Shields are large and often ornate, requiring special attention when painting. It is easier to paint them separately and glue them on to the models afterwards. Some shields have a moulded design which you can paint, others are plain, without a design at all. This gives you an opportunity to create and paint your own design. Start by painting the background colour first and paint your shield design over the top (you'll see lots of ideas in this book). Don't worry about highlighting the shield, flat colours are just fine.

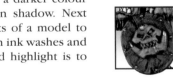

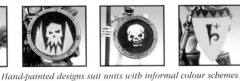

Hand-painted designs suit units with informal colour schemes.

Models within a unit can be made to look more individual by varying shield designs.

Simple heraldic designs characterise Bretonnian troops.

Examples of moulded shield designs.

BUILDING REGIMENTS

Regimental Leader

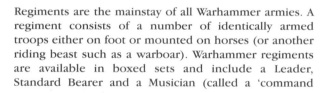

This unit of 24 Empire Spearmen is arranged in four ranks, six models wide. The more ranks a unit has, the better it fights in close combat. In the front rank are the Leader, Standard Bearer and Musician.

Regiments are the mainstay of all Warhammer armies. A regiment consists of a number of identically armed troops either on foot or mounted on horses (or another riding beast such as a warboar). Warhammer regiments are available in boxed sets and include a Leader, Standard Bearer and a Musician (called a 'command group'). In order to make the Leader of a unit stand out from the rest of his troops it is usual to arm him differently from the rest of the unit, with a sword instead of a spear for example.

Drummer

As well as using moulded banners, you can easily make plastic or paper ones yourself.

BANNERS

Although most Warhammer regiments come with moulded banners, some models have banner poles that you can glue a paper banner to. Some units come with a paper banner already supplied but you can always have a go at making your own. If you feel confident, you can copy a design or make up your own, drawing it in pencil first and then filling in the design with paint. Tracing a design from a book is also a good idea. Carefully cut out the design and glue it to the banner pole with superglue.

Cavalry are amongst the most powerful and splendid looking troops in an army. When putting them together you'll need to pay particular attention to how they rank up. Some modellers cut and reposition the mounts on their bases to get them to fit together as a unit.

The basics of painting a regiment of cavalry are no different from painting a unit of troops. As you may only have a few mounted troops in your army, you can spend a lot more time on your cavalry than your troops. We recommend you paint the rider and the mount separately and then glue them together afterwards.

These Ghouls have been carefully angled on their bases and arranged in a specific order to get them to rank up.

RANKING UP

Even before you think about painting your regiments make sure that they stand next to each other easily. Some dynamically posed models may need to be carefully positioned on their bases to fit into the ranks of troops. This is particularly true of command models such as the Standard Bearer. Sometimes the whole regiment may be full of such models and you will need to pay special attention when assembling them.

How you arrange the models in your regiment to make a solid block is easy. Start with the Standard Bearer and then put the regiment Leader and Musician on either side. Next decide how wide you want the unit to be. If you want a narrow frontage of say four or five models simply add models on either side of the command models. You may prefer to give your missile troops a wider frontage so that more models can fire. Then add models behind the front row to make several ranks.

With a little imagination it's easy to assemble models in a variety of different poses. These troops are all made from parts in the Empire Militia regiment box.

To set up a regiment of 20 Skaven, with a frontage five broad and four ranks deep, start with the Leader, Standard Bearer and Musician. Put two ordinary Skaven on either side and place one rank behind the other to make a solid block of troops.

This Skaven regiment has been set up in a movement tray large enough for 20 miniatures with 20mm bases. ▶

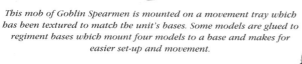

This mob of Goblin Spearmen is mounted on a movement tray which has been textured to match the unit's bases. Some models are glued to regiment bases which mount four models to a base and makes for easier set-up and movement.

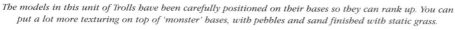

The models in this unit of Trolls have been carefully positioned on their bases so they can rank up. You can put a lot more texturing on top of 'monster' bases, with pebbles and sand finished with static grass.

Position models on their bases so they rank up together. Even miniatures that rank up easily, like these Empire Spearmen, need putting in the right places in a unit, those with spears advancing going at the front.

The bases on this regiment of Empire troops are textured with sand painted brown. The texture was then highlighted by drybrushing. Static grass has been glued in clumps on top and the edge of the base painted Goblin Green.

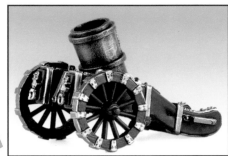

War machines may seem a little intimidating to paint at first, but they are really two pieces in one: the weapon itself and its carriage. Paint each part separately and assemble them afterwards.

PAINTING MORE THAN ONE MODEL AT A TIME

When it comes to painting regiments of troops rather than individual warriors, here's a Top Tip: Always clean up and assemble the whole regiment first, then start painting a single rank at a time. Line up your models and start by painting at one end and move down the line. Don't try to complete one model after the other, start with one colour and paint all the same parts on the models that colour. For instance, all the tunics may be red, all the trousers blue, etc. By the time you've finished painting the last model, the first will be dry and you'll be able to start on the next colour. This way you don't have to wait around for your models to dry.

You may want to do any ink washes and highlighting as you go along or, if you prefer, leave them all until the end. If you make a mistake don't worry, just paint over it. This is easier to do as you go along rather than at the end. Do not be concerned about painting every detail on a unit as you'll usually not see them on the table top. It's the overall effect of the unit which matters. Spend more time on your army General and Wizard as these highly detailed individuals benefit from having more painting time lavished on them.

PAINTING BASES

Once you've finished painting all your models, it's time to paint the bases. Traditionally, gamers paint their bases Goblin Green but there are no hard and fast rules – you can try Bestial Brown or Bubonic Brown for instance. Pick a colour that matches your battlefield. Paint the whole base your chosen colour, trying not to get any colour on the feet of the model. If you finish all the bases the same way across the whole of your army this will really help to unify the force on the tabletop.

FINISHING BASES

Models really look good with some 'texture' added to the top of their base. Paint some PVA glue onto the top of the base and stick on your chosen texture. Coloured flock is nice and quick to add to a base as it doesn't need painting. A lot of gamers like to use sand to texture their bases instead of flock, painted and drybrushed to make a hard wearing surface. They also often mix in small pieces of grit to look like stones.

Some gamers like to add static grass, a long flock which, when mixed with other textures, looks particularly good. Neatly finished bases can turn even the simplest painted miniatures into a battle-ready force.

BASING MINIATURES

One way to base miniatures is to use flock. Start by painting the base all over, in this case with Goblin Green. Be careful not to get any paint on the feet. Once the paint is dry, paint PVA glue over the top of the base. Put the top of the base into some flock for a few seconds. Take it out and tap the base to get rid of any excess flock. If there is any flock on the feet, brush it away with a damp paint brush before it dries.

CHOOSING AN ARMY

We've looked at how to put together regiments of troops and now you're ready to think about the next stage, collecting a whole army. You'll have to think about a mighty warrior who will lead the regiments you have already painted. Generals have the best armour and magic weapons in the whole army and they commonly ride a huge monster as well. Once you've decided on your General, how about collecting more units, cavalry, monsters or artillery.

The great thing about Warhammer armies is that they can all be different from each other, as different as the gamers who collect them. For instance, one Empire General might prefer to field as many regiments of foot troops as he can, whilst another prefers lots of cavalry. Yet another wouldn't dream of taking to the battlefield without as many cannons as he could muster. Everyone has their own preferences. How these preferences are arrived at depends on the individual. One gamer, when collecting his army, will look at the background of the army and pick a force that clearly reflects that. Another will pick a force to suit his own personal style of play, even at the expense of character. A lot of gamers pick the race whose character most suits their fighting style. Someone who favours close combat will choose a Chaos or Orc army. Someone who loves the Skaven obviously prefers an army of weak troops full of wacky weapons!

Dwarf armies are full of stalwart, armoured warriors who are better at defending than attacking.

Chaos Warrior armies are made up of elite troops who are extremely well armoured and deadly in hand-to-hand combat.

Empire Army General

The army's General is the centrepiece of any force and represents the gamer on the battlefield. Players pick the most imposing model they can for their General. Some gamers like to convert their General to make a unique character, like this massive Orc Warlord, right.

The Bretonnian army is very colourful and dynamic, with powerful knights backed up by foot troops.

Skaven armies feature lots of foot troops supported by unusual special units and powerful war machines.

TERRAIN

Now that you are on your way to collecting a Warhammer army, it's a good idea to consider the field of battle that your valiant force will fight on. A lot of gamers fight their first battles on the floor; after all, there's usually lots of space to fight on. With a little imagination, a pile of books becomes a hill. Once you get bored of the dog eating your models you can move on to using the dining room table. Cover it with a sheet of green cloth or a Battle Mat and place your hills of books underneath to give a contoured look.

MAKING TERRAIN

Games Workshop makes excellent terrain pieces – trees, hills, hedges and even card buildings – the ruined Empire outpost in the Warhammer boxed game is excellent for setting the scene for a battle. The next step for a lot of gamers is to make their own terrain. *How to make Wargames Terrain* (available from Games Workshop stores and Mail Order) gives lots of great ideas for terrain pieces as well as ways of making the most of what you have to hand. The exciting thing about making terrain is that you can make great terrain models out of junk: card, old Citadel models, stones or pebbles. You name it, with just a little imagination anything can be turned into a gaming piece for your battlefield.

You can use stuff straight from the garden, like these small stones to make a cairn.

Most battlefields will have common terrain features – trees, hills, hedges, boulders, etc. However, this doesn't stop you from collecting terrain that really sets the scene for your battle, such as an High Elf tower or a mausoleum for an Undead army.

WARGAMES TABLES

You can use the floor, a kitchen table covered in a green cloth, a Battle Board (available from Games Workshop) or a specially constructed gaming table to fight your games of Warhammer on.

Green cloth over a table.

Green painted table.

The Perry twins have been collecting miniatures for many years and have built up a large collection of fully modelled terrain boards.

AN ORC ENCAMPMENT

This terrain was made for our Orc army and is created from pieces of balsa wood, polystyrene tiles and spare plastic weapons on thick card bases. Books are available about terrain building from Games Workshop as well as articles in White Dwarf magazine with more information on how to make terrain specifically for your army.

The cloth walls of this Orc hut were made by soaking kitchen towel in watered down PVA glue.

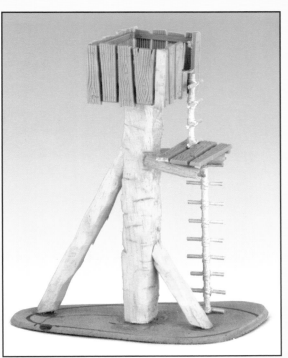

A watch tower carved from balsa wood.

An outer wall made from plastic and metal Citadel miniatures, combined with balsa wood embedded in modelling putty.

A Dwarf army clashes with the Skaven.

A High Elf warhost against a force of Chaos Warriors.

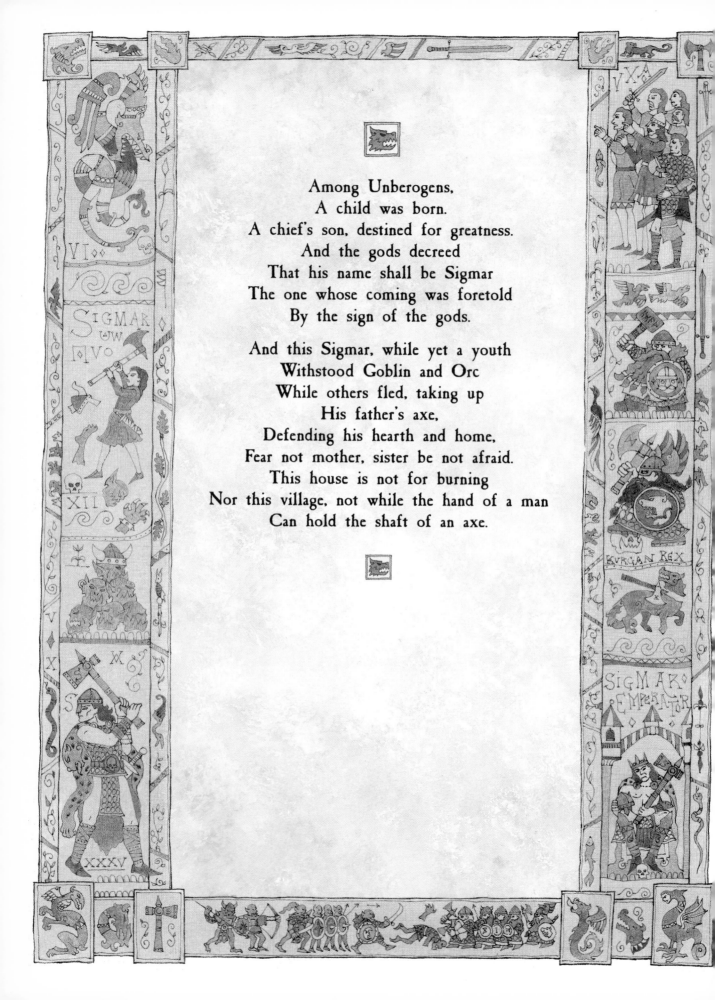

Among Unberogens,
A child was born.
A chief's son, destined for greatness.
And the gods decreed
That his name shall be Sigmar
The one whose coming was foretold
By the sign of the gods.

And this Sigmar, while yet a youth
Withstood Goblin and Orc
While others fled, taking up
His father's axe,
Defending his hearth and home,
Fear not mother, sister be not afraid.
This house is not for burning
Nor this village, not while the hand of a man
Can hold the shaft of an axe.

RULES

Characteristics
Units
The Turn
Movement
Shooting
Close Combat
Psychology

Welcome to Warhammer, the game of fantasy battles. Warhammer is a game of combat in which players take command of painted miniature armies complete with infantry regiments, cavalry squadrons and lumbering war machines.

This book contains all the information you will need in order to play Warhammer, as well as background information, advice on collecting and painting an army, running a campaign, and much more besides.

TABLETOP CONFLICT

In Warhammer, the opposing factions – the armies – are represented by models, assembled and painted by you.

Your tabletop becomes part of the Warhammer world, be it the steaming jungles of Lustria, the wind-swept plains of Kislev or the forbidding forests of the Empire.

The aim of the game is to outfight your opponent, which requires a mixture of both skill and luck. You'll soon learn how to arm and design your army effectively, and how to exploit the terrain to your best advantage.

You'll probably want to expand your basic force as you play more games. This is easy as there are lots of models available for all the armies and new miniatures will be coming out all the time. With these

If you kill one man you are murderer.

If you kill ten you are a monster.

If you kill a hundred you are a hero.

If you kill ten thousand you are a conqueror!

Boyar Alexandr of Kislev

you can expand your army, equip your heroes with different weapons and armour and hire mercenaries to join your force.

NEW PLAYERS

If you're new to Games Workshop games you'll be reassured to know that finding other players is not normally a problem – you'll be surprised how many there are!

There may be a Games Workshop store near you where you can buy models, paint and games supplements. However, Games Workshop stores are not just shops, they are hobby centres, where the staff will happily help you to learn the rules, show you how to paint and suggest ways to develop your army.

WHAT YOU WILL NEED

As well as this book, you will need the following items to play Warhammer:

MODELS

You will need enough miniatures of the appropriate race/type to represent the warriors in your army. It is a good idea to work out your army on paper first and then purchase the miniatures that you require.

As you will see in the section called Warhammer Armies, each army fights in a particular way – some contain expert archers while others are better in close combat or have mighty magicians. When choosing which army you want to lead you could choose one that reflects your preferred playing style, or you could read The Warhammer World section and choose one that really captures your imagination. A good way of picking an army is simply to pick the one with the models you like the best.

PLAYING SURFACE

You will also need something to play your battles on. Any firm, level surface is best, such as a tabletop or an area of floor – most kitchen tables will do. It's a good idea to use an old sheet or blanket to protect the table from scratches.

Some players make a special gaming board from chipboard or other similar material (divided into two or more pieces for ease of storage) which they can use on top of a table to extend the playing area.

Whatever you use, you will find that an area approximately 6' x 4' is about right for most battles.

TEMPLATES

Breath weapons of certain creatures like Dragons, as well as the shots of certain war machines, use templates to represent the area affected. There are three templates you need: a teardrop shaped flame template and two round templates with 3" and 5" diameter respectively.

At the back of the book we have included templates which you can photocopy and use in your games.

Life is a spark of light in the midst of endless darkness. We cling to love and hate, joy and pain, belief and fear, for they make us feel alive. Some of us are glorious, mighty men who will forge legends and burn like fiery stars in the darkness, casting the brief hope of life to this world.

But in the end we will have to give up everything we have, and descend back to the endless, dreamless darkness, to be forever forgotten.

Belannaer the Wise

TAPE MEASURE

For measuring ranges you will need a tape measure marked in inches, or a couple of plastic range rulers.

OTHER EQUIPMENT

You will also need pens and paper to record your regiments' weapons and other details.

DICE

All dice rolls use a standard six-sided dice (usually shortened to D6). Sometimes you will be asked to modify the result of the dice roll. This is noted as D6 plus or minus a number, such as D6+1 or D6-2. Roll the dice and add or subtract the number indicated to get the final result. You may have to roll a certain number of dice in one go. For example, 2D6 means roll two dice and add the scores together. You may also come across the term D3. As there is no such thing as a three-sided dice, use the following method for determining a score between 1 and 3. Roll a D6 and halve the score, rounding up: 1 or 2 equals 1, 3 or 4 equals 2 and 5 or 6 equals 3.

To play Warhammer you will need lots of six-sided dice, as well as an Artillery dice and a Scatter dice.

SPECIAL DICE

Special dice symbols are used to represent occurrences of luck and misfortune. From this point onwards these are referred to as MISFIRE and HIT. The corresponding symbols are shown below:

MISFIRE   **HIT**

Warhammer uses two special dice: the Artillery dice marked 2, 4, 6, 8, 10 and MISFIRE, and the Scatter dice marked with arrows and HIT symbols. These dice are used to represent the effects of various war machines such as cannons and stone throwers.

RE-ROLLS

Sometimes the rules allow you a 're-roll' of the dice. This is exactly as it sounds – pick up the dice you wish to re-roll and roll them again. The second score counts with a re-roll even if it is a worse result than the first, and no single dice roll can be re-rolled more than once, regardless of the source of the re-roll.

CHARACTERISTICS

In Warhammer there are many different types of warriors, from ordinary archers and spearmen to lordly knights riding mighty chargers. There are monstrous creatures too, some quite small such as Goblins and others that are huge such as fire-breathing Dragons.

To represent these in the game, we have nine characteristics that describe the various aspects of their physical or mental make up.

MOVEMENT ALLOWANCE (M)
Often simply called Move this shows the number of inches a creature can move on the tabletop under normal circumstances. Eg, a Goblin with a Move of 4 (M4) can move 4".

WEAPON SKILL (WS)
Defines how accomplished or skilled a warrior is with his weapons, or how determined and vicious a monster is. Weapon Skill is rated on a scale of 1 to 10 and the higher the score the more likely the fighter is to hit an opponent in close combat. An ordinary human has WS3 whilst a battle-hardened leader might have WS4, WS5 or possibly even higher!

BALLISTIC SKILL (BS)
This shows how good a warrior is with ranged weapons such as bows or handguns. Ballistic Skill is rated on a scale of 1 to 10 and the higher this value is, the easier a creature finds it to hit with missile attacks.

Some monsters have natural weapons that can be used at range (they might spit venom, for example) and their BS is used to determine whether they hit or not.

STRENGTH (S)
Shows how strong a creature is. Strength is rated on a scale of 1 to 10. An exceptionally puny creature might have a Strength characteristic of 1, while a mighty Giant might have S7 or even higher. Most Men have S3. Strength tells you how hard a creature can hit and thus how easily it can hurt an opponent it has struck.

TOUGHNESS (T)
Toughness is a measure of a creature's ability to resist or withstand physical damage and pain, and reflects such factors as the toughness of a creature's flesh, hide or skin, or the depth of its fur. Toughness is rated on a scale of 1 to 10 and the tougher a creature is, the better it can withstand an enemy's blows.

WOUNDS (W)
Shows how much damage a creature can take before it dies or is so badly hurt that it can't fight any more. Most Men and human-sized creatures have a Wounds characteristic value of 1. Large monsters are often able to withstand several wounds that would slay a smaller creature and so have W2, W3, W4 or more.

INITIATIVE (I)
This is rated on a scale of 1 to 10 and indicates how fast a creature can react. Creatures with a low Initiative score (such as Orcs with I2) are slow and cumbersome whilst creatures with a high Initiative score (eg, Elves with I6) are quicker and more agile. Humans have I3. In close combat, Initiative dictates the order in which creatures strike, since faster creatures will attack before slower ones.

ATTACKS (A)
Indicates the number of times a creature attacks during close combat. Most creatures attack only once and have an Attacks value of 1, although some monsters or warriors of exceptional skill may be able to strike several times and have A2, A3 or more.

LEADERSHIP (LD)
A creature with a high Leadership value is courageous, steadfast, and self-controlled. A creature with a low value is the opposite! Leadership is rated on a score of 1 to 10. Humans have a Leadership value of 7, which is average, whilst cowardly Night Goblins have only a Leadership value of 5.

0 LEVEL CHARACTERISTICS

Some creatures have been given a value of '0' for certain characteristics which means that they have no ability whatsoever in that skill. This usually applies to creatures unable to use missile weapons, so they have BS0, but it might equally well apply to other characteristics too. For example, an ordinary horse has no Attacks (A0).

If any creature or object has a Weapon Skill of 0 then it is unable to defend itself in close combat, and any blows which are struck against it will automatically hit.

If at any time a model's Strength, Toughness or Wounds are reduced to 0 or below, it is considered slain and removed from play.

CHARACTERISTIC PROFILES

Every creature in the Warhammer world has a characteristic profile which lists the value of its different characteristics. The examples below show the profiles for an Orc and a Man.

	M	WS	BS	S	T	W	I	A	Ld
Orc	4	3	3	3	4	1	2	1	7

	M	WS	BS	S	T	W	I	A	Ld
Human	4	3	3	3	3	1	3	1	7

As you can see, an Orc and a Man are similar in many respects. They both move at the same speed – 4", and they both have the same Weapon Skill and Ballistic Skill values which means they are very evenly matched in combat. Both have the same Strength value, so they can deliver blows with equal potency. When it comes to Toughness however the Orc wins over the Man – the Orc's value is 4 compared to 3. This is not a vast difference, but it does make the Orc better able to withstand blows and gives it the edge in any hand-to-hand fighting. Both creatures have 1 Wound, which is the normal value for man-sized creatures. The Orc loses out however when it comes to Initiative. This is not a terrible disadvantage, but it does mean that the Man will get to strike his blows before the Orc does when they get stuck into hand-to-hand fighting. Both races have the same Leadership of 7 – which is about average.

SAVES

A creature's saving throw gives it a chance to avoid being harmed when struck or shot. Most creatures have a saving throw based on what kind of armour they are wearing, so their saving throw may be improved if they are equipped with better armour. Other creatures, such as the reptilian Lizardmen, receive an armour saving throw for having scaly skin, while others may have a thick skin or chitinous shell which grants them an armour save.

Some troops are protected by magic or are incredibly tough by nature. These creatures have what is known as a Ward save, a special type of save which can save them from almost any type of damage.

Armour saves are taken by rolling a D6. If a creature has a 3+ armour save, it can normally avoid any wound it suffers by rolling 3 or more on a D6.

CHARACTERISTIC TESTS

Often during a battle, a model will have to take a test on one of its characteristics. In order to pass the test, the model has to roll a D6 and obtain a result equal to or lower than the value of the characteristic involved. Note that if a 6 is rolled, then the model will automatically fail the test regardless of the characteristic's value.

LEADERSHIP TEST

Tests that are made against the Leadership characteristic of a model are done slightly differently to other tests. In the case of a Leadership test, roll two dice and add the results together. If the result is equal to or less than the model's Leadership value, the test has been passed.

UNITS

Warhammer allows you to fight battles with armies of troops, war machines and monstrous beings. It is up to you as the commander of your forces to find the best way to use your cavalry and infantry to achieve victory. The Citadel miniatures used to play Warhammer are simply referred to as models in the rules that follow. Each model is an individual playing piece with its own capabilities and characteristics.

In most cases, models band together into units. A unit will usually consist of several models, but a lone heroic character, a single, very large and powerful model such as a chariot, a monstrous creature like a Dragon or Great Cannon and its crew are also considered to be a unit.

Units have different capabilities and are divided into several types as explained below. For example, when the rules refer to cavalry units, all troops that fall under the category of cavalry must follow those rules.

Units are arranged in a formation that consists of one, two, three or more ranks. As far as possible, the unit always has the same number of models in each rank and, where not possible, it is always the rear rank that is left short. The last rank is filled from the centre.

INFANTRY

Infantry includes all units of foot troops, be they Dwarfs, Elves, Men, or any other of the myriad Warhammer races fighting on foot. A typical infantry regiment is at least 10 strong but can include 20, 40 or even more! Infantry forms the backbone of most Warhammer armies.

CAVALRY

As well as units of warriors fighting on foot, the armies of Warhammer include troops riding horses, giant wolves, and other creatures. The term cavalry refers to riders mounted on horse-sized creatures which have only one Wound in their profile. Bigger creatures are referred to as monsters and these have special rules as described later. Cavalry operates much in the same way as an infantry unit, although it moves faster than foot troops, and often the steeds ridden by the riders can fight as well. Rules for cavalry are discussed where appropriate.

A cavalry model is treated in all respects as a single model. Should the rider be slain the entire model is removed from battle. Cavalry models always use the rider's Leadership for all tests that require it. When the model is attacked, it is the rider's Toughness and Wounds that are used. The mount's Toughness, Wounds and Ld are never used, but are included on its profile because these creatures sometimes appear on their own.

WAR MACHINES (see p.118-125)

These are usually huge, lumbering machineries of destruction, such as the Great Cannons of the Empire, Stone throwers of the Orcs or bizarre and deadly Doomwheels of the Skaven. War machines are often fielded together with their crew and form a unit on their own. Some small war machines, such as Skaven Warpfire Throwers, are regarded as infantry instead of war machines and follow the rules that are given for infantry.

CHARIOTS (see p.126-128)

Many races make use of chariots pulled by creatures such as horses, boars or reptilian Cold Ones. Chariots move faster than infantry, roughly at the same speed as cavalry. A chariot's crew, as well as the creatures pulling it, are considered an integral part of the chariot, and if it is destroyed they are killed along with it. Powerful characters can also ride in chariots. In most cases, chariots fight individually.

MONSTERS (see p.103-105)

Creatures such as Giants, Pegasus, Dragons, Chimeras or War Hydras are called monsters. These are creatures that fight as units of one model, and move individually, their size, strength and magical nature making them a match for units of lesser troops. Sometimes monsters are ridden by powerful Heroes, and follow a slightly different set of rules.

BANNERS, MUSICIANS & CHAMPIONS

Units of troops commonly include a Standard Bearer who carries the unit's banner and a Musician such as a hornblower or drummer. It is also usual for units to be led by a Champion, an experienced and able warrior.

The Champion, Standard Bearer and Musician are placed in the front rank of the unit whenever possible. When a unit turns to face its side or rear, they are automatically rearranged in the new front rank.

As we shall see later, a unit can also be joined by a character, in which case these models are also arranged into the front rank alongside the Champion, Standard Bearer and Musician. Don't worry about this for now – the rules for characters are explained later.

UNIT STRENGTH

Warhammer has several rules (such as outnumbering, panic, etc) where the unit with greater impetus, size or hitting power gains an advantage over its opponents. To establish the relative power of all these different creatures, you need to determine **Unit Strength**. In most cases this is worked out by simply counting the number of models in a unit. However, some huge creatures such as Trolls, war machines, chariots, etc, are individually clearly more powerful than a single man on foot! These creatures have a different Unit Strength.

Orc Boar Chariot

A War Machine, in this case an Empire Cannon

A Wood Elf Forest Dragon with rider

Four ranks of Orcs

A single rank of Empire Pistoliers cavalry

Unit Strength table

TROOP TYPE	UNIT STRENGTH
All Infantry	1
Characters on foot	1
Unit flyers (Warhawks, etc)	1
(All models not listed elsewhere automatically have a Unit Strength of 1).	
Cavalry *(ie, all models on 25mm x 50mm bases)*	2
Chariots	4
War Machines including crew *(ie, Cannons, Stone Throwers, Mortars, Bolt Throwers)*	3
Ogres, Trolls, Minotaurs, Kroxigor, Chaos Spawn, Snotling bases, etc *(ie, models on 40 mm or larger bases that are not monsters (as described opposite), including characters of these races)*	3
Monsters including Giants, Hipporiffs, Dragons, etc *(ie, a Griffon with 4 Wounds has a Unit Strength of 4).*	Original number of Wounds
Ridden Monsters *(including war beasts such as Stegadons and War Hydras)*	1 per rider + Unit Strength of Monster

The table that appears opposite gives you the Unit Strength value of each troop type. The Unit Strength listed is for each model in a unit. To figure out the Unit Strength of an entire regiment, count the number of models in the unit and multiply it with the appropriate number given. In the case of several types of models with different Unit Strengths in the same unit, simply add these together.

Eg, a unit of three Ogres has a Unit Strength of 9 (3x3=9).

FACING

All models taking part in the battle are assumed to face directly forward from the front of their base. This applies equally to units of troops as to large monsters fighting on their own. This is important because a model can only see things that lie in a 90° arc in front of it. Being able to see the enemy is vital when it comes to shooting and deciding whether units can charge their foe.

The facing rule is shown on the diagram opposite. It is worth remembering this rule right from the start as it is very important.

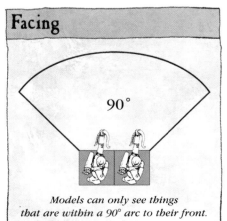

Facing

90°

Models can only see things that are within a 90° arc to their front.

THE TURN

Battles are fought between two opposing sides – two armies that will struggle for supremacy using all their armed might and cunning. The warring armies are commanded by kings and generals, wizards and heroes. Their model counterparts are commanded by you – the player.

In a real battle lots of things happen at once and it is very difficult to tell exactly how the battle is progressing at any one moment. The fortunes of each side sway throughout the battle as one side charges and then the other, roaring with fury and bloodlust as they throw themselves upon the enemy. Mighty war-engines lob their cargoes of death towards their cowering foes and clouds of arrows darken the turbulent skies.

In Warhammer we represent the howling maelstrom of action in turns, in a similar way to chess or draughts. Each player takes one complete turn, then his opponent takes a turn. The first player then takes another turn, followed by the second player again, and so on: each player taking a turn one after the other until the battle is over.

To decide which side takes the first turn it is usual for both players to roll a D6 and the player who rolls highest goes first. See the Scenarios section for more about different ways of setting up a battle and deciding which side has the first turn.

Within the turn, actions are performed in a fixed order – this is called the **turn sequence**. Each turn is divided up into phases during which the player moves all his units, shoots all his missiles, resolves all close combat, and so on.

When it is your turn, it is up to you to keep track of where you are in the turn sequence. If you forget, your opponent should be able to remind you. Each turn is divided into the following phases. These phases are always completed in the order given below, and all actions in that phase must be resolved before moving onto the next phase.

WHO GETS THE FIRST TURN

Which player gets the first turn of the game can be determined in number of different ways. Normally both players roll a D6 and the player with the highest score can decide to move first or second. Sometimes the scenario you are playing will decide it for you. (See Scenarios, p. 196).

1. START OF THE TURN

The rules often call upon a player to make tests or actions at the start of a turn. These are mostly psychology tests (as discussed in the Psychology section), or special rules that apply to a specific race such as the Animosity rule for Orcs & Goblins.

2. MOVEMENT

During the Movement phase you may move your models as defined in the rules for movement.

3. MAGIC

In the Magic phase your Wizards may cast spells. The full rules for spellcasting and magic are described later in this book (see the Magic section).

4. SHOOTING

During the Shooting phase you may fire any missile weapons as described in the rules for shooting.

5. CLOSE COMBAT

During the Close Combat phase all troops in close combat fight. This is an exception to the normal turn sequence in that both sides fight, not just the side whose turn it is.

IMPROVISING

Warhammer is an involving game, with many different races, weapons, and endless possibilities. In a game of this size and level of complexity there are bound to be certain occasions where a particular situation lies outside the rules as they are written. This is inevitable, as it would be impossible to cover every circumstance without writing many hundreds, if not thousands, of pages of dull and pedantic text. Warhammer players should feel free to improvise where necessary, resolving situations in a friendly and mutually agreeable manner, and evolving the game far beyond the published rules if they wish.

When you come across a situation in a battle that is not covered fully by the rulebook, be prepared to interpret a rule or come up with a suitable rule for yourselves.

When a situation of contention arises, players should agree on a fair and reasonable solution and get on with the game as quickly as possible. The most common way of resolving any disputes is for both players to roll a D6 to see whose interpretation applies in that instance.

After the game has finished, sit down and discuss what happened with your opponent and see if you can both reach an agreement incase the same situation ever arises again. Remember, you're playing to enjoy a challenging battle with friends, where the spirit of the game is more important than winning at any cost.

EXCEPTIONS

There are exceptions to the general turn sequence when things are worked out as they occur rather than in any strict order. Quite often the actions of one player will trigger the sudden appearance of a particular troop type, or activate some special weapon or occurrence. Examples of this are springing a bear trap or sinking into quicksand – consequences resulting from movement which may be conveniently resolved there and then. Inevitably, there will be the odd occasion when events can be worked out in one phase or another with little real difference.

 In that dread desert, beneath moons' pale gaze, the dead men walk. They haunt the dunes in that breathless, windless night. They brandish their weapons in mocking challenge to all life, and sometimes, in ghastly dry voices, like the rustling of sere leaves, they whisper the one word they remember from life, the name of their ancient, dark master.

They whisper the name... Nagash.

from the Book of the Dead
by Abdul ben Rachid

MOVEMENT

During the Movement phase, or Move phase, you get the opportunity to move your forces around the battlefield. As with the turn sequence, the things that you can do within the Movement phase are performed in a strict order. An overview of each part of the sequence is given below and further rules governing movement are discussed in the section entitled Moving Troops.

1. DECLARE CHARGES

If you want any of your troops to charge, you must declare this at the very start of the Movement phase.

2. RALLY FLEEING TROOPS

If any of your troops are fleeing, you can attempt to rally them after declaring charges.

3. COMPULSORY MOVES

Move troops that are subject to a compulsory movement rule.

4. MOVE CHARGERS

Move charging troops and resolve other movement resulting from the charge.

5. REMAINING MOVES

Move the rest of your troops.

DECLARE CHARGES

At the start of your Movement phase, the first thing you must do is declare which units will charge. Except in a few unusual circumstances explained later, you are never forced to charge. It is always your decision which units, if any, will charge the enemy.

However, charging is the only way that models are normally allowed to move into close combat. If you want to attack an enemy then you must charge him – you cannot simply move your model into close combat without declaring a charge first. All charges are declared at the start of your Movement phase, in any order you wish.

To declare a charge, indicate which unit is charging and nominate one enemy unit that it is going to attack. For example, you might declare that your Empire Knights unit is charging your opponent's Orc Warriors unit.

A unit may only declare a charge if at least one model in the unit can see at least one enemy model in the opposing unit. It is not necessary for every model to be able to see an enemy – the whole unit is able to charge the enemy so long as one model can do so. For line of sight see Facing, p41.

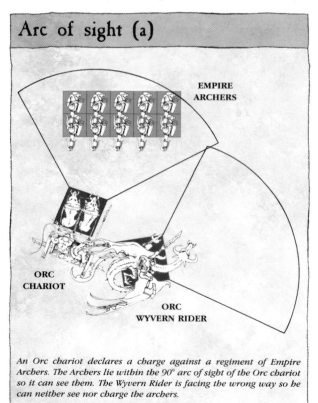

Arc of sight (a)

An Orc chariot declares a charge against a regiment of Empire Archers. The Archers lie within the 90° arc of sight of the Orc chariot so it can see them. The Wyvern Rider is facing the wrong way so he can neither see nor charge the archers.

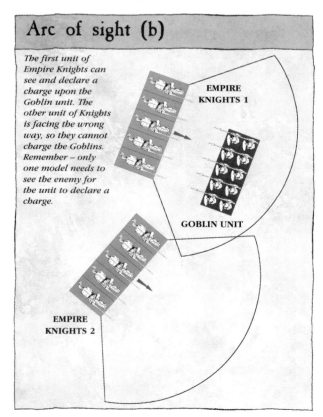

Arc of sight (b)

The first unit of Empire Knights can see and declare a charge upon the Goblin unit. The other unit of Knights is facing the wrong way, so they cannot charge the Goblins. Remember – only one model needs to see the enemy for the unit to declare a charge.

Troops can only charge up to a predetermined distance – this is called a **charge move** and is explained later. When you declare a charge you must do so without measuring the distance to the target, you must rely on your estimate of the distance to ensure that your troops can reach their target.

When deciding whether to charge you must also take into account any terrain that might slow you down, as described later. Deciding whether to charge or not calls for a good judgement of distances!

CHARGE RESPONSES

After you declare your charges, but before you measure whether chargers are within range, your opponent declares how each charged unit will respond. A charged unit has three response options: **stand & shoot**, **hold**, or **flee**. Units already engaged in close combat may only hold.

STAND & SHOOT

If the charged unit has missile weapons and the chargers are more than half their original charge move away, then troops can shoot at the chargers as they advance. For example, a unit of Knights with Move 7 can be shot at if they charge a unit of Archers that is more than 7" away, but cannot be shot at if it charges a unit 7" or less away. Work this out immediately before moving chargers – refer to the Shooting section for rules governing missile weapons (p.61).

Treat stand & shoot responses which fail to hit the enemy because chargers are too close, etc, as a hold response instead.

HOLD

A unit can stand fast and receive the charge, representing individual troopers bracing themselves for the inevitable impact. This is the usual response of troops who do not have missile weapons or who are too close to the enemy to use them.

FLEE

Flee means just that – when your unit sees the enemy thundering down upon them, they turn tail and run! This is a rather desperate option as once troops begin to run they tend to carry on going, and may run away from the battlefield altogether, whether you want them to or not.

As soon as a unit declares that it is fleeing, it is moved directly away from charging enemies by 2D6" if its Movement characteristic is 6" or less, or by 3D6" if its Move is more than 6". The fleeing unit is repositioned facing directly away from the chargers. Move the fleeing models immediately by the distance indicated by the dice roll. This is explained further in the rules for fleeing models in the Close Combat section.

RALLYING

Having declared charges and charge responses, the player whose turn it is now has the opportunity to rally any of his units that are currently fleeing. Troops are normally forced to flee when they are defeated in close combat, if they are frightened by large monsters, or if they have suffered some other unusually traumatic experience. Fleeing troops are of no fighting value unless they can be rallied, which means they come to their senses and stop fleeing in readiness to fight once more.

Because fleeing usually results from close combat the rules for fleeing troops can be found in the Close Combat section of this book. In the Rally phase of his turn, a player makes a test to determine whether his fleeing units manage to rally. If they rally then they remain where they are for the turn but may immediately adopt a new fighting formation facing in any direction. If the fleeing troops fail their Rally test and continue to flee then they are moved next along with other compulsory movement.

COMPULSORY MOVES

After the player has attempted to rally any units that are fleeing, it is time to make any compulsory moves that the rules require.

Generally speaking, a player can move his units how he wishes within the confines of the rules governing movement. However, sometimes troops go out of control for some reason, either because they are overcome by sheer terror, because they are compelled by magic, or because they are disorientated or confused. The player has no control over the movement of these troops and so these are referred to as **compulsory moves**.

The most common kind of compulsory move is fleeing. Fleeing troops always first flee away from their enemy and in subsequent turns towards the nearest table edge, and they always move a randomly determined distance.

All compulsory movement is done now before other movement takes place. This gives troops moving in this fashion the opportunity to get in the way, block lines of advance and do all sorts of other annoying things.

 All life consists of highly organised matter, governed by the laws of nature. Thus all life is a struggle against Chaos, a struggle that is ultimately destined to be lost.

Albrecht of Nuln

MOVE CHARGERS

Once any compulsory moves are complete, it is time for the player to move any units that have declared a charge. They are moved one at a time, in the order that the charges were declared.

Chargers are moved towards their target in accordance with the movement rules given later. When troops charge, they move twice as fast as normal, representing a run or gallop, and this double speed move is called a **charge move**. For example, troops with a normal Move of 4" per turn have a charge move of 8".

Front, flank & rear zones (a)

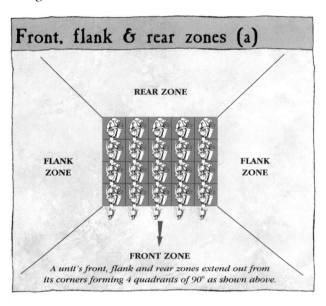

A unit's front, flank and rear zones extend out from its corners forming 4 quadrants of 90° as shown above.

FLANK & REAR CHARGES

Sometimes you may find that your models are able to charge an enemy unit in the flank or rear. This is particularly good because an attack from an unexpected direction will sometimes throw the enemy into a panic and might give you an advantage in combat too. A charging unit's position at the start of the Movement phase determines whether it charges into the flank, the rear or the front of the enemy unit.

If the charging unit is in the target's frontal zone when the charge is declared then it charges into the front. As units generally begin the game facing each other, this is the most common situation that will arise. However, if the charging unit comes from the flank zone, it charges into the side; if in the rear zone, it charges into the rear. See the diagrams below for more clarification.

REMAINING MOVES

Once compulsory moves and charges have been resolved, it is time to move the rest of your troops. Generally speaking, you do not have to move troops at all if you do not want to, or you can move them as short or as great a distance as you like up to their permitted maximum move distance.

The rules governing movement, the encumbering effects of weighty barding, hindering terrain, obstacles to movement, and manoeuvring units around the battlefield are covered in the following section.

Front, flank & rear zones (b)

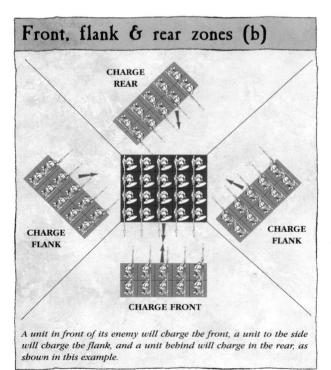

A unit in front of its enemy will charge the front, a unit to the side will charge the flank, and a unit behind will charge in the rear, as shown in this example.

Front, flank & rear zones (c)

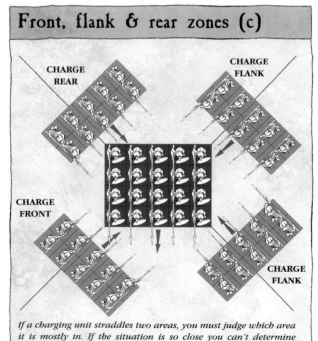

If a charging unit straddles two areas, you must judge which area it is mostly in. If the situation is so close you can't determine where a unit should charge then roll a dice to decide.

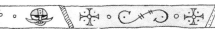

MOVING TROOPS

This section contains all the common rules for moving armies on the tabletop. The same rules govern almost all movement, including the movement of chargers and most compulsory moves. Any exceptions that apply to chargers and fleeing troops are discussed separately. Also, a few creatures move in a special way, flying monsters for example. These are exceptions to the usual rules which, for the sake of convenience, are discussed elsewhere.

Moving an army is an important and often decisive part of the Warhammer game. When opposing commanders are well matched, movement can be as challenging and as satisfying as a game of chess. However, unlike a chessboard, the tabletop is not divided into exact squares. Instead movement is determined using a measuring tape or ruler.

The nature of the game, the varied terrain it is fought over and the stability of the models themselves means that it is impossible to be absolutely accurate about the movement of troops – the odd fraction of an inch will inevitably disappear as lines are neatened and models edged together. On the whole, this need not cause concern during play as it is better to keep the game flowing rather than worrying about unavoidable imprecision. It is recommended that where a move is especially important or an exact measurement is critical, it is good practice to agree what you are doing with your opponent before moving troops.

> Though the gates that stand between the mortal world and the immortal Realm of Chaos are now closed to me, still I would rather die having glimpsed eternity than ever to have stirred from the cold furrow of mortal life. I embrace death without regret as I embraced life without fear.
>
> Unknown Chaos Spawn

MOVEMENT RATE

The normal Movement rate of a model is defined by its Movement (M) characteristic value.

During their Movement phase, units can move up to their Movement rate in inches. For example, Men have a Movement characteristic of 4 and so may move up to 4". Elves, naturally faster and nimbler of foot, move up to 5". You do not have to move the full distance allowed, or even at all if you prefer, but you cannot move further than your normal Move rate unless charging, marching, pursuing or fleeing (all of these types of move are discussed later).

Troops riding mounts with barding move more slowly because the weight of their gear impedes movement. A cavalry mount with barding suffers a -1" move penalty.

For example, a Knight riding a horse can normally move 8". If the horse is wearing barding then the Knight moves 8"-1" (for the horse's barding) which equals a move of 7".

Wheeling a unit

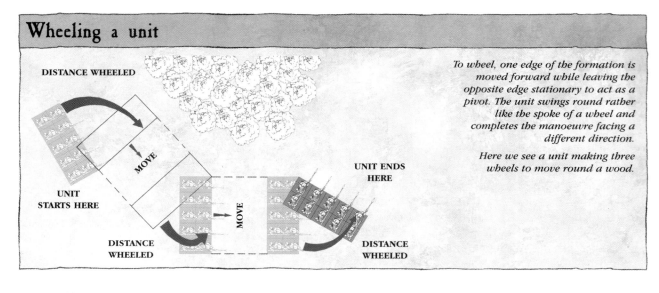

DISTANCE WHEELED

MOVE

UNIT STARTS HERE

DISTANCE WHEELED

MOVE

UNIT ENDS HERE

DISTANCE WHEELED

To wheel, one edge of the formation is moved forward while leaving the opposite edge stationary to act as a pivot. The unit swings round rather like the spoke of a wheel and completes the manoeuvre facing a different direction.

Here we see a unit making three wheels to move round a wood.

Turning a unit

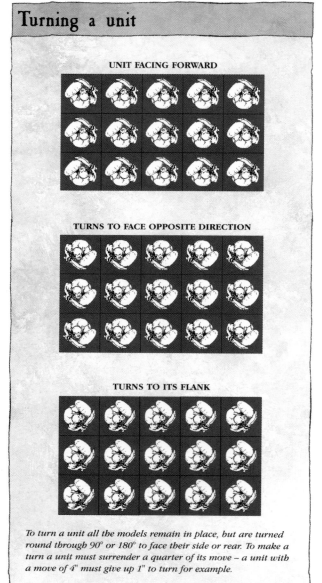

UNIT FACING FORWARD

TURNS TO FACE OPPOSITE DIRECTION

TURNS TO ITS FLANK

To turn a unit all the models remain in place, but are turned round through 90° or 180° to face their side or rear. To make a turn a unit must surrender a quarter of its move – a unit with a move of 4" must give up 1" to turn for example.

Changing formation

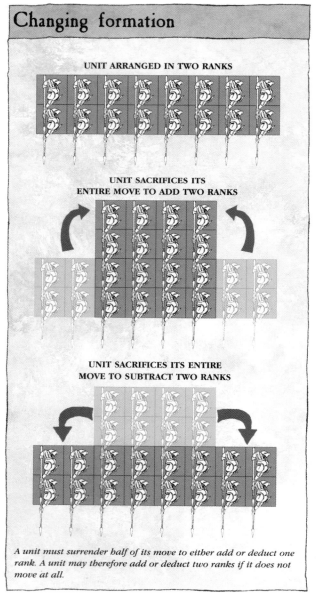

UNIT ARRANGED IN TWO RANKS

UNIT SACRIFICES ITS ENTIRE MOVE TO ADD TWO RANKS

UNIT SACRIFICES ITS ENTIRE MOVE TO SUBTRACT TWO RANKS

A unit must surrender half of its move to either add or deduct one rank. A unit may therefore add or deduct two ranks if it does not move at all.

MANOEUVRE

Troops move and fight in a tight formation of one or more ranks. Such a formation is often referred to by an appropriate title such as a **regiment** or, in the case of cavalry, a **squadron**, or it can simply be called by the cover-all term – **unit**.

When a unit moves around the battlefield it must maintain its formation, which means that models are not free to wander off on their own. The formation can move straight forward as a body perfectly easily, but if it wishes to change direction then it must make a **manoeuvre**.

There are three specific types of manoeuvre that enable a unit to turn about or rearrange its ranks: **wheel**, **turn** and **change formation**. In addition there is a fourth special manoeuvre called **reforming**.

WHEEL

To wheel, the leading edge of the formation moves forward, pivoting round one of the front corners. The unit swings round like the spoke of a wheel and completes the manoeuvre facing a different direction.

When it wheels, the entire unit counts as having moved as far as the outside model. Once the wheel is complete, you may use any movement that the unit has remaining.

For example, a unit of Empire Spearmen might wheel 2" to the left and move 2" straight forward, for a total move of 4".

A unit can wheel several times during its move as long as it has enough movement to do so and is not charging. A unit that is charging is only able to wheel once to align itself to the enemy, as described later.

TURN

To turn a unit, all the models remain in place but are turned around through 90° or 180° to face their side or rear. To make a turn, a unit must surrender a quarter of its move.

For example, a unit with a Move of 4" must give up 1" in order to turn.

A unit is allowed to turn several times during its move unless it is charging or marching.

When a unit is turned to face its side or rear, its leader is automatically rearranged into the front rank along with the Standard Bearer, Musician and any other characters that are in the unit. If there is not enough space within the ranks, models can be rearranged into the rear ranks as the player wishes.

CHANGE FORMATION

A unit of troops can also change its formation by adding or reducing the number of ranks in which it is deployed. For example, a unit that consists of two ranks may increase its depth to three ranks by moving models from the front two ranks to form a new third line.

A unit must surrender half of its move to either add or deduct one rank. A unit may add or deduct two ranks if it does not move at all.

When redeploying ranks in this way it is important to remember that a unit always has the same number of models in each rank, except for the rear rank which may contain the same or fewer models. A rear rank is still a rank whether it is full or contains only one model, although only ranks of four or more models are considered to be of any value in close combat, as described later.

REFORM

A unit of troops can change the direction in which it is facing and rearrange its formation all at once by means of a manoeuvre called reforming. The leader issues the order to adopt a new formation and the troops mill about until they assume their new positions.

A unit of troops can reform during its Movement phase as long as it is not in close combat, and is otherwise free to move as it wishes. The player declares that the unit is reforming and regroups it into a new formation. Keeping the centre of the unit the same, arrange the unit into a new formation of as many ranks as you please facing whichever direction you wish, as long as none of the models in the unit move more than twice their Movement rate (ie, Men with Move 4 can move up to 8"). Character models, Standard Bearers and Musicians must still be placed in the front rank of the unit as normal.

A unit which reforms cannot move that turn because it takes the entire Movement phase to reform. Also, reforming troops cannot shoot with missile weapons that turn because they are too busy assuming their new formation. Other actions, such as Wizards casting spells, are still allowed.

TERRAIN

Troops only move their full Movement rate over unobstructed ground. They will slow down if impeded by broken ground such as bushes or woods. Terrain is divided into four types to simulate this: **open**, **difficult**, **very difficult** & **impassable** terrain.

OPEN TERRAIN

Open terrain is clear ground that doesn't impede movement at all. The battlefield is basically all open terrain unless otherwise indicated. This will normally include hills, as long as they are not too steep, as well as features such as roads, paths, gateways and other firm surfaces.

DIFFICULT TERRAIN

Difficult terrain includes the following:

Brush, scrub and other clinging vegetation.
Debris, wreckage, loose rocks and boulders.
Fords, streams and shallow water.
Marshes, bogs and thick mud.
Freshly ploughed, flooded and muddy fields.
Sand dunes and areas of deep sand.
Stairs, steps and ladders.

Steep or treacherous slopes. This can include particular hills if both players agree before the game, otherwise hills are considered to be open terrain.

Woods, orchards, growing crops and dense foliage.

Troops cross difficult ground at half speed, so if your unit has Move 4 then it can only move 2" in a wood.

If troops move over open ground and difficult terrain during the same turn, then their movement over open ground is at full speed and movement over difficult ground is reduced to half speed as normal. For example, a Man moves 2" across open ground and then enters a wood. He now has 2" of his move left. This is covered at half speed as it is difficult terrain, so he can only move a further 1" through the wood.

VERY DIFFICULT TERRAIN

Very difficult terrain includes areas that are even more arduous to move through, such as the following:

Thick woods packed with briars and thorns.

Almost sheer slopes that need to be climbed on hands and knees.

Fast flowing but still fordable rivers.

Very difficult terrain reduces movement to quarter speed. Fractions are rounded up to the nearest 1/2" to prevent unnecessary complication.

IMPASSABLE TERRAIN

Impassable terrain is terrain so difficult to move through that it cannot be crossed during the course of a battle. It includes terrain features such as rivers, lakes, impenetrable swamps and sheer cliffs. Troops must go round impassable terrain.

Players should decide before the battle begins whether certain terrain features will be difficult, very difficult or impassable during the course of the battle.

OBSTACLES

Obstacles are things such as hedges, fences, walls and trenches that troops must clamber over to cross. Although obstacles may be similar in some respects to difficult ground, in that a hedge and a wood might both contain trees, there is an important difference. Obstacles are basically linear barriers, such as a wall, which troops must cross over before they can proceed. Difficult terrain describes an area of ground such as a bog or marsh that slows down a unit's overall speed.

It takes a model half of its move to cross an obstacle. So if a model has Move 4 it must surrender 2" to cross a hedge or a wall. If a model has insufficient move left to cross an obstacle it has reached then it must halt in front of it. The model does not count as being half way across if it has 1" of its 4" Move remaining, for example. Where an entire unit of troops is attempting

Most bizarre of monsters is the dreaded Chimera: it's body is a size of a house, and has wicked claws longer than daggers. It's tail lashes like an iron whip, and it's huge leathery wings carry it through the skies.

This loathsome creature has three heads. One of them is horned, like a head of a ram: other is like that of a vast lion: the third head is the most frightening of all: it that of a scaled dragon, and it belches forth noxious smoke and scorching fire.

Chimera hunts in the northern wastes, and meat of men is it's delicacy: it will hunt relentlessly through day and night to capture it's prey.

From Grimoire Beterricus

to cross an obstacle, the penalty continues to apply to the whole unit as long as any of the models are crossing.

Sometimes the front of a unit may end up on one side of a linear obstacle and the back part on the other side. This is fine. Place the part of the unit which has crossed on the far side of the obstacle and leave the part that has yet to cross on the other side. As long as the ranks on both sides are in contact with the obstacle, this is perfectly acceptable. Once troops have moved over the obstacle, the unit's ranks are returned to base contact. Remember that the unit suffers a half move penalty until all its troops have crossed the obstacle.

If a wall, hedge or fence has a gate in it then it is assumed to be open unless otherwise agreed, and troops may move through the gate without penalty.

If a unit's formation is divided by an obstacle then it may not manoeuvre by turning or wheeling, and it may not change its formation. The unit must cross the obstacle before it can do any of these things.

Bear in mind that a unit of troops can suffer from reduced speed for moving over difficult terrain and the half Move penalty for crossing an obstacle. If troops are moving at half their normal speed, of 2" across difficult terrain (eg, a freshly ploughed field) they must still surrender a half of their move to cross a hedge or fence, a -1" penalty in this case.

CHARGING

Chargers are moved after compulsory movement and before you move the rest of your army. Make sure you complete all charges before moving other troops. Chargers move at double their normal Move rate, but must make the usual deductions for crossing terrain and obstacles. For example, mounted Knights have Move 7 and so can charge up to 14". If moving over difficult terrain, such as a muddy field, they move at half their speed, reducing their charge distance to 7".

Before you move a charging unit check that your opponent has declared his response and that troops electing to flee have been moved and troops electing to stand & shoot have done so. Measure the distance between the chargers and their target.

A FAILED CHARGE

If the enemy has fled, or if you have estimated your charge incorrectly, your troops might not be able to move far enough to reach their intended target. If this is the case, the charge has failed.

If a charge fails, the unit is moved at its normal Move rate rather than double speed. The unit is moved directly towards the intended target as if it were charging but halts once it has covered its normal Move distance. This represents when troops have begun to charge before realising it is impossible to reach their enemy; consequently their movement peters out as they lose impetus and enthusiasm.

A unit that fails its charge cannot shoot with missile weapons that turn, though Wizards may cast spells.

MANOEUVRING DURING A CHARGE

A charging unit cannot turn or change formation. This is because the troops are running or galloping once the charge has begun and are unable to execute delicate manoeuvres even if they were able to hear the orders of their leaders above the din.

The following rules govern manoeuvres during a charge:

1. When a unit charges an enemy the player must endeavour to bring as many models from the charging unit into combat as possible. This can sometimes be achieved by moving the chargers straight forward, but often it will be necessary to wheel slightly to face the enemy. This is a very important rule, so be sure to get it right from the start!

2. During a charge a unit can wheel once. It can, and indeed must, wheel in order to maximise the number of charging models able to fight. Note that the unit does not have to wheel if this would mean that it cannot reach its enemy.

If chargers need to wheel towards their target, execute the wheel as already described, measuring the distance wheeled as you normally would. This distance counts as part of the total distance charged. For example, if a unit can charge 12" it might wheel 4" to bring models to face the enemy and then move up to 8" towards them.

Once a unit has completed any required wheel it is moved straight forward towards the enemy and stops as soon as the two units touch.

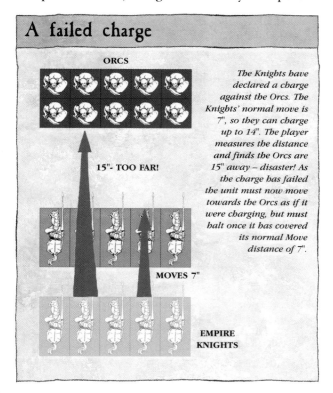

A failed charge

ORCS

15"- TOO FAR!

MOVES 7"

EMPIRE KNIGHTS

The Knights have declared a charge against the Orcs. The Knights' normal move is 7", so they can charge up to 14". The player measures the distance and finds the Orcs are 15" away – disaster! As the charge has failed the unit must now move towards the Orcs as if it were charging, but must halt once it has covered its normal Move distance of 7".

ALIGNING THE COMBATANTS

Once the charging unit is in contact it is automatically aligned against its enemy as shown in the diagram below to form a battle line. This extra alignment move is free.

If it is impractical to align a unit properly because of interposing terrain, other models, or whatever, then it is acceptable to re-align the charged unit as well (or instead) so that the battlelines remain neat. A confusing situation may arise when interposing terrain or models make it impossible to align the whole unit, for example. Rather than clutter the rules with endless clarifications, we have included further examples in the back of this book.

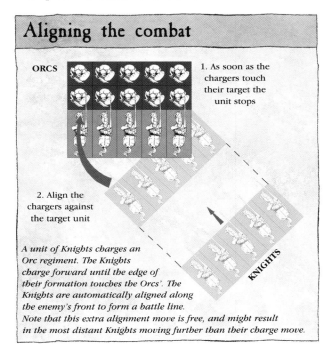

Aligning the combat

ORCS

1. As soon as the chargers touch their target the unit stops

2. Align the chargers against the target unit

A unit of Knights charges an Orc regiment. The Knights charge forward until the edge of their formation touches the Orcs'. The Knights are automatically aligned along the enemy's front to form a battle line. Note that this extra alignment move is free, and might result in the most distant Knights moving further than their charge move.

KNIGHTS

MOVING ENGAGED UNITS

Once opposing units are engaged in close combat they may not move away until one side or the other breaks or is destroyed. Units already engaged in close combat at the start of their turn cannot move but must continue to fight in the Close Combat phase.

CHARGE REACTIONS

If a charged unit stands & shoots, it is possible that it may cause sufficient casualties on the charging unit to force an immediate Panic test. Panic tests and other special psychological tests are explained in the Psychology section. This might result in a charge being brought to a halt before contact is made with the enemy. That is why it is important to work out fire from enemies who stand & shoot before moving chargers. If the chargers are out of missile range at the beginning of their charge then work out missile casualties at the maximum range of the weapon.

If a charged unit flees as it is charged then it will move directly away from its chargers either 2D6" or 3D6" depending on whether its Movement rate is up to 6" or more than 6", as explained later. It may be that fleeing troops move too far for the chargers to catch them, in which case the chargers move their normal Move rate exactly as for any other failed charge.

If fleeing troops do not move far enough away to avoid their attackers then they are in deep trouble! If the chargers have sufficient movement to catch them then the entire fleeing unit is destroyed. The chargers only need to catch one model to destroy the whole unit as it flees. Chargers move their full charge move, moving past the point where the enemy was caught if necessary. The fleeing troops are run into the ground or scattered beyond any hope of recovery. See the rules for fleeing troops in the Close Combat section for more details.

REDIRECTING A CHARGE

If a charged unit flees, it can happen that another enemy unit is now within the charging unit's reach. If this fresh enemy unit is within range then the player is allowed to redirect the charge, though he does not have to. He must declare that his unit is charging against the new target, and the target must make a response as normal. If this unit flees as well then the charging player is not allowed to redirect his charge again.

If there is a choice of units that can be charged, the charging unit must go after an enemy that is nearest to the original target unit.

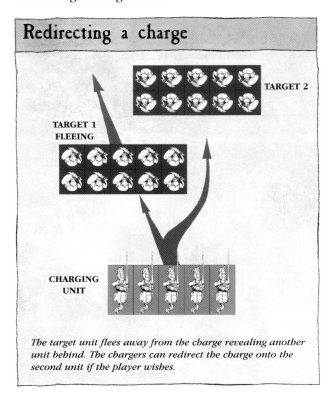

Redirecting a charge

TARGET 2

TARGET 1 FLEEING

CHARGING UNIT

The target unit flees away from the charge revealing another unit behind. The chargers can redirect the charge onto the second unit if the player wishes.

PANIC

Troops who are charged in the flank or rear whilst they are already fighting other enemy who engaged them on the previous turn(s) must take a Panic test to see whether their nerve holds, as described later. This test is taken as soon as it is established that chargers are within range, but before moving any troops. The rules for Panic tests and other psychological tests are explained in full in the section on Psychology.

COMBAT BONUSES

If a unit is charged in the flank or rear by a unit with a unit strength of five or more then it loses any rank bonuses that it would otherwise have in close combat. Units that are ranked up in depth normally fight better because the troops in the rear ranks are able to physically support those in the front, lending their weight to the formation, but a unit which is charged in the flank or rear will lose this advantage. See the Close Combat section for details of combat results and how rank bonuses work. If a unit is attacking an enemy in the flank or rear, it gains the advantage of fighting a formation unprepared to fight in that direction. Consequently, the attackers receive extra combat bonuses, as described in the Close Combat section.

ODDBALL STUFF

A charge can sometimes trigger extra movement from the enemy. For example, Goblin Fanatics will leap out of their units as soon as enemy approach within 8". This happens out of the normal sequence: the charge is halted as soon as the chargers move within 8" and the Goblin Fanatics are moved and any damage they cause is worked out straight away. It is up to the player to say that he has out of sequence movements or actions to perform at the appropriate moment.

FLANK AND REAR CHARGES

Being charged from a direction you cannot see and thought was safe is a frightening thing for even the bravest of troops. With his field of vision narrowed by his position in the ranks, the average soldier has only a limited knowledge of what is happening on the battlefield. If the enemy has somehow got round behind him he might reasonably assume that the battle is lost. Doubt will be sown in his mind and he may become disoriented and confused. His fighting efficiency may even become impaired. If he is fighting in close combat, he might panic and flee, thinking that the enemy is upon his unguarded back.

Individual models can turn to face the chargers and avoid this test and any other penalties, unless they are already engaged in close combat.

MARCHING

Marching at the double allows troops that are away from the main fighting zones to move more rapidly. This represents the swift movement of reserves to a critical area by means of a rapid march and helps to ensure that units do not get stranded away from the fighting.

Marching troops move at twice their normal Movement rate with weapons sheathed or shouldered. They are literally 'going at the double'. A unit that is on the march is not prepared for combat so marching is not suitable for a unit that is close to the enemy. In reality, no troops would approach the enemy with their weapons unready to defend or attack with.

Troops can march if there are no enemy models within 8" of them at the start of the turn. If there are enemy models (fleeing enemies do not count) anywhere within 8" at the start of the turn, the unit is too busy preparing to fight and so cannot march. Note that the marching unit can move closer than 8" to an enemy as it moves.

A unit on the march cannot change formation or turn as this would disrupt its movement. It can wheel as normal, as you might imagine a column of troops would in order to follow a route or path, for example.

A marching unit cannot move through difficult or other obstructive terrain or cross obstacles. It must stop if it comes to these features.

A unit that is on the march cannot shoot missile weapons during the Shooting phase. It is unprepared for combat and any weapons it carries are not ready to be used. Any Wizards with the unit can still cast spells.

INDIVIDUAL MODELS

Units which consist of models that move individually, such as Giants or large monsters with or without riders, can march move in the same way as units of troops.

In the case of individual models their speed bonus is not due to them 'marching' in formation but takes account of their freedom to move, breaking into a run, and so forth.

SNAKING

A unit deployed in a column with models lined up one behind the other can move very easily. The lead model is not restricted by troops either side and so can choose a snaking path which twists about. This is called **snaking**. Trailing models are placed so that they follow the path of the lead model. This a special type of movement unique to long lines of troops. It isn't a very practical formation for fighting, but it is very handy for threading your way through buildings and between obstacles.

1" APART

Players will sometimes find that the movement of troops results in the tabletop becoming quite crowded, especially when several different units are engaged in close combat fighting. It is obviously important to establish what units are actually fighting and which are close by but not engaged, eg, perhaps merely passing by.

For this reason, opposing troops are kept at least 1" apart when they are not fighting. Models which would otherwise approach to within 1" of an enemy without engaging them are simply halted 1" away. Remember that units may only engage in close combat by means of a charge, except in exceptional circumstances. These are clearly indicated in the rules.

This rule is ignored during charge moves – a charging unit may approach within 1" of any enemy. This is done for the purposes of game mechanics.

MAGIC

After movement is resolved, it is time for the Magic phase. If you are new to the Warhammer game we recommend that you ignore magic for now and familiarise yourself with the rules for shooting and close combat. If you wish to learn how magic works, turn to p.134.

BATTLE OF THE IRON CRAG

Hear me manlings, and honour heroes of your folk. I, Duregar of Karak-Hirn speak to you now of the Battle of Iron Crag. It was the day of Grimnir, five and a half thousand years after the founding of Karaz-a-Karak, when the combined armies of Reikland and Dwarfs fought the hordes of Orc Warlord Grothak One-Eye.

The men bore the brunt of the attack, falling in their hundreds, yet not giving an inch of ground. They stood alone on the hill, and withstood the avalanche of steel and green-skinned monsters, showing spirit to match the bravery of long-bearded Dwarf warriors.

The massed fire of our Thunderers saved the last five of them, and the charges of the Ironbreakers broke the foe. For the honour of our allies we built a mound of the heads of the Orcish scum as a warning to those invaders who come to pillage our lands.

It was King Alrik, the bearer of the great hammer of Karak-Hirn, who lead the Dwarfs into victory. He was said to have slain three dozen of the foe alone that day.

The birds of prey came to peck the eyes of the fallen enemies, an apt fate for those who would come and defile the land of our ancestors. Our own dead we carried to be buried in the Halls of the Dead beneath the mountains.

It was the hand guns of the Dwarfs, such as this, which brought victory in the Battle of the Iron Crag. This one is a masterpiece with a spring-loading mechanism, made by the great Engineer Thorik of Karak-Hirn.

A skilled Dwarf Thunderer can slay a Goblin from two hundred paces with such a weapon!

SHOOTING

Once the Movement and Magic phases are over, it is time to work out any shooting that is to be done. Troops armed with bows, crossbows or other missile weapons may shoot at any enemy targets they can see. Unless otherwise mentioned, each model can only make one shooting attack in each Shooting phase. You may also shoot with any war machines such as stone throwers, cannons, etc. The rules for these are covered later.

You always start shooting with any weapons that require you to guess the range of the shot (such as cannons and stone throwers for example). Guess all the ranges of these before measuring any of them. Otherwise, there is no particular order in which shooting must be resolved.

Nominate one of your units that you want to shoot with and select the enemy target you wish to shoot at. For example, in the situation shown in the diagram on the right, you might choose to shoot with your Empire Archers at the Goblin Wolf Riders or the unit of Goblin Spearmen. Once you have declared your target, measure the range and resolve shooting using the rules described. Continue until you have shot with everything able to do so, including any war machines you may have.

RANGE

All missile weapons have a maximum range which indicates the greatest distance that they can shoot. If your declared target lies beyond this maximum range, your shots will automatically miss. This is why you must pick your target before measuring the range.

Missile weapon range

Short Bow	16"
Bow	24"
Long Bow	30"
Crossbow	30"
Repeating Crossbow	24"
Sling	18"
Javelin	8"
Thrown axe	4"
Thrown knife, dart	6"
Handguns	24"
Pistol	8"

Selecting a target

Goblin Wolf Riders

Goblin Spearmen

NOMINATE 1 ENEMY TARGET!

Empire Archers

The unit of Empire Archers can shoot at the Goblin Wolf Riders or the Goblin Spearmen.

For example: The Empire player is using bows, which have a range of 24". He declares that he is opening fire on the nearest Orc unit. When he measures the distance, he finds that the Orcs are 25" away. His hail of arrows therefore falls short of the jeering greenskins.

It often happens that some models in a firing unit will be within range and other models in the unit will be out of range. If this is the case then only those which are in range can shoot and the remainder automatically miss.

These ranges are the maximum distances that the weapons can fire. Missiles lose power and accuracy long before they reach their maximum range, so ranges are divided into two types: **short range** and **long range**.

Short range is up to and **including** half the maximum range of the weapon.

Long range is between half and maximum distance of the weapon.

For example: Short range for a short bow is up to 8". A target that is at more than 8" counts as being at long range.

As we shall see later, there are modifiers that make it much more difficult for a weapon to hit a target at long range.

WHO CAN SHOOT AND LINE OF SIGHT

The direction of the front of the model's base is assumed to be the actual direction faced by the creature it represents. Common sense dictates that a model cannot shoot at something it cannot see. To represent this, a target must lie within a 90° arc projected from the front of the shooter. Where models are on square bases, this can be imagined easily by projecting a line through the corners. This is called the **line of sight** and it determines which opponents the model can shoot at or charge.

A shooter's line of sight may be blocked if there is anything between him and his intended target which obscures his line of sight. Thus, interposing models or scenery may block a model's line of sight to a target. Because of this, except as noted later, only models in the front rank of a unit are able to shoot, as those behind will not be able to see past their friends.

Imagine a real battlefield with its contours, morning mists and haze of dust. Picture the woods and hedges that obscure vision, the sudden fall of ground that hides the enemy, and the distances that blur friend with foe. Towering over our miniature battlefield we are unaware of all this, but the troops represented by our models would not be so lucky. Just as their real life counterparts cannot see through hills or hedges, we must assume that our models cannot see behind corresponding scenic features.

As it is impossible for us to say exactly what everyone's scenery looks like, it is not practical to be definitive about which kinds of terrain block line of sight. You must be prepared to use your own judgement within the following guidelines.

Perhaps the easiest way of checking what a model can see is to get down over the table and take a model's eye view, but be reasonable about this, as in reality it would be much more difficult to see enemy troops than over a perfectly flat, mist-free gaming table.

Hills, large boulders and buildings obscure sight over level ground. If an interposing hill or house completely obscures a line of sight to a model on the other side of it, you may not see through it and so cannot shoot at the model on the other side.

Hedges and walls block line of sight over level ground. However, a model placed directly behind and touching an obstacle is assumed to be able to see and shoot over the obstacle, with head and shoulders clearly visible. Such a model can shoot but also be seen and shot at.

Woods block line of sight if the shooter and the target lie on either side of the wood. It is only possible to see through up to 2" of woodland, so if a model

inside a wood is within 2" of the edge, he can see out and shoot and he can also be seen and shot at (a -1 penalty applies). If it is further than 2" inside the wood, a model can

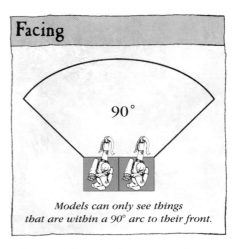

Facing

90°

Models can only see things that are within a 90° arc to their front.

neither be seen by models outside nor can he see them. If both target and shooter are inside the wood then the missile range is reduced to the farthest they can see – which is 2".

Troops, either friendly or unfriendly, block line of sight. It is not possible to shoot directly through one model to hit another. This does not apply if a target behind normal-sized models (such as Men or Orcs) is defined as a *large target*. Snotlings or Goblins can't block line of sight to a Giant, for example! This works vice versa – a Dragonrider, for example, can shoot at targets over interposing friendly models which are not large.

Note that this does not allow large creatures to charge through any interposing models!

HILLS & ELEVATED POSITIONS

Hills are tactically important positions, overlooking the entire battlefield and giving war machines and missile-armed troops an excellent opportunity to shoot at the enemy. Many battles have been won or lost depending on a General's ability to exploit the tactical use of hills.

MISSILE FIRE FROM HILLS

Troops on a hill can draw a line of sight from an elevated position. To determine what the troops can see, you should get down over the table and take a model's eye view. Therefore, most of the time your troops may be able to see over troops that are on the ground below, and over other obstacles that are lower than the hill.

Troops on a hill are considered to be in a good position to fire, so can fire with one additional rank compared to missile-armed troops on flat ground. This means that most bowmen can shoot with two ranks if they are on a hill.

COVER

Troops who are in base contact behind certain terrain features, such as hedges or walls, can take advantage of cover. This makes them harder to hit because they can duck back out of the way, leaving arrows to splinter against a wall or tree. There are two sorts of cover: **hard** cover and **soft** cover.

HARD COVER

This offers real physical protection as well as partially concealing the target from view. The corner of a building, a large rock, walls and wooden palisades are all types of hard cover. Troops positioned at windows and doors also count as being behind hard cover.

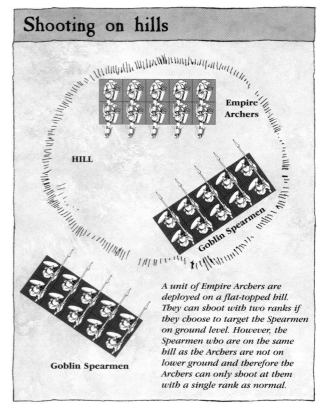

Shooting on hills

A unit of Empire Archers are deployed on a flat-topped hill. They can shoot with two ranks if they choose to target the Spearmen on ground level. However, the Spearmen who are on the same hill as the Archers are not on lower ground and therefore the Archers can only shoot at them with a single rank as normal.

A model positioned at the corner of a building so that he is peeking round is protected by hard cover and models in trenches or pits are also in hard cover.

SOFT COVER

Although it partially shields a target from view, soft cover provides scant protection against incoming missiles. You can hide behind a hedge, but a crossbow bolt or arrow will go straight through it. Hedges and woodland provide soft cover and troops within woods automatically count as being in soft cover.

SHOOTING & CLOSE COMBAT

Units in hand-to-hand fighting are far too busy to use missile weapons and therefore may not shoot.

Players are not allowed to shoot at targets that are engaged in close combat. The risk of hitting their own comrades is far too high.

TEMPLATES

Sometimes some weapons (such as stone throwers) may deviate and hit units already in close combat. As described later, some of these weapons utilise a template to determine how many models are hit by a falling stone, a gout of Dragon fire, and so on. Normally, models under the template are considered targets and will be hit. See the section on War Machines for details.

If a template ends up in such a way that it touches only models from one side, and none of the models it touches are actually fighting (ie, in base contact with their enemy), then all casualties are worked out exactly as normal. The shot has struck in such a way that all hits fall on that unit.

If a template ends up so that it touches models from either side that are fighting, or models from both sides whether fighting or not, then work out the number of hits as normal but distribute them equally to both sides. The shot has fallen in the thick of the fighting and both sides suffer the consequences.

STAND & SHOOT

If a charge is declared against a unit with missile weapons it can respond by shooting at the charging unit but only if the charging unit is more than half its charge distance away. This reaction is called **stand & shoot**. The shots are worked out once all charges have been declared and before the chargers are moved. Work out the shots at the measured range and apply the -1 to hit modifier for shooting at a charging target.

A unit which stands & shoots does so out of the normal turn sequence, in the other side's Movement phase before chargers are moved. Note that chargers who begin their move within half their charge distance of the enemy cannot be shot at in this way. They are too close, and there is insufficient time for the unit to shoot at their enemy.

If the chargers start their charge beyond the maximum range of the shooting unit's missile weapons, the shots are made at the maximum range of the weapons. The archers let loose as soon as their enemies are within range.

Dividing shots

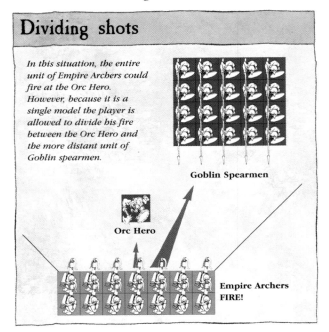

In this situation, the entire unit of Empire Archers could fire at the Orc Hero. However, because it is a single model the player is allowed to divide his fire between the Orc Hero and the more distant unit of Goblin spearmen.

Goblin Spearmen

Orc Hero

Empire Archers FIRE!

DIVIDING SHOTS

In most circumstances, a unit of troops takes aim and shoots at a single target, such as a unit of enemy troops, a huge monster or chariot, obeying the command of their leader who is assumed to direct the unit's fire.

A unit may divide its fire between two or more enemy targets if it is impossible for all the models to shoot at a single target. For example, it might be that no single target is visible to all shooters either because it is obscured or because it is so close to the unit that it lies outside the arc of vision of some of the shooting models.

In the case of individual enemy models, such as large monsters, Heroes, Goblin Fanatics and similar, it is permitted to divide shots against these and other more distant targets, even if the entire unit could shoot against the single enemy model. This allows a shooting unit to spread its fire against a group of single models.

HITTING THE TARGET

The chance of a shooter scoring a hit on his target depends on his Ballistic Skill, or BS. The higher the individual's Ballistic Skill, the greater his chance of hitting.

To determine whether you hit, you must roll a D6 for each model that is shooting. Note that the number of Attacks a model has will not affect the number of shots – each shooter can shoot only once unless the weapon he carries has a special rule which allows it to fire more rapidly.

Count how many models in your unit are shooting and roll that number of dice. It is easiest to roll all the dice at once, although you don't have to. If there are a lot of models shooting, you might need to roll several batches of dice. The following table shows the minimum D6 score you will need to hit.

Ballistic Skill	1	2	3	4	5	6	7	8	9	10
To hit score	6	5	4	3	2	1	0	-1	-2	-3

If you score equal to or greater than the number required, you have hit. If you score less, you have missed.

For example: You fire with five Goblin Archers. Goblins have BS 3, so you need a score of at least 4 to hit. You roll 5 dice and score 1, 2, 2, 4, and 6 which equals 2 hits and 3 misses.

Of course, you cannot roll less than 1 on a D6, so troops with BS 6 or more will have a negative to hit score. However, in Warhammer no troops ever hit automatically, so a roll of 1 on a D6 always fails, regardless of the dice modifiers and Ballistic Skill of the model.

SHOOTING

TO HIT MODIFIERS

Shooting isn't simply a matter of pointing your weapon at the target and letting fly. Factors other than your Ballistic Skill affect the chance of hitting, such as range and cover as already discussed. There are other factors too, some of which make it easier to hit and others that make it harder. These are called **To Hit** modifiers, and they are cumulative.

Factors that make it easier are added to your dice roll. Factors that make it harder are subtracted from your dice roll.

All shooting to hit modifiers are cumulative. So, if you are shooting at long range at a target behind soft cover, your chance of hitting is reduced by -2. This means that with BS 5 you would need to roll a 4 to hit instead of the 2 normally required.

For example: Ten Goblin Archers fire at a unit of Elves. Their targets are 10" away. To make matters worse, the Elves are standing behind a hedge – soft cover! The Goblins are armed with short bows, so their targets are at long range (short range for these weapons is 8" or less). Because their BS is 3, the Goblins need 4s to hit, but since their targets are in cover and at long range, they suffer a penalty of -2. So each archer needs to roll a 6 to hit (6-2=4). The player rolls ten dice and manages to get two 6s – two hits!

+1 SHOOTING AT A LARGE TARGET

A large target is anything which in real life would be massively tall or which is especially bulky. Giants are large targets, for example, while Men, Orcs, Elves, Ogres, Cannons and the vast majority of troops are not. In every case, a creature's description in the relevant Army book will inform you whether it is a large target or not. Cavalry riders are not considered to be large targets if they are riding horses, wolves, boars or comparable beasts. Dragons, Greater Daemons and certain war machines are large targets.

-1 SHOOTING WHILE MOVING

If the shooter moved during the Movement phase (or during the Magic phase via the effect of a spell) then his chance of hitting is reduced. Even a simple turn or change of formation is enough to reduce his concentration and so counts as movement for this purpose.

-1 SHOOTING AT A CHARGING ENEMY.

If a model is charged and elects to stand & shoot at his attacker then his chance of hitting is reduced. While the enemy thunders towards him, his aim will be distracted and his shot hurried as he abandons his weapon to take up a sword.

-1 SHOOTING AT LONG RANGE

If the target lies at over half your maximum range you are less likely to hit. Sometimes you will find some of the shooters are within short range and some are at long range. If this is the case, you must roll two batches of dice, one for each range band.

-1 SHOOTING AT A SINGLE MODEL OR AT SKIRMISHERS

If the target is a single man-sized model (including characters) on foot then this penalty applies. The penalty also applies when shooting at enemy in a skirmish formation or at any single man-sized model on its own. See the section on Heroes and Wizards for a complete explanation of the rules for shooting at character models, and see the section on Skirmishers for rules regarding skirmishing troops.

-1 TARGET IS BEHIND SOFT COVER

If the target is behind soft cover then the chance of hitting it is reduced.

-2 TARGET IS BEHIND HARD COVER

If the target is behind hard cover, the chance of hitting it is drastically reduced.

WOUND CHART

	Target's Toughness									
Weapon's Strength	**1**	**2**	**3**	**4**	**5**	**6**	**7**	**8**	**9**	**10**
1	4	5	6	6	N	N	N	N	N	N
2	3	4	5	6	6	N	N	N	N	N
3	2	3	4	5	6	6	N	N	N	N
4	2	2	3	4	5	6	6	N	N	N
5	2	2	2	3	4	5	6	6	N	N
6	2	2	2	2	3	4	5	6	6	N
7	2	2	2	2	2	3	4	5	6	6
8	2	2	2	2	2	2	3	4	5	6
9	2	2	2	2	2	2	2	3	4	5
10	2	2	2	2	2	2	2	2	3	4

7+ TO HIT

If to hit modifiers result in a required score of 7 or more when shooting then it is still possible to score a hit, though very unlikely. As it is impossible to roll a 7 on a D6, you will first need to roll a 6 and then, for each shot scoring a 6, you will need to roll a further score as shown on the chart below. So, for example, in order to score an 8, you must roll a 6 followed by a 5 or more. If you require a score of 10 or more then it is impossible to hit the intended target.

```
7 . . . . . . . . . . 6 followed by a 4, 5 or 6
8 . . . . . . . . . . . . 6 followed by a 5 or 6
9 . . . . . . . . . . . . . . . 6 followed by a 6
10+ . . . . . . . . . . . . . . . . . Impossible!
```

WOUNDS

Not all hits will wound their target – some might glance off armour or merely graze their target. Some creatures are so tough that arrows do not easily pierce their flesh, or are so resilient that they are able to ignore missiles sticking out of their body. Once you have hit your target, roll again to see if he has been wounded. To do this compare the weapon's Strength with the target's Toughness. The Strength values of common missile weapons are given on the right; the target's Toughness 'T', is included in its profile.

Roll a D6 for each hit scored and consult the Wound chart above. Find the weapon's Strength and look down that row. Then scan along to the column for the target's Toughness. The number is the minimum score on a D6 needed to score a wound. Where the value is 'N' this indicates that the target is too tough for you to hurt. N stands for no effect – or no chance!

WEAPON STRENGTH

The following examples show the strength of various missile weapons. They are included here as examples: the section on Weapons describes all missile and close combat weapons in more detail.

WEAPON	STRENGTH
Shortbow	3
Bow	3
Longbow	3
Repeater Crossbow	3
Sling	3
Crossbow	4
Handgun	4

Continuing our earlier example: The Goblin player, having scored 2 hits on the Elves, consults the table. His ladz' short bows are S 3. The Elves are T 3. He sees that he needs to roll 4s or more to wound an Elf. He rolls a 4 and a 2, wounding one Elf.

SAVES

If a creature is wounded by a hit, it still has a chance of avoiding damage by making a save roll on a D6. There are two types of saves: **armour saves** and **Ward saves**. These are explained below.

ARMOUR SAVE

Models that are wounded still have a chance to avoid damage if they are wearing armour or carrying shields, or if they are riding a horse or similar creature. These models have an armour saving roll.

Roll a D6 for each wound suffered by your troops. If you roll greater than or equal to the model's armour save, the wound has been deflected by its armour.

For example: A warrior carrying a shield and wearing light armour has an armour save of 5+, so he must roll a 5 or 6 to be saved by his armour.

Cavalry models automatically have an armour save of 6 even if the rider is wearing no armour. This represents the extra protection afforded by the mount. If the rider is armoured then his armour save will be +1 better than it would be if he were on foot.

For example, a Man wearing light armour and carrying a shield has an armour save of 5+ on foot and 4+ when mounted.

Note that this bonus only applies to cavalry and not to characters or other models riding monsters. Rules for monsters and riders are discussed in the section on Monsters.

To continue our example from above, the Goblin archers have scored 1 wound on the Elf troops. Since the Elves are wearing light armour and have shields their armour saving throw is 5+. The Elf player rolls a 2. Not surprisingly he has failed. If he had scored a 5 or 6, the arrow would have bounced off and the Elf would have been unharmed.

Armour saves

Armour Worn	Armour Save	Armour Save if Cavalry
None	None	6+
Shield or light armour	6+	5+
Shield & light armour or heavy armour only	5+	4+
Shield & heavy armour	4+	3+
Riders with shield & heavy armour, riding armoured mounts.	–	2+

Armour save modifiers

Some weapons or creatures are so powerful that they can punch right through armour, so armour provides less protection against them. Such attacks confer modifiers that are subtracted from the foe's armour saving throw. This is shown by the table below.

For example: A crossbow (S4) hits a warrior wearing light armour and shield. Normally he would need to roll 5 or 6 to make his save and avoid taking the wound but, because of the crossbow's enormous hitting power, -1 is subtracted from his dice roll. Therefore, he must now roll a 6 to save.

Save modifiers

Strength of hit	Reduce armour save by
3 or less	None
4	–1
5	–2
6	–3
7	–4
8	–5
9	–6
10	–7

Maximum save

Observant readers will have noticed that the best save on the Armour saves chart is a 2+ on a D6 but it is possible to get a better save. Magic armour is one way to improve the wearer's armour save to 1+ or even less! However a roll of 1 will always fail, so even a model with a 1+ or better armour save will suffer a wound if it rolls 1 when taking its armour save.

The advantage of a 1+ save is that it offers better protection against weapons with save modifiers. For example, a model with a 2+ save hit by a S4 attack saves on a 3+, while a model with a 1+ save will save on a 2+.

WARD SAVES

Some troops types and creatures are protected by more than mere physical armour. They may be shielded by magical charms or blessings, given protection by the gods of the Warhammer world, or perhaps they are just astoundingly lucky.

Models with this sort of protection are referred to as having a Ward save or Ward. This type of save is quite different from an armour save and it is very important to understand the difference from the beginning.

Wards represent magical or divine protection which can save a warrior when armour would be of no use at all. Unlike an armour save, a Ward is **never** modified by Strength modifiers, etc. Even if a hit ignores all armour saves, a model with a Ward may still try to make its Ward save as normal. A model may only ever make one Ward save against each wound it has suffered.

Sometimes a model has both an armour save and a Ward save. In this case, the model must take the armour save first and, if it is failed, the model is allowed to try to make a Ward save. No model can ever try to make more than one Ward save against a wound it has suffered. If a model has two Ward saves for any reason, use the better Ward save.

REMOVING CASUALTIES

Most human-sized troops can only sustain one wound before they fall casualty. Some models can take several wounds before they become casualties, but these are the exceptions rather than the norm. The number of wounds a model can sustain before it falls casualty is indicated by its Wounds value or 'W' on its profile.

CASUALTIES

Where troops have only a single wound, casualties are removed as follows. If a unit of troops is hit and suffers wounds which it does not save then for each wound, one model is removed as a 'kill'. Although it is convenient to think of casualties as slain, individual warriors are not necessarily dead, they may be temporarily knocked out, incapacitated, or simply too badly wounded to carry on fighting. For our purposes, the result is the same so we treat all casualties as if they were killed and remove them.

Although casualties would really fall amongst the front rank, for the purposes of gameplay remove models from the rear rank of the unit. This keeps the formation neat and represents rear rankers stepping forward to cover gaps in the line. If the unit is deployed in a single rank then casualties are removed roughly equally from either end, representing the troops gathering about their leader and standard.

MULTIPLE WOUND CASUALTIES

If models have more than 1 Wound, casualties are removed as follows. Imagine that a unit of Minotaurs suffers 5 wounds from arrow fire. Minotaurs are huge creatures and each model has 3 Wounds. The arrows would fall randomly among the unit, possibly wounding several creatures, but for our purposes we shall remove whole models where possible. So, 5 wounds equals 1 model dead (3 wounds) with 2 wounds left over. The wounds left over are not enough to remove another model, so the player must make a note that 2 wounds have been suffered by the unit. If the unit takes another wound from some other attack then another Minotaur model is removed. It is obviously important to keep a record of wounds taken by units such as this.

CAVALRY CASUALTIES

In the case of cavalry models, all shots are worked out against the rider. If the rider is slain, the mount is removed as well. This is a convenient and practical way of representing cavalry, as it dispenses with the need for individual dismounted riders and loose mounts. Obviously some riders are dead, horses bolt and run away, and some mounts are killed, throwing their riders to the ground. But these things can be left to the imagination while models are removed as a single piece. Note that this only applies to ordinary cavalry (mounts which have 1 Wound) and not to monsters with riders. Monsters have more than 1 Wound on their profile and are covered by the rules for Monsters (see p.103-105).

PANIC TESTS

It is very difficult for troops to keep their nerve while people around them are falling to arrow fire. To simulate this, any unit taking substantial casualties may be called upon to take a Panic test. A Panic test is a Psychology test described in the section on Psychology along with other effects such as *fear*, *terror*, etc.

FAST DICE ROLLING

You will have gathered by now that it is necessary to roll quite a few dice to resolve shooting – whole handfuls at once in fact! This doesn't take as long as you might imagine because all the dice are rolled together. The most practical way of going about this is to take as many dice as you have troops shooting and roll them all at once. So, if you're shooting with ten Archers roll ten dice. Then pick out any dice which score a hit and re-roll them to wound. So, from ten dice rolled, four might typically score hits. These are re-rolled and may score 2 wounds, for example.

Dice which score wounds are picked out and handed over to your opponent to take his saving throws with. This same system applies when working out close combat damage too.

Dwarf warrior of Karaz-a-Karak

CLOSE COMBAT

Once shooting has been resolved it is time to deal with the brutal cut and thrust of close combat, hand-to-hand fighting or mêlée, as it's sometimes called. Once engaged in close combat, units cannot move or shoot missile weapons, they must stand toe-to-toe with their enemy until one side is destroyed or forced to flee. Regardless of which player's turn it is, all models that are in contact with the enemy must fight. The Close Combat phase is therefore an exception to the normal turn sequence in that both sides take part in the fighting.

Like the Movement phase, the Close Combat phase follows a set order or sequence as outlined below.

1. Fight Combats

Each unit involved in combat fights as explained in the rules that follow. Fight all the combats before working out results.

2. Results

Work out which side has won each combat and by how much. The losing side will have lost by 1, 2 or more 'points' as explained later.

3. Break Tests

Each unit that loses in combat must take a Break test. Any units failing their Break test are deemed 'broken' and a note is made or models are turned round to show this. Take all Break tests now.

4. Panic Tests

If any friendly units have broken then units nearby must take a Panic test as described in the Psychology section. Take any required Panic tests now.

5. Flee!

Units which have broken or failed their Panic test must flee away from their enemy. Move all newly fleeing troops now.

6. Pursue

Units whose enemies have broken and fled that turn are allowed to pursue them and might possibly catch and destroy them.

7. Redress Ranks

At the end of the Close Combat phase, formations are tidied up ready for the next phase.

Examples of combat

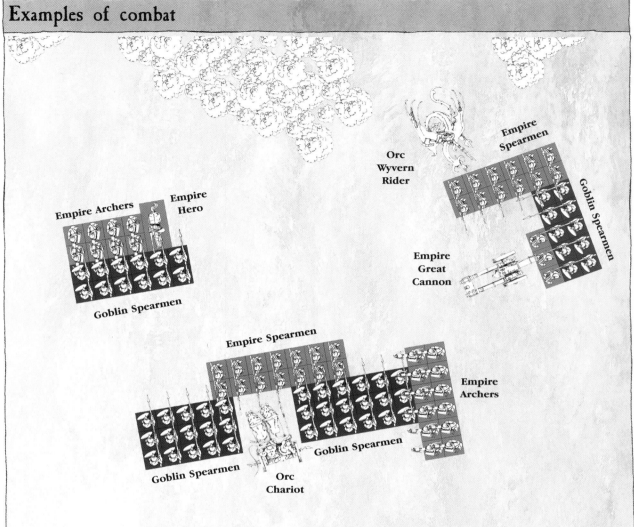

On this part of the battlefield there are three separate combats: one between two units and an Empire Hero on the left; a huge fight between two units of Empire troops, two units of Goblins and a Orc Chariot below; and a combat between two opposing units, an Orc Wyvern Rider and the crew of an Empire Great Cannon on the right.

COMBATS

Work out each combat one at a time – resolve the fighting for all of the troops involved in one combat before moving on to the next combat.

A combat is often a fight between a single unit of troops from each side, but it is possible that several units, monsters and Heroes may become involved. In the case of several combats being fought at once, the player whose turn it is determines the order combats are resolved.

So long as fighting units are interconnected, they are participating in the same combat. All the combat results for such a combat are worked out at the same time.

 Kill them with swords, kill them with lances and spears, kill them with the bolts of your crossbows. Kill their warriors, kill their women and their children, their elderly and their sick. Kill their hounds, cattle and their livestock. But above all, kill with pleasure.

Captain Daerkhil of the Black Ark Bringer of Joyous Oblivion prior to the punitive Dark Elf raid on the coastal town of Bergsburg. There were no survivors.

WHO STRIKES FIRST?

In the desperate hack and slay of close combat the advantage goes to the best and fastest warriors, or those who have gained the extra impetus of charging into combat that turn. To represent this, combatants strike blows in a strict order.

Troops who have charged that turn automatically strike first. Otherwise, all blows are struck in strict order of Initiative (I). Combatants with a higher Initiative strike first followed by those with a lower Initiative. This is important because if a model is slain before it has a chance to strike, it obviously cannot fight back. Striking first is a big advantage, which is why it is better to charge your enemy rather than allow him to charge you.

If opposing troops have the same Initiative then the side which won the combat in the previous turn may strike first. If this doesn't apply, you should roll a D6 and the player who scores highest goes first.

For example: A bunch of Orc Boar Riders charges a group of Elf Spearmen. The Elves have an Initiative of 6, while the Orcs only have Initiative 2. The Orcs strike first because they charged. Next turn, the Elves will go first because of their higher Initiative.

Vast, merciless and darker than midnight was that army, and the mere sight of it struck fear into the hearts of the bravest of us. Above the black-clad regiments whipped the banners of the Blood God, decorated with twisting runes which seemed to writhe as if alive. Cold steel glittered amongst their ranks, and they were led by their Champions whose weapons screamed for blood. They marched towards us in full armour without tiring, without slowing. They beat great drums that made the earth shake as they marched.

Arrows we fired did not deter them. We prepared a shieldwall and they smashed it aside as if the soldiers within it were small children. The cavalry that charged them was crushed. No swordmaster could best even one of them in single combat. They shrugged off wounds that would have slain any mortal man in an eyeblink. The skulls of our comrades they carried in their belts.

And I still remember their warcry. "Blood for the Blood God! Skulls for the throne of Khorne!" Even as they died they still chanted, drowning out the screams of the dying and the blaring of our horns. "Blood for the Blood God!" And at the end of the day only I survived, buried under a mound of headless corpses.

These are the Warriors of Chaos. Tremble o sun, cry out your pain o earth! For these are the enemies we must defeat if our world is to be saved.

WHICH MODELS FIGHT

A model can fight if its base is touching the base of an enemy model even if it only touches at the corner. Even models attacked in the side or rear may fight. If you wish, they may be temporarily turned in the ranks to indicate that they are doing so.

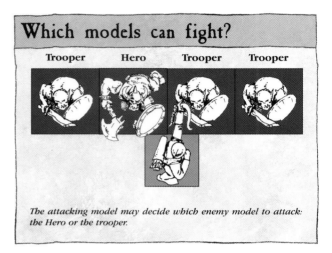

The attacking model may decide which enemy model to attack: the Hero or the trooper.

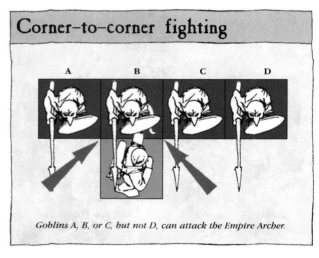

Goblins A, B, or C, but not D, can attack the Empire Archer.

If a model is touching more than one enemy, it can choose which to attack. If a model has more than 1 Attack, it can divide its Attacks as the player wishes so long as this is made clear before rolling to hit. For example, if faced with an enemy Hero and an ordinary enemy warrior you might decide to attack the warrior because he is easier to kill, or you could take the outside chance of slaying the Hero.

In the case of cavalry mounts that have their own Attacks, such as Warhorses and Giant Wolves, the rider's Attack and the mount's Attack are worked out separately. This means that some cavalry models have two lots of Attacks: the rider's Attacks and the Attacks of his mount.

In any case, models in base contact with the enemy may not choose to avoid attacking their enemies.

TO HIT CHART

	Opponent's Weapon Skill									
	1	2	3	4	5	6	7	8	9	10
1	4	4	5	5	5	5	5	5	5	5
2	3	4	4	4	5	5	5	5	5	5
3	3	3	4	4	4	4	5	5	5	5
4	3	3	3	4	4	4	4	4	5	5
5	3	3	3	3	4	4	4	4	4	4
6	3	3	3	3	3	4	4	4	4	4
7	3	3	3	3	3	3	4	4	4	4
8	3	3	3	3	3	3	3	4	4	4
9	3	3	3	3	3	3	3	3	4	4
10	3	3	3	3	3	3	3	3	3	4

Attacker's Weapon Skill (row labels)

HITTING THE ENEMY

To see whether any hits are scored, roll a D6 for each model fighting. If you have more than 1 Attack with your troops then roll a D6 for each Attack. For example, 10 Elves have 1 Attack each so roll 10 dice, but 10 Minotaurs have 3 Attacks each so roll 30 dice.

The dice roll needed to score a hit on your enemy depends upon the relative Weapon Skills of the attacker and his foe. Compare the Weapon Skill of the attacker with the Weapon Skill of his opponent and consult the To Hit chart above to find the minimum D6 score needed to hit.

If you look at the chart, you will see that if your warrior's Weapon Skill is greater than that of his enemy, you hit him on a dice roll of 3+. Otherwise your model will hit on a 4+, unless the enemy's Weapon Skill is more than double yours, in which case you require a 5+.

Sometimes modifiers apply to these rolls, but, unless it is specifically stated that hitting a model is impossible, an unmodified roll of 6 always hits.

CAVALRY

When you are fighting against cavalry, all blows are struck against the rider using the rider's Weapon Skill and never against the mount. A mount fights using its own Weapon Skill if it has its own Attack.

DEFENDED OBSTACLE

Troops lining up behind a wall, hedge or other obstacle can adopt a position to defend it. The front rank is moved right up against the obstacle to show this. Enemy wishing to attack the defenders can do so by charging them as normal. Attacking models don't have to physically cross the obstacle, indeed they are unable to whilst it is defended. Instead, the front rank is positioned on the opposite side to the defenders.

If attacking an enemy behind a defended obstacle, a 6 on a D6 is needed to hit them. This penalty applies to a unit attacking troops that have already taken up position behind the defended obstacle. The penalty does not apply to both sides in the combat even though the obstacle lies between them. The defending side has the advantage of already taking up a good position with its weapons sticking out or over gaps in the hedge or wall, whilst the other side must mount an assault in the face of a wall of sword points or spear tips. Flying models attacking enemy behind defended obstacles ignore the penalty.

The attacking side continues to suffer the '6 to hit' penalty until it wins a round of combat. Once the attackers have won the combat, they are assumed to have climbed over or onto the wall, and further combats are fought as normal. Chariots cannot charge models across defended obstacles, they would just be smashed to pieces.

WOUND CHART

	Target's Toughness									
Weapon's Strength	1	2	3	4	5	6	7	8	9	10
1	4	5	6	6	N	N	N	N	N	N
2	3	4	5	6	6	N	N	N	N	N
3	2	3	4	5	6	6	N	N	N	N
4	2	2	3	4	5	6	6	N	N	N
5	2	2	2	3	4	5	6	6	N	N
6	2	2	2	2	3	4	5	6	6	N
7	2	2	2	2	2	3	4	5	6	6
8	2	2	2	2	2	2	3	4	5	6
9	2	2	2	2	2	2	2	3	4	5
10	2	2	2	2	2	2	2	2	3	4

WOUNDS

Not all successful hits are going to harm your enemy – some may rebound from bones or bounce off tough hide, while others may cause only superficial damage which doesn't prevent the creature fighting. Once you have hit your foe, you must roll again to see whether your hits inflict wounds.

This procedure is the same as is described for shooting. Consult the Wound chart above, cross referencing the attacker's Strength with the defender's Toughness. Both values appear on the profiles of the creatures that are fighting. The chart indicates the minimum score required on a D6 to cause a wound. Note that where the table shows an 'N' this indicates that the target is too tough to be hurt. N stands for no effect.

WEAPONS MODIFIERS

Unlike hits from shooting, the Strength value of the attacker is used to determine wounds rather than the Strength of the weapon itself. However, some weapons confer a bonus on the attacker's Strength. For example, Bretonnian Knights that are charging with lances receive a +2 bonus to their Strength. These bonuses are discussed together with other special rules in the section on Weapons.

SAVES

Combatants that are wounded have a chance to avoid suffering any damage if they are wearing armour, carrying shields or have a Ward save. This is exactly the same as described for shooting, and the same rules apply.

REMOVING CASUALTIES

Close combat casualties are removed in the same way as shooting casualties. Although casualties fall amongst the rank that is fighting, it is more convenient to assume that models in the rear ranks will step forward to fill any gaps that appear. It is therefore more practical to remove casualties straight from a unit's rear ranks.

Models that fall casualty are not removed from the tabletop immediately, but are placed behind their unit. This is because when it comes to working out who has won the combat you will need to know how many casualties have been caused during it. Also, models which are removed before they have had a chance to attack may not do so, and models that are stepping forward from rear ranks to replace them can't attack that turn. This means that any casualties inflicted will reduce the number of enemy left to fight back. You need to know exactly how many models were killed that combat round who cannot attack back.

EXCESS CASUALTIES

It can sometimes happen that a unit causes more casualties than there are enemy models in base contact with it. When this happens, the excess casualties are removed as normal. This represents the attackers springing forward and following up their assault by striking over the fallen bodies of their foes. Such is the ferocity of their attack and the surprise caused by their success, the excess casualties are struck down where they stand and have no chance to attack back.

RESULTS

For each separate combat you must determine which side has won. Do this once all the units engaged in the combat have fought.

Begin by adding up all the wounds caused by each side in the combat. It does not matter which particular units suffered the wounds, just add them all up. Do not forget to add the wounds taken by big creatures that have not been removed as casualties. Do NOT count the wounds that were saved by armour or Ward saves.

The side which has inflicted the most wounds wins the combat. The other side has lost. If both have inflicted the same number of wounds then the result is a draw.

However, a side can claim extra bonus points under certain circumstances – for example, if it has a Standard Bearer, if it is attacking the enemy in the flank, or if it is fighting from higher ground.

Each bonus point is added to the number of wounds inflicted. So, for example, if both sides cause 3 wounds

then the result is a draw, but if one side has a standard it adds +1 to its score, beating the enemy by 4 points to 3. These bonus points can make all the difference between winning and losing the combat. The Combat Resolution Bonus chart on p.73 summarises bonus points.

Once both sides have established their total points, including the number of casualties caused and bonus points, compare the values to discover which side has won the combat.

The higher that the winner's score is compared to the loser's score, the bigger and more decisive the victory. An 8 point against a 7 point victory is only a slight win, for example, because the difference in scores is only 1 point. An 8 point against a 2 point victory, however, is extremely decisive, as the difference in scores is a whopping 6 points. This difference in scores is important because it is used when working out whether a defeated enemy stands his ground or turns and flees.

COMBAT RESULTS

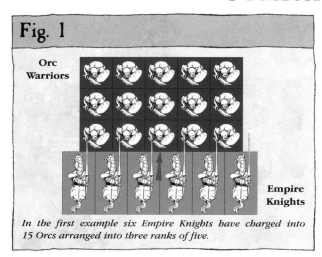

Fig. 1

In the first example six Empire Knights have charged into 15 Orcs arranged into three ranks of five.

Fig. 2

This time the Goblins strike first as they have charged, inflicting one casualty on the Knights. The Knights strike next as their Initiative is higher than that of the Orc Warriors, and they kill three of their enemies. In reply the Orcs inflict a further casualty on the Knights.

To work out which side has won count up the wounds caused by each side. The Orcs and Goblins have caused 2 against the Knights' score of 3. However, the Orcs & Goblins receive a rank bonus of +3 from the Goblin unit. Note that only one bonus is added from ranks, and it is always from the deepest unit participating. In addition the Goblins are making a flank attack and so earn an extra +1 and the Orcs & Goblins outnumber the Knights 40 to 6 (a further +1). The Orcs & Goblins' total is therefore 2 (wounds) + 3 (ranks) +1 (flank) +1 (outnumber) = 7 against the Knights' 3. The Orcs & Goblins win by a difference of 4.

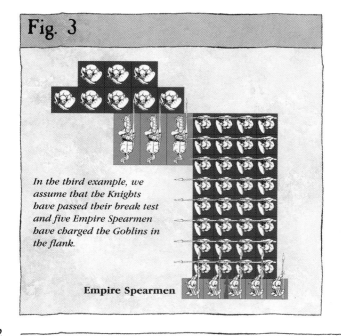

Fig. 3

In the third example, we assume that the Knights have passed their break test and five Empire Spearmen have charged the Goblins in the flank.

Empire Spearmen

Fig. 1

Let us imagine that the Knights inflict 4 wounds, striking down four of the Orcs.

In reply the remaining Orc Warrior inflicts 1 wound and kills a single Knight.

To decide who wins the combat each side adds up the number of wounds it has caused. In this case the Knights score 4 and the Orcs 1. However, the Orcs have +2 from their extra ranks and they outnumber the Knights (Orcs' Unit Strength is 11, Knights' Unit Strength is 10), for a final score of 4.

The combat is a draw.

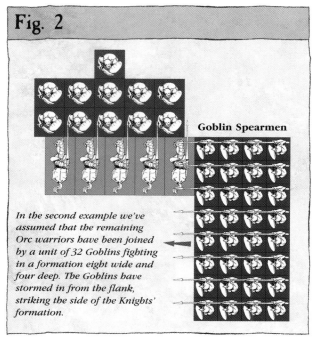

Goblin Spearmen

In the second example we've assumed that the remaining Orc warriors have been joined by a unit of 32 Goblins fighting in a formation eight wide and four deep. The Goblins have stormed in from the flank, striking the side of the Knights' formation.

Fig. 3

The Spearmen strike first as they have charged, inflicting two casualties on the Goblin unit. The Knights strike next causing one casualty on the Orcs, the Orcs kill one Knight, whilst the Goblins fail to kill any Knights but the models fighting on the flank manage to kill one spearman. The wounds inflicted by each side amount to 3 caused by the Empire and 2 caused by the Orcs & Goblins.

The Orc & Goblin force loses their rank bonus from the Goblins because they have been charged in the flank – nor are there sufficient Orc Warriors remaining to provide an extra rank. Also, the Orcs & Goblin's flank bonus is lost because both sides now have one unit fighting to a flank cancelling each other out. The Orcs & Goblins earn an extra +1 for the outnumber bonus.

The total scores are therefore 3 on each side and the result is a draw!

COMBAT RESOLUTION BONUSES

This table is used to determine the combat resolution score. All of these are cumulative apart from where otherwise noted. Some magic items and exceptional circumstances may affect the combat resolution score; this is clearly indicated in their description.

Bonus Situation

+1   Extra Rank

If your formation is a unit at least four models wide then you may claim a bonus of +1 for each rank behind the first at the start of a round of close combat, up to a maximum of +3. The bonus can be claimed for an incomplete last rear rank so long as it contains at least four models.

Fast cavalry and skirmishers never gain a bonus for extra ranks (p.117 & p.116).

If you have several units fighting in a combat, count the bonus from the unit with the largest number of ranks. Do not add up the bonuses from all the units fighting.

This bonus is lost if the unit is charged in the flank or rear by an enemy with a Unit Strength of five or more. Note that this applies only as long as the unit which charged is in combat with the enemy – if they break and flee, or are reduced to a Unit Strength of less than five, the unit regains its rank bonus.

+1   Outnumber enemy

If the combined Unit Strength of your troops in combat is greater than the combined Unit Strength of your enemies you receive a +1 bonus.

+1   Standard

If any of your units includes a Standard Bearer (either a unit Standard Bearer or a Battle Standard Bearer) in its front rank then you may add a +1 bonus.

Note that if several standards are involved in the combat (a unit Standard or a Battle Standard) then you still only add +1, not +1 for each standard. Rules for standards are described later.

Bonus Situation

+1   High Ground

If you are fighting from a higher position than your enemy, for example, your troops are occupying the crest of a hill, then you may add a +1 bonus. This bonus is only granted if your fighting rank is on higher ground than your enemy.

+1   Flank Attack

If you are fighting against an enemy unit's flank, you may add a +1 bonus so long as your unit has a Unit Strength of five or more.

Note that you only count +1 even if both flanks of the enemy are engaged.

If both sides have troops attacking in the flank then the side with the most number of flanking units gets the bonus. The bonus is only applied once, regardless of how many flanking units are involved in the combat.

+2   Rear Attack

The same comments apply as for a flank attack to units attacking in the rear. This bonus and the bonus for a flank attack are cumulative, so if you are attacking in the side and rear you will receive a bonus of +3.

+1   Overkill

If a character fighting in a *challenge* (see p.99) kills his opponent and scores more wounds than the enemy has then each excess wound scores a +1 overkill bonus towards the combat result up to a maximum of +5.

This bonus only applies in a challenge as described in the Characters section.

LOSERS TAKE A BREAK TEST

The side that loses a combat must take a test to determine whether it stands and fights or turns tail and runs away. This is called a Break test. You need to take a separate Break test for every unit involved in the combat.

Depending on which units pass and which fail their test, some may break and flee whilst others stand their ground. Troops which are better led, braver, and more professional are more likely to stand firm, whilst wild, temperamental troops are far more likely to run for it.

Take the test as follows. Firstly, nominate which unit you are testing for. Roll 2D6 and add the scores together. Add the difference between the winner's and loser's combat score. If the total is greater than the unit's Leadership (Ld) value then the unit is broken. Broken units will turn tail and flee once all combat on the entire battlefield has been worked out. Until all combat has been worked out, simply turn a few of the rear rank models round to remind you that the unit is broken.

For example: A unit of Elf Archers is fighting a unit of Goblin Spearmen. The Goblins inflict 3 wounds on the Elves, and the Elves inflict 4 wounds on the Goblins. However, the Goblin player has four complete ranks in his formation, each extra rank adding +1 to his score, and his troops outnumber the Elves, adding another +1. This gives him 3 + 4 = 7 points against the Elves' score of 4.

The Elves have therefore lost the combat, even though they have caused more casualties – the vast numbers of Goblins pressing from the back have overwhelmed them. The

Elves must therefore take a Break test adding +3 to their dice score, because the difference between the scores is 3. Elves have a good Leadership value (8) but with the extra +3 modifier on the dice, the player will have to roll 5 or less to stand and fight. The player rolls 2D6 and scores 7. The +3 modifier brings his total to 10 which is greater than the unit's Leadership, so the Elves are broken.

PANIC TESTS FOR BREAKS

Once all defeated units have taken a Break test, each remaining unit that is within 6" of friendly units which have broken or been wiped out is called upon to take a Panic test, as described in the Psychology section. This represents the spread of panic amongst the army as friendly units collapse and turn tail and run. Panic is a special psychological effect, and the full rules for Panic are covered in the following section of the rulebook. However, it is worth bearing in mind at this stage that Panic tests must be taken once all Break tests are complete, but **before** fleeing troops are moved.

FLEEING TROOPS

Once you have completed all of the Break tests resulting from combat that turn and have taken all necessary Panic tests, it is time for broken and *panicked* troops to flee. Fleeing troops turn directly away from their enemy and run as fast as they can. If they were engaged by several opponents, they flee away from the enemy unit with the highest Unit Strength. They abandon their formation and run from their enemy in a complete rout, blindly scrambling over the ground in their efforts to avoid destruction.

Even though the fleeing unit moves in a disorganised mob, for the purposes of moving the fleeing troops, it is convenient to keep them in formation.

MOVE FLEEING TROOPS

It is difficult to say precisely how far fleeing troops will run because they are no longer fighting as a body but milling around in a frightened mob. To represent this, dice are rolled to establish how far the fleeing unit moves. If the unit normally moves 6" or less roll 2D6. If the unit moves more than 6" roll 3D6. The result is the distance covered by the fleeing troops. Due to their disrupted formation, they ignore any penalty for obstacles and terrain (apart from impassable terrain).

Move the fleeing unit directly away from its enemy, so that the closest part of the unit is 2D6" or 3D6" away and facing in the opposite direction. Fleeing troops will move round friends where possible, but will move straight through friends if no other venue of escape remains. Individual fleeing models that would otherwise end up in the middle of a friendly unit are instead placed to the side or beyond them if this is the only option.

A fleeing unit is destroyed if caught by pursuers, as described under Pursuit.

SUBSEQUENT ACTIONS OF FLEEING TROOPS

If they are not destroyed then fleeing units continue to move 2D6" or 3D6" during their subsequent Movement phases. This is their **Flee roll**. They must attempt to leave the battlefield as quickly as possible, which often means that they will move towards the nearest table edge. This is a 'compulsory move' so fleeing troops are moved before other troops once charges have been declared (see the Movement section). Due to their disorganised formation they ignore penalties for obstacles and terrain (except for impassable terrain).

A unit which is fleeing cannot fight, shoot or use magic – it can only flee. Where there is room, it will move round obstacles that block its path, including units of troops. Fleeing troops will not move within 4" of enemy unless they have no other choice – if they are surrounded, for example.

If any models from a fleeing unit leave the table edge then the entire unit is considered to have left the battlefield and is removed from play. Troops have scattered beyond recovery or have found places to hide themselves until the battle is over.

If enemy troops successfully charge a unit that is already fleeing then the unit automatically flees from the charge. The unit makes its 2D6" or 3D6" Flee roll just like any other unit fleeing from a charge. The charging enemy destroys the fleeing troops if it catches them. If they do not catch the fleeing troops then the charge has failed (see Movement for the rules relating to charges and charge reactions).

RALLYING

A fleeing unit must attempt to stop fleeing by taking a Rally test in its Movement phase. This represents the efforts of leaders and brave individuals to call a halt to the rout, bring the troops to their senses and restore order. This is called **rallying**.

RALLY TEST

Rally tests are taken in the Movement phase after charges have been declared but before further movement has occured (see the sequence at the start of the Movement section).

To take a Rally test roll 2D6. If the score is equal to or less than the unit's Leadership (Ld) then the unit stops fleeing and has rallied. The unit must spend the remainder of the turn *reforming* and may not shoot or fight, though the player may rearrange its

formation and turn it to face in whichever direction he chooses. Any rallying characters may cast spells as normal. If a fleeing unit has suffered a great many casualties it will be unable to rally – its warriors are too demoralised and are interested only in escape. A unit must have at least 25% of its original number of models surviving to be able to rally. If a fleeing unit has less than 25% of its original number left, the unit cannot rally and will continue to flee until it leaves the table or is destroyed. Other models, such as characters, may never join a fleeing unit. A character cannot leave a unit which is fleeing, so cannot be rallied if a unit he has joined flees with less than 25% of its original number left.

PURSUIT

If a unit wins a combat and all the enemies it is fighting flee, then the victorious unit must normally pursue. The troops surge forward, hacking at their retreating foes as their backs are turned, cutting them down as they run and scattering them before their uncontrolled fury. Note that a unit will only pursue if all the enemies it is fighting flee – if one enemy unit breaks and flees whilst another fights on then the victorious troops cannot pursue. Like fleeing, pursuit is a hectic and uncontrolled affair, so dice are rolled to determine how far the pursuing unit moves.

PURSUIT MOVE

Once fleeing troops have been moved, victorious units will pursue. To find out how far they pursue, starting with the unit with the highest Unit Strength, roll 2D6 or 3D6 in exactly the same way as for fleeing troops. This is their **Pursuit roll**. If a victorious unit scores equal to or greater than the Flee roll scored by the unit it is pursuing then the fleeing unit is completely destroyed – all the troops are cut down as they run or they are scattered beyond hope of regrouping. Pursuers are moved the full distance indicated straight towards the fleeing troops, and through their position if their pursuit move is especially long. If the pursuers do not roll a sufficently high score to catch the fleeing unit then no further casualties are caused and the pursuers are simply moved the distance indicated towards their fleeing enemies. Pursuers always move their full pursuit distance unless their pursuit takes them into contact with fresh enemy (see p.76). During a pursuit move, pursuers ignore any penalties for obstacles and terrain (apart from impassable terrain) – their victory has given them the extra impetus to chase their fleeing enemies.

Note that units do not continue to pursue in subsequent turns; pursuit is a single bonus move which is made when a beaten enemy flees. One unit can only pursue one fleeing enemy unit, even if it broke several units in close combat.

PURSUIT INTO FRESH ENEMY

Assuming that pursuers do not encounter any fresh enemy, they move the distance indicated by their dice roll and thereafter are ready to fight normally. So, in their following turn they may charge, march or move normally exactly like any other unit, and no penalty is imposed because of their pursuit move.

It sometimes happens that pursuers move so far that they hit a fresh enemy unit. The pursuers are carried forward against the enemy unit as they chase their fleeing enemy. This is treated as if it were a new charge. However, this will only happen if your direct pursuit move would take you into contact with the enemy. The pursuing unit has no choice in the matter, they must charge against the fresh enemy. The unexpectedly attacked unit can only respond to the charge by holding; any attempt to flee, stand & shoot, or do anything else amidst the confusion of running bodies is deemed impossible. They must make any necessary Psychology tests immediately.

If the new enemy causes *fear* or *terror* (see the Psychology section), the pursuers do not have to make a test – they are gripped by the excitement of the chase and are ready to fight any enemy! Note that psychology will apply as normal in the subsequent turns – only the tests required to charge opponents who cause *fear* or *terror* are ignored.

Since pursuit into fresh enemy is treated as a new charge, all rules governing charges apply. Specifically, the pursuers must endeavour to bring as many charging models into combat as possible. This means that it will often be necessary to wheel slightly in order to face the enemy.

The resulting combat is worked out in the following turn. The pursuers are charging and so get all the usual benefits and bonuses as if they had charged that turn, even though their charge occurred during the close combat phase of the previous turn. A fleeing

I watch you. I see the hatred in your eyes, well hidden behind courtly graces. I listen. I know the terrible darkness that hides behind your well rehearsed lies. I wait for you at the edge of sanity. I taste the pain in your mind, the yearning to end this charade. I make my home in the darkest pits of your soul. In the shadows I bide my time. I patiently wait for you to open your eyes and realise that it is by my will alone that you draw breath. For I am Tzeentch and you are my puppet who dances to my tune.

unit is destroyed even if its pursuers subsequently charge a new enemy, as long as the pursuing unit's Pursuit roll scores equal to or greater than the fleeing unit's Flee roll.

RESTRAINING PURSUIT

A player may decide that he would prefer his unit did not pursue a fleeing enemy. Normally a unit must pursue if it is able to do so, but, before rolling to see how far the enemy flees, the player may attempt to halt the pursuit by making a test against the unit's Leadership (Ld). This represents the unit's leader calling to his troops to hold, while their natural inclination is to run after the enemy and cut them down. Roll 2D6. If the score is equal to or less than the unit's Leadership value then the test is passed and the unit may remain stationary instead of pursuing.

A unit does not have to pursue if it is defending a wall, hedgerow or a comparable obstacle or fortification. As pursuit would force the unit to abandon its secure position there is obviously an incentive to stay put! In such a case, the player can choose whether to pursue or not without the need of a dice roll.

PURSUIT OFF THE TABLE

A unit which pursues its fleeing enemy off the table returns to the same point from which it left the table, in the same formation in its following Movement phase, facing directly towards the battlefield. The unit may not charge, as it has missed its opportunity to declare charges, but may move its full Move that turn, and it may shoot and otherwise participate in the game as normal. In any case, the unit counts as having moved and so will suffer a -1 penalty to any shooting.

REDRESS THE RANKS

Once fleeing troops and pursuers have been moved, it is time to tidy up the formations of fighting units in preparation for the next phase. This will not always prove necessary, as much depends upon the casualties inflicted and the combat results.

Remember, a unit must always contain the same number of models in each rank as the first, except for its rear rank which may contain fewer. The process of redressing the ranks is intended to ensure that this remains true after combat, and also affords victors the chance to adjust their formation by expanding their frontage or lapping round as described opposite.

FLEEING UNITS

Units which have fled, abandon their formation and so have no opportunity to redress their ranks at this time. The unit forms a rough block or mass of troops, and models are arranged in a higgledy-piggledy manner to show their disorganised status. Fleeing units do not take further Psychology tests – they must test to Rally in their Movement phase.

UNITS TAKING CASUALTIES

Casualties are usually removed from the back of a unit's formation, in which case the unit is left exactly as it is. Remember, a unit engaged in combat cannot move in its Movement phase and so has no opportunity to change its formation.

If a unit is fighting in a single rank, forming a line of troops, then casualties are removed from either end. If this results in an enemy who is attacking the side of the formation becoming separated from the combat, then compensate for this by moving one or both units so that they remain in contact where possible.

If a character model is fighting as part of a unit's formation, perhaps leading the unit into battle, then his death will leave a gap in your front rank. In this case, move a model forward from the rear rank to fill the gap, or, if the unit is fighting in a single rank, move a model from one edge. See the section on Characters for more detail.

EXPAND FRONTAGE

If a unit wins the combat, models can be moved from rear ranks and placed in the front rank to increase the width of the formation so that more models can fight. The formation's width can be increased by up to two models on either or both flanks.

Lapping round

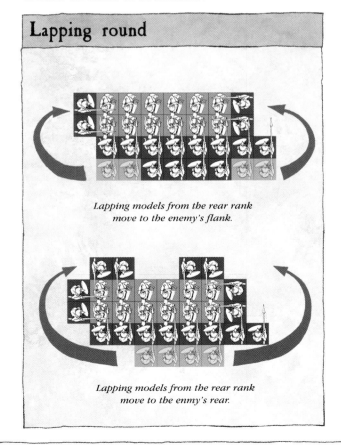

Lapping models from the rear rank move to the enemy's flank.

Lapping models from the rear rank move to the enmy's rear.

Expand frontage

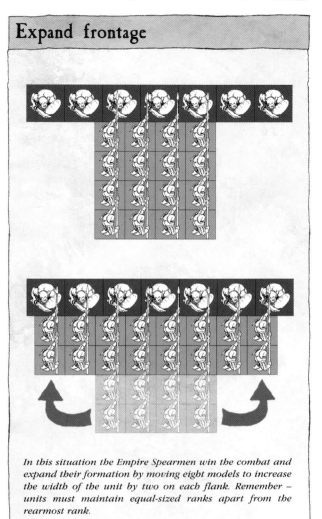

In this situation the Empire Spearmen win the combat and expand their formation by moving eight models to increase the width of the unit by two on each flank. Remember – units must maintain equal-sized ranks apart from the rearmost rank.

LAPPING ROUND

If a unit wins the combat and its formation already extends to the enemy's flanks then models may be moved from the rear ranks round the sides of the enemy unit. These extra models are described as **lapping round**. You may move up to two models around each flank, assuming that there is room and that the flank is not blocked by another unit, buildings, or terrain. Once models have covered the enemy's flanks, further models may be lapped around the rear should they win a further turn. In this way, it is possible to extend your line and surround an enemy unit completely.

If a unit which is lapping around is successfully charged by fresh enemies that can reach them, the lapping models will immediately return to the rear rank of their formation. The chargers will be moved into contact with the reformed unit if their charge reach is sufficient. If they can no longer reach the charged unit because models in it have been moved to the rear ranks, the charge counts as having failed.

COMBAT BONUSES

Models that are lapping round the flank or rear are ignored for purposes of establishing a unit's rank bonus in close combat. Lapping round models in this way might therefore reduce your rank bonus by reducing the number of ranks fighting.

However, units which are lapping round do receive the extra bonuses for flank and rear attacks so long as the entire unit has a Unit Strength of 5 or more. This means that, in most cases, it is well worth lapping round whenever you can. Note that models lapping around an enemy unit's flanks or rear do not negate the enemy unit's rank bonus – only a new charge into the flank or rear of a unit negates its rank bonus.

DEFEAT IN COMBAT

If a unit is defeated in close combat then any models already lapping round are immediately returned to the rear rank of their formation. They have been driven off by the enemy and forced to regroup behind the unit's main body.

WHICH MODELS CAN FIGHT

All models touching base-to-base are allowed to fight in close combat, so troops along the sides of 'flanked' units can fight back against troops that are lapping round. Players might wish to physically turn the models round to face their enemies in order to show this, although it is not strictly necessary to do so.

"Hail to the mighty tomb guards who are before me. They who have stood guardian to my tomb chamber for eternity! For I Settra, Lord of Kings has awakened to command ye! Hail to the sentinels, turn now your heads to face the foe! Arise, ye Sphinxes who crouch beside the monuments of the king; your prey has been found. Hail to the commanders of the right and the left flanks, lead forth your regiments. Fill the air with the sound of your chariots pursuing the foe! Your standards are pleasing to the gods, see how the sun god shines upon them. See how they gleam after the darkness of the tomb. Hail to the Liche Priests, ye who have loyally served without counting the years. Ye who raised up your incantations to strengthen my spirit!"

Settra the Tomb King

OVERRUN RULE

Sometimes a powerful unit is capable of smashing through an enemy in a single round of close combat. In such cases, the thundering charge of the victorious unit will sweep it forward as it cuts down its pitiful enemies.

In Warhammer this is represented by the **Overrun rule**. This rule stops individuals and small units from stopping a unit of charging Knights in its tracks, for example.

OVERRUN

If all of a unit's opponents are slain in the first round of close combat then it is allowed to make an Overrun move as if it had broken its enemies. This will be 2D6" or 3D6" depending on the Movement value of the unit (like with fleeing and pursuit). The unit moves forwards in a direct line (ie, towards and through the position where the destroyed enemy unit was). Note that the victorious unit does not have to make the Overrun move – the player may elect to keep his troops stationary if he wishes.

Sometimes the Overrun move allows the unit to hit a fresh enemy unit. This is treated as if it were a new charge, and all the rules governing charges apply. In this case, the Overrunning unit has no choice in the matter, it must charge against the fresh enemy. The unexpectedly attacked unit can only respond to the charge by holding; any attempt to flee or stand & shoot is impossible. When moving an overrunning unit into contact with the enemy, the player must endeavour to bring as many models from the charging unit into combat as possible. This can usually be achieved by moving them straight forward, but it will sometimes be necessary to wheel the unit slightly to face the enemy.

If the new enemy or the overrunning unit causes *fear* or *terror*, neither unit has to make a Psychology test – the overrunners are too exultant and the charged unit is too surprised! Note that psychology will apply as normal in subsequent turns – only tests required to charge opponents who cause *fear* or *terror* are ignored.

The resulting combat is worked out in the following turn. The overrunning troops are charging and so get all the usual benefits and bonuses, just as if they had charged that turn, even though their charge actually occurred during the Close Combat phase of the previous turn.

Assuming that overrunning troops do not encounter any fresh enemy, they move the distance indicated by their dice roll and thereafter are ready to fight normally. So, in their following turn they may charge, march or move normally exactly like any other unit, and no penalty is imposed because of pursuing.

PSYCHOLOGY

It is an unfortunate fact that in the heat of battle troops often don't respond as you, their commander, might want them to. Faced with terrifying supernatural foes, their courage might fail, or they could simply be too dim to understand the orders they have been given. The hatred engendered by age-long feuds can overwhelm military discipline and leave troops overcome with bloodlust at the sight of their ancestral foes.

As the army commander, it is your duty to know about these things and take them into account in your plans. If you do not then you may find that you are defeated before you even begin.

The Psychology rules represent these factors in the game and call upon the player to make occasional tests to determine whether his troops are affected by adverse psychology, such as fear or terror. Most Psychology tests are made in the same way, so we'll describe the procedure first before we look at the individual psychological factors.

TAKING PSYCHOLOGY TESTS

When taking Psychology tests, roll 2D6 and compare the result to the Leadership value of the unit taking the test. If the result is less than or equal to the unit's Leadership score, the test is passed and all is well. If the result is greater than the unit's Leadership score then the test has been failed.

Players will immediately realise that a Psychology test is taken in the same way as a Break test in close combat and uses the same characteristic, namely the Leadership value. However, a Break test is not a Psychology test. The two are quite separate. This is an important point to remember because some bonuses will apply specifically to Break tests and others will apply specifically to Psychology tests.

USING RIDER'S LEADERSHIP

In the case of models such as cavalry, chariots and heroic individuals riding monsters, it is the rider's Leadership that is used and not that of the mount or monster. If a chariot has several crew, use the Ld of the crew member with the highest Ld value.

USING LEADERS' LEADERSHIP

If a unit of troops is led by a character then the entire unit may choose to test against his Leadership value. Characters often have better Leadership values than ordinary troops, so a regiment led by a superior character will be less prone to the effects of psychology. See the Characters section for rules concerning characters and units of troops.

THE ORDER OF TESTS

Many Psychology tests are taken at the start of the player's turn. For example, Panic tests caused by friends fleeing nearby and Stupidity tests are both taken at the start of the turn. When a player is called upon to take different tests at the start of the turn then do them in the same order as they are listed here. So, if a unit is obliged to take a Panic and a Stupidity test then take the Panic test first, and only if this is passed will it be necessary to take the Stupidity test.

Two hundred years before the time of Emperor Karl Franz, it seemed that the world had come to an end. There was a war like none before, the only one which alone is known as the Great War – the Great War against Chaos.

For the first time in many long millennia the Four Gods of Chaos set aside their endless rivalries and marshalled their armies to end the rule of mortals once and for all. From the Northern Wastes came the Hordes of Chaos. Armies of barbarians worshipping the Four Powers, numberless misshapen Beastmen, monstrous Chaos Spawn and Shoggoths, the feared Dragon Ogres woken from their eternal slumber by the Storm of Chaos. The earth shook under the cloven hoofs of nameless Chaos beasts. In the wake of their coming the Dark Gods sent their legions to war: endless cohorts of screaming Daemons, footsoldiers of the Ruinous Powers. It was the greatest army ever to march upon the lands of the Old World.

The followers of the Dark Gods laid waste to the cities and towns of Kislev and defeated every army sent against them. Bolgasgrad, Petragrad, Kinsk and Praag were all burned to the ground and their inhabitants put to the sword. The Dwarf hold of Karak Vlag was lost, never to be heard from again. With each victory the borders of the Realm of Chaos swelled, claiming more of the mortal lands. It seemed that the very end of time had come, and all life was doomed to decay into a seething mass of lost and screaming souls, eternally enduring the forms thrust upon them by the uncaring gods of Chaos.

But then a man emerged from the lands of the Empire, lands ravaged by disunity and rivalry for the Throne of the Emperor. From the City of Nuln came a man who would unite the Empire and ultimately defeat the armies of Chaos, throwing back the dark tide. He was Magnus, later known as the Pious, Saviour of the Empire.

PSYCHOLOGY TESTS

Warhammer uses the following psychology rules:

a) Panic   b) Fear
c) Terror   d) Stupidity
e) Frenzy   f) Hatred
g) Stubborn

PANIC

This is the most common and most important psychological effect. Battles are often won or lost because an army panics and flees, even though it may not have been beaten in combat. Troops who see their friends run can easily lose their nerve and flee themselves, causing other troops to lose heart until the whole army is fleeing in blind panic.

A unit must take a Panic test in the following circumstances:

1) Fleeing friendly unit is within 4" at the start of the turn.

2) Friends within 6" break from close combat or are destroyed.

3) The unit is charged in the side or rear whilst engaged in combat.

4) Fleeing friends are destroyed by chargers who are within 4".

5) The unit suffers 25% casualties from shooting or magic.

6) A unit is wiped out by shooting within 4".

Note that most Panic tests are taken at the end of each phase, and you only need to take one Panic test per unit in each Shooting, Close Combat or Magic phase, etc, even if there are multiple reasons to take Panic tests.

1) Fleeing friendly unit within 4" at the start of the turn

A unit must test at the start of its turn if there is one or more units of fleeing friends within 4". However, the unit does not have to test if its Unit Strength is equal to or higher than the combined Unit Strengths of all fleeing friendly units within 4". For example, a unit of

20 Spearmen does not have to test if a unit of five cavalry is fleeing past them. However, if the cavalry unit was 12 strong, the Spearmen would have to test for *panic* as the Unit Strength of 12 cavalry is 24 (12x2=24).

2) Friends break from close combat within 6".

Test at the end of the Close Combat phase if one or more friendly units break within 6" as a result of being defeated in close combat. Measure from the closest point of the broken unit. In order to avoid confusion between units which are fleeing from combat and units which are fleeing as a result of panic, work out all combat results first and then take all resultant Panic tests. A unit only needs to take one Panic test on account of breaking friends in each Close Combat phase, regardless of how many units of friends break within 6". The same test must also be taken if a friendly unit within 6" is destroyed in close combat, unless it is a single model with less than 5 Wounds on its original profile, in which case no test is necessary. Although a unit which is destroyed cannot be broken as it no longer exists, its destruction is still extremely unnerving for friends nearby!

3) Charged in the side or rear while engaged in combat

A unit must test if it is fighting in close combat at the beginning of the turn, and is charged in the side or rear by an enemy unit with a Unit Strength of 5 or more. Make the test as soon as the charge is declared and determined to be within reach. No test is required if the charging unit is unable to reach its target unit. Also, no test is required if the charging unit amounts to fewer than five models.

4) Fleeing friends destroyed by chargers within 4"

If a friendly unit flees from a charge and is caught and destroyed then all friendly units within 4" of the final position of the fleeing troops must take a Panic test once all charges are complete but before close combat starts.

No test is needed if the unit outnumbers its destroyed friends, in the same way as described for point 1.

5) 25% Casualties from shooting or magic

A unit must take a Panic test if it suffers 25% of its current number as casualties in the enemy's Shooting phase or Magic phase. Only a single test per Shooting or Magic phase is required, and all the tests are taken at the end of the current phase. Example: A unit of 12 models must test if it suffers three or more casualties from shooting.

War machines do not have to test if they lose one or more of their crew, and neither do ridden monsters if they lose their rider, or vice versa.

This test must also be taken by a charging unit if its enemies stand & shoot and inflict 25% casualties. This may result in the charging unit panicking before it contacts its target, in which case it has been forced to flee from the hail of arrows unleashed by the defenders.

This test must also be taken if the unit suffers 25% casualties from randomly moving enemies, magical effects or unusual terrain types as might be included as 'special rules' by the players. This is intended as a 'catch-all' to cover units that suffer high casualties from something other than normal close combat, shooting or magic. Some good examples include casualties inflicted by a crashing Gyrocopter, whirling Goblin Fanatics, or Squig Hoppers, which cause casualties as they move. These Panic tests are taken at the end of the phase.

6) Unit wiped out by shooting or magic within 4"

If a unit is completely wiped out by missile fire or magic, any friendly units within 4" of the destroyed unit must take a Panic test at the end of the phase.

PANICKING UNITS

A unit that fails a Panic test will flee in the same way as described for units which break in close combat or which flee from a charge.

Fleeing troops abandon their formation and are moved in a rough mass or mob 2D6" or 3D6" away from the enemy and/or source of *panic*, but the player is allowed to decide exactly where to flee within these guidelines. See the Close Combat section for rules governing fleeing troops.

PANICKING AT THE START OF THE TURN

Note that if a unit panics at the start of its turn because of fleeing friends within 4", *terror*, etc, then it may not attempt to rally that turn. The unit must flee during the compulsory movement part of its Movement phase.

PANICKING IN CLOSE COMBAT

If a unit is engaged in close combat and panics then the normal Flee and Pursuit rules apply. The fleeing unit can therefore be pursued if its enemy won the preceding combat, and consequently the fleeing unit may be destroyed in the same way as a unit that breaks following defeat in combat. If the enemy did not win the previous combat (or the two have not yet fought for some reason) the enemy cannot pursue.

Note that a unit which panics and flees from combat does not cause other units to *panic* as a result (ie, because friends break from close combat within 6"). A test is only required for friends that are defeated in combat and then broken as a result.

VOLUNTARY TESTS

It is conceivable that a situation occurs where both players agree a Panic test is in order, even though the rules don't strictly require it. This is most likely to happen if fighting a scenario you have invented, perhaps where ambushers spring a trap, where boulders are thrown from cliffs, or some such circumstance which the players have contrived.

If both players agree a Panic test can be taken to represent the unsettling situation the unit is in.

FEAR

Fear is a natural reaction to huge or especially ugly and unnerving monsters. Some creatures inspire *fear* as is indicated in their relevant Army book and these include large and disturbing monsters such as Trolls as well as supernatural horrors such as Skeletons.

A unit must take a Fear test if it is faced by one of the the following situations:

1. IF CHARGED BY A FEAR-CAUSING ENEMY

If a unit is charged by an enemy that it *fear*s then it must take a test to see if can overcome that fear and carry on fighting. Test when the charge is declared and the unit is determined to be within its charge range.

If the test is passed, the unit can fight on as normal. If the unit fails its test and its Unit Strength happens to be lower than the charging enemy, it will flee.

If the unit fails its test but its Unit Strength is higher than the charging enemy's, it will fight on as normal but must roll 6s to score hits in the first turn of close combat.

2. IF A UNIT WISHES TO CHARGE A FEARED ENEMY

If a unit wishes to charge an enemy that causes *fear* then it must take a test to overcome its fear first. If the unit is unfortunate and the test is failed, it may not charge or shoot and must remain stationary in that Movement phase.

DEFEATED BY FEAR-CAUSING ENEMY

A unit defeated in close combat is automatically broken without a Break test if it is fighting an enemy that it *fear*s and its Unit Strength is lower than the victorious enemy. If the *fear*-causing enemy does not have a higher Unit Strength then a Break test is taken as normal. See the Close Combat section for details of combat results, Break tests and fleeing troops. Note that this rule applies whether the unit has passed any Fear tests or not.

TERROR

Some monsters are so huge and threatening that they are considered to be even more frightening than those described by the Fear rules. Such creatures cause *terror*.

Troops who are confronted by monsters or situations that cause *terror* must test to see whether they overcome their terror. If they fail, they are completely terrified and are reduced to gibbering wrecks. Troops only ever test for *terror* once in a battle. Once they've overcome their terror they are not affected again.

If a creature causes *terror* then it automatically causes *fear* as well, and all the rules described for fear apply. However, you never have to take a Terror and a Fear test from the same enemy or situation – just take a Terror test: if you pass the Terror test then you automatically pass the Fear test too. As any unit of troops only ever takes one Terror test in a battle, any subsequent encounters with terrifying monsters or situations will simply count as *fear*.

1. A unit must make a Terror test if charged by or wishing to charge an enemy that causes *terror*.

2. A unit must make a Terror test at the start of its turn if there is an enemy which causes *terror* within 6".

FLEE!

A unit which fails its Terror test will flee away from the source of its terror as if it had failed its Break test in close combat or had decided to flee from a charge.

A unit being charged will flee immediately like any unit which flees from a charge.

A unit attempting to charge or failing a test at the start of its turn will flee in the compulsory movement part of its Movement phase.

A unit which flees in terror because of an enemy within 6" at the start of its turn may not attempt to rally that turn. It will flee in the compulsory part of its Movement phase, in the same way as a unit which panics because of fleeing friends within 4" (see Panic).

Remember that only a single test is ever made for *terror* by any unit during the whole game, whether it is made because of a charge or because the unit finds itself within 6" of a terrifying monster.

FEAR AND TERROR LIABILITIES

Obviously a large monster is less likely to suffer from *fear* or *terror* itself. There is no way a huge Dragon is going to be scared of a Troll, for example. These special liabilities also apply to any rider of a large monster (or a steed) too, so a Dragon rider wouldn't be afraid of a creature that would frighten him were he on foot. They also apply to units that are accompanied by *fear* or *terror* causing creatures: a Skink unit with a Kroxigor would be immune to *fear*, for example.

The following rules apply:

A creature that causes *fear* is not affected by enemies that cause *fear*. Faced with an enemy that causes *terror*, a *fear*-causing monster only suffers *fear*, not *terror*. For example, a Troll causes *fear* and a Dragon causes *terror*. The Dragon is not at all worried by the Troll, but the Troll *fears* the Dragon.

A creature that causes *terror* is not affected by *fear* or *terror* at all. For example, a Dragon rider is completely unworried by *fear* or *terror* because his mount causes *terror*.

It sometimes happens that an enemy unit of ordinary troops is led by a mighty Hero or a monster which causes *fear* or *terror*. In this situation, test for *fear/terror* if a charge will result in the charged unit fighting the Hero or monster in question.

In the case of *terror* a unit must also test if it is within 6" of the creature at the start of its turn, but not necessarily because it is within 6" of a unit that the terrifying creature is in. If the unit is charging a unit of enemy troops in the side or rear, so that the charging unit won't have to fight a terror-causing monster, then the unit does not have to test for terror. This is common sense – if you don't have to confront the beast then no test is required.

STUPIDITY

Many large and powerful creatures are unfortunately rather stupid. Even some otherwise quite intelligent creatures act stupidly now and again because they are readily confused or distracted, or perhaps because they are drugged or have been knocked insensible. The Stupidity rules represent the sort of slow wittedness or dumb behaviour which some especially

The Halfling is but half as tall as a man but hath a greater appetite. He dwells in a hole burrowed out of the hill. He is oft times grumpy except when he feasts. He delights mostly in eating and drinking and telling of bawdy tales. He is a goodly shotte with the bow and hath a dislike for Goblins and other sneaking things who would raid his foodstore. The Halfling is sturdy and round and hairy and sayeth little for he knoweth that a mouth is for eating with.

The Halflings do dwell in their own land which is called the Moot. It lieth in the midst of the Empire and is well hidden among woods. Here do they till the soil and grow an abundance of food, such that they feed the hungry cities of the Empire for a tidy sum of gold.

Ye Halflings do not oft display valour save when the foe approacheth the baggage wagons wherein is stored the provisions. Then do they wax most wrothful and show expertise in fighting.

From the Grimoire Aurus

stolid or stubborn beasts are prone to. Creatures that are *stupid* are indicated in the Army books and include such monstrous creatures as Trolls.

Stupid creatures must make a test at the start of their turn to see whether they overcome their stupidity. Make a test for each unit of *stupid* troops. If they pass the test by rolling their Leadership value or less on 2D6 then all is well and good – the creatures behave reasonably intelligently and can move and fight as normal. Nothing untoward has occurred beyond a bit of drooling and the odd spontaneous cackle.

If the test is failed then all is not well. The following rules apply until the creatures' following turn when they must test once more to see whether they are overcome by stupidity. In addition, a Wizard subject to being *stupid* cannot cast spells if he fails the test.

1) If already in close combat, half of the *stupid* creatures in base contact with the enemy suddenly stop fighting. They stare around blankly and wonder where they are. If the unit has an odd number of models or if a *stupid* creature is fighting on its own then roll a D6. If the result is 4 or more, the odd model fights; if not, it stands around vacantly. Note that only *stupid* creatures are affected. If a unit contains *stupid* creatures and other creatures (a unit of Trolls led by a Goblin Chieftain, for example) then the other creatures are not affected. The controlling player decides which individual creatures in combat cannot fight.

2) If not in close combat, the unit momentarily forgets what it is doing. Move the unit directly forwards at half normal speed (for example, Trolls with Movement 6 would move 3" forward). Any enemy troops encountered are automatically charged. If there are friends in the way, both units blunder into each other and their ranks become confused, in which case both units are pinned in place for the rest of the turn and neither may move further. This counts as compulsory movement and so occurs before other movement, but after charges have been declared (see the Movement section). Creatures within the unit that do not suffer from being *stupid* must also move as described – they are carried along by the movement of the rest of the unit and risk being trampled if they attempt to do otherwise.

FURTHER PSYCHOLOGY

Creatures affected by *stupidity* are quite unaware of anything happening around them, such is their state of confusion. Until they are no longer *stupid* they ignore all further Psychology tests. This means that *stupid* creatures cannot be affected

by *panic*, *fear*, etc, but they can still be broken in close combat by failing a Break test exactly as normal. *Stupid* troops that flee are not affected by stupidity until they have rallied, after which they must take Stupidity tests at the start of each of their subsequent turns.

STUPIDITY AND RIDERS

It sometimes happens that a cavalry rider or a monster rider will be riding a *stupid* creature, for example a Dark Elf riding a Cold One. If a rider's mount is *stupid* then he will have to test for stupidity at the start of his turn, but the rider's Leadership characteristic is used rather than that of the mount. If the test is failed, the rider is obliged to hang on while the creature behaves in whatever bizarre manner the rules dictate, but the rider can fight normally if he gets the opportunity.

FRENZY

Certain warriors can work themselves into a fighting frenzy, a whirlwind of destruction in which all concern for personal safety is ignored in favour of mindless violence. Many of these frenzied warriors are drugged or tranced, and have driven themselves into a psychotic frenzy with chanting, singing, yelling and screaming. These troops are described as *frenzied*. In the case of mounted troops, *frenzy* only affects the riders. No Psychology test is required for frenzy, and the following rules apply automatically:

After charges have been declared, measure to see if any enemies are within charge reach of any *frenzied* troops (ie, within the unit's charge move and in their normal charge arc). If so, the *frenzied* unit **must** charge that enemy. The player has no choice in the matter; the unit will automatically make its charge move. This automatic charge is done after charges have been declared, but you may declare normal charges with your *frenzied* troops if you wish. If there are several eligible units within the charge reach of the *frenzied* unit, the controlling player may decide which unit to charge.

Frenzied troops and characters fight with +1 extra Attack during close combat. Models that have 1 Attack on their profile therefore have 2, troops with 2 Attacks have 3, and so on. If models have an extra weapon then they will receive +1 extra Attack for this as normal, so if they have 1 Attack on their profile, they would receive 2+1= 3 Attacks in total.

Frenzied troops and characters must pursue fleeing enemy whether the player wants them to or not. They even pursue if they are defending an obstacle. Unlike other troops, they may not attempt to hold back as they are far too crazed with battle lust. If they wipe their enemy out in the first Close Combat phase, they will always overrun their opponent. Frenzied troops may not elect to flee if they are charged – their bloodlust overcomes their concerns for safety.

OTHER PSYCHOLOGY

Frenzied units are not affected by other psychology. So long as they are *frenzied*, they are immune to *panic, fear, terror, hatred* etc, and do not have to make these tests. Note that this immunity only extends to Psychology tests. It does not include Break tests in close combat which must still be taken as normal. Frenzied troops cannot flee as a charge reaction – they are too consumed by their eagerness to fight!

DEFEATED IN COMBAT

Troops that are defeated in close combat, as determined by the combat results, are no longer *frenzied*. Their exuberant, crazed frenzy has been thoroughly beaten out of them and they continue to fight as ordinary warriors for the remainder of the battle.

HATRED

Hatred is a powerful emotion and instances of hatred and rivalry are commonplace in the Warhammer world. There are grudges borne over centuries, racial animosity bordering on madness, and irreconcilable feuds that have left generations of dead in their wake. Some races hate other races with such bitter conviction that they will fight with astounding fury. Like frenzy, no Psychology test is taken for *hatred*.

Troops fighting in close combat with a *hated* foe may re-roll any misses when they attack in the first turn of any combat. This bonus only applies in the first turn of a combat and represents the unit venting its pent up hatred on the foe. After the initial round of blood-mad hacking they lose some impetus and subsequently fight as normal for the rest of the combat.

Troops who *hate* their enemy must always pursue them if they flee. They cannot attempt to avoid pursuit by testing their Leadership as other troops can. They must even pursue if behind a defended obstacle.

STUBBORN

Some troops will fight on in close combat almost regardless of casualties. This can be because they consider themselves to be elite, have taken severe vows to hold their ground in combat or are simply too dumb to flee when defeated by superior troops! Sometimes troops will fight stubbornly against certain enemies because of honour, vows or racial animosity, and fight normally against other enemies. These troops are referred as being *stubborn*.

The following rules apply:

Stubborn troops take all Break tests on their unmodified Leadership value. They do not reduce this value regardless of any combat results, how many casualties they have suffered or other combat bonuses. This means, for example, that *stubborn* troops with a Leadership value of 9 will only ever break on the roll of 10 or more when making a Break test. If a *stubborn* unit contains characters with higher Leadership values than the rank-and-file troops who are not themselves *stubborn*, the character's Leadership value can be used to take the test, but it is still subject to the normal modifiers for a Break test. Use either the Leadership value of the character leading the unit or the unit's own Leadership value, depending on which results in the higher value for passing a Break test.

Characters that are part of a *stubborn* unit but are not *stubborn* themselves will not have to take a separate Break test – they benefit and gain from the determination of the troops around them! *Stubborn* units led by *stubborn* characters can use the character's unmodified Leadership value for Break tests. Note that any troops who are not *stubborn* but are led by a *stubborn* character may use his Leadership value for Break tests, but the roll is modified as normal.

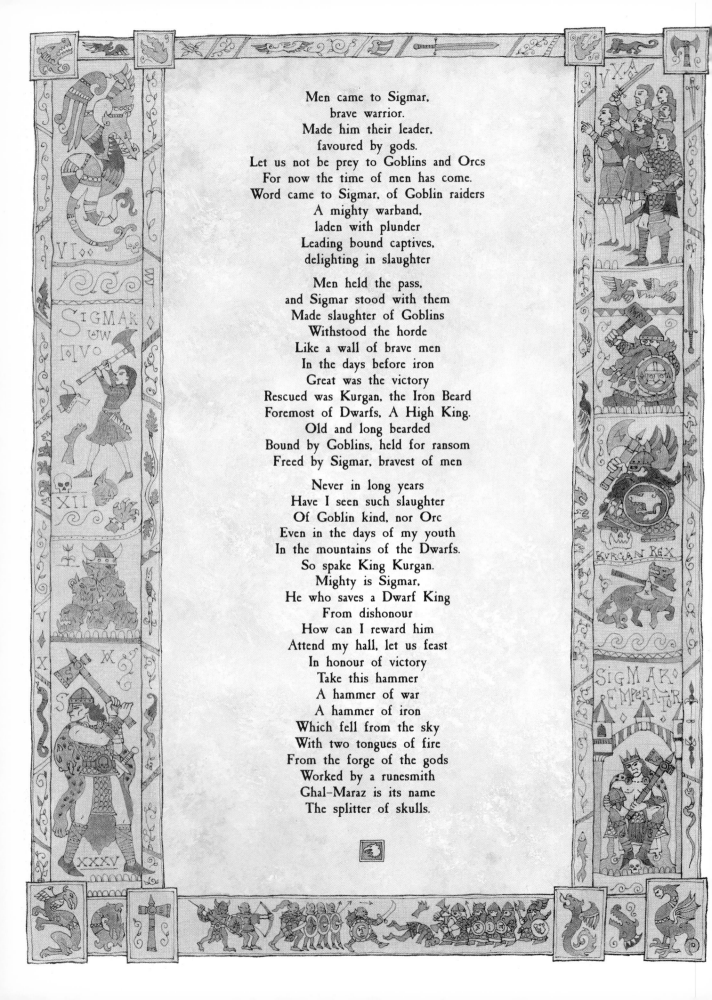

Men came to Sigmar,
brave warrior.
Made him their leader,
favoured by gods.
Let us not be prey to Goblins and Orcs
For now the time of men has come.
Word came to Sigmar, of Goblin raiders
A mighty warband,
laden with plunder
Leading bound captives,
delighting in slaughter

Men held the pass,
and Sigmar stood with them
Made slaughter of Goblins
Withstood the horde
Like a wall of brave men
In the days before iron
Great was the victory
Rescued was Kurgan, the Iron Beard
Foremost of Dwarfs, A High King.
Old and long bearded
Bound by Goblins, held for ransom
Freed by Sigmar, bravest of men

Never in long years
Have I seen such slaughter
Of Goblin kind, nor Orc
Even in the days of my youth
In the mountains of the Dwarfs.
So spake King Kurgan.
Mighty is Sigmar,
He who saves a Dwarf King
From dishonour
How can I reward him
Attend my hall, let us feast
In honour of victory
Take this hammer
A hammer of war
A hammer of iron
Which fell from the sky
With two tongues of fire
From the forge of the gods
Worked by a runesmith
Ghal–Maraz is its name
The splitter of skulls.

ADVANCED RULES

Weapons
Characters
General & Battle Standard Bearer
Monsters
Flyers
Standards, Musicians & Champions
Special Rules
Skirmishers
Fast Cavalry
War Machines
Chariots
Buildings

WEAPONS

In a grim and dangerous world, warriors employ many different types of weapons against a multitude of foes. From the fine swords of the Elves to the sharp axes of the Dwarfs, every race has weaponry fitted to its preferred style of fighting. Few individuals manage to avoid violence in this perilous world. The rest wage war.

WEAPONS AND UNITS

It is usual for all the models in a unit to carry the same weapons. So, a unit will be a unit of Spearmen, a unit of Halberdiers, a unit of Crossbowmen, etc. It is acceptable for a unit to include a minority of models that are differently armed for the sake of a varied and interesting appearance, but the whole unit still counts as being armed as the majority. Where models are varied in this way, it is important that the overall appearance of the unit is not misleading.

All troops and characters are assumed to carry hand weapons, such as swords, long daggers, axes, clubs, maces and comparable weaponry. In addition, some troops carry another weapon such as a spear, Great Axe, or halberd. At the start of the first turn of a combat, troops can choose which of their weapons to use. Whichever weapon they use must be used for the entire combat. Eg, troops armed with Great Axes may opt to fight with their swords if they do not wish to suffer the penalty of striking last, but must then fight with swords for the duration of the entire combat.

SPECIAL COMBAT RULES

Before we look at the rules for individual weapons we shall consider two exceptional but important cases. In both instances these rules only apply to warriors fighting on foot and not to mounted warriors or warriors fighting from chariots. They cover warriors fighting with a weapon in each hand and warriors fighting with hand weapons and shields.

FIGHTING WITH A WEAPON IN EACH HAND

Some warriors carry two hand weapons, one in each hand, and can rain down even more blows on their enemy. This could include a sword in both hands, an axe and sword, a sword and long dagger, or any combination of hand weapons described in the Weapons section.

If a warrior on foot fights with a hand weapon in each hand, he receives +1 extra Attack to account for his second weapon. Eg, if the warrior's Attack characteristic is 1, he has 2 Attacks, if his Attack characteristic is 2, he has 3 Attacks, and so on.

FIGHTING WITH A HAND WEAPON AND A SHIELD

Some warriors carry a hand weapon in one hand and a shield in the other, and so are able to defend themselves easily by deflecting blows by means of either their shield or hand weapon. Any hand weapon is good for this, whether it is a sword, an axe, a club, pistol butt, etc.

If a warrior on foot fights with a hand weapon and shield, he may increase his Armour save by a further +1 in close combat. Eg, if he has a shield and light armour and a sword, his armour save is increased from 5+ to 4+ when fighting in close combat. This only applies in close combat, not against wounds suffered from shooting, magic, or other means.

SPECIAL WEAPON RULES

Different weapons have advantages and disadvantages in different circumstances. Some require both hands to use but are very powerful, some missile weapons have long range but take a long time to load, and so on. These qualities are represented by the special weapon rules described here. Rules for individual types of weapon are listed later in this section.

STRENGTH BONUS

Some weapons give their wielders a Strength bonus in close combat or when shooting. This is clearly indicated in the weapon's profile. For example, a halberd has a +1 Strength bonus, so if used in close combat by a warrior with a Strength of 3, any hits caused are resolved with a Strength of 4. Note that this Strength bonus only applies when the warrior is using the weapon – his Strength characteristic remains unchanged for other purposes.

Some Strength bonuses only apply in the first turn of a combat. This reflects the fact that the weapons are especially cumbersome or exhausting to use. This restriction is indicated in the weapon's description.

Some Strength bonuses only apply in the first turn of a combat and only if the user has charged that turn. These are weapons that rely upon the impact of the charge to pierce the foe. This restriction is indicated in the weapon's description.

REQUIRES TWO HANDS

Some weapons require two hands to use in close combat. These weapons usually have a long shaft. Note that all Great Weapons require two hands to use and are sometimes known as 'double-handed weapons' for that reason. However, Great Weapons are not the only weapons that require two hands to use.

If a weapon requires two hands to use then it is not possible to simultaneously employ a shield or another weapon. If a shield is carried then it must be slung across the warrior's back or dropped behind him whilst he fights in close combat.

STRIKES LAST

Many weapons, such as the Great Sword favoured by some Empire troops or the Great Axes of the Dwarfs, are very heavy and require considerable training and stamina to wield. Such a weapon is described by the term **strikes last**.

Troops armed with a weapon that strikes last will always strike last during close combat where they would otherwise strike in Initiative order. Note that troops that charge will still strike first in the initial turn of close combat, as charging troops always strike first rather than in Initiative order. For example, troops armed with Great Axes will strike first on the turn they charge and strike last thereafter.

FIGHT IN RANKS

Spears and similar weapons are well suited to fighting in deep formations. Weapons used for fighting in ranks enable troops in a second or subsequent rank to fight in close combat as well as the warriors in the first rank who are actually touching the enemy. For example, a unit of Spearmen can fight in two ranks – warriors in the second rank can stab past their comrades using their long spears.

If a unit is entitled to fight in this way then any model in a second or subsequent rank can fight if it is behind a model that is engaged in close combat to its front. Extra ranks cannot fight to their side or rear but only to their front. Where a weapon can fight in two or more ranks, this is indicated in the weapon's description, for example, 'spears fight in two ranks'.

In order to employ all of its additional ranks as described, a unit must not have moved in that turn. If a unit has moved, if it has charged for example, then it fights with one less rank than it otherwise would. For example, a unit of Spearmen can normally fight in two ranks, but will fight with only one rank if they charge. The unit will be able to fight with the extra rank during subsequent rounds of close combat.

Note that troops armed with weapons which fight in ranks can fight with the extra ranks only against opponents engaged to their front, not against enemies fighting in the formation's flank or rear.

MULTIPLE SHOTS

Some missile weapons enable their users to shoot several times in each Shooting phase – known as **multiple shots**. The number of times the weapon can fire is given as part of its description. Eg, a Dark Elf repeater crossbow can fire two shots in each Shooting phase so is noted as having 2 x multiple shots. These weapons can either fire once without penalty, or several times with a -1 to hit penalty for each shot.

Note that a model's Attacks characteristic has no effect on the number of shots it can make. The Attacks characteristic refers to close combat attacks only.

THROWN WEAPON

Some warriors carry missile weapons which are designed to be thrown, such as javelins or throwing axes. These generally have a short range, but as they are aimed individually, they can be very accurate.

Thrown weapons do not suffer the usual to hit penalties for shooting at long range or for moving and shooting. Note that this doesn't entitle the warrior to throw his missile if he charges or marches, it is simply that the usual -1 to hit penalty for moving whilst shooting does not apply.

Where march you, men of Reikland,
Where carry you halberds and swords?

We march to war for our Emperor
And Sigmar, our saviour and lord.

Tomorrow we go to war
to face the hosts of Chaos.

Tomorrow we will be buried
in the cold graves that await us.

And when this war is done,
and my body lies on the field at night

Hear my prayer, save my soul,
Lord Sigmar take me to your light.

Old Soldier's song from Reikland

MOVE-OR-FIRE

Some missile weapons take a long time to load, such as crossbows and handguns. So, a model that is armed with a move-or-fire weapon may not fire his weapon if he has moved at all during that turn. It doesn't matter if the model was forced to move by some compulsory action or by magic. Any movement will prevent the model from shooting, even the simple act of turning round.

ARMOUR PIERCING

Certain weapons, most notably blackpowder weapons such as handguns, are even better at penetrating armour than their Strength value suggests. Therefore, the enemy Armour save is reduced by an additional -1. For example, an Armour piercing weapon that has Strength 4 would have a -2 Armour save modifier rather than -1.

LIST OF WEAPONS

Listed on the following pages are some of the many and varied types of weapon used by warriors in the Warhammer world. The weapons that are covered here are those most commonly and universally used rather than a comprehensive list. Unusual weapons and weapons which are specific to individual races or armies are covered in the Army book for that particular race.

CLOSE COMBAT WEAPONS

Close Combat weapons are just that… weapons which are used in close combat. Most warriors carry at least a hand weapon of some kind and many carry something more potent in addition. In close combat, warriors fight using their own Strength characteristic to resolve hits, but modified as indicated for the weapon they use.

HAND WEAPON
(SWORD, AXE, MACE, CLUB, ETC)

The term 'hand weapon' is used to describe any stabbing, cutting or bludgeoning weapon held in one hand and not otherwise covered by the rules. As such it includes swords, axes, clubs, maces and long daggers.

Rules: No special weapon rules apply to hand weapons but they do have the advantage that they can be used in combination with each other (see 'Fighting with a weapon in each hand') or with a shield (see 'Fighting with a hand weapon and shield').

GREAT WEAPON
(GREAT SWORD, GREAT AXE, ETC)

Great Weapons are especially large and heavy weapons that are wielded with both hands. As well as Great Swords this includes the similarly heavy Great Hammer, Great Axes, and such like. A blow from a Great Weapon can cut a foe in half and break apart the thickest armour.

Rules: +2 Strength bonus; requires two hands; strikes last.

FLAIL

The flail is a cumbersome and heavy weapon that is wielded with both hands. It consists of heavy weights, often spiked, attached to a pole or handle by means of heavy chains. A flail drains the user's stamina quickly, but is very destructive in the hands of a skilled warrior.

Rules: +2 Strength bonus in first of combat; requires two hands.

MORNING STAR

This is a single-handed weapon that consists of one or more spiked balls on a chain. Like the larger flail that it resembles, a morning star is a tiring weapon to use so its advantage lies in the first round of combat.

Rules: +1 Strength bonus in first turn of combat.

HALBERD

The halberd is a heavy bladed weapon mounted on a sturdy shaft. The steel blade has a point like a spear as well as a heavy cutting edge like an axe. It is held in both hands and used to chop as well as thrust, so it is a very adaptable and extremely effective weapon for infantry.

Rules: +1 Strength Bonus; requires two hands

SPEARS (INFANTRY)

Spears are used by troops on foot to form a solid mass of spear points. Because stationary spearmen can fight in two ranks they are ideal defensive weapons.

Rules: Fight in two ranks.

SPEARS (CAVALRY)

All cavalry, monster riders and chariot riders armed with spears can employ them to ride down enemy troops with, spitting them as the horsemen ride into their ranks.

Rules: +1 Strength bonus in first turn of combat when charging.

LANCE

All cavalry, monster riders and chariot riders armed with long lances can employ this deadly weapon with devastating effect.

Rules: +2 Strength bonus in first turn of combat when charging.

PISTOL (hand-to-hand)

A pistol is an exceptional weapon in that it can be used both in close combat and for shooting at a distance. For this reason it is included in both the Close Combat and Missile lists. Pistols are primitive weapons that employ a noxious and rather unreliable form of gunpowder to propel a small lead or stone bullet.

In close combat, a pistol can be used in one hand whilst the other hand holds either a hand weapon or another pistol. In this respect the pistol acts like a hand weapon and uses the 'Fighting with a weapon in each hand' rule, conferring +1 additional Attack.

In the first turn of a combat engagement, a pistol counts as having Strength 4 and also has an Armour piercing attack, reducing the enemy's Armour save by a further -1. This applies to all attacks if a model carries a pistol in each hand, but only to the single additional attack if a warrior is fighting with a hand weapon and a pistol. This represents the pistol's shot. In second and subsequent rounds of the engagement the wielder uses the heavy butt of his pistol/s like a club, so after the first round, a pistol is considered to be equivalent to an ordinary hand weapon (see rules above).

For example, a warrior who is fighting with a pistol in each hand fights with Strength 4 and the Armour piercing modifier in the first turn of combat and fights as with hand weapons thereafter. However, a warrior with a sword in one hand and a pistol in the other strikes one Attack with the pistol (Strength 4/Armour piercing) and remaining Attacks with the hand weapon in the first turn of combat, but in subsequent turns he counts as having only hand weapons.

Rules: Strength 4 in the first turn of combat, Armour piercing in the first turn of combat.

MISSILE WEAPONS

Missile weapons are bows, crossbows and similar weapons whether simple or primitive like a javelin or more complex and advanced like hand guns and pistols.

SHORTBOW

Shortbows are small, short-ranged bows which are favoured by Goblins. Some cavalry also carry a shortbow because it is easier to shoot from horseback.

Maximum range: 16"; **Strength:** 3; **Rules:** –

BOW

The bow is carried by most races and used extensively in warfare. It is a compact, long-ranged weapon that is cheap to make and easy to maintain.

Maximum range: 24"; **Strength:** 3; **Rules:** –

LONGBOW

A longbow is a dangerous weapon made of alternating layers of either yew or elm. A skilled archer can hit an enemy from three hundred paces.

Maximum range: 30"; **Strength:** 3; **Rules:** –

CROSSBOW

A crossbow consists of a short, strong bowstave mounted on a wooden or steel stock. It takes a long time to load and wind a crossbow for each shot, but the crossbow bolt has tremendous range and power.

Maximum range: 30"; **Strength:** 4; **Rules:** Move-or-fire

REPEATER CROSSBOW

Used almost exclusively by the Dark Elves of Naggaroth, the repeater crossbow is a lighter, less powerful type of crossbow that has a magazine of bolts which allows a single bolt to drop into place ready for firing as the string is drawn. A repeater crossbow can fire a hail of shots in the time it takes to shoot one ordinary crossbow bolt.

Maximum range: 24"; **Strength:** 3;

Rules: 2 x Multiple Shots

SLING

Slings are not often used on the battlefield because of their short range. The weapon consists of a looped string of cloth or leather into which a stone is placed.

Maximum range: 18"; **Strength:** 3;

Rules: 2 x Multiple Shots if enemy is within 9".

JAVELIN

The javelin is a light spear designed for throwing, and javelin armed warriors often carry several to last them throughout the battle. The javelin is too flimsy to be used in hand-to-hand fighting. It is not a very common weapon as it has a short range, but the multitudinous reptilian Skinks of Lustria use javelins extensively.

Maximum range: 8"; **Strength:** As user;

Rules: Thrown weapon

THROWING STAR/KNIFE

Throwing stars and knives are small, easily concealed weapons. Consequently they are favoured by assassins and lightly armed infiltrators. A perfectly balanced knife is not suitable for close combat, but is deadly in the hands of a skilled thrower.

Maximum range: 6"; **Strength:** As user;

Rules: Thrown weapon

THROWING AXE

Some Dwarf warriors use heavy-bladed throwing axes. These weapons are keenly balanced so they can be thrown accurately despite their weight. Even so, the strongest warrior cannot throw such a weapon very far, but if a throwing axe hits its target the effect is devastating.

Note that throwing axes cannot be used in close combat – or if used they simply count as hand weapons. Normal axes carried as hand weapons cannot be thrown either!

Maximum range: 6"; **Strength:** As user;

Rules: Thrown weapon, Strength bonus +1

HANDGUN

A handgun is a simple firearm consisting of a metal barrel mounted on a wooden stock. The gunpowder charge is ignited by poking a length of burning cord, or match as it is called, into a small touchhole. Some of the more advanced versions made by Dwarfs have levers and springs which hold the burning match and triggers which release the firing mechanism and fire the gun.

Handguns are not terribly reliable weapons, as occasionally the gun barrel tends to explode violently apart or the powder fails to ignite. Handguns, however, do have a long range and hit very hard, making a mockery of even the thickest armour.

Maximum range: 24"; **Strength:** 4;

Rules: Move-or-fire, Armour piercing

PISTOL (shooting)

A pistol is simply a small version of a hand gun fired by a spring mechanism. We have already described how a pistol can be used in close combat. In addition a pistol can shot up to a distance of 8".

Note that although a model may carry several pistols he may only shoot one in the Shooting phase.

Pistols do not suffer the usual to hit penalties for shooting at long range or for moving and shooting.

Maximum range: 8"; **Strength:** 4;

Rules: Armour piercing

WEAPONS SUMMARY

Missile weapons table

Name	Max. Range	Strength	Rules
Shortbow	16"	3	–
Bow	24"	3	–
Longbow	30"	3	–
Crossbow	30"	4	Move-or-fire
Handgun	24"	4	Move-or-fire, Armour piercing
Pistol	8"	4	Armour piercing
Repeater crossbow	24"	3	2 x multiple shots
Sling	18"	3	2 x multiple shots if enemy within 9"
Javelin	8"	As user	Thrown weapon
Throwing axe	6"	As user	Thrown weapon, +1 Strength bonus
Throwing knife/throwing star	6"	As user	Thrown weapon

Close Combat weapons table

Name	Rules
Hand weapon	Special combat rules
Great Weapon	Requires two hands; strikes last; +2 Strength bonus
Flail	Requires two hands; +2 Strength bonus in first turn
Halberd	Requires two hands, +1 Strength bonus
Spear (infantry)	Fights in two ranks
Spear (cavalry)	+1 Strength bonus in the first turn when charging
Lance	+2 Strength bonus in the first turn when charging
Morning star	+1 Strength bonus in the first turn
Pistol	Strength 4; Armour piercing in the first round of combat

93

CHARACTERS

The Warhammer world would not be what it is without the presence of potent individuals, great Heroes, valiant Champions, mighty Wizards and black-hearted Necromancers. These individuals add an entirely different aspect to the game either as valuable leaders, or powerful individuals able to fight against vast numbers of lesser mortals. These models are known as **characters**.

Heroic individuals vary tremendously: some are tougher, meaner and more powerful than the average warrior. Others are faster than a typical member of their race, stronger and more skilled with weapons, or are natural leaders with the power to inspire. Whilst others have special powers, skills or abilities, such as the Dark Elf Beastmasters or Imperial Engineers.

In most cases they are known by different names appropriate to their nation or race. Orc characters, for example, are known by the 'Orcy' titles of Big Bosses and Warbosses, while the leaders of the Empire are known as Elector Counts and Warrior Priests.

Of course, these types of valiant individuals cannot really represent every nuance of distinction between mighty warriors, bold leaders and cunning wizards, but it does enable us to fight with comparably powerful characters, whether they are goodly, honourable knights or are the most rotten-hearted perpetrators of evil.

Characters often have superior characteristic values compared to ordinary members of their race. For example:

	M	WS	BS	S	T	W	I	A	Ld
Human	4	3	3	3	3	1	3	1	7

	M	WS	BS	S	T	W	I	A	Ld
Elector Count	4	5	5	4	4	3	5	3	9

From these examples it is clear that characters are quite different from ordinary troops.

TYPES OF CHARACTERS

Characters such as Wizards and Generals are represented by individual models, which fight as units in their own right. However, as we shall see, one of the most useful abilities of independent characters is to join other units in battle, so that they can bolster the battleline where needed. Some characters also have the ability to cast spells. In game terms, all such characters are called **Wizards**.

WIZARDS

Magic is everywhere in the Warhammer world, it permeates all living creatures and every inanimate thing. Its power is there to use for good or ill. Magic is almost as important as the fighting abilities of warriors, for it can make the difference between victory and defeat. As a consequence, mighty rulers and noble lords employ their own Wizards to protect them and fight on their behalf. Some of the races are even ruled over by powerful Wizards.

In the Empire, the Emperor himself encourages the study of magic so that he may have powerful battle Wizards to help fight his wars. In Ulthuan in the far west, the High Mages of the Elves practice the most potent of all sorceries. Even Orcs and Goblins, low minded as they are, have Shamans who can blast the enemy with raw magic. Of all the intelligent races of the Old World only the Dwarfs have no Wizards. Their skills lie in the manufacture of fabulous magical artefacts and enscribing runes of power.

There are many different types of Wizard but they all have a Power Level ranging from 1 to 4. The Power Level of a Wizard represents his ability to cast spells and determines the number of spells he has. These four Power Levels are not intended to represent every possible variation in an individual's abilities; they are useful categories that enable us to match comparable Wizards against each other.

The complete rules for Wizards, spellcasting, and many magic items are covered by the Magic section of this book. Refer to this section for a description of how magic works in the Warhammer game.

MOVING CHARACTERS

A character model is moved and fights as an individual piece, except that he may also join up with and fight alongside units of troops as described below.

When a character moves on his own he can ignore any penalties for crossing terrain and obstacles (apart from impassable terrain), and because he is not part of a larger formation he does not have to change direction by turning or wheeling – he can change direction freely as he moves. So, a character can move a fraction of his Movement distance, head off in another direction, move a little more, change direction again, and so on.

CHARACTERS AND LINE OF SIGHT

Characters on foot are able to move and see freely and can therefore see, charge and shoot 360° around themselves.

However, if a character is mounted on a steed such as a horse, in a chariot or rides a monster like a Griffon, he must follow all the normal rules for line of sight (ie, the character has a 90° arc of sight). He must also still be able to see his enemy when charges are declared. Just like other troops, he cannot dash round the side of a unit to charge it in the rear if he begins his move in front of it. Also, such a character (whether he is riding in a chariot, on a steed or a monster) must take into account penalties for terrain as normal. This is because a mounted character is not as manoeuvrable as a character on foot.

Characters on foot who have 5 or more Wounds in their original profile also have to follow the normal rules for arc of sight (see above). This is because these characters are so massive and cumbersome.

COMPULSORY MOVES

As characters can turn freely as they move they can also be turned to face any direction once they have moved – in order to see a target the character intends to shoot at, for example.

The exception to this rule is if the character makes a compulsory move, such as a charge, flee or pursuit move, in which case the model must finish its move facing the direction of travel. Obviously, in this situation the character is far too preoccupied with what is in front or behind him to worry about looking round for fresh targets.

MARCHING

Characters moving on their own are allowed to march just like formations of troops, although in their case this represents their freedom to move about the battlefield as they will, natural dynamism and an uncanny ability to be in the right place at the right time (in true heroic fashion!). Individual characters can march at double their normal Movement distance, even if within 8" of any enemy models, and they also ignore penalties for terrain or obstacles, apart from impassable terrain.

CHARACTERS AND UNITS

INDEPENDENT CHARACTERS JOINING UNITS

Apart from Champions, who always fight as part of their regiment as described elsewhere in this book, characters can move and fight on their own. In effect, they are individual units of one model. During the battle, a character can join a unit of ordinary troops, in which case he becomes part of that unit until he leaves it.

To join a unit of troops, a character has only to move so that he is touching it. Once he has joined the unit, the model is automatically placed in its front rank. Note that a character will inevitably use up a proportion of his move to reach the unit he is joining. If the unit has not already moved then its further movement is limited to that fraction remaining to the character. Any movement lost represents time wasted waiting for the character.

If there is no room for the character in the front rank of the formation (because the Standard Bearer, Musician and Champion take up all the available positions, for example), he is placed in the second rank of the unit. As long as the character remains in the back ranks he cannot fight (even with a spear), use magic or magic items, nor can the unit use his Leadership value for tests. In effect, he is out of the game. Only if the character is engaged in close combat (via a flank or rear charge, for example) can he fight back normally.

Characters may not join units which are in close combat, although they may obviously join the battle by charging their enemies (if allowed to by normal circumstances). Characters may not join a fleeing unit.

INDEPENDENT CHARACTERS LEAVING UNITS

Except in the circumstances noted below, a character who is part of a unit of troops can leave during the Movement phase. A character is able to leave one unit of troops and join another in the same turn if you so wish, but he is unable to join and leave the same unit in the same turn.

A character may never leave or join a unit of troops while it is subject to a compulsory movement rule. For example, he cannot leave a unit which is fleeing, which has declared a charge, which has rallied that turn (because it cannot move) or which is engaged in close combat.

As mentioned above, if a character is with a unit when it declares a charge he must charge with it. However, if the unit he is with does not declare a charge, a character may declare a separate charge of his own and therefore leave the unit by charging out of it.

Once close combat has begun, a character will not be able to leave a unit he has joined until all the fighting is over and any compulsory movement, such as fleeing and pursuit, has been resolved.

INDEPENDENT CHARACTERS MOVING WITH UNITS

If a character forms part of a unit of troops then the unit as a whole will dictate his maximum movement. He simply moves along like an ordinary member of the unit. If the character moves more slowly than his unit then the whole unit will have to slow down so that he can keep up with them.

MOVING CHARACTERS
WITHIN ENGAGED UNITS

If a unit is engaged in combat and a character is positioned in the formation in such a way that he is unable to fight, perhaps because he is in the front rank and the formation has been charged in the rear, or because the enemy unit is smaller and the character is stranded beyond the fighting, then the player is allowed to move the character into a position where he can fight in his next Movement phase. Simply swap the character for an ordinary trooper model that is already fighting. This can mean that the character loses the chance to fight in the first turn of combat. Note that a character may not replace another character who is already engaged in close combat.

Although the above rule allows a character to move within a unit in order to fight an enemy, he cannot move once he is already fighting. For example, he cannot move from the front to the rear if he is already fighting to the front, he must stay where he is and fight the enemy he is touching. Nor can a character move into a non-fighting rank to avoid fighting unless he is deliberately refusing a challenge, as described later.

SHOOTING AT INDEPENDENT CHARACTERS

The Shooting rules are written from the point of view of units of troops firing upon other units of troops. A character moving around on his own is treated as a unit consisting of one model. In this respect, a character is a viable target just like a regiment of infantry.

However, in reality a lone individual would be likely to escape the notice of the enemy on the battlefield, being strewn as it is with stragglers from destroyed regiments making their way back to camp, and the inevitable confusion and debris of conflict. The following rules represent the fact that characters are harder to shoot at than larger units of troops.

PROXIMITY TO
FRIENDLY TROOPS

A character model which is more than 5" from a friendly unit of five or more models can be shot at without any restrictions. Characters who are prone to jumping up and down right in front of the enemy are just asking to get killed, so it serves them right if they get shot!

A character model within 5" of a friendly unit of five or more models can only be picked out as a target if he is the closest target. This restriction enables characters to move around behind the battlelines without attracting an unrealistic and unreasonable

amount of missile fire. Note that if the character is riding a horse or similar mount then he can still be singled out as a target if all the friendly units within 5" are infantry. The same applies if the character is riding a monster or is much larger than any friendly units within 5".

If a character is part of a unit which consists of at least five rank-and-file models of similar size in total then he cannot be shot at. Any shots against the unit will hit ordinary troopers and not the character. If the unit drops in size to less than five rank-and-file models, then further hits are allocated before rolling to wound. Divide the number of hits evenly between all the members of the unit (including the characters), and randomise any excess hits. If the number of hits the unit suffers is smaller than the number of models in a unit, randomise which models are hit.

So, for example, if a unit with three rank-and-file models and two characters suffered seven hits, then each model would suffer a single hit, and you would roll to wound and take saves immediately. Allocate the remaining two hits between any survivors randomly.

By order of the great god Khorne
whose name I called upon extolling his glory,
he commanded
that I should assail my enemies.

When the command of Khorne,
my lord, came to my ears
From Wastes I departed
to Kislev I marched straightaway.

The boyars of Kislev
mustered their fighting men against me,
offering resistance in battle.

I grasped in my hand the mighty axe,
the weapon which Khorne had granted me.
Like a lion I raged
I butchered them like sheep
with my terrible weapon.

Not a man among them escaped.
Their corpses I skewered on stakes,
with their skulls I covered
the altar of Khorne.

From the monolith of Gerther von Stahl,
the Exalted Champion of Khorne

PICKING OUT
INDEPENDENT CHARACTERS

If a character is substantially larger than the troops he is with or near to, then he can be picked out as a target regardless of the rules just given. If a character rides a horse then he will stand out amongst a unit of infantry, if he rides a Dragon or is mounted in a chariot he will be an obvious target amongst a unit of cavalry, and so on.

TO HIT PENALTY

When deliberately shooting at a man-sized character model on foot there is a -1 to hit penalty, as described in the Shooting section. This is because the normal chance of hitting assumes that the target is massed up in ranks. This is not the case when you are shooting at a single character, especially if there are other potential targets to distract the shooter's attention.

Note that this -1 does not apply if you are shooting at a character who is riding a steed or a monster, as described in the Monsters section. In such a case, the

shooter does not suffer the -1 penalty and benefits from the +1 to hit modifier if the monster ridden by a character is defined as a large target.

CLOSE COMBAT

When a unit closes with its enemies in close combat, character models will inevitably find themselves confronted by enemy troops. As described in the Close Combat section, models can attack any enemy models whose base they are touching.

Troopers confronted by character models will usually have the option of attacking a character or ordinary enemies, as bases will usually overlap slightly when models move into combat. Where a player has a choice of attacking characters or ordinary troops, he must nominate which model(s) he is striking against before rolling to hit.

DIVIDING ATTACKS

Characters often come face-to-face with enemy characters, and the same choice applies to them as to other models – they may attack any enemy whose base they are touching. If a character has more than 1 Attack he can divide his attacks among characters and ordinary troops as described in the Close Combat section. The challenge is an important exception to this rule as described below.

EXCESS WOUNDS

As with combat between ordinary warriors, casualties inflicted by a character can extend beyond the models the character is touching. If a character has say, 4 Attacks and is facing two enemy troopers then his attacks are worked out against these. However, if the character scores sufficient wounds to slay three or four models then the enemy unit loses three or four troopers, not just two.

Don't be fooled by the fact that models are static and the battle lines rigid and straight. What is represented is real combat! Heroes are just the type to strike boldly left and right, stepping forward to deliver fresh attacks, cutting down foes who step forward to fill a gap.

If a character attacks an enemy character, or another individual model such as a monster, then any excess wounds caused by those attacks are not carried over onto ordinary troopers fighting alongside. The attacker has

chosen to concentrate his attacks on a single special foe and any wounds left over are wasted and do not count towards the result of the combat. The exception to this rule is during the challenge as described next.

CHALLENGES

In each turn before working out any close combat, each side is allowed to issue challenges. The challenge represents one-on-one combat between powerful rivals, the final showdown between mighty adversaries in the midst of battle.

ISSUING A CHALLENGE

One challenge can be issued in each combat that is being fought. For each combat, start with the player whose turn it is. The player chooses one character model from those fighting to issue a challenge with.

The second player has the option of refusing or meeting a challenge. If he refuses then no challenge takes place, and the refusing player must retire a character from the combat as described below. The challenger fights normally in the following combat. If the challenge is accepted, the player selects one of his characters from those already fighting in the combat to take up the challenge.

If the player whose turn it is does not issue a challenge then his opponent may issue one himself. The other player may then accept or decline in the same way. However, note that a challenge cannot be issued unless there is a character to fight – ordinary troopers or monsters cannot take up a challenge.

Note that in order to participate in a challenge, either to issue it or to meet it, a character must be fighting in combat already. This means that the model must actually be positioned base-to-base against an enemy model. A character who is not already fighting, for example because he is in the front of a formation which has been attacked in the rear, cannot take part in a challenge.

REFUSING A CHALLENGE
(Boo Hiss!)

If a challenge is refused then the declining player must retire one character nominated by his opponent. The retiring character is removed from the engaged rank and placed at the back of the formation. The retired character may not fight or do anything else that turn. The unit may not use his Leadership for any tests during the same turn either, noone likes a coward! The (so called) Hero has chosen to hide away behind his fellows rather than face the challenger one-on-one. The retired character is automatically returned to a fighting rank at the end of that Close Combat phase ready to fight in the following turn. He is positioned in the same place as before.

FIGHTING A CHALLENGE

Once a challenge is accepted, the character who accepted the challenge is moved in the ranks so that the two protagonists are opposite each other. If the models are especially large it may be more convenient to remove them altogether and place them beside the fighting units.

When combat is worked out, these two will fight together. No other models may attack them even if their bases are touching, and no other models may shoot at them or use magic to attack them.

Once the challenge is underway no further challenges may be issued in that combat until one character is slain. The challenge might therefore last over several turns of combat.

If characters are riding monsters or steeds which have their own attacks then these fight during the challenge as well as their rider. If the character is riding in a chariot then the crew and creatures do not fight in the challenge at all (see chariot rules).

SINGLE CHARACTER CHALLENGES

Sometimes a single character, possibly mounted on a huge monster, will attack a unit of troops. If the single character finds himself challenged he cannot refuse as he has no formation to hide behind.

OVERKILL!

Excess wounds caused when attacking characters are normally discounted because all the effort of these attacks goes into fighting the character. As any excess wounds are not inflicted they are not counted towards the combat result. However, any excess wounds scored when fighting a challenge do count towards the combat result (up to a maximum of +5), even though they are not actually inflicted. This is called the **Overkill rule**.

This represents the situation where troops are watching their hero boldly (or deperately!) battling for his life against his adversary. All eyes are focussed on the mighty clash and both sides are yelling encouragement. If the troops see their champion crushed to a bloody pulp before their eyes they will inevitably get a bit upset and might decide to turn tail and run rather than stick around for a dose of the same.

In practical terms, the Overkill rule means that it is a positive advantage to crush a challenged enemy as overwhelmingly as possible. It also means that players will benefit if they meet a challenge with as powerful a character as possible. Players are advised to avoid taking on especially dangerous opponents with lowly Champions, although, of course, even the most modest character will generally do better than an ordinary warrior.

LEADERSHIP & UNIT PSYCHOLOGY

CHARACTER'S LEADERSHIP

If a unit of troops is led by a character it may use the character's Leadership value for any Leadership-based tests it has to take, including spells which are resisted by using the Leadership value of the target. Where a unit includes several characters, use the highest Leadership amongst them. This is a very important rule, as it provides units of poor troops with the leadership that they need. This is especially true of Goblins, which are all but useless without a proper character to lead them. Leadership is important because it is used for Psychology tests, Rally tests, and also for Break tests in combat.

INDEPENDENT CHARACTERS AND UNIT PSYCHOLOGY

While a character is with a unit of troops he is considered to be part of that unit in all respects. This means that if the unit flees then he must flee along with them at the same speed, if the unit pursues then he must pursue with them as well, if the unit declares a charge then he must charge as part of it. Some implications of this are discussed in the following paragraph.

If a unit of troops *panics*, or is forced to flee because of a Fear or Terror test, then any character who is part of the unit must also flee even if he is immune to *panic, fear* or *terror*. If the unit is affected by *frenzy* or forced to pursue because of *hatred*, the character must move along with the unit but does not benefit from any bonus unless he is affected by *frenzy/hatred* himself. In other words, a character does not go into a *frenzy* just because he is with a unit that can do so, although he has no choice but to accompany them when they charge.

If a unit is affected by *stupidity* any characters must move as the unit moves, although the character can fight normally unless he is *stupid* himself. Remember, a character cannot leave a unit when it turns *stupid* and stands still or moves stupidly because such a unit is bound by a compulsory movement rule, the character must therefore stay put. We can imagine he is trying to goad the stupid creatures into activity, or perhaps he is pinned down or hemmed in by the dribbling brutes and unable to move of his own volition.

If a character is liable to a Terror or Fear test which doesn't apply to the rest of the unit, he can ignore any tests. For example, if a character who is subject to *fear* is in a unit of *fear*-causing troops, such as Ogres, and is charged by enemies who cause *fear*, he does not have to take a Fear test.

STONE THROWERS, CANNONS & CHARACTERS

Some shooting weapons, such as stone throwers, have an area template that the firer can place anywhere he wants. This allows the player to deliberately aim his shot at a character. Cannons also allow you to choose exactly where to aim shots, and so can be aimed directly against characters, as do the breath weapons of Dragons, for example.

In the case of missile weapons that can be aimed in this way, there is a special rule which allows characters to either jump out of the way, throw themselves to the ground, or somehow avoid destruction by their amazing luck or uncanny reactions. This is intended to prevent characters becoming targets for these weapons in a manner which is unrealistic, unfair and definitely unheroic!

This rule applies to all missile weapons which work in a different way to ordinary shooting, and which are not therefore restricted by the rules regarding shooting at characters described above.

"LOOK OUT, SIR!"

A character model who is part of a unit of five or more rank and file models may be lucky enough to avoid death from cannon shot, a boulder from a stone thrower, or any other attack using a template (such as spells which use templates), thanks to a warning shouted by a comrade. Possibly one of his companions shoves him out of the way, or pushes him to the ground. A warrior spots the fateful missile heading towards his leader, and shouts "Look out, Sir!" or some such warning, and hopefully alerts the character in time for him to duck or adroitly avoid the hurtling missile. The missile slips past the character and hits the man standing beside or behind him.

If a character is part of a unit of models of similar size (cavalry models cannot benefit from this rule in a unit of infantry, for example) and is hit by cannon fire, a stone thrower, or other missiles not governed by the normal target restriction, then roll a D6.

On the roll of a 1, the character fails to hear the warning and is hit. Work out damage as normal.

On a roll of 2 to 6, the character is alerted to the danger and avoids the missile. The character is not hit and the missile strikes another model instead, so transfer the hit onto the closest rank-and-file model in the unit.

Note that some magic spells work like conventional shooting, in which case the normal rules for shooting at characters with arrows, etc, will apply. In other cases, magic works in different ways, either like cannons or stone throwers or differently altogether. This is covered further in the Magic section.

CHARACTERS
RIDING MONSTERS

If a character is riding a creature that causes *fear* or *terror*, then the entire combined model of rider and mount is assumed to cause *fear* or *terror*. The rider is only affected by *fear* and *terror* in the same way as the mount he is riding and any tests that are required are taken using the rider's Leadership. See the Psychology section for a detailed explanation of how this works. For example, a Dragon causes *terror* and so is unaffected by *fear* or *terror* – it is a huge monster and is hardly likely to be upset by smaller, less frightening creatures. A Dragon rider is also immune to *fear* and *terror*. Perched on top of a huge Dragon his courage is bolstered beyond the point where he has to worry about such things.

MOUNTS AND PSYCHOLOGY

If a monster is subject to some inhibiting psychological effect, such as *hatred* or *stupidity*, then the appropriate tests must be made. However, all Leadership tests can be taken using the rider's Leadership characteristic. This represents the rider's ability to control the beast and impose his own will over the creature's natural instincts.

If the monster is affected by *frenzy, stupidity, hatred,* etc, it will carry its rider along with it, but the rider himself is not affected by the psychological reaction. So, if a monster goes *stupid* and is unable to fight, this does not affect the rider who continues to fight on as normal.

The same rule applies to monsters pulling chariots: any Psychology tests are taken using the best Leadership value of the chariot's crew.

SHOOTING PENALTIES

Remember that a character riding a large monster does not benefit from the -1 to hit penalty when being shot at. This penalty only applies when shooting at roughly man-sized characters on foot. Also, the rider and large monster will suffer from the +1 to hit bonus when shot at if they represent a large target.

SPECIAL CHARACTERS

The Warhammer Army books include several different types of characters, be they Wizards or Heroes. However, we can easily imagine all kinds of wild individuals with different characteristic values from those given in the army lists. The characters described above are 'standard' types. They are typically representative of their race, and of the sort of Heroes and Wizards you can expect to find in a Warhammer army. Variant types of character, those differing from the standard types, are referred to as 'special characters'.

Special characters are the Warhammer equivalent of famous warleaders and mages, individuals renowned amongst their own kind and abhorred by their enemies. For example, they can be the mighty leaders of nations, such as the Emperor Karl Franz of the Empire, Orc and Goblin Warlords such as Grom the Paunch of Misty Mountain, Malekith the Witch King of the Dark Elves, Hotek the renegade Priest of Vaul and many more besides. There are also important military leaders and high ranking nobles, such as Bretonnian Dukes, Elector Counts from the Empire, and devious Skaven Seers. All of these special characters are quite different from the standard types. Some are better fighters than others, but some are better leaders, while many carry specific magical weapons or ride large monsters.

Numerous special characters are described in the Warhammer Army books and other Warhammer supplements and, of course, players can get together and make up their own if they wish. After all, who can resist the temptation to create a mighty leader of armies in their own image, to paint and perhaps even model him to suit their heroic vision, to name and invent a past for their character, and to fight him in battle after battle!

GENERALS & BATTLE STANDARDS

Every army has a heroic character to command it. We refer to this character as the **General**, although this is only to distinguish him from other heroes. He might be an Orc chieftain, a Bretonnian duke, an Elector Count of the Empire, etc. Many armies are commanded by the ruler of their entire nation. For example, the Emperor of the Empire and King of Bretonnia are mighty warriors who are ever ready to ride out at the head of their forces.

The General of your army is always the character with the highest Leadership value. If several characters have the same value then choose one to be the General at the start of the battle. He is in command of the whole army and represents you personally. The General is an important character because he can inspire others to fight on where otherwise they might turn and flee.

GENERAL'S LEADERSHIP

Any unit within 12" of the General model may use the General's Leadership value instead of its own when making a Leadership-based test. This means that a unit near the General can use his superior Leadership when testing for Break tests in close combat, when attempting to rally, for Psychology

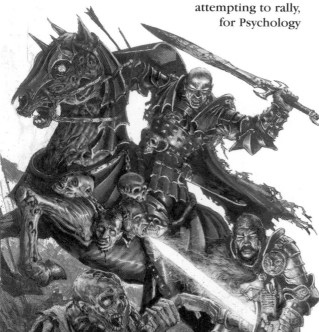

tests such as *fear* and *panic*, and for any other Leadership-based test. This rule ceases to apply if the General is fleeing.

THE BATTLE STANDARD

A General can be accompanied by a special Standard Bearer carrying either his personal banner or the Battle Standard of the army itself. This Battle Standard does not have to move along with the General but it is most useful when he is close by.

An army's Battle Standard is usually carried by a character model who has appropriately heroic characteristics. Unlike ordinary standards the Battle Standard cannot be passed on if its bearer is slain. Should the bearer be slain then the Battle Standard can be captured in the same way as a unit banner. See the rules concerning standards for details.

COMBAT BONUS

A Battle Standard Bearer can join a unit of troops in the same way as any other character. If he is with a unit that is fighting in close combat then the unit receives an extra +1 combat bonus when working out combat results if the Battle Standard Bearer is placed in the front rank of the unit.

Troops fighting alongside their banners only receive +1 no matter how many banners are involved. A unit with both a Standard Bearer and the Battle Standard Bearer will only receive +1 Combat Result bonus.

RE-ROLL BREAK TESTS

Any unit within 12" of the Battle Standard may retake a failed Break test. The unit is only allowed to retake any Break test once, a re-roll may never be re-rolled.

If the General is within 12" of the unit as well then it will also benefit from being able to use his Leadership value. These two factors combined, the General's Leadership and the opportunity to re-take a failed throw, mean that units near to the General and the Battle Standard will tend to hold their ground come what may.

Note that a Battle Standard allows a unit to retake a failed Break test – and only a Break test. It does not entitle a unit to retake any other Leadership test, such as a Psychology test or a test to rally.

MONSTERS

The Old World is a vast and untamed place where wild and monstrous creatures roam the dark forests and tall mountains. There are many creatures roughly human in appearance, though a little larger than a man, such as Orcs, Trolls, and Minotaurs, but there are also bigger and more bizarre monsters: Griffons, Dragons, Manticores, to name but a few.

It is with these monsters that this section of the rules is concerned. Monsters may be ridden to battle by mighty Heroes and Wizards. Many of these beasts must be hand reared by their master if they are ever to accept a rider, so the great leaders of the Old World pay vast sums to adventurers who collect eggs or hatchlings from the nests of Griffons and other winged monsters. This is a dangerous profession, and for many a fatal one, but it ensures that the Emperor's zoo in Altdorf gains fresh creatures to rear on behalf of the nobles and Wizard Lords of the Empire.

Monsters are powerful elements of the army. Some monsters develop loyalty and devotion to their masters and will willingly fight for them, while others are placed under enchantments or simply driven forward towards the enemy in the hope that they will attack the right side.

MONSTERS AS UNITS

Monsters can fight as if they were a unit consisting of one model. They do not have to turn or wheel to change direction, but can pivot about on the spot without penalty. They require line of sight if they want to charge or shoot, just like units of troops.

MONSTER MOUNTS

Monsters are most commonly employed as mounts for characters. A monster and its rider or riders count as a single model in the same way as a cavalry model, although different rules apply.

Horses, wolves, warboars and other similar sized creatures that only have 1 Wound are covered by the rules already described for cavalry. As you will recall, a mounted Knight is a cavalry model. If the Knight is slain then the complete model is removed including the horse he is riding. To represent the value of the horse and to make cavalry appropriately resilient an extra +1 is added to the Knight's saving throw, but otherwise no account is made of separate casualties for mount and rider.

This system is fine for these smaller creatures, but obviously wouldn't work for big monsters such as Dragons which are far larger and much more difficult to kill than a horse or a wolf.

If a mount has 2 or more Wounds then it is classed as a **monster** and the following rules are used for riders and mounts. These rules would therefore apply to a Hero riding a Griffon, a Wizard mounted on a Wyvern, a Dragon and its lordly rider, and so on. No additional +1 is added to the rider's saving throw, as the advantages of riding the monster are worked out in other ways instead.

SHOOTING AT A MONSTER MOUNT

As a single model, the monster and its rider are considered to be a single target. It is not possible to shoot specifically at either the rider or the mount. All shots are taken against the whole model and any hits are randomised between the rider and monster as described below.

SHOOTING AT CHARACTER RIDERS

When you shoot at a character riding a monster the usual restrictions for shooting at characters apply, as explained in the section on Heroes and Wizards. However, some monsters are so big that the chance of being able to find a unit of comparably sized creatures to shelter inside or nearby is rather slim. A character riding a monster is therefore easy to pick out as a target. If the monster is a large target, the enemy adds +1 to his 'to hit' score.

The normal -1 to hit that applies to man-sized characters on foot does not apply to characters who are riding steeds or monsters. The whole target is simply so obvious that there is no doubt as to where the character is! You might wish to re-read the rules for shooting at characters in the Characters section to clarify this.

RANDOMISE HITS

When shooting at a monster and its rider, roll to hit the model as normal, adding +1 if the monster is a large target. Once you have established how many hits have been scored you must apportion them between the rider and the monster. For each hit scored roll a D6; on a roll of 1-4 the monster has been hit. Roll to wound the monster as normal. On a roll of 5 or 6 the rider has been hit. Roll to wound the rider as normal.

"There are countless worlds beyond the void of chaos, endless kingdoms to conquer, cities to sack, forests to burn, warriors to slay in their millions. But by Khorne, I have chosen this world to conquer, and conquer it I shall, even if it takes a thousand millennia."

Khastarax, Daemon Prince of Khorne

Work out wounds separately on the rider and his mount. Take any saving throws due to the target as normal. Most monsters do not have an armour saving throw as they have no armour, but some have scaly hide which confers a equivalent save. Riders are permitted saves for their armour, but remember that they do not receive the additional +1 save as cavalry troops do when riding smaller creatures.

If a monster has two or more riders (a very unusual combination) then randomise hits to see which rider is hit and work out any resultant wounds on that individual. If models are glued in place (as is likely) it will be necessary to make a note of any casualties suffered.

EXCESS WOUNDS

If a rider is slain and suffers more wounds than he has on his characteristic profile, excess wounds are discounted. They are not carried through onto the monster, nor onto a second rider if the monster has two riders. Similarly, any excess wounds inflicted on the monster are discounted, they are not carried over onto the rider.

 "The only good stunty is a dead stunty, and the only thing better 'n a dead stunty is a dyin' stunty who tells yer where to find 'is mates."

Black Orc Warboss Morglum Necksnapper

CLOSE COMBAT

In close combat, the enemy is faced with a deadly monster and, more often than not, a potent Hero as well. The monster will attack using its own characteristics, and the rider attacks separately using his characteristics. As the monster and rider are likely to have different Initiative values they might strike their blows at different times. These attacks are worked out entirely normally, one batch for the rider and one batch for the monster.

ENEMY ATTACKS

When it comes to attacking back, the enemy will be faced with two potential targets, the rider and the monster. The enemy can choose to direct his attacks against either the rider or the monster, and can distribute attacks between them in any way he likes.

The opposing player must state how many attacks are against the monster and how many are against the rider before he rolls any dice, otherwise all attacks are assumed to be against the rider.

Attacks are worked out exactly as normal, and the score required to hit will depend upon the relative values of the monster or the rider's Weapon Skill, like all hand-to-hand fighting.

SLAIN RIDERS & MONSTERS

Wounds must be recorded separately for the rider and his mount. If the mount is slain the rider may continue to fight on foot if you have a separate model to represent him. If the rider is slain, the monster will behave in an erratic fashion, possibly going wild and attacking either its own side or running rampant amongst both armies. Remember that these big monsters are often hand reared by their masters, and are likely to go uncontrollably wild if their rider is slain. Take a Leadership test against the monster's own Leadership (you may not use the Leadership value of the General for this even if he is within 12").

If successful, the player may control the monster as normal for the rest of the game. If the test is failed, roll a D6 and consult the chart opposite. Note that if the monster's rider is killed in close combat, you should resolve the combat first (ie, fight the combat until one side is broken or destroyed, resolve fleeing and rallying, etc.). If the monster is victorious than make the Leadership test on the first turn when the monster would be free to move and act normally.

VICTORY POINTS

Victory points are rewarded separately for the monster and the character riding it (see p.198).

Monster reaction chart

D6 Reaction

1-2 The monster makes for the nearest table edge as fast as it can and tries to leave the battlefield. The monster will avoid any troops or scenery blocking its way and will attempt to go round them to find an escape route. If attacked, the monster will fight back, but it will not charge of its own volition unless it is forced to do so by a Psychology rule. It will not use any breath or other range weapon. Once it has left the table, the monster will not return.

3-4 The monster attacks the nearest target that it can see, favouring enemy if there is a choice of two equally distant targets. It must charge if able to do so, and if unable to charge must move towards the nearest target it can see as fast as possible. Once in close combat it will fight, pursue, etc, normally. It will use any breath or other range weapon to attack the nearest troops if able to do so.

5-6 The monster remains steadfastly where it is, guarding the fallen body of its beloved master. The monster will not move but it will face towards and use any breath or similar ranged weapon to attack enemy who approach within range. If the monster is engaged in close combat it will fight, but it will not pursue fleeing enemy. It is unbreakable and immune to Psychology. The monster will remain by its master to the end, faithfully protecting him against harm or capture.

"Ere now! Wot do you think you're doin'?" bellowed the big Black Orc Boss. Furtive Goblin faces turned round and flinched instinctively. 'Nuffink Boss, just 'aving a bit of grub is all,' whimpered the bravest of the greenskins. 'Don't give me that. Yer up to sumfink...' The towering Orc looked round suspiciously. 'Where's Ratgash? You 'aven't... 'et im?' There was a shocked silence.

"Et Ratgash,' the Goblin sounded hurt. "Et Ratgash. That's disgustin' Boss. E's one of us ladz.'

'Besides,' squeaked another greenskin, "E's all grease and gristle 'im. Give us all innagestion e' would.'

'Then who is this then?' The Black Orc pointed a damning claw towards the meal. 'And none of yer lies or I'll give yer sumfink a whole lot worse than innagestion.'

'Er... Gitter, Boss. One of Maggot's lot. But 'e was dead when we found 'im.' The Goblin paused a moment. 'Corse 'e claimed 'e was just sleepin'... but that lot is all liars ain't they.' The Goblins nodded in unison. No Goblin really trusted another, and with good reason.

'Carry on then,' pronounced the Black Orc. 'And you'll save me a leg if you know what's good for you!'

FLYERS

Some creatures in the Warhammer world have wings and can fly, soaring quickly from one side of the battlefield to the other. Representing such creatures poses a few problems on the gaming table. As it is impractical to suspend heavy models over the tabletop the following rules are intended to capture the feel of fast moving aerial combat in a practical manner without worrying unduly about the third dimension.

FLYERS

All models capable of flight have the special rule Fly on their army list entry they belong to. For the sake of convenience they are termed as **flyers**. Flyers are moved during the player's Move phase along with other models.

There are two types of flyers: flying monsters and flying units. They share the same rules apart from a few expections given later. All flyer models are on square bases like other troops in Warhammer. This is more convenient and makes it easier to resolve close combats between flyers and other unts.

AIR AND GROUND MOVEMENT

Most flyers are also capable of moving along the ground by walking or running. If a flyer has a Movement value this represents its ground movement in the same way as any other model. When moving along the ground using its Movement characteristic the usual movement rules apply, as described in the Movement section. A flyer may choose to fly or move along the ground, but cannot do both in the same turn.

AERIAL MOVEMENT

In Warhammer, flight is represented by a 'long swoop' or 'glide' of up to 20". The flyer starts off on the ground, takes off, flies to where it wishes to go, and then lands. Flyers, therefore, begin and end their movement on the ground. Flyers never need to wheel or turn, but can always make their move in a direct line. Of course, they still need to see any target they want to charge or shoot at and have a 90° arc of sight to their front, as normal.

Flyers do not benefit from the extra Move distance conferred on ground moving models for charging or marching. The flying move is never doubled and flyers charge at normal speed as explained below.

FLYING CHARGES

A flyer may charge an enemy within its 20" flight move. The charge must be declared in the normal way and the enemy has the usual response options. The flying move is not doubled like a ground charge is. Note that a flyer must be able to see its intended target when charges are declared as normal, and can fly over models and scenery which would stop the charge of a normal model. Flyers that charge their enemy are placed into base contact with

the enemy unit in a normal manner (ie, flyers are positioned to the sides if the attack comes from the flank, to the rear if it comes from behind, etc).

MOVE PENALTIES AND RESTRICTIONS

Flyers suffer no movement penalties for changing direction, overflying scenery, or crossing obstacles. They may overfly other models, including enemy troops, without penalty. Flyers may not move, land in or take off from within a wood. If flyers wish to enter a wood, they must land outside it and walk inside using their ground movement in the next turn. Note that this applies to any terrain that both players consider would prohibit flying.

Flyers may not land on top of enemy formations – if they wish to attack an enemy they must engage in combat as described above.

WORKING OUT COMBAT

Close combat between flyers and their enemies is worked out in the same way as other combat, because flying monsters land at the end of their flying charge and then fight normally on the ground. Work out casualties for both sides and calculate the combat results as normal. The losing side must take a Break test and, if it fails, must flee just like in any other combat.

FLEEING FLYERS

The distance flyers flee is usually based on their flying Move rather than their ground Move. The normal flee distance for flyers is therefore 3D6" in common with all models whose move is more than 6". If flyers must flee along the ground due to some constraint which prevents them from flying, for example, if they are in the middle of a wood, then they flee 2D6" or 3D6" depending on their Movement characteristic, just like other troops.

Flyers pursue fleeing enemy in exactly the same way as ordinary troops. Their normal pursuit rate is therefore 3D6" and the same comments apply as for fleeing.

UNITS OF FLYERS

Most flyers are monsters, but some units of troops can fly too. Such units are clearly identified in their army lists. They follow all the normal rules for flyers given above, apart from the exceptions noted below.

SKIRMISH

Flying units always operate as skirmishers (see p.115).

CHARACTERS

Characters can never join units of flyers, even if they ride flying creatures. This is because characters ride large flying monsters, which are nowhere near as manoeuvrable as the light, fast creatures of flying units and will slow them down considerably.

STANDARDS, MUSICIANS & CHAMPIONS

So far we have described units as consisting of identical rank-and-file troops. However, more often than not, warriors march to war under the leadership of a captain or some other officer, to the accompaniment of a drum or horn and beneath the fluttering standards of their cities and rulers. The regiments of the Empire march under flags bearing the arms of their Electors and their Emperor. Bretonnians go to war before the glittering heraldic banners of their lords and King. Orcs wave banners covered in glyphs proclaiming the might and power of their chieftains.

Standards and drums also have a practical value: they are used to signal to the troops, direct their unit's movement and provide a highly visible point around which formation changes and manoeuvres can be made. The rules that follow represent the boost that Standards and Musicians give to a unit's fighting prowess.

POSITION WITHIN THE UNIT

The unit's Standard Bearer, Musician, Champion and any characters within it, must be placed in the front rank. When the unit turns round to face the side or rear, its Champion, together with the Standard Bearer, Musician and any characters in the unit, are automatically rearranged into the new front rank.

Except, as discussed elsewhere, these special models, including any characters that have joined the unit, are always positioned in the front rank, with the Standard Bearer in the middle. Only if all the character models cannot fit into the front rank alongside the Musician and Standard Bearer are they placed into the second rank. Characters in the second rank cannot take part in close combat in any way unless they are directly engaged, via a flank charge for example.

STANDARDS

A unit of troops may carry a standard which might take the form of a flag, banner, totemic idol or similar device. The standard is carried by a Standard Bearer. He is assumed to be armed and armoured like the other models in the unit and fights in exactly the same way. Although the model might actually lack a shield or substitute a spear for a sword, such things are ignored as making no difference to the unit's overall fighting ability. The Standard Bearer also has to carry a banner as well as fight, but he is chosen from the meanest and most determined individuals in the unit, and this more than makes up for any disadvantage suffered because of the weight and inconvenience of his standard or difference in his armour or weaponry.

The enemy cannot specifically attack Standard Bearers or Musicians as he can character models. Standard Bearers are not normally removed as casualties, as it is assumed that if the Standard Bearer were killed another warrior would pick up the banner and take his place. Therefore, the player can always remove an ordinary warrior in preference to a Standard Bearer, even if the ordinary warrior is not in base contact with the enemy.

COMBAT RESULT BONUS

If a unit includes a Standard Bearer then it will be more determined than ever to beat its foe. A unit which has a Standard Bearer may therefore add +1 to its combat result when deciding which side has won a close combat. See the Close Combat section for a complete description of how to work out which side has won a combat.

CAPTURING STANDARDS

If a unit is defeated in close combat and subsequently breaks and flees then the enemy automatically captures its standard if they pursue. The standard is captured regardless of whether the pursuers catch and destroy the fleeing troops. Standards are also captured if an enemy unit is completely destroyed in close combat.

If victors do not pursue then the standard is lost in the tide of battle but it is not captured. In either case, the Standard Bearer model is removed from the unit, and in the case of a unit which is not destroyed, it is replaced with an ordinary trooper model.

Note that standards are only lost if the unit is defeated and broken in close combat, not if the unit flees after it has *panicked* or because of a failed Fear test.

Captured standards may be placed behind the unit which captured them and carried about as trophies for the rest of the game. Trophies have no fighting value; they are merely used to indicate that the unit has captured its adversary's flag. The player's Standard Bearer model is surrendered for the duration of the game and his jubilant enemy places it behind his unit to proclaim his victory (or removes it from the table if this is more convenient).

Trophies may be recaptured along with the defeated unit's own standard if it breaks and flees from combat. Captured trophies may therefore be recaptured by defeating the unit that has them, thereby avenging their initial loss and restoring them to a proper place of honour.

Once the game is over, a player can claim extra Victory points for standards he has captured and still holds, as described in the Scenarios section.

MUSICIANS

An army marches under its banners but it does so to the beat of drums and the call of blaring horns. A unit of troops may include a Musician model, either a horn blower or a drummer, to accompany it into battle. Like Standard Bearers, Musicians fight just like an ordinary member of their unit, even if the model itself has slight variances in armour or weaponry. Also like Standard Bearers, the player does not have to remove Musicians but can substitute an ordinary model instead. Unlike Standard Bearers, Musicians are not removed automatically when a unit breaks and flees from combat. Their instruments are somewhat lighter and less cumbersome than a weighty standard. Musicians cannot be captured as trophies.

A Musician model is placed in the front rank of its unit. His effect on the fighting ability of the unit is not as great as a Standard Bearer but is useful nonetheless.

RALLYING AND DRAWN COMBATS

If a unit of troops has a Musician in its front rank then an inspiring horn blast or rousing drum beat can turn retreat into a stalwart defence.

A fleeing unit with a Musician will gain a +1 Leadership bonus in any attempt to rally (note that a unit's Leadership cannot be increased to more than 10 in this way). Also, if close combat is drawn but one side has a Musician and the other doesn't, the side with a Musician wins the combat by one point. If both sides have a Musician then the result is still a draw.

CHAMPIONS

A unit of troops can often include a single Champion. He can be bought as an upgrade to a normal model in the unit as described in the Warhammer Army books. Champions are often extremely strong, tough or astute members of their race, and comrades look up to them and take pride in their prowess. Champions of units have various names depending on the army they fight for; Orc Champions can be called Bosses, while Empire Champions can be called Sergeants or Marksmen, for example. No matter what their name, Champions always follow the same rules.

Although powerful, Champions are not characters but members of their regiment and always fight as part of it, moving, attacking, fleeing and pursuing alongside the unit as a whole. If the unit has any special rules which apply to it then these also apply to the Champion. Unlike characters, a Champion never moves and fights on his own, and can never leave his unit or join another one. They are effectively another model in the unit with enhanced characteristics. If killed in close combat, any excess wounds caused against them are carried over to normal rank-and-file models in the unit.

The Champion is always armed and equipped in the same way as the rest of his unit, unless otherwise noted. The Options entry in each army list tells you whether you can upgrade one of the unit members to a Champion. Except where noted elsewhere, the Champion is always placed in the front rank along with the unit's Standard Bearer and Musician.

Unlike Standard Bearers and Musicians, you can direct attacks against Champions and kill them – if a Champion is removed as a casualty he is not replaced by another Champion. Even though they are not characters, Champions are subject to the following rules which govern characters: they can accept and issue challenges and benefit from the 'Look out, Sir!' rule. See the Characters section (p.94) for details.

BATTLE OF THREE TOWERS

I remember well the day when the armies of the Empire mustered to defend their land against the Lords of Ulthuan. I marched to battle amongst the ranks of the Stirland halberdiers, and fought against the Elves, hand-to-hand, from dawn till dusk.

We know not whether the foe came for plunder or the secrets of the bygone ages. But they were upon us in an instant, an army of spearmen in glittering mail coats, cohorts of keen-eyed Elven archers and silver-helmed knights, and even two great serpentine dragons like which the world has not seen in many ages.

See the great skull of a Dragon Araugnir now stands here in the Hall of Trophies. The great Wyrm was slain by the Nuln battery of Great Cannons. Their captain was decorated for their bravery with the Laurels of Victory after the battle.

The blade you see before you was a trophy from the duel between Grand Master Heydrich and the Elven prince commanding the enemy. The Lord of Templars vanquished the Elven Lord and it was this decisive fight which finally broke the spirit of our foes and made them retreat from the field leaderless.

SPECIAL RULES

Many troops in the Warhammer game have unique and unusual abilities and skills. These range from supernatural abilities, such as the regenerative powers of Trolls and the fiery breath of Dragons, to the natural protection gained by Lizardmen from their scaly hides.

In the game these abilities and special skills are represented by special rules. Any creature may have one or more special rules and, unless otherwise mentioned, the effects from special rules are cumulative.

The following list is by no means exhaustive, but it does detail the most common special rules and should serve as a good reference source.

SCOUTS

These troops are skilled at sneaking forwards to scout out the enemy before the main force arrives. By making the best use of cover, advancing at night, or with other troops providing a diversion, they are able to deploy ahead of the rest of the army.

Scouts are set up after both armies have been deployed. They can be set up anywhere on the table, at least 10" away from the enemy and must be out of the sight of any enemy troops and in or behind interposing terrain (not out in the open!). If both armies contain troops with this ability, each player should roll a D6, with the player scoring the highest choosing whether he deploys before or after the enemy's Scouts. Two opposing groups of Scouts cannot be set up within 10" of each other.

Alternatively, Scouts can be placed on the controlling player's deployment zone like any other troops, after deployment of both main armies is finished.

IMMUNE TO PSYCHOLOGY

Some warriors and creatures in the Warhammer world are almost completely fearless, or such grizzled veterans that scenes which would make lesser troops panic have no effect on them.

Troops that are immune to psychology are never affected by *fear, terror, frenzy* or any other Psychology rules. Troops immune to Psychology may never flee as a charge reaction – they are far too proud and brave to do this! These troops still have to take Break tests as normal.

UNBREAKABLE

Some creatures are utterly fearless and will never give up a battle, no matter how hopeless the situation might be. This could be because of the troops'

extreme bravery, or because the creatures fighting are not truly alive.

These troops never break in close combat, and they are also immune to *panic, terror* and *fear* or any other Psychology rules. If defeated in close combat (even by *fear*-causing creatures that outnumber them) unbreakable troops continue to fight on regardless of results. They may never, however, declare that they are fleeing as a charge reaction, as they will literally die fighting under any circumstances.

SCALY SKIN

Some creatures, the reptilian Lizardmen in particular, have tough, scaly skin which acts exactly like armour. This save can be variable. Lizardmen Skinks, for example, have a scaly skin save of 6+, while mighty Dragons could have a save of 3+ or more! The effectiveness of the scaly skin can be combined with armour, so a model with a 5+ scaly skin save and a shield would have a 4+ save. Note that scaly skin is an armour save for all intents and purposes, and may be modified by high Strength, etc.

KILLING BLOW

Some warriors have honed the craft of killing into an art. Tales are told of the master swordsmen of the White Tower who can decapitate a man with one stroke of their blade – their victims barely registering the sword leaving its scabbard.

If a model with the Killing Blow special ability rolls a 6 when rolling to wound, he automatically slays his opponent without recourse to a saving throw, apart from Ward saves.

This attack is only effective against roughly man-sized opponents such as Men, Orcs, Elves, Beastmen, etc.

It has no effect on big creatures such as Ogres or Dragons, or things like swarms which consist of several creatures. It can be used against models mounted on steeds or monsters as long as the riders themselves are roughly man-sized.

REGENERATION

A creature with this ability may try to regenerate any wound on a D6 roll of 4+. Only one attempt may be made on each wound to regenerate it.

Troops that are able to can regenerate damage if not too badly hurt. Work this out as follows. When attacked in close combat, shot at, or the target of spells, calculate the number of wounds suffered as normal. Once all attacks for the phase have been made, the creature may try to regenerate. Roll a D6 for each wound suffered during that phase. If a 4 or more is rolled, that wound has regenerated. You may only try to regenerate any single wound once. Any regenerated wounds are reinstated, and models removed as casualties are replaced if enough wounds are regenerated.

The results of combat, panic, etc are worked out after creatures have regenerated (the number of wounds inflicted does not include any that are regenerated).

For example, three Trolls (which can regenerate) are fighting five Empire Knights. The Knights strike first and inflict 5 wounds, enough to kill one Troll and cause 2 further wounds. The remaining two Trolls inflict 3 wounds on the Knights. The Trolls now test to regenerate and successfully regenerate 3 wounds. The 3 wounds are reinstated, the 'killed' Troll is replaced, and the 2 wounds suffered are noted down. The Knights have scored only 2 wounds in the end while the Trolls have inflicted 3. Assuming no other combat bonuses apply, the Trolls have won.

Fire

The flesh of a regenerating creature cannot regenerate if it has been burnt. If a regenerating creature or unit sustains one or more wounds from a flame attack it cannot regenerate any wounds during the remainder of the battle, not even those inflicted by ordinary weapons.

MAGIC RESISTANCE (1-3)

Some supernatural creatures are resistant to magic, or are protected by divine mystic powers or mighty sorcerers.

A creature with magic resistance will be difficult to harm with magic. The number in the brackets indicates the maximum number of extra dice that may be rolled when trying to dispel each spell that affects the magically resistant creature. For details of dispelling see the Magic section.

POISONED ATTACKS

Some warriors of the Warhammer world use lethal toxins to envenom their weaponry. The Dark Elf Adepts of Khaine and the Skinks of the steaming jungles of Lustria are the most noted exponents in the use of poisoned weapons.

A warrior with poisoned attacks will wound his target automatically if he scores a 6 when determining whether he hits his opponent in the Shooting or Close Combat phases. Armour saves are taken as normal. Unliving targets (such as war machines) are immune to poison as are some troop types. These are clearly defined in their description.

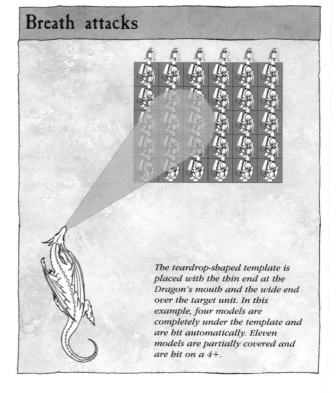

Breath attacks

The teardrop-shaped template is placed with the thin end at the Dragon's mouth and the wide end over the target unit. In this example, four models are completely under the template and are hit automatically. Eleven models are partially covered and are hit on a 4+.

BREATH WEAPON

Fiery Dragons and the dreaded Hydras and Chimeras of the Chaos Wastes, as well as some even more bizarre creatures, have the ability to breathe fire, noxious gas, lightning or even stranger breath weapons.

A model with a breath weapon may use it in the Shooting phase. Use the Flame template, placing the broad end over your intended target as you wish and the narrow end next to the creature's head. Any model that lies completely under the template is hit automatically – models whose bases lie partially under the template are hit on a 4+. The strength and any special effects of the breath weapon will be detailed in the entry for each individual creature. Characters under the template are eligible for 'Look out, Sir!' rolls if they are in a unit.

Breath weapons may not be used as a stand & shoot charge reaction, and neither can they be used in close combat. A creature with a breath weapon needs time to belch forth its flames!

FLAMMABLE

Some creatures, such as Undead Mummies and Treemen, burn easily. A flammable creature hit by a flaming weapon or fiery spell will take double wounds, so every wound suffered by a flammable creature will be doubled to 2 wounds. Take any saves before multiplying the wounds.

SKIRMISHERS

A skirmish is an encounter between small groups fighting in loose or dispersed formation rather than formal ranks and files. Such an encounter might take place over a broad area of woodland or a group of buildings, where skirmishers can spread out to infiltrate the wood or occupy buildings. In a battle, only specified troops are allowed to skirmish, as indicated in their Army book. However, any units can adopt a skirmish formation in order to enter buildings, as described in the Buildings section.

FORMATION

A unit which can skirmish never moves in a rigid formation of ranks and files. Instead, it moves as a loose group or rough line. This enables skirmishers to move more quickly and to take advantage of minor folds in the ground, scrub, and other small features to shelter from shooting. The Warhammer Army books indicate which units are able to skirmish.

1" APART

Skirmishers are deployed on the battlefield in a formation consisting of a loose group. Models in a skirmishing unit are positioned up to 1" apart so that they are not touching each other.

FACING

A skirmishing unit does not have a specific facing and can see all round (ie, it has an arc of sight of 360°). Skirmishers can declare charges or shoot in any direction.

MOVING

Troops in skirmish formation move in a loose group with models up to 1" apart. Should the group be split as a result of casualties, or should individuals become divided from it for some reason, the player must rectify this in his next Movement phase.

MANOEUVRES

Skirmishing models are moved in the same way as individual character models. The unit does not turn or wheel and instead each model is moved in any direction without penalty. Once movement is complete, the entire unit must form a loose group or line with models no more than 1" apart.

OBSTACLES AND DIFFICULT TERRAIN

Skirmishers move around obstacles or over rough ground more easily than troops in formation. They suffer no movement penalties for crossing obstacles or for moving over difficult or very difficult ground.

DOUBLE PACE

Because they are not restrained by a close formation, skirmishers can move up to double their normal pace despite the proximity of enemy troops within 8". So, a skirmishing unit with a Movement characteristic of 4" moves up to 8" rather than 4".

Skirmishers do not double their 'doubled' move to charge or march. They simply move up to double their Movement rate all the time. Their standard move value is still used to work out pursuit and fleeing distances.

SHOOTING AND MOVING

Skirmishers moving faster than their standard Movement characteristic value are assumed to be concentrating on moving and are unable to shoot that turn. They are running too fast and do not have time to stop and shoot at their enemy.

SHOOTING

Skirmishers can shoot in any direction, though individuals models can be pivoted on the spot so that the unit looks more realistic (this does not count as movement).

Thanks to their special training and loose formation, skirmishers do not block the line of sight of other members of their own unit (including characters that have joined the unit).

Note that units of skirmishers block the line of sight to other units (see diagram). It is not possible to see through the gaps between skirmishing models.

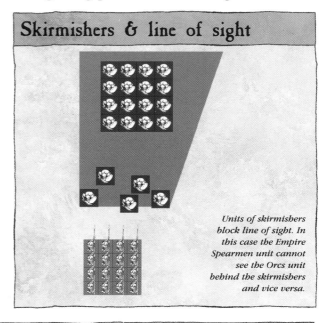

Skirmishers & line of sight

Units of skirmishers block line of sight. In this case the Empire Spearmen unit cannot see the Orcs unit behind the skirmishers and vice versa.

An enemy shooting at a skirmishing target suffers a -1 to hit penalty in the same way as if they were shooting at a single man-sized model. See the Shooting section for to hit modifiers.

If a character is fighting as part of a skirmishing unit of troops the -1 to hit penalty is applied only once, not twice.

CLOSE COMBAT

A unit of skirmishers may charge an enemy that is visible to at least one of its models when charges are declared. To decide which side of the enemy is charged, follow the normal rules: the skirmishers will charge the enemy in the arc where most of the skirmishers are when the charge is declared. All models within charge reach are moved individually towards their foe and arranged into a fighting line.

When the maximum number of models has been brought into base-to-base contact with the side charged (including models fighting corner-to-corner), remaining skirmishers will begin to form up in ranks behind the first line of models in base contact with the enemy.

Any models unable to reach the enemy (because they don't have enough movement or because there is no space left in the fighting line) are placed in the rear ranks so that the unit forms up in what looks like a regular formation behind the models that have formed the fighting line (see diagram).

If the skirmishers are charged, the enemy is brought into base contact with the closest skirmisher and then the enemy unit is halted. The skirmishers immediately form up following the rules explained above and then the enemy will proceed with further charges. The charging enemy models attack first in the ensuing Close Combat phase as normal.

Skirmishers will remain in this formation as long as the combat continues, and adopt the loose formation as soon as combat ends.

SKIRMISHERS IN COMBAT

Skirmishers fight in a normal formation of ranks and files but, due to their nature as extremely light troops, they lose most of the normal bonuses that apply to units who fight in ranks.

Skirmishers receive no combat bonus for additional ranks in their formation.

Skirmishers do not negate the rank bonus of other units if they charge them in the flank or rear.

CHARACTERS

A character on foot can join a skirmishing unit and fight with it. No other characters (mounted, riding in chariots, etc) can join skirmishing units.

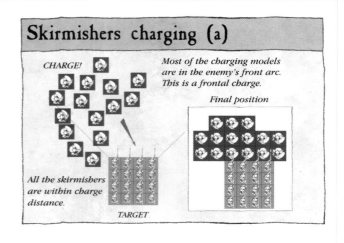

Skirmishers charging (a)

CHARGE!

Most of the charging models are in the enemy's front arc. This is a frontal charge.

Final position

All the skirmishers are within charge distance.

TARGET

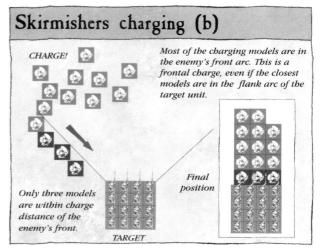

Skirmishers charging (b)

CHARGE!

Most of the charging models are in the enemy's front arc. This is a frontal charge, even if the closest models are in the flank arc of the target unit.

Final position

Only three models are within charge distance of the enemy's front.

TARGET

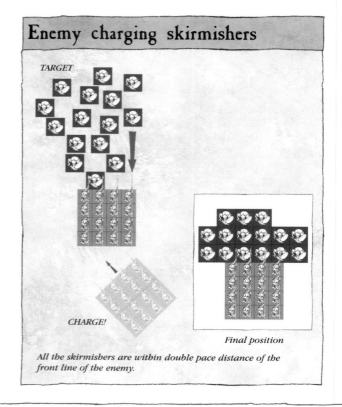

Enemy charging skirmishers

TARGET

CHARGE!

Final position

All the skirmishers are within double pace distance of the front line of the enemy.

FAST CAVALRY

Fast cavalry (sometimes called light cavalry) are riders of exceptional prowess, trained in lightning-fast manoeuvres and flank attacks. They are more lightly armed and armoured than heavy knights, but make up for this with their flexibility.

Troops that are **fast cavalry** are indicated in their relevant Army book. In battle, they act as scouts and outriders for the army, as well as harrying the flanks of enemy formations with their missile weapons.

FORMATION & MOVEMENT

A fast cavalry unit uses regular formations as do other cavalry and suffers penalties in difficult terrain. In fact they follow all of the normal rules for units apart from the exceptions detailed below. Fast cavalry receives no bonus for ranks.

FREE REFORM

Unless it charges, the fast cavalry unit is permitted to reform at any time during its Movement phase without incurring any penalties to its Move distance. See the rules for reforming (p.49). Note that none of the models in the fast cavalry unit can move more than their maximum move distance despite the free reform.

SHOOTING

CHOOSING A TARGET

Although it may sound unlikely, a well-trained horseman can turn completely around in his saddle and shoot behind him while moving forwards! When they are shooting, fast cavalry can fire all round regardless of the direction in which the model is pointing. Note that for charging, stand & shoot reactions, etc, the model needs to be facing the enemy as normal.

SHOOTING AND MOVING

Fast cavalry armed with missile weapons are expert at shooting from horseback (or wolfback!) and can therefore shoot even when marching. The normal -1 penalty for moving applies.

FLEEING FAST CAVALRY

Fast cavalry is extremely good at escaping from combat and regrouping. Unlike normal troops, a unit of fast cavalry which chooses to flee as a charge reaction and subsequently rallies at the beginning of their next turn may reform facing in any direction and is free to move during the Movement phase. If the chargers fail to catch the fast cavalry unit which declared flee as a charge reaction then the charge is a failed charge as normal. If the flee move of the fast cavalry does not take them beyond the charge reach of their enemies, the unit is destroyed as normal.

CHARACTERS AND FAST CAVALRY

Mounted character models may join fast cavalry units and move with the unit, but do not benefit from any of the special shooting rules.

Turning fast cavalry

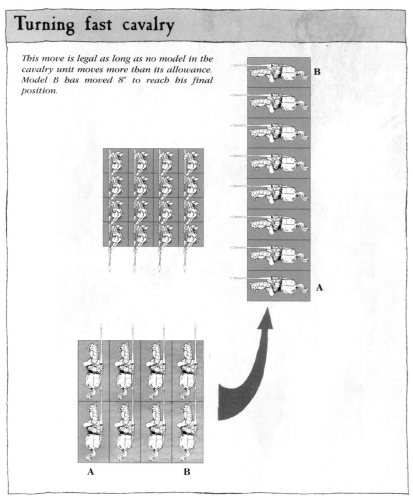

This move is legal as long as no model in the cavalry unit moves more than its allowance. Model B has moved 8" to reach his final position.

WAR MACHINES

War machines are an important part of many armies in the Warhammer world. Amongst the most spectacular of these engines of destruction are the gigantic cannons of the Empire and Dwarfs, but their manufacture is difficult and the secrets of gun casting and gunpowder manufacture are carefully guarded. Orcs and other less sophisticated races build gigantic stone throwers which lob boulders high into the air to come crashing down upon enemy formations or behind city walls. Bolt throwers are powerful giant crossbows that can send a spear-sized bolt clean through several ranks of enemy, skewering each in turn. These are all relatively common war machines that can be found in several armies, and thus their rules are included here.

MODELS

A war machine comprises the machine plus a crew, which is usually two or three crewmen. The crew are based separately, unlike with the model of a chariot or a ridden monster where the crew or riders are likely to be physically glued to the chariot or mount. This is necessary because a war machine's crew can be forced to flee from their machine, either because they are broken in combat or because they panic. Crew must be kept within 1" of the machine to count as crew.

MOVING A WAR MACHINE

The machine's crew can wheel, carry or move their machine, perhaps to gain a better position to fire. Note that a war machine may not march or charge.

AIMING A WAR MACHINE

A player may freely pivot a war machine to face any direction he likes before shooting. Apart from this, a war machine or the crew may not move and fire.

CHARACTERS

A character model may join a war machine in the same way as he might join a unit of troops. Note however, that war machines never include their own Champions – only units of troops are able to have Champions. The war machine benefits from the associated character's Leadership value in the same way that a unit of troops would.

"There are no problems that cannot be solved with cannons."

Chief Engineer Boris Kraus of Nuln

In the case of war machines, the character must be positioned within 1" of a specific machine for the purpose of allocating damage from shooting hits. However, only crew can operate a machine, a character cannot.

Characters do not actually become crew when they join a war machine and are never hurt should the machine malfunction. They are sensible or experienced enough to keep sufficient distance between themselves and the dangerous mechanism to be safe.

COMBAT

The crews of the war machines described over the following pages all fight in the same way, so rather than repeat ourselves several times over, the rules have been collated for ease of reference. Note that some of the war machines described in the Warhammer Armies books have their own special rules and those will be included with the appropriate army lists.

SHOOTING AT WAR MACHINES

When shooting at a war machine, shots are worked out against the entire model (both crew and machine) and any hits scored are randomised between the crew and war machine.

When shooting at a war machine, the shooter does not receive any bonus or penalty to his to hit score, unless a war machine is a large target. In which case the normal bonus of +1 to hit for large targets applies. This will be clearly indicated in the army list entry of each war machine.

Once hits have been established, randomise where they strike by rolling a D6. If 1-4 is the result, roll to 'wound' the machine. If the result is a 5 or 6, roll to wound a crewman.

Once all crew are slain, if they flee, or once the machine is destroyed, further hits do not need to be randomised but will strike a crewman or the machine as appropriate.

HITS FROM TEMPLATES

Any shots from stone throwers, or weapons that use a template, are worked out as follows. If a crewman lies under the template, he is hit. If the machine lies under the template, it is hit.

HITS ON CREW/CHARACTERS

Usually a machine's crew are identical, so it is not necessary to determine which is hit, but if a machine includes a character he may be hit by shots directed at the machine. In this case, randomise any crew hits to determine whether the character is hit. For example where there are two crew and a character roll a D6: 1-2=crewman A, 3-4=crewman B, 5-6=character.

CHARGE RESPONSES

If charged, a war machine's crew can either hold or flee but cannot stand & shoot as the machine is too cumbersome to allow this.

HOLD

In close combat, the crew will defend their machines. Models are moved so that they are interposed between their machine and the chargers in order to fight the enemy that comes into contact with the machine.

Enemy models can divide attacks between crew, characters or the machine that they are touching. The machine itself does not fight.

FLEE

If a machine's crew flees from a charge then the chargers can either continue to charge past the machine in order to destroy its crew or, if the player prefers, they can stop when they reach the machine and attack it. The machine itself does not flee as such, but is abandoned by its crew and any associated characters.

FLEEING CREW

If crew flee from close combat, their machine is abandoned. The victors must ignore it in order to pursue unless the player elects to restrain pursuit and passes the required Leadership test to do so.

Note that once they are separated from their war machines, crewmen become a fleeing unit. Consequently, the number of crewmen fleeing is used as the basis for any Panic tests on friendly troops nearby. For the purposes of rallying, the original number of crewmen is considered to be the original size of the unit.

ATTACKING A MACHINE

A war machine that is attacked in close combat is assumed to have a WS of 0 and is therefore hit automatically.

An enemy that is attacking an abandoned war machine is not considered to be engaged in combat. No combat results are worked out and the attackers are free to move away from the war machine as they wish.

ABANDONED MACHINES

An abandoned machine can be re-crewed by crew members from any other war machine from the same side if their own machine has been destroyed or if they abandon their machine. The entire crew may deliberately abandon a war machine in order to crew another. Crew models will not fight away from a machine and, if they are charged whilst not serving as crew, they will always flee.

WAR MACHINES AND VICTORY POINTS

In games where Victory points are awarded for fleeing or destroyed units, a war machine is considered to be destroyed for the purposes of calculating Victory points if either the machine has been destroyed or its entire crew has abandoned the machine (whether they have fled, been killed or moved away).

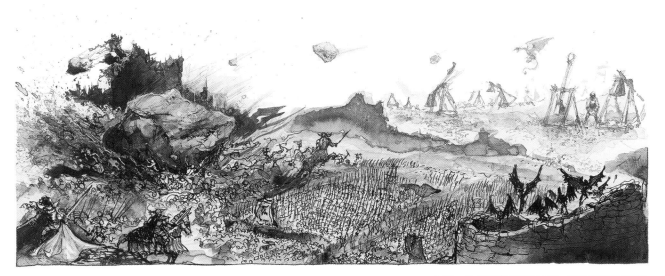

STONE THROWERS

These are powerful and destructive weapons that lob large boulders into the air, sending them crashing through enemy ranks. Many races in Warhammer use these devices. Not all are built in the same way: some use a massive counterweight to catapult their missile into the air while others use torsion power like a giant crossbow. The bigger the engine, the larger the rock it can throw and the more damage it can do. The very largest stone throwers can hurl a projectile big enough to knock down buildings and even city walls!

Work out the results of stone throwing in the Shooting phase. To work out damage you will need the small 3" round template. The stone is not as big as the template of course (that would require a very large engine indeed) but it shatters on impact sending shards of sharp stone over a wide area.

Pivot the stone thrower on the spot so that it is pointing in the direction it is going to shoot. The crew do not need to be able to see their target, but they must see that there are enemy in the direction they are firing. Then declare how far the rock is to be fired. Do this without measuring the distance to that target, so try to guess the range as accurately as possible. Once you have made your guess, place the template directly over that spot where you have guessed.

For example: A stone thrower is firing at a unit of Bretonnian Knights that are in front of the player. He makes his guess and declares that the stone thrower is firing 28" directly towards the centre of the Knights. He then measures 28" towards the target. If he has made a good guess the template will lie over its intended target. If not, there's still a chance the stone may veer off course and hit something.

To decide whether the missile lands where it was aimed roll the Scatter dice and the Artillery dice.

The Scatter dice is the dice marked with arrows on four sides and the HIT symbol on two sides. If a HIT is rolled then the missile lands exactly where it was aimed. If an arrow is rolled then the missile veers off in the direction shown by the arrow.

'S' funny,' muttered the Orc. 'Da uvver ones didn't do that.'

'Er, Boss,' wheedled the Goblin, tugging on the Orc's sleeve. 'Boss. That was Skragit, tha... urk!'

'Wot?' Growled the big Orc, grabbing the Gobbo by the throat and lifting him up to head height. The Gobbo began to go blue, but managed to point one trembling finger towards the arcing 'rock' that was now falling towards the enemy. 'Oh,' said the Orc, dropping the Goblin and turning to watch the 'rock' land in the midst of a regiment of humies. 'I was wonderin' why it was screechin'.'

Misfire chart

D6 Result

1 DESTROYED!

The engine cannot stand the strain placed upon it and breaks under the tension as it is fired. Bits of wood and metal fly all around, the stone tumbles to the ground splintering the engine and throwing debris into the air. The engine is destroyed and its crew slain or injured. Remove the engine and its crew.

2-3 DISABLED

The normal smooth running of the machine and its crew is disrupted by some accident or freak occurrence. A rope snaps and lashes about wildly, a crewman sets the machine up wrongly so that it pulls itself apart, or maybe a careless operator has become entangled in the mechanism. The engine does not shoot this turn and cannot fire next turn either while the damage is repaired. To help you remember, it is a good idea to turn the machine round to face away from the enemy. In addition, one of the crew is slain – caught by a snapping rope, entangled in the machinery, or thrown high into the air in place of the stone!

4-6 MAY NOT SHOOT

A minor fault prevents the machine shooting this turn. A crewman drops the stone as he lifts it into position, maybe a ratchet jams or a rope loosens. The machine is unharmed and may shoot as normal next turn.

The Artillery dice is marked 2, 4, 6, 8, 10 and MISFIRE. If a Misfire has been rolled then something has gone wrong – roll a D6 and consult the Misfire Chart above. A Misfire roll automatically cancels out the whole shot regardless of the Scatter dice result. If a number on the Artillery dice is rolled then this is the distance in inches the missile veers off target as shown by the arrow on the Scatter dice. Move the template the distance indicated in the direction shown by the arrow. If a HIT has been rolled then the numbers are ignored; a number simply indicates that the shot has not misfired.

For example: The player guesses bang on and the template lies directly in the middle of the chosen target. He then rolls both dice. The Scatter dice shows a HIT! It has landed right on target. The Artillery dice score is 4 – the number indicates that nothing is amiss and the shot lands exactly where it was aimed. If the Artillery dice had been a MISFIRE then the whole shot would have been messed up as described on the Misfire chart.

Number of models hit

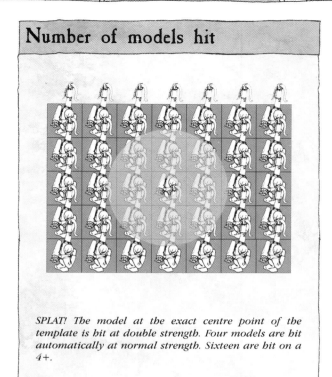

SPLAT! The model at the exact centre point of the template is hit at double strength. Four models are hit automatically at normal strength. Sixteen are hit on a 4+.

DAMAGE

Once it is established where the stone lands damage can be worked out. Any model that lies completely under the template is hit automatically – models whose bases lie partially under the template are hit on a 4+. See the diagram above for details.

You will have to use your judgement and common sense to decide exactly which models lie under the template – sometimes it is not easy to judge precisely.

Once it has been worked out which models are struck, work out damage in the usual way. Roll for each target to see whether it has suffered damage. Stone throwers have a Strength of 4 or more, so they cause damage on the roll of a 3+ or 4+ against most Human or similarly sized targets. Refer to the To Wound chart for details. A damaging hit from a stone thrower causes D6 wounds, but as most creatures have only 1 Wound it is not necessary to take this dice roll. It is, however, useful when attacking characters and big monsters.

Any single model which lies directly at the *centre* of the template suffers 1 automatic hit at *twice* the stone thrower's usual Strength – the stone lands directly on top of that model. This means that a stone thrower can potentially slay even a large monster or a powerful character.

No armour saving throw is permitted against wounds from a stone thrower. When a big rock lands on you, you are squashed regardless of what armour you may be wearing! Ward saves may be taken as normal.

PROFILES

Stone throwers vary in design – some are much bigger than others, whilst some may be positively monstrous! However, most stone throwers use the following profile:

	RANGE	STRENGTH	DAMAGE	SAVES
Stone Thrower	60"	4(8)	D6	No armour save

Being large, solid devices, stone throwers are difficult to destroy. However, it's possible for them to become the target of other engines of war or they may be attacked by large monsters. Stone throwers therefore have a profile like a creature with a Toughness value and a number of Wounds which they can sustain before they are destroyed. As with other details, these might vary in specific cases, but a typical engine has the values shown here.

The Movement rate is the speed which the stone thrower can move with its full crew – if any crew are slain then its speed is reduced proportionally. A machine cannot move and shoot in the same turn except to turn to face its target. Generally speaking, war machines have such a long range that it is pointless moving them about.

Movement	Toughness	Wounds
As crew	7	3

LOSS OF CREW

A stone thrower requires a full crew to work it properly – to carry stones, push the machine round to bear on its target, and so on. If one crewman is slain then the rest can just about get by without slowing up the machine noticeably. If two or more crewmen are slain then the remaining crew will be unable to cope and the stone thrower will have to miss a whole turn before it can shoot again. This is in addition to any penalty imposed by a Misfire result. Obviously, the engine requires at least one crewman to work, so the machine will become useless should they all be slain.

STONE THROWER SUMMARY

1) Declare target and guess range.
2) Position the 3" template and roll Scatter and Artillery dice.
3) If the Artillery dice is a MISFIRE, refer to Misfire Chart, otherwise...
   a) If the Scatter dice is a HIT, the stone has struck home.
   b) If the Scatter dice is an arrow the stone has landed in the direction shown 2", 4", 6", 8" or 10" away from the aiming point as shown on the Artillery dice.
4) All models completely under the template are hit automatically, those partially under are hit on a 4+.
5) Work out hits as normal. Models are allowed no armour saving throw from a stone thrower.

CANNONS

Cannons are dangerous, if sometimes unpredictable, weapons whose manufacture is limited to human and Dwarf experts. When they work, cannons can shatter the most determined enemy, pouring deadly shot into his massed formations, levelling his cities and toppling huge monsters. But cannons often go wrong. Weaknesses in the casting methods can leave minute cracks or other deficiencies which cause them to explode when fired, or gunpowder can fail to ignite or may explode prematurely. Despite the occasional spectacular accident, cannons are extremely potent weapons that have been instrumental in winning more than one battle on behalf of their users.

Cannons are fired in the Shooting phase along with any other missile weapons. To fire a cannon, it must first be turned on the spot so it points in the direction of the intended target. Then the player must declare how far the cannon is going to shoot – eg, 24", 30", 32", etc.

The cannonball travels the distance that the player has nominated, plus the score from the Artillery dice. Roll this dice and add the score to the distance that has been declared. The cannonball travels the total distance towards the target and will either land short, pass straight over, or hit depending on how accurately the player guessed the range and what effect the dice has.

Remember the dice will always add at least 2" to an estimate, and can add up to 10", so you should aim a few inches short of the target.

Once it is established where the cannonball hits, place a small coin or other marker directly over the spot. The cannonball does not stop where it hits the ground but bounces straight forward and cuts a line through any targets in the way. To determine how far the cannonball bounces, roll the Artillery dice again and mark the spot where the cannonball comes to land. Any models between the points where the ball

A war rages across the Old World: It is a war between Law and Chaos. Between steel and forest. Between truth and lies. Between fathers and sons. Between life and death. It is a world where the din of battle never grows silent, and for each warrior who falls in battle ten youths take up arms. It is a grim world filled with peril and danger. Take up your arms. It is time for war.

strikes the ground and where it eventually comes to land are hit by the flying cannonball. This line is considered to be a template for rules purposes (such as 'Look out, Sir!' rolls).

When a cannonball collides through a unit, only one model per rank is hit. The diagram below shows how this works.

Any model struck by a cannonball takes a Strength 10 hit resolved in the normal manner. If the cannonball wounds its target then it causes not 1 wound but D3 or D6 wounds depending on the size of the cannon. As most models have only 1 Wound anyway it will not be necessary to roll this extra dice, but it is important when it comes to rolling for Heroes, big monsters, and engines of war which can take several wounds. Wounds caused by cannon shot cannot be saved by armour. If a cannonball hits a model which has several parts then resolve which part of the model is hit just like shooting with bows, etc.

No armour saving throw is permitted for wounds caused by cannons. If a cannonball hits you, no amount of armour is going to do you any good. Ward saves can be taken as normal.

For example: A cannon is fired at a unit of Goblins that is in front of the player. He makes his guess and declares that he is aiming 12" directly towards the middle of the Goblin unit. Having made his guess the player then rolls the Artillery dice and scores a 4, which equals 4". This makes a total of 16". He measures 16" towards the Goblins and places a marker where the ball hits. If he has guessed well this will be just in front of them. The ball now bounces forward the score of the second Artillery dice roll. This time he rolls an 8 and the ball bounces 8" straight through the Goblin unit hitting all the models in the way.

GRAPESHOT

Instead of firing a normal shot, cannon crew can declare at the beginning of the Shooting phase that they are going to use grapeshot. In that case, place the Flame template straight in front of the gun. All models under the template (even if only grazed by it) suffer a Strength 4 hit (1 wound, -2 save modifier).

MISFIRES

The Artillery dice is rolled twice when a cannon is fired, so there are two chances of rolling a Misfire result. However, the two results will be different. If a Misfire result is rolled on the first dice, the cannon has literally misfired and may explode. If a Misfire is rolled on the Bounce roll then this merely indicates that the ball has stuck in the ground and does not bounce.

If a Misfire is rolled as the cannon is shot then consult the Misfire chart on the following page.

Misfire chart

D6   Result

1   DESTROYED!

The cannon explodes with a mighty crack. Shards of metal and wood fly in all directions leaving a hole in the ground and a cloud of black smoke. The cannon is destroyed and its crew slain or injured. Remove the cannon and its crew.

2-3   MALFUNCTION

The powder fails to ignite and the cannon does not fire. The crew must remove the ball and powder before the cannon can shoot again – which takes another turn. The cannon therefore cannot fire either this turn or the next turn. It is a good idea to turn the cannon round to indicate this.

4-6   MAY NOT SHOOT

A minor fault prevents the cannon from firing this turn, perhaps the fuse is not set properly or maybe the crewmen mishandle the loading procedure. The cannon is unharmed and may shoot as normal next turn.

If you roll a Misfire on your Bounce roll then the cannon is unharmed, the misfire result merely indicates that the cannon ball has stuck in the ground where it hits. If the shot lands on top of a model then that particular model is hit as normal, but there is no further bounce damage.

PROFILES

Cannons are hand forged by master craftsmen, and each is different with little standardisation in the way of calibres or length. Individual cannons can be huge, but most are either large cannons, such as the Empire Great Cannon, or smaller cannons.

Details are given below for typical examples. The difference between the two types is **range** and **damage**. Bigger cannons carry a larger charge and so have a longer range and cause more damage.

Machine	Range	Strength	Damage	Saves
Cannon	48"	10	D3	No armour save
Great Cannon	60"	10	D6	No armour save

Cannons are cast from iron or bronze and are built into solid carriages. They are very difficult to destroy, although the enemy may try to attack them with other war machines, large monsters or magic, for example. Therefore they have a profile with a Toughness value and number of Wounds which they can sustain before they are destroyed. As with other details these may vary, but the typical cannons have a value shown here.

The Move rate is the speed that the cannon can be moved by a full crew, assuming that the cannon's carriage has wheels. A cannon which does not have wheels cannot be moved. If any crew are slain, the cannon's speed is reduced proportionally.

A cannon cannot move and shoot in the same turn except to turn to face its target. Cannons have such a long range it is pointless moving them.

Movement	Toughness	Wounds
As crew	7	3

Firing a cannon

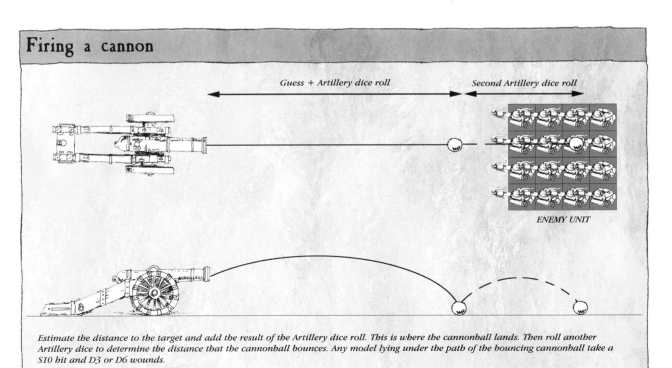

Guess + Artillery dice roll

Second Artillery dice roll

ENEMY UNIT

Estimate the distance to the target and add the result of the Artillery dice roll. This is where the cannonball lands. Then roll another Artillery dice to determine the distance that the cannonball bounces. Any model lying under the path of the bouncing cannonball take a S10 hit and D3 or D6 wounds.

LOSS OF CREW

A cannon requires a full crew to work properly – to carry cannonballs, load gunpowder, push the machine round to bear on its target, and so on. If one crewman is slain then the rest can just about get by without reducing the rate of fire. If two or more crewmen are slain then the remaining crew will be unable to cope, so when it shoots the cannon must miss a whole turn before it can shoot again. This is in addition to any penalty imposed by a Misfire result.

Obviously the cannon requires at least one crewman to work it, so the machine becomes useless should they all be slain.

CANNON SUMMARY

1) Align the cannon on the target and declare the distance you are aiming.

2) Roll the Artillery dice and add the score to the distance aimed. The cannonball travels forward this distance before striking the ground.

3) If you roll a MISFIRE refer to the Misfire chart. Otherwise, mark the point where the cannonball strikes the ground and roll the Artillery dice to establish the bounce distance. All models in the path of the bounce are hit.

4) If you roll a MISFIRE for the Bounce roll, the cannonball sticks in the ground and does not bounce.

5) Work out the effect of hits normally. Models have no armour saving throw for a cannon hit.

BOLT THROWERS

Bolt or dart throwers are large crossbows that shoot a spear-sized missile. They are so large that they are mounted on their own stand, often with wheels so they can be pivoted easily. A crew of two or more is required to wind back the powerful torsion arms and position the huge bolt ready for firing. On the whole, these weapons are nowhere near as large or cumbersome as stone throwers and cannons.

Bolt throwers are fired in the Shooting phase along with other missile weapons. To fire a bolt thrower it must first be turned on the spot so that it points towards its intended victim. The bolt travels straight forward and (hopefully) hits the first target in its path. In a unit of troops this will always be a regular trooper. Only if there are no rank-and-file troops in the first rank hit by the bolt will it be necessary to randomise which model in the first rank is hit.

To determine whether the bolt strikes its target, roll a D6 to hit using the crew's BS in the same way as bow shots, crossbows, and other missile weapons. The usual modifiers apply, except no penalty is imposed for turning the machine, as it is designed to be used in this way. See the Shooting section for details.

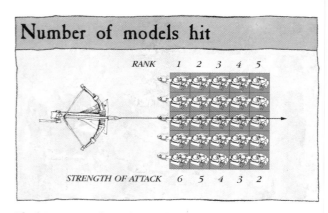

Number of models hit

RANK 1 2 3 4 5

STRENGTH OF ATTACK 6 5 4 3 2

If a hit is scored work out damage as described below. If the shot misses then the bolt hits the ground or sails into the air and comes down harmlessly somewhere else.

WORKING OUT DAMAGE FROM HITS

A bolt thrower is a powerful weapon which can hurl its bolt through several ranks of troops, piercing each warrior in turn. If it hits then resolve damage against the target using the bolt thrower's full Strength of 6. If the model hit in the first rank is slain then the bolt hits the trooper in the second rank directly behind: resolve damage on the second model with a Strength of 5. If the second rank trooper is slain then a model in the third rank is hit: resolve damage with a Strength of 4. Continue to work out damage as the bolt pierces and slays a model in each rank, deducting -1 from the Strength for each rank pierced.

A model damaged by a bolt thrower sustains not 1 but D3 wounds, which means that even large monsters can be hurt or slain by a hit from a bolt thrower. Armour saves are not allowed for hits from a bolt thrower because the missiles are so fast and deadly that any armour is pierced along with its wearer. As saves are not taken, a target with only 1 Wound will be slain if it takes damage, there is no need to roll the D3 to decide the number of wounds. Remember that Ward saves can be taken as normal against damage from a bolt thrower.

PROFILES

The bolt thrower hurls a sharp spear which causes considerable damage. The chart below shows its details.

Range	Strength	Damage	Armour saves
48"	6 -1 per rank	D3	No armour save is allowed

Bolt throwers are made from solid wood and iron. They have a profile like a creature, with a Toughness value and a number of Wounds which they can sustain before they are destroyed.

The Movement rate is the speed which the bolt thrower can be moved by its full crew. If a crewman is slain, the bolt thrower's speed is reduced proportionally. A bolt thrower cannot move and shoot in the same turn except to turn to face its target.

Movement	Toughness	Wounds
As crew	7	3

LOSS OF CREW

Some bolt throwers have a crew of two and if one crewman is slain then the remaining crewman can just about get by without slowing up the machine noticeably. Should a bolt thrower require a larger crew, then the loss of a second crewman will reduce its rate of fire to every second turn in the same way as for stone throwers and cannons.

BOLT THROWER SUMMARY

1) Align the bolt thrower on target and roll to hit.

2) Resolve damage at Strength 6. No armour save is allowed for a hit from a bolt thrower.

3) If the target is slain roll damage against the second rank at Strength 5.

4) Continue rolling for damage until you fail to slay the target or run out of ranks.

5) Deduct -1 from the Strength for each rank already pierced.

OTHER WAR MACHINES

Stone throwers, bolt throwers and cannons are common to several armies, but in addition there are many strange war machines that are available only to specific armies. These are described in the Warhammer Armies books together with the special rules that apply to them. Examples include flame cannons which spout a sheet of flames, devastating multiple-barrelled organ cannons, and the deadly Skaven warpfire throwers.

Some of these unique war machines are so different that they have entirely new rules, but others are similar to the machines described above in that they consist of a weapon and its crew.

In general, when shooting at such machines, all hits are randomised between the machine and crew in the same way as hits on stone throwers, cannons and bolt throwers. Also generally speaking, when in close combat with such machines the same rules apply as to the crews of stone throwers, cannons and bolt throwers. Exceptions to these procedures are described together with the special rules for the weapons in the appropriate Warhammer Armies books.

CHARIOTS

Chariots are capable of charging into the midst of enemy units, cutting them down like wheat with their scythed wheels. Most chariots have at least two crew with two creatures pulling the chariot – these creatures are normally horses, but many races of the Warhammer world utilise far more powerful and dangerous beasts. For example, Goblins capture and harness ferocious wolves to their chariots, while Orcs favour brutal, snorting warboars, and the chariots of the ruthless Dark Elves are pulled by croaking Cold Ones.

THE CHARIOT MODEL

A chariot, including its crew and the creatures pulling it, are considered to be a single model in the same way as a powerful character riding a large monster. Chariots can move and fight individually in the same way as character models or large monsters. Each chariot is, in effect, a unit of one model. However, note that spells which move individual models cannot move chariots as this would make them far too powerful.

Chariots have separate characteristics for the chariot itself, the crew, and the creatures pulling it, but some characteristics are not included in the profile as they are never used.

EXAMPLES OF CHARIOTS

Goblin Wolf Chariot

	M	WS	BS	S	T	W	I	A	Ld
Chariot	–	–	–	5	4	3	–	–	–
Crew	–	2	3	3	–	–	2	1	6
Giant Wolves	9	3	–	3	–	–	3	1	–

Armour save: 5+

High Elf Tiranoc Chariot

	M	WS	BS	S	T	W	I	A	Ld
Chariot	–	–	–	5	4	4	–	–	–
Crew	–	5	4	3	–	–	5	1	8
Elven Steeds	9	3	–	3	–	–	4	1	–

Armour save: 5+

Beastman Tuskgor Chariot

	M	WS	BS	S	T	W	I	A	Ld
Chariot	–	–	–	5	5	5	–	–	–
Crew	–	4	3	3	–	–	3	1	7
Tuskor	7	3	–	4	–	–	2	1	–

Armour save: 4+

CHARIOT UNITS

Some armies, most notably the army of the Tomb Kings, can group several chariots together into a unit. These are treated exactly as cavalry, though they can never gain a rank bonus. If chariots can be grouped into units, this is clearly indicated in the army list.

Any standard carried in a chariot gives its usual benefit in close combat (normal +1 Combat result bonus) and if a banner carried in a chariot is a magic banner, the magical effect of the standard applies as normal.

MOVING CHARIOTS

A chariot moves at the same speed as the creatures that are pulling it. Chariots of the Old World are massive, lumbering war machines and can therefore never march, although they double their move when charging in the same way as other models do. When moving a chariot simply measure the distance and move it. There is no need to turn or wheel, though the chariot still has to have a line of sight to any enemy that it is going to charge. In effect, chariots can turn to face any direction without reduction to movement.

Each chariot is pulled by two or more creatures. Their characteristics are listed in the chariot's army list entry as they affect the speed of the chariot and because the creatures fight in the Close Combat phase.

OBSTACLES & TERRAIN

Chariots cannot voluntarily move over obstacles or difficult terrain, except to cross a river at a bridge or a ford, that is safe to cross. A chariot compelled to move over terrain it cannot normally move through is likely to be damaged as its wheels strike rocks, its body becomes entangled in undergrowth, or it careens over a wall. If forced by circumstances into difficult terrain or over an obstacle, the chariot sustains D6 S6 hits. Apply these as hits from close combat and all the hits are directed toward the chariot. Chariots sometimes have to cross obstacles or difficult terrain, for example, if they are forced to flee from close combat. Chariots cannot charge over obstacles.

CHARIOT'S WEAPON SKILL

A chariot does not have a separate Weapon Skill, so when it fights in close combat, the enemy compares his Weapon Skill against that of the chariot's crew. If the chariot has crewmen with different Weapon Skill values then always use the highest.

SHOOTING AT CHARIOTS

When you want to fire at a chariot, treat it like any other unit. One of your units can choose it as a target and must direct all its shooting at it. Roll to hit and to wound against the chariot in the same way as against troops. Any hits scored are targeted towards the chariot as a whole, unless any characters are riding in the chariot (see Characters in Chariots). Some chariots are large targets and you therefore get a +1 to hit bonus when shooting at them. If the chariot is a large target then this is clearly indicated in the army list entry.

DESTROYED CHARIOTS & HIGH STRENGTH HITS

Just like any other creature, a chariot can only suffer a certain number of wounds before it is destroyed. Roll to wound as normal, and take any saves that apply as explained below. A chariot has a pool of Wounds which represent the chariot itself, its crew and the creatures pulling it. When a chariot loses its last Wound, remove the whole model from the battlefield.

If a chariot is hit and wounded by an attack which is of Strength 7 or more, it is destroyed automatically with no armour saving throw allowed – even the most strongest chariot can be blown apart if hit by a cannonball!

If a chariot is destroyed, all of its crew are automatically killed. Any characters in the chariot (see below) will suffer a single S5 hit if it is destroyed. If they survive, they may continue to fight on foot. Survivors are placed within 2" of the place where the chariot was. If the chariot was in close combat before it was destroyed, any surviving characters will continue the fight on foot.

CHARIOT SAVES

Most chariots have an armour save, just like troops, to take into account their heavy construction and the protection they offer to their crew. The army list entry clearly indicates the armour save value of each chariot.

CHARACTERS IN CHARIOTS

Characters can ride chariots in much the same way as large monsters. When shooting at a chariot, the hits are randomised between the character riding the chariot and the chariot itself. Roll a D6: on a roll of 6 the attack hits the character. Work out damage in the normal manner, except that the character either gains a +2 armour save bonus for riding the chariot or can use the armour save value of the chariot, whichever is the highest.

In close combat, enemies can choose whether to attack either the chariot or the character riding it (see overleaf).

CHARIOT ATTACK

Chariots are heavy, lumbering machines, which cause considerable damage when they charge. In addition to this, the crew and steeds pulling the chariot may attack, making a chariot extremely dangerous in combat when it charges.

IMPACT HITS

When a chariot charges a unit, it causes D6 hits with its own Strength. The number of hits is increased by +1 if the chariot is equipped with scythed wheels. These hits are inflicted first, before the close combat begins, and any wounds caused by the charging chariot count towards the combat resolution as normal. Remove any casualties as detailed in the Close Combat section. Like other casualties of close combat, the models killed by the impact hits do not get to fight.

The main danger from a chariot comes during its charge, so it is vitally important that it isn't outmanoeuvred and charged by the enemy. Chariots caught out in this way get no impact hits and are likely to be overwhelmed.

Impact hits against a unit of troops are worked out against the troops rather than against any characters in the unit (including the unit Champion). If a chariot charges against a single character on his own then the impact hits will obviously strike the character, but in other cases it is assumed that the character is canny enough to avoid the crushing chariot.

If a chariot charges another chariot ridden by a character, or a monster ridden by a character, the impact hits are never worked out against the character but rather against his chariot or mount. Crew and creatures pulling the chariot may attack the rider as normal.

CREW ATTACKS

Chariot crew may fight against enemy in contact with the chariot whether to its front, side or rear. They strike blows in normal Initiative order and attack during a charge, exactly like other warriors. All crew (usually two) fight, including the driver.

Crew and chariots may also shoot any of their missile weapons in the Shooting phase as normal (unless engaged in close combat) though a -1 to hit penalty applies if the chariot moves.

CREATURE ATTACKS

The creatures pulling the chariot may fight if they have their own attacks. Giant Wolves, for example, have their own attacks. Due to restrictions of harness and reins, creatures can only attack enemy directly in front of them. Work out attacks in Initiative order, but they will attack first during charges as normal.

ATTACKING CHARIOTS IN CLOSE COMBAT

You may choose to attack either the chariot (this includes crew and creatures pulling it) or a character riding in it (if present). In the case of characters, the protection of the chariot increases their armour save by +2 or use the chariot's armour save. Otherwise combat against characters in chariots is resolved in the normal manner. Attacks in close combat against the chariot are resolved exactly like they would be for shooting, (except that you roll to hit comparing your Weapon Skill against the highest WS of the chariot crew), and then record any wounds suffered.

CHARIOT CHALLENGES

A character in a chariot may issue or meet a challenge. He is considered to have stepped down from the chariot and the challenge is worked out as if the character was on foot. Any impact hits from the chariot are worked out against the unit rather than the character, as are the attacks of the creatures pulling the chariot and the rest of the crew; they are not part of the challenge. Only if the enemy character was on his own when the chariot charged are impact hits, crew and creature attacks worked against him.

FLEE AND PURSUIT

Chariots flee and pursue exactly like ordinary troops. If broken in close combat or forced to flee, they move 2D6" or 3D6" depending on their speed. If caught by pursuers, they are destroyed. Similarly, they pursue fleeing enemies at the same rate and will destroy them if caught.

VICTORY POINTS

Chariots yield Victory points for each individual chariot destroyed. Calculate Victory points for characters riding chariots separately.

CHARIOT UPGRADES

As indicated in the Warhammer Army books, some chariots can be upgraded as summarised below:

Chariot upgrade summary	
UPGRADE	EFFECT
Extra crewman	+1 additional crew attack per extra crewman
Extra steed	+1 additional steed attack per steed
Scythed wheels	+1 to impact hits

BUILDINGS

Buildings provide interesting terrain features on the battlefield. Not only are they attractive but they can also be important from a tactical point of view. Towers might overlook the battlefield providing an excellent vantage point for archers, Wizards or war machines. Troops deployed in buildings will be hard to winkle out and are able to defend their position against a much more numerous enemy. However, a good General knows that it is not always profitable to occupy buildings just because they are there, as it is easy to waste vital time taking a village that the enemy then ignores or circumvents. Players must weigh the tactical considerations for themselves, and decide whether or not a particular building has any tactical value. One way is to simply treat buildings as difficult terrain.

MOVING INTO AND AROUND BUILDINGS

It is not possible for units of troops to enter buildings, courtyards, or small walled fortifications in a conventional formation. In order to do so they automatically break into a skirmish formation (see the Skirmishers section). Although only specified types of troops can skirmish on the battlefield, any troops can skirmish in and around buildings.

ENTERING A BUILDING

Models may enter a building in their Movement phase by moving through an unguarded door or window which is judged to be large enough to accommodate them. A unit of troops may be divided between several buildings, or a building and the surrounding area. Models can leave a building through an unguarded door or window in the same way, but are not allowed to enter and leave the same building in a single turn.

INSIDE A BUILDING

The number of models it is possible to place inside a building will depend upon its size. If the model building has roofs and floors that can be removed, then the models can be placed physically inside, which simplifies matters considerably. However, most buildings do not offer this kind of facility, so players must decide before the game how many models the building can contain. Obviously, models that are too large to fit into the building cannot do so – a Dragon or Troll is simply too large to fit into a cottage!

Unless your buildings have removable roofs and floors you will need to keep a separate record of where models occupy a building. This can be done in any suitable manner, for example by writing down how many models are inside on a scrap of paper and placing the piece of paper under or beside the building. Point out to your opponent where troops are moving into buildings to avoid any confusion later on.

Except where buildings are really huge, you will not need to move troops about inside. Models inside the building are assumed to be wherever you wish, and can shoot from any windows, doors or other openings as opportunity permits. However, if a building is very large, roughly speaking more than 6" along any side, then this can lead to unreasonable situations. If a building were 24" long for example, it would be ridiculous to allow a model to romp from one end to the other in a single turn. Should you wish to employ such grandiose buildings then you must be prepared to either make them in such a way that models can be placed inside, or record movement within them by means of graph paper charts or maps, noting down where models are each turn.

SHOOTING

Models that are inside buildings can shoot from arrow slits, windows, doors or other openings. Up to two models may shoot from a single opening. Models on flat roofs, parapets, balconies or suchlike can also shoot. Troops occupying a building do not all have to shoot at the same target but shoot as individuals choosing permissible targets as you wish.

Models which have shot from windows or other openings in their own turn can be seen and shot at by the enemy in their turn. Models inside buildings benefit from the advantage of being behind hard cover (-2 to hit) as well as being in skirmish formation (a further -1 to hit).

FIGHTING INSIDE BUILDINGS

A unit that wishes to attack an enemy-held building must adopt a skirmish formation in order to move through doors or windows. This is automatically accomplished as soon as the charge is declared. Attackers can move straight through any unguarded doors or ground floor windows but must stop if there is a defender guarding the entrance.

Up to two models per side can fight across a window or doorway. The defenders benefit from the rule for fighting across defended obstacles, so the attackers will need 6s to hit regardless of their Weapon Skill characteristic (WS) until they win a round of combat.

When both sides have troops inside a building, and assuming that models cannot physically be placed inside the building model itself, it will be necessary to resort to a map or ground plan. Quickly draw out a rough ground plan of the building noting the position of windows and doors. Place the ground plan as near to the gaming table as possible. The defender places his models onto the ground plan and attackers are transferred over as they move into the building. Further movement and combat can then be resolved on the plan, and models transferred back to the gaming table as they leave the building.

DESTRUCTION

Buildings are very tough but not so tough that they cannot be destroyed by large machines or monsters. To represent this, buildings are given a Toughness value and a number of Wounds in the same way as other constructions such as war machines and chariots. As it is not strictly appropriate to talk about 'Wounds' in this context we refer to them as Damage points instead – remember that Damage points and Wounds are exactly the **same** thing.

LARGE BUILDINGS

If a building is very large it would be inappropriate to destroy it all at once. You might prefer to divide it up into several portions and consider each separately. Eg, a Lord's manor house could have a main hall and two wings. This would conveniently divide into three parts for the purposes of recording damage.

DAMAGE ON BUILDINGS

The chart below lists types of buildings and suggests Toughness values and Damage points for them. As many gamers make their own buildings you may prefer to tailor each building's values to its appearance.

Building chart

Type of building	Toughness	Damage pts
Mud or straw huts, light wooden shacks/outhouses	5	2
Timber or brick house or log built cabin	7	5
Stone house	9	5
Stone tower or fortification	10	10
Heavily reinforced & barred door	6	1
Secured fortress gate	8	5

If a building sustains its full quota of Damage points it collapses. Models inside a collapsing building must make their basic armour saving roll or they are trapped and slain. Models which pass their armour save may be moved outside the building.

We have included values for a variety of buildings as well as heavy doors and fortress gates, as you may wish to experiment with games where defenders shut the doors of their tower or castle whilst defenders attempt to batter down the defenses (see also the Siege rules in the Appendix section). Ordinary domestic doors are not considered to offer any significant defence.

AND FINALLY...

This section includes many suggestions and ideas rather than reams of hard and fast rules. This is simply because it is impossible for us to imagine what kind of scenery you have available or might wish to construct. Ambitious players might want to construct a whole townscape of temples and palaces, sorcerer's towers, public squares and who knows what! Rules for castles, keeps and towers are discussed in the Siege section.

If you make your own buildings, you will no doubt want to incorporate interesting features such as spiral stairways, sweeping bridges, gatehouses, drawbridges and so on. For example, a winding staircase could take half a turn to climb or a turn if it is very long, or a narrow corridor could allow passage to only four models per turn. Such matters are left to players to determine as they feel appropriate.

Then fame and renown
Of Sigmar, hammer bearer
Of the high king of the Dwarfs
Spread far and wide.
Sigmar the chief, mighty lord
Of Unberogens, and other tribes
Of Mankind.
Except for Teutogens
Who is this Sigmar?
Let us wage war on him!
Men against men, pleasing to Orcs.
Yet the gods shook their heads
Let Sigmar prevail. Let tribes be united
Let mankind be well led.
And vanquished was, the Teutogen chief
And for Sigmar was his hall.
Lord of all tribes, leader of Men.

MAGIC

Magic
Spell Lists
Magic Items

MAGIC

This section introduces such things as mighty Wizards, magical spells and sorcerous items into the Warhammer game. In the Warhammer world, magic is a very real force – a force to be both feared and respected. Only beings that possess awesome mental and physical power can even hope to bend the powers of magic to their will. Lesser persons would be consumed in an instant – their minds torn apart by unfettered energies and their souls dragged to the darkest underworld by cackling daemons. Even the most accomplished sorcerers walk a narrow path between ultimate power and eternal damnation.

You will learn much from the pages that follow about how magic works in the Warhammer world, about the different kinds of spells, and about the ever present dangers of meddling with dark, sorcerous forces. Before we begin, let us make sure that we are properly prepared!

WIZARDS

In the Warhammer game we commonly refer to a model able to cast spells as a Wizard. Some races use different terms, such as Sorcerer, Mage, Shaman or Seer, but all of these and others are considered to be types of Wizard. Their use in the game is covered by the rules described on the following pages.

SPELLS

In the player's Magic phase, his Wizards can cast spells. These can be terribly destructive, or powerfully protective, or might confer special abilities on the caster or other models. A comprehensive list of spells is given later.

In the furthest north, beyond the boundaries of sanity and the laws of nature, stands the wrecked gateway of the Old Ones, oozing with darkness and spewing forth mutating energy: the raw stuff of chaos. It is a bleeding wound, a tear in the fabric of reality, a gateway to another dimension. The shattered gate appears as a great ring circled by stone machineries, dwarfing the mountains around it. It is covered in runes of unimaginable potency, that glow in the darkness, their dancing shapes altering reality. From the dark reaches of the gateway pours out the winds of magic and mutating clouds of warpstone dust.

Some races have their own unique types of spell which they can use instead of those in this book. These are not described here as there are a great many, and they are only of specific interest to a player who owns that particular army. They are therefore included in the Warhammer Army book for each race.

MAGIC ITEMS

A magic item is an artefact or device imbued with magical power. Such items are not common in the Warhammer world and their extraordinary value and arcane nature means that they often take the form of treasured heirlooms belonging to noble houses or powerful magical covens. The kings and lords of the Old World possess many such devices but rightly fear to use them, except in the most dire circumstances.

We have provided a short list of magic items in this book. These are items of a relatively general type, the kind of artefacts which can be made and duplicated by an accomplished artificer of magic. However, most magic items are unique and their nature is strongly bound to the race that manufactured them. You will find many more magic items specific to each race described in the Warhammer Army books.

WIZARD LEVELS

No two Wizards in the Warhammer world are identical in power or knowledge, but in the game we divide Wizards into four degrees of ability called **Levels**.

Level 1: Wizards of the First Level are those of basic ability, although they are mighty practitioners of magic in everyday terms.

Level 2: Wizards of the Second Level are experienced spell casters whose powers are significantly greater than mere First Level Wizards.

Level 3: Wizards of the Third Level are great sorcerers of a kind rarely seen on the battlefield except in times of dire need.

Level 4: Wizards of the Fourth Level are the most mighty of all Wizards, the very equals of kings amongst the realms of sorcery.

The higher a Wizard's Level, the greater his ability to draw magical power from the swirling winds of magic, either for his own use or that of his fellow Wizards.

Each Wizard begins the game with one pre-generated spell for each Magic Level he has. We'll explain how to generate spells later. For now it is sufficient to know that First Level Wizards have one spell, Second Level Wizards have two spells, and so on.

CASTING SPELLS

In a player's Magic phase, which follows the Movement phase, each of his Wizards can attempt to cast each of his spells only once. Spell casting is determined by rolling dice, and the number of dice available to roll limits the number of spells that can be attempted. Fleeing or dead Wizards cannot attempt to cast spells.

Wizards cannot cast spells at units in close combat, unless specifically noted in the spell's description.

POWER DICE

At the start of the Magic phase, the player whose turn it is takes two dice and adds one further dice for each First Level Wizard, two dice for each Second Level Wizard, three dice for each Third Level Wizard, and four dice for each Fourth Level Wizard in his army. Some magic items also add bonus dice. All of these dice are called **Power dice**. The dice are expended throughout the Magic phase when rolling to cast

spells, so it is important that all of the Power dice are placed in a pile directly in front of the player where they can be seen, or alternatively placed into a cup, a box or some other convenient place where they will not get mixed up with other dice used in the game. Alternatively, the players may wish to use different coloured dice to represent Power dice. Fleeing or dead Wizards do not generate Power dice.

Power dice chart

LEVEL	NO. OF POWER DICE
Basic	2
Each First Level Wizard	+1
Each Second Level Wizard	+2
Each Third Level Wizard	+3
Each Fourth Level Wizard	+4

DISPEL DICE

At the same time as the player whose turn it is makes a pile of Power dice, his opponent makes a pile of Dispel dice. To do so, he takes two dice (four in the case of a Dwarf army) and adds one further dice for each First or Second Level Wizard, or Dwarf Runesmith or Runelord in his army regardless of Level, and two dice for each Third or Fourth Level Wizard in his army. As with Power dice, magic items can add to the Dispel pile. As with Power dice, the Dispel dice can be placed into a cup, box or some other convenient place where they will not get mixed up with other dice used in the game. The Dispel dice are expended throughout the Magic phase when attempting to dispel spells that have been cast by the opposing player. Fleeing or dead Wizards do not generate Dispel dice.

Dispel dice chart

LEVEL	NO. OF DISPEL DICE
Basic	2
Each First Level Wizard	+1
Each Second Level Wizard	+1
Each Third Level Wizard	+2
Each Fourth Level Wizard	+2

Once the players have gathered the appropriate number of dice into their Power dice pile or Dispel dice pile the player whose turn it is can begin to cast spells.

HOW TO CAST A SPELL

To cast a spell, a Wizard chooses and nominates one of his spells to cast and then declares the target of the spell.

Each spell has an associated casting value which varies from a minimum of 3 to a maximum of 15. When a Wizard attempts to cast a spell, the player can roll a number of dice from his Power dice pile equal to the amount indicated in the table below. So, for example, a First Level Wizard may only roll a maximum of two dice to cast a spell. The result is the total of the dice rolled.

For example, if one dice scores 4 the result is 4, if two dice score 4 and 6 the result is 10, if three dice score 3, 5 and 6 the result is 14.

Spell casting chart

Level of Wizard	Maximum Power dice rolled for a single spell
1	2
2	3
3	4
4	5

If the result equals or exceeds the spell's casting value the spell is successfully cast. If the result is less than the spell's casting value, it is not cast. In either case, all dice rolled are 'expended' and removed from the Power dice pile. As can be appreciated, the chances of casting a spell can be increased by rolling more dice, but doing so will reduce the number remaining and hence the chances of casting further spells.

If a spell is successfully cast, the opposing player can make one attempt to dispel it. He rolls as many Dispel dice as he wishes and compares the total of the scores with the score rolled by the caster's Power dice. If the result is equal to or higher than the caster's score, the spell is dispelled – it is not cast and has no effect. As Dispel dice are rolled they are expended, reducing the player's ability to dispel further spells.

MINIMUM 3 TO CAST

No matter how powerful a Wizard might be, he cannot cast a spell where the total of the dice result is less than 3. A result of 1 or 2 is always considered a failure, despite any modifiers. This is true regardless of any bonuses that might apply in any form, whether from a magic item or some other source. When rolling to cast a spell, a result of 1 or 2 is always a failure.

MISCASTS AND IRRESISTIBLE FORCE

So far we have seen that spells are cast by rolling a result equal to or more than the required casting score. In addition, there are two special rules that apply to all Wizards when they cast spells: these are **Miscasts** and **Irresistible Force**.

When rolling to cast a spell, if the player rolls two or more 1s, the spell is a Miscast. The spell automatically fails to cast regardless of the total result. Something goes horribly wrong. Refer to the Miscast table to discover what horrible fate has befallen your Wizard.

When rolling to cast a spell, any result of two or more natural 6s means that the spell has been cast with Irresistible Force. The spell is cast successfully and the enemy cannot attempt to stop it working, as described below. It cannot be resisted!

As astute readers will have realised, the chances of rolling a Miscast or Irresistible Force is increased by rolling more dice. Such is the nature of magical power! If a spell miscasts and is cast with Irresistible Force at the same time (eg, from four dice the player rolls two 1s and two 6s) then the spell counts as a Miscast. Miscasts take precedence in this case.

With Miscasts and Irresistible Force it is the actual dice scores that are considered, irrespective of bonuses and before any re-rolls from magic items are taken. A re-roll cannot cause a spell to be cast with Irresistible Force, nor can it prevent a Miscast.

DISPELLING A SPELL

Compared to our mundane world, the Warhammer world is drenched in magic. The very rocks of the planet are soaked with sorcerous power, the trees draw their sustenance from waters steeped in magic, and the air itself is impregnated with raw sorcery. Small wonder then that the creatures which live in the Warhammer world have developed a certain natural immunity to magic – an ability to resist the influence of magic upon their minds and bodies. Were this not the case then all life would have since mutated into abhorrent forms and the world would be overrun with slithering tentacled monstrosities.

To represent this natural ability to resist the influence of magic, we have the **Dispel roll**. After a player has cast a spell, his opponent can immediately make one attempt to dispel it using any number of his Dispel dice. Some magic items may allow a second attempt, or a re-roll, but these are exceptions and in normal circumstances only one attempt can be made to dispel a spell. You will notice that it does not matter who or what the spell has been cast at, it can always be dispelled.

In addition, the result can be increased further by the use of magic items. Any number of magic items can be combined to boost the score, but the player must declare that he is using any magic items **before** he makes the Dispel dice roll. It is not permitted to roll the dice and then decide to use a magic item retrospectively. Many of these magic items can only be used once, or a limited number of times, so it is important to be clear about whether you are using them or not before rolling the dice.

To dispel a spell, the player must score the same number or higher than the caster scored to cast the spell. For example, if the caster used four dice and got a result of 20, the dispelling player must score 20 or more on his Dispel dice to dispel the spell.

The crash of Dwarven boots echoed down the valley as rank upon rank of Longbeards, Hammerers and Ironbreakers marched along to the martial beat of the drums and the rising notes of war horns. On the hillsides above them dark shapes flitted from shadow to shadow. The Dark Elf scouts whistled to each other in the manner of birds, reporting the slow progress of the Dwarf King's army. They could see him now, borne upon his throne which was carried on the shoulders of four sturdy Dwarf veterans. As the Dwarf column reached the centre of the pass a piercing howl echoed across the mountains.

On the summit of Mount Blood, Morgir smiled grimly at her second-in-command Kherith.

'We'll give them a few more minutes, I want the rock fall to cut the King off from retreat. They will be caught like rats in a trap. Are your riders ready for the charge?'

'Yes, my lady! They wait in the copse to the east, and will charge as soon as the ground starts to tremble.'

'The King must not escape, I have need of him. His blood will be useful to me when I seize power from my brother. Dwarf blood, I am told, is very rich, and the blood of their High King will be a most useful bargaining tool with my master.'

The Dark Elf Knight shuddered despite himself. He dared not think what could possibly make Morgir more powerful. The screams of her rituals echoed around the tower on the dark nights, and the unearthly voices of the beings she summoned would vibrate through the black stone like an earthquake.

Morgir started to chant, gesturing frenziedly with her hands. The air grew hot and dry and Kherith felt the moisture being pulled from his body. A dark aura surrounded the sorceress now, and as she traced her arms through the air faint shadows were left in their wake. With a hideous screech Morgir snatched a dagger from her belt and plunged it into the acolyte standing beside her. As the Dark Elf's life bubbled away into the rough grass his mistress spoke the final incantation and the ground began to shake.

As the trees around them toppled to the ground Kherith's Knights charged from the woods, ahead of them the hillsides collapsed. A massive wall of rock and dust plunged into the valley bringing screaming death onto the heads of the Dwarf rearguard. The splintering of wood and the screech of tortured metal echoed harshly in the midday air, as the Dwarf's artillery train was crushed.

Screaming her triumph, Morgir lashed out at the bewildered Dwarfs with a bolt of darkness. As the magic arced down towards the valley floor the spell suddenly dissipated. Frowning, the Sorceress closed her eyes, seeking out what was amiss. There! Another wizard! Opening her eyes she scanned the Dwarfs' ranks and spotted a splash of red beside the High King, an Imperial Wizard of the College of Bright Magic. Even as she watched she saw a massive fireball hurtle into her Knights, smashing them from their saddles and turning the scattered woods into a massive ball of flame.

Summoning up the energies for another spell, Morgir laughed aloud. She still had plenty of power left and the Dwarf King's blood would be hers!

DOUBLE 1 AND DOUBLE 6

Trying to control massive magical energy to dissipate an enemy spell is extremely taxing and difficult, and can easily go wrong. Therefore, just as with casting spells, if two or more of the Dispel dice come up as 1s, the attempt to dispel a spell automatically fails. Regardless of how many bonuses you might have accrued from magic items, etc, a roll of two or more 1s is always a failure. If a player rolls two or more 6s when dispelling a spell, the dispel succeeds automatically. Note that an automatic fail takes precedence over an automatic success when dispelling a spell.

IRRESISTIBLE FORCE

As we have already noted, if two or more 6s are rolled when casting a spell, the spell is considered to have been cast with (adopt deep booming voice now) **Irresistible Force**! A spell cast with Irresistible Force is irresistible just like it says… you cannot dispel the spell and no Dispel roll can be attempted.

DWARFS

Dwarfs are legendarily resistant to magic and a Dwarf army always adds two extra Dispel dice to its pile. A Dwarf army therefore starts with four dice plus one per Runesmith or Runelord in the army.

MISCASTS

If a player rolls two or more 1s when rolling Power dice to cast a spell, this is a **very** bad thing. Something has gone terribly wrong with the spell. The Wizard, and by extension the player, is about to find out what kind of terrible consequences occur when foolish creatures dabble in things best left alone. We said that magic is a dark and dangerous power and how telling those words will become as you take 2D6 and roll on the Miscast table! Note that a Miscast spell never succeeds regardless of the actual number rolled by the Wizard.

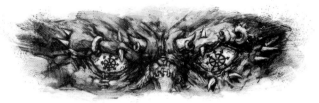

The Miscast table given below is a general table which is used for all races that do not have a specific table in their own Warhammer Army book. Some races derive their sorcerous powers from specific, and usually very nasty, gods or daemons, for which specific, and usually very nasty, Miscast tables are provided in the appropriate Warhammer Army books.

Miscast table

Roll 2D6 as your opponent cackles maniacally

2D6	Result
2	The collected magical power explodes in a ball of energy. Models in base contact, friend or foe, suffer one Strength 10 hit, as does the casting Wizard.
3	There is an explosion of dazzling colours and sulphur as the Wizard loses the control of the spell. The caster is blasted D6" in a random direction (use the Artillery dice to determine the direction) and cannot cast further spells until he rolls a 6 on a D6 at the start of his Magic phase. If blasted into another model he stops and both take one Strength 10 hit. If blasted into a wall, wood, or solid object, the caster takes one Strength 10 hit.
4	The magical energies escape as the Wizard loses his concentration. The opposing player may immediately cast any one of his own spells of the same casting difficulty rating or less. No casting roll is required – the spell is automatically cast – but it can be dispelled by the player whose turn it is by using Power dice in the same way as Dispel dice. A player needs to beat the basic casting value of the spell to dispel it.
5	The caster is knocked off his feet by a sorcerous explosion. He cannot shoot or attack this turn, is hit automatically in close combat and cannot cast any magic this turn or in his next turn, but is otherwise unaffected.
6-7	The caster loses control of his spell and struggles to keep the magical energies in check. He cannot cast any more spells in this Magic phase.
8-9	A massive vortex of power drains away the sorcerous energy. Any remaining Power dice held by the player are removed and the Magic phase ends.
10	The caster is racked by sorcerous power and suffers 1 wound with no saves allowed.
11	Ravaged by the power of Chaos the Wizard loses some of his power. The caster's Magic Level is reduced by -1 and he cannot attempt to cast the spell that he has miscast for the rest of the battle. If the caster's Magic Level is reduced to 0 he can cast no further spells for the rest of the battle, but he still counts as a First Level Wizard for the purposes of calculating the number of Dispel dice only.
12	The caster's mind is ravaged by the power of a hideous Daemon who's attention the spellcaster has drawn. The spell he attempted to cast is successful and counts as having been cast with Irresistible Force, but the caster cannot cast any more spells for the duration of the battle, and generates no Dispel or Power dice.

CHARACTERS AND UNITS AS TARGETS OF SPELLS

Note that characters on their own, large monsters, war machines, etc, are classed as units as well, so spells that target units can be cast on these targets. Characters in units cannot be targeted separately unless otherwise noted.

A unit is considered to be the target of a spell if any of the models in the unit are affected by the spell.

NATURAL DISPELS AND MAGICAL DEFENSES

Some units have a natural resistance to magic, or they are protected from hostile magic by magical artefacts they possess.

These often add Dispel dice to attempts to counter any spells. These dice may be used on their own as well – for example a unit may carry a magic standard which gives two Dispel dice against any spells which affect the unit. These can either be used on their own against any spell targeted against the unit, or in combination with Dispel dice from Wizards or other sources.

SPELLS WITH TEMPLATES

Certain spells utilise one of the templates provided with the game.

When using templates, any models whose base is completely under the template are considered to be affected by the spell. Models whose bases are not covered by it have been lucky enough to escape.

FLEEING WIZARDS

Fleeing Wizards are not allowed to cast or dispel spells. Fleeing Wizards do not add any dice to the Dispel dice or Power dice pool. Note that Wizards who are rallied before the Magic Phase **are** allowed to cast spells and can dispel as normal. Dispel dice can even be used if the player has no Wizards.

SPELLS IN PLAY

Most spells are cast instantly and their effect is worked out at once. For instance, the Fire Ball spell is cast, it strikes a target and damage is resolved. In this case, the spell has no further effect in the game during the same Magic phase, and the spell cannot be cast again in that Magic phase.

Some spells last for longer than this and they are said to *Remain in Play* or *Last One Turn*. These spells cannot be cast again while they remain in play.

DISPELLING SPELLS IN PLAY

After a player has finished casting his spells, his opponent is allowed to dispel any spells that remain in play (unless they were cast in the same Magic phase) if he has any Dispel dice left. Note that he only needs to beat the casting value of the spell in question – he does not have to beat the original casting score. In addition, these spells can be dispelled in the player's own Magic phase using any Power dice not being used to cast spells, as Dispel dice. Follow the same rules as given above. Note that a spell that was originally cast with Irresistible Force can be dispelled as normal in subsequent turns if it remains in play.

Magic phase sequence

1. CAST
The player decides that one of his Wizards is casting a spell. He nominates the target of the spell and decides how many Power dice he wants to use to cast the spell. The number of Power dice he can use is limited by the caster's level.

To cast a spell successfully, the caster must roll equal to or greater than the casting value of the spell. Add the results of the dice together to determine how difficult the spell will be to dispel.

If two or more of the dice come up as 6s, the spell is cast with Irresistible Force and cannot be dispelled. If any two or more dice come up as 1s, the spell is Miscast (refer to the Miscast table).

2. DISPEL
The opposing player may attempt to counter the spells using one or more of his Dispel dice. He will have to roll equal to or greater than the score rolled by the casting player. If two or more dice come up as 1s, the dispel automatically fails.

3. SPELL FAILS OR SPELL SUCCEEDS
Apply the effect of the spell if it succeeds.

4. CAST AGAIN
Provided that he has more spells to cast and more Power dice remain, the player whose turn it is can cast again.

5. DISPEL ANY SPELLS IN PLAY
Once the first player has finished casting his spells, the opposing player may dispel any spells in play if he has any Dispel dice left.

The casting player may use any remaining Power dice that he has to try to dispel spells in play.

The Battle of Blood Gorge

Blood Gorge was my first battle, and damn near my last. See this scar, and this? My empty sleeve, and this patch where my eye should be? They were all gained on that black day.

The Orcs had been restless all summer and finally swept down from the mountains like a Spring flood, smashing aside the militia, burning and pillaging all they could reach. By the time we'd mustered our scattered forces they were withdrawing with their loot back into the mountains. It was in Blood Gorge that we caught them, uncounted Orcs and numberless Goblins, eager for battle. I was young then, like you are now, and proud to lead the valiant but doomed Wolfenberg Halberdiers.

We fought like Unberogens, slaughtering dozens of the foul Orcs, but there were always more. Mind you, it's not just scars that I have from that day. No, I have other reminders of that grim battle. See here, the battered Orc shield I took from the dead hands of the beast that slew Beckmann. The cunning Orc had caught his halberd blade with it and disarmed him. I was too late to save Beckmann, but not to pay the brute back. Here too is the sword I finished that day with. Took it from one of our dead. Always carry two weapons lad, that's a lesson I learned the hard way. If I hadn't picked this up I'd not be talking to you now. See the fine pommel and the gold work? Forget 'em and look at the blade. Finest Estalian steel. That's what matters. That's what'll bring you back home. That's also what I used to relieve one of their spell casting witches of his head after he'd turned my hammer into a snake. This bird skull totem was his. And the Book? No I can't read any of it either. Magical, I'd say. Took it from the witch too, but it was loot. Not an Orc thing. Every time I look at it my eyes go funny, so now I don't. Head hurts? That's magic for you.

And this takes pride of place. The helmet that belonged to the biggest of the scum. The one who killed most of my brave lads. No, I'm fine, just got something in my eye. Yes, like I said, the Orc's helmet. It took a bit of a battering, but then so did the pair of us. Still, it's me with his helm and not the other way about, and for that I truly thank Sigmar. Now run along and play...

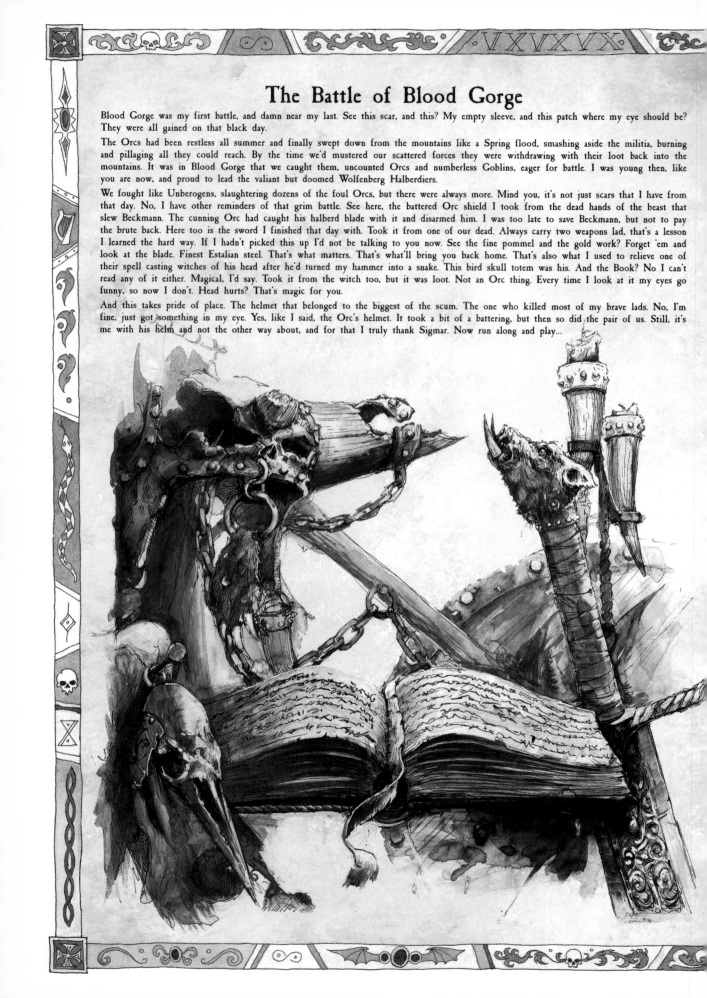

SPELL LISTS

The Warhammer rulebook describes eight different kinds of magical lore each of which is represented by six spells making a total of 48 individual spells. Each Lore is based upon one of the eight magical traditions of the High Elves whose learning far exceeds that of any other race in the Warhammer world. The men of the Empire learned their sorcery from High Elf mages and so use the same system as their basis of study – though their knowledge is by no means as great.

The sorcery of the other races of the Warhammer world is also based upon one or more of the eight kinds of magic but often includes spells unique to a particular race. The Warhammer Army books contain further spell lists for specific armies where appropriate. There are two other types of magic which do not directly concern us here – High magic and Dark magic. These are described in the Warhammer Army books for the High Elves and Dark Elves respectively.

THE EIGHT LORES OF MAGIC

The Eight Lores of Magic are listed here by the names that they are referred to in the following pages. These are not the only names by which they are known, by any means, but these terms will serve our purposes perfectly well.

The eight different Lores of magic in Warhammer are: Fire, Metal, Shadow, Beasts, The Heavens, Light, Life, and Death.

SELECTING SPELLS

The Warhammer Army books describe exactly which kinds of Lore are used by the different Warhammer races and provide further race specific spells in most cases. Those given here are used primarily by the Wizards of the Empire and by Elves, but form the basis for the magic of other races too.

All Wizards follow one particular kind of magical Lore. Where permitted, an army can include Wizards who follow different Lores or several of the same – this is up to the player.

Wizards have one spell for each Magic Level. Wizards of the First Level have one spell, Wizards of the Second Level have two spells, Third Level Wizards have three spells and Wizards of the Fourth Level have four spells.

The standard procedure for selecting spells is for each player to randomly generate a spell or spells for each of his Wizards before both sides deploy their troops.

This is normally done openly and opponents will therefore be aware of which spells their opponent has generated. A Wizard can always substitute one of his spells with the first spell that is on the list. For example, a Level 1 Wizard who chooses to use Fire magic and rolls a 5 (getting the Conflagration of Doom spell) could substitute this spell with the Fire Ball spell.

Players who wish to adopt some other method of selecting their spells, such as choosing spells or secretly generating random spells, are perfectly welcome to come to an arrangement between themselves. The spell lists include random generation charts and players declare before the battle which Lore of Magic each of their Wizards is using before generating any spells.

If both sides are using Wizards, roll a dice to see who generates his spells first. Start generating spells with the highest Level Wizards. If two Wizards in the same army are using the same Lore of Magic, they may gain duplicates of spells, but no single Wizard can have the same spell twice.

Two Wizards on opposing sides may use the same spell lists, thus both sides may have the same spells.

FIRE BALLS AND OTHER MAGIC MISSILES

Many spells are described as *magic missiles* – for example, Fire Ball. In this case, the Wizard conjures a ball of flame and hurls it at a target. All magical missiles are thrown, hurled, or projected in this fashion.

A magic missile can only be cast at a target if it would be a viable target according to the rules for shooting. For example, the Wizard must be able to see the target, and individuals can only be picked out from surrounding units in the same circumstances as archers, crossbowmen or comparably armed individuals can do so. Unless otherwise noted, magic missiles hit their targets automatically.

A Wizard cannot cast these spells if he is engaged in close combat.

CANCELLING SPELLS

It is quite possible for the effect of one spell to contradict the effect of another. For example, a unit which has a spell cast upon it by one Wizard which prevents it from moving might subsequently have a spell cast upon it by another Wizard that obliges it to move. In these cases, the most recent spell automatically dispels the previous spell.

The source of all magic is the bright realm whose airs form the substance of change and which is known to the wise by the name of chaos. All life lies balanced between the order of timeless idealised forms and the chaos of endless change. Order and chaos in equal measure and strength. Few understand this, for most men are flawed by ambition, desire and vanity so that their souls are blind to what is most pure and noble. So it is that many are drawn to the vice of wizardry. These fools scoff at danger, mistaking the wisdom of the aged for fear, and wise prudence for the coward's terror. It is as a warning that I write this. Reader! Mark well my words and let my fate be a lesson to all who would meddle with the powers of change.

As the dread Rune of Chaos has eight arrows so eight winds blow from chaos into the lands of time and, hence, through the minds of men. Upon each wind daemons ride into the world. Their whispering is the noise of the wind and their laughter rattles at our doors. These are the names of the Eight Winds of Chaos: Aqshy the Wind of Fire, Chamon the Wind of Change, Ghur the Wild Wind, Hysh the Serpent Wind, Azyr the Celestial Wind, Ulgu the Shadow Wind, Ghyran-the Wind of Life, Shyish the Wind of Death.

From these winds the sorcerers of this earth distil their spells, calling upon the aid of daemons and their minions as travel upon the winds of magic. Thus, in centuries past, grew the great traditions of sorcery which are practiced to this day for good or ill. These are their names as they are known to me.

From the Wind of Aqshy comes the Lore of Fire or Pyromancy.

From the Wind of Chamon comes the Lore of Metal or Alchemy.

From the Wind of Ghur comes the Lore of Beasts.

From the Wind of Hysh comes the Lore of Light.

From the Wind of Azyr comes the Lore of the Heavens or Astromancy.

From the Wind of Ulgu comes the Lore of Shadow.

From the Wind of Ghyran comes the Lore of Life.

From the Wind of Shyish comes the Lore of Death or Amethyst.

THE LORE OF FIRE

Fire magic is practiced in varying degrees of accomplishment by several races of the Warhammer world. In the Empire its secrets are kept by the Wizards of the Bright Flame, or Pyromancers, whose fire-topped towers rise above the city of Altdorf.

All of these spells are considered to be *Fire* attacks and cause double damage against flammable creatures (see the section on special rules, page 114). To randomly generate a spell roll a D6 and consult the chart below. If you roll the same spell twice for the same Wizard, roll again.

D6	Spell	Casting Value
1	Fire Ball	5+
2	Flaming Sword of Rhuin	6+
3	Fiery Blast	8+
4	Burning Head	9+
5	Conflagration of Doom	11+
6	Wall of Fire	12+

FIRE BALL   Cast on 5+

The fire ball is a *magic missile* with a range of up to 24". If successfully cast, the Fire Ball hits its target and causes D6 Strength 4 hits.

FLAMING SWORD OF RHUIN
Remains in play   Cast on 6+

This spell can be cast by the Wizard on himself. It can be cast even if the Wizard is in close combat. Once it has been cast, the spell lasts until the Wizard attempts another spell.

A magical flaming blade materialises in the Wizard's grasp. This counts as a magic weapon. The Wizard gains +1 additional Attack to his profile for the duration of the spell. All the Wizard's attacks will hit on a basic score of 2+ and he adds +3 to his Strength whilst using the *Sword of Rhuin*. Whilst he has the Flaming Sword, the Wizard must use it as his sole weapon, he cannot combine it with other weapons.

FIERY BLAST   Cast on 8+

The Fiery Blast is an especially dangerous *magic missile* – it is an upmarket version of the Fire Ball, being both more powerful and harder to cast. The Fiery Blast has a range of up to 24". If successfully cast, the Fiery Blast hits its target and causes 2D6 Strength 4 hits.

BURNING HEAD   Cast on 9+

A phantasmic flaming head shoots 18" from the caster in a straight direct path, laughing insanely as it burns a trail of destruction in its way. Each model that lies in the direct path of the Burning Head suffers a Strength 4 hit.

CONFLAGRATION OF DOOM   Cast on 11+

This can be cast on any enemy unit anywhere on the table. If successfully cast, the target bursts into flames taking D6 Strength 4 hits. The target can take further hits depending on how long the fire burns. To represent this both players roll a D6. If the casting player's dice score is lower than or equal to his opponent's, the flames go out and nothing else happens, but if he rolls higher, add the dice roll to the number of hits caused. Both players then roll a further D6 and repeat the process until the casting player rolls equal to or less than his opponent. Once the casting player fails to roll higher, the fire goes out and no further hits are caused.

WALL OF FIRE
Remains in Play   Cast on 12+

This spell has a range of 24" and can be cast on an enemy unit which is visible to the caster and which has no models (friend or foe) within 1" of its front rank (though walls, hedges and other scenic features don't matter).

A wall of fire rises in front of the unit. To represent this take some cotton wool or paper and place this in a line up to 1" thick in front of the unit.

The unit suffers 1 automatic hit for each model (including characters) in its front rank. For example, six models in the front rank would suffer 6 hits. Each hit is resolved with a Strength of 4.

Once it is cast, the Wall of Fire remains where it is until it is dispelled, or until the Wizard chooses to end it (which he can do at any time), attempts to cast another spell or is slain. No further hits are caused by the Wall of Fire unless a unit tries to move through it, in which case each model that moves through the Wall of Fire suffers a further Strength 4 hit.

The Wall of Fire does not block the line of sight of archers and chargers, nor does it reduce a unit's Movement rate.

THE LORE OF METAL

In the lands of Men, the Lore of Metal is more commonly known as Alchemy. It is practiced by many races, but few are as devoted to it as Men. If there is truth in common talk then there are many fortunes won by means of alchemical sorcery. The Alchemists of the Golden Order at Altdorf have the Emperor's ear in all matters of state and war – or so it is said by ordinary folk of the town.

To randomly generate a spell, roll a D6 and consult the chart below. If you roll the same spell twice for the same Wizard, roll again.

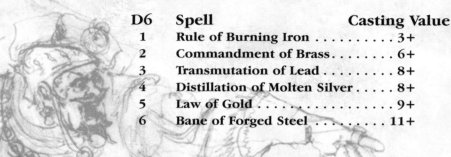

D6	Spell	Casting Value
1	Rule of Burning Iron	3+
2	Commandment of Brass	6+
3	Transmutation of Lead	8+
4	Distillation of Molten Silver	8+
5	Law of Gold	9+
6	Bane of Forged Steel	11+

RULE OF BURNING IRON — Cast on 3+

Burning Iron is a *magic missile* with a range of up to 24". If successfully cast, the spell hits a single model (chosen by the caster) and causes 1 S3 hit if the target has no armour save or a save of 6, 1 S4 hit if the target has an armour save of 5+, and 1 S5 hit if the target has an armour save of 4+ or better. This is a *Fire* attack and causes double damage against flammable targets.

COMMANDMENT OF BRASS

Lasts 1 turn — Cast on 6+

This spell has a range of 24" and can be cast on an enemy war machine or chariot which is visible to the caster and which is not already engaged in close combat. If successfully cast, the machine cannot move or shoot until the end of its own following turn. If forced to flee for whatever reason, the spell is broken and the unit flees.

TRANSMUTATION OF LEAD — Cast on 8+

This spell can be cast on an enemy unit that is within 24", and which is engaged in close combat. If successfully cast, the enemy's armour, weapons and other equipment are transmuted to lead for the duration of the ensuing Close Combat phase. The affected unit suffers a -1 to hit penalty in close combat, and armour saves suffer a -1 penalty during that turn's Close Combat phase.

DISTILLATION OF MOLTEN SILVER   Cast on 8+

The Distillation of Molten Silver is a *magic missile* with a range of up to 24". If successfully cast, a squall of molten silver hits the target and causes 2D6 Strength 4 hits. This is a *Fire* attack and causes double damage against flammable targets.

LAW OF GOLD — Cast on 9+

This spell can be cast on an enemy unit that is within 24" of the caster. The opposing player must nominate one magic item carried by any model in the unit. The caster rolls a D6: on the roll of 1-4 the item cannot be used until the end of enemy's next turn, on a 5 or 6 the item cannot be used for the rest of game. The Law of Gold has no effect on a unit that does not include any models with magic items.

BANE OF FORGED STEEL — Cast on 11+

This spell has a range of 12" and can be cast on an enemy unit which is visible to the caster. If successfully cast, the enemy's weapons begin to crumble and rust away. No weapon bonuses or penalties apply to the affected unit for the remainder of the battle. For example, a unit wielding Great Swords will not get their +2 Strength bonus in combat for the rest of the battle, but will now not have to strike last. A unit with missile weapons may not shoot for the duration of the entire battle. Affected units are assumed to use hand weapons instead. War machines and magic weapons cannot be affected by the Bane of Forged Steel – only ordinary weaponry carried by troops.

THE LORE OF SHADOW

In the land of the Empire, Wizards of the Shadow call themselves Grey Wizards, as if to distance themselves from the sinister reputation of their sorcery. They are more often called Trickster Wizards by the common folk, who mistrust and fear them. Shadow Lore is the magic of deceit and illusion, of trickery, concealment and darkness.

To randomly generate a spell, roll a D6 and consult the chart below. If you roll the same spell twice for the same Wizard roll again.

D6	Spell	Casting Value
1	Steed of Shadows	4+
2	Creeping Death	6+
3	Pelt of Midnight	7+
4	Shades of Death	8+
5	Unseen Lurker	10+
6	Pit of Shades	11+

STEED OF SHADOWS   Cast on 4+

This spell may be cast upon the Wizard himself or any single friendly independent character model within 12" of him – the spell can only be cast on a model on foot (it won't work on a mounted model or a model riding in a chariot, for example).

If successfully cast, the model can make a normal flight move of up to 20". The model can fly out of close combat if desired, but cannot fly into close combat unless positioned so that it could do so by making a normal aerial charge (for example, it must not be engaged in combat already and must be able to see the target).

CREEPING DEATH   Cast on 6+

The Creeping Death is a *magic missile* with a range of up to 24". If successfully cast, the Creeping Death hits its targets and causes D6 Strength 3 hits. No armour saves are allowed against wounds caused by the Creeping Death.

PELT OF MIDNIGHT

Remains in play   Cast on 7+

This spell can be cast on a friendly unit that is within 24" of the caster. If successfully cast, all subsequent shooting directed at the unit requires a 6 to hit. All weapons which use a Scatter dice to hit will scatter automatically when targeted at the unit.

Once it is cast, the Pelt of Midnight continues to work until it is dispelled, or until the Wizard chooses to end it (which he can do at any time), attempts to cast another spell or is slain.

SHADES OF DEATH

Remains in Play   Cast on 8+

This spell affects a single friendly unit within 6" of the Wizard which is not engaged in close combat. The unit now causes *fear*.

Once it is cast, the Shades of Death continues to work until it is dispelled, or until the Wizard chooses to end it (which he can do at any time), attempts to cast another spell or is slain.

UNSEEN LURKER   Cast on 10+

This spell can be cast on a friendly unit that is within 24", and which is not already engaged in close combat. The unit can immediately make a move of up to 8" in the same way as a normal move made in the Movement phase. The unit can charge an enemy within 8" if opportunity permits, and the same rules apply as for a normal charge made during the Movement phase. The enemy can only respond by holding their ground – the Unseen Lurker conceals the charger's intent until it is too late to respond in any other way.

PIT OF SHADES   Cast on 11+

The Pit of Shades can be cast on any one unengaged enemy unit anywhere on the table. If successfully cast, the ground falls away beneath the unit's feet toppling them to their doom.

Take the 3" template and place it over a single target enemy unit. All models in the target unit completely under the template are automatically hit and those touched by it are hit on a 4+ on a D6. Models hit suffer 1 Strength 3 hit. In addition, the player whose unit is affected rolls a D6: on a score of 1-3 the unit climbs out of the pit (this counts as moving for the purposes of shooting, etc) and moves at half speed next turn, on a score of 4-6 the unit is unaffected. The pit closes up after the unit has clambered out of it.

THE LORE OF BEASTS

The Lore of Beasts is the magic of Shamans and animal spirits. It is a sorcery of wild and primitive races, of creatures that shun the cities of Men, and of Men who have turned their backs upon the ways of their own kind.

To randomly generate a spell, roll a D6 and consult the chart below. If you roll the same spell twice for the same Wizard, roll again.

D6	Spell	Casting Value
1	Buccos the Oxen Stands	5+
2	Adlos the Eagle's Cry	6+
3	Ursos the Bear's Anger	6+
4	Corvos the Crow's Feast	7+
5	Kinos the Beast Cowers	8+
6	Lupens the Wolf Hunts	9+

THE OXEN STANDS   Cast on 5+

This spell can be cast on any friendly fleeing unit on the tabletop. If successful, the unit is rallied immediately.

THE EAGLE'S CRY   Cast on 6+

This spell can be cast on an enemy cavalry unit, swarm, chariot or a single ridden or unridden monster which is within 24" of the caster and which is not engaged in close combat. If successful, the creature/s become momentarily wild and uncontrollable.

The affected unit must take an immediate Leadership test. If passed, the unit suffers a -1 Movement penalty during their next Movement phase (-2" if it marches or charges). The Movement of flyers is reduced to 12". If failed, the unit/monster immediately makes a compulsory move of 2D6" directly towards its own side's table edge, but halts if this move brings it into contact with a friendly unit, impassable terrain, or within 1" of any enemy. If the unit moves off the tabletop, it counts as having fled the battle.

THE BEAR'S ANGER
Remains in play   Cast on 6+

This spell can be cast by the Wizard on himself while he is in close combat. He becomes as wild and powerful as a mighty bear. He adds +3 Attacks, +2 Strength, and +1 Toughness to his characteristics. He cannot wield a weapon whilst using this spell.

Once cast, the spell lasts until the end of the next combat engagement which the Wizard takes part in, until it is dispelled, until the Wizard chooses to end it (which he can do at any time), attempts to cast another spell or is slain.

THE CROW'S FEAST   Cast on 7+

Corvos the Crow's Feast is a *magic missile* with a range of up to 24". If successfully cast, a flock of crows mobs the spell's target and causes 2D6 Strength 3 hits.

THE BEAST COWERS   Cast on 8+

This spell can be cast on any enemy unit of cavalry, a chariot, a ridden monster, a lone monster such as a Great Eagle, or a swarm. The target of the spell must be on the tabletop and must be engaged in close combat.

If successfully cast, any creatures in the unit (but not their riders) will cower and therefore require 6s to hit in that turn's Close Combat phase. If 6s are required anyway, the creatures may not attack.

THE WOLF HUNTS   Cast on 9+

This spell can be cast on any friendly unit of cavalry, a chariot, a ridden monster, a monster on its own, or a swarm. The target must be within 24" of the caster and must not be engaged in close combat.

If the spell is cast successfully, the unit moves 2D6" towards the nearest enemy that it can see. If no enemy are visible then it will not move. If in doubt as to which enemy unit is nearest, the caster may choose but must do so before rolling the distance. If the distance is sufficient to reach the enemy, the unit is deemed to have charged and all the normal charging rules apply, except that the enemy can only stand their ground – no other charge response is possible due to the speed of the spell.

THE LORE OF THE HEAVENS

In the cities of Men, the Lore of the Heavens is called Astromancy. It is the magic of the sky and stars, of portents, fate and the movement of heavenly bodies.

To randomly generate a spell, roll a D6 and consult the chart below. If you roll the same spell twice for the same Wizard, roll again.

D6	Spell	Casting Value
1	Second Sign of Amul	5+
2	Portent of Far	6+
3	Forked Lightning	7+
4	Uranon's Thunder Bolt	9+
5	Storm of Cronos	9+
6	Comet of Casandora	10+

SECOND SIGN OF AMUL   Cast on 5+

This spell can be cast by a Wizard and gives the player a chance of re-rolling dice during the remainder of his own turn.

If successfully cast, roll a D3 to determine the number of re-rolls the player can make. Each re-roll entitles the player to take any single D6 dice (including one of the dice rolled on a 2D6, 3D6, etc.) he has rolled and roll it again. Any dice can be re-rolled but the player cannot re-roll a re-rolled dice… he only gets one chance to overcome a duff roll. Any re-rolls not used by the end of the turn are wasted.

PORTENT OF FAR   Cast on 6+

This spell can be cast on a friendly unit that is within 12" and which is engaged in close combat.

If successfully cast, all subsequent dice rolls of a 1 made either to hit or to wound by that unit can be re-rolled that turn. Re-rolled scores of 1 stand – you cannot re-roll a re-rolled dice.

FORKED LIGHTNING   Cast on 7+

This spell can be cast on any enemy unit on the tabletop. If successfully cast, the unit is struck by lightning causing D6 Strength 4 hits. These hits are distributed exactly like hits from shooting.

URANON'S THUNDER BOLT   Cast on 9+

This spell can be cast on any enemy unit on the tabletop. If successfully cast, the unit is struck by a thunder bolt causing D6 Strength 4 hits with no armour save possible. These hits are distributed exactly like hits from shooting.

STORM OF CRONOS   Cast on 9+

This spell can be cast on all enemy units which are visible to and within 12" of the caster. If successfully cast, all enemy units within range and sight are affected. Each unit takes D6 Strength 4 hits, distributed exactly like shooting.

THE COMET OF CASANDORA
Remains in Play   Cast on 10+

This spell can be cast upon any fixed point on the tabletop. If successfully cast, place a suitable marker over the exact spot affected – a small coin is ideal for this.

Once cast, the player rolls a D6 at the start of each player's turn (ie, at the start of his turn and at the start of his opponent's turn). On a score of 1-3 nothing happens, but place another marker on the first. On the score of a 4-6 the spot is struck by a comet. All units from either side which are within D6" multiplied by the number of markers already placed are struck by the comet. Each unit struck by the comet takes 2D6 Strength 5 hits. For example – if there are two markers in place and the D6 roll is a 4, all units within 4 x 2 = 8" are struck. If the spell is dispelled while in play, all the markers are removed.

THE LORE OF LIGHT

The Lore of Light is a magic of bright and radiant power, of the solar wind, and of life giving energy. Wizards who practice this art are sometimes called White Wizards or Heirophants. It is the magic of solar rituals, carefully guarded secrets and ancient ceremonies.

To randomly generate a spell, roll a D6 and consult the chart below. If you roll the same spell twice for the same Wizard, roll again.

D6	Spell	Casting Value
1	Pha's Illumination	5+
2	Shem's Burning Gaze	5+
3	Urru's Dazzling Brightness	6+
4	Ulzah's Healing Hand	7+
5	Karu's Guardian Light	8+
6	Amshu's Blinding Light	9+

PHA'S ILLUMINATION

Remains in Play   **Cast on 5+**

This spell can be cast by the Wizard on himself. Once it has been cast, the spell lasts until the Wizard attempts another spell or until it is dispelled.

The Wizard is swathed in power. Regardless of his characteristics, he has 3 Attacks and Strength 5 whilst this spell lasts. He cannot wield a weapon whilst using this spell. No magic weapons can be used to attack him whilst the spell lasts. Once cast, the spell lasts for the duration of the combat engagement until it is dispelled, until the Wizard chooses to end it (which he can do at any time), attempts to cast another spell or is slain.

BURNING GAZE   **Cast on 5+**

Shem's Burning Gaze is a *magic missile* with a range of up to 24". If successfully cast, the Burning Gaze hits its targets and causes D6 Strength 4 hits.

Burning Gaze is a *flaming* attack and so causes double damage on *flammable* targets, etc.

DAZZLING BRIGHTNESS   **Cast on 6+**

This spell can be cast on any enemy unit that is engaged in close combat and which is within 18" of the caster. If successfully cast, the target unit is dazzled and its WS characteristic is reduced to 1 for the duration of that turn's Close Combat phase.

HEALING HAND   **Cast on 7+**

This spell can be cast upon the Wizard himself or upon any friendly model anywhere on the tabletop that has already suffered one or more wounds.

If successfully cast, the model regains all its lost Wounds. In the case of a monster and its rider, choose one as the target of the spell. This spell has no effect on Undead models, Chaos Daemons, war machines, chariots or other unliving units.

GUARDIAN LIGHT

Remains in Play   **Cast on 8+**

This spell affects all friendly units that are within 12" of the caster. If successfully cast, all these units are now immune to psychology, and fleeing units automatically rally.

Once cast, the spell remains in play until it is dispelled, until the Wizard chooses to end it (which he can do at any time), attempts to cast another spell or is slain.

BLINDING LIGHT

Lasts one turn   **Cast on 9+**

This spell can be cast on an enemy unit which is visible to and within 24" of the caster, and which is not engaged in close combat. If successfully cast, the unit is momentarily blinded and its Movement characteristic is reduced by half (rounding down) and its WS and BS are reduced to 1. This lasts until the end of the unit's following turn.

THE LORE OF LIFE

The Lore of Life is the magical lore of the growing earth and as such is bound to the changing seasons. Few creatures of any race understand the nature of growing things as do these Wizards. It is a form of magic that exists in all water and vegetation and which is strongest when it is close to places where rivers run and where woods and forests grow most abundantly.

To randomly generate a spell, roll a D6 and consult the chart below. If you roll the same spell twice for the same Wizard, roll again.

D6	Spell	Casting Value
1	Siodh Silverhyl, Mistress of the Marsh	6+
2	Bheortaine Briartangle, Father of Thorn	7+
3	Olannan Rattledor, the Howler Wind	7+
4	Keirnu Oakenclub, Master of the Wood	7+
5	Rulainn Boulderfist, Master of stone	8+
6	Mhadh Gathersquall, the Rain Lord	9+

MISTRESS OF THE MARSH　　Cast on 6+

This spell can be cast upon an enemy unit that is within 12" of a river, stream, bog, or any other water feature on the tabletop which has been identified as such before the game. If there are no such features in range, it can be cast on any enemy unit within 6" of the caster. It cannot be used against a unit that is engaged in close combat. If successfully cast, the ground beneath the unit is turned to swamp and the unit moves at half speed until the end of its own following turn. If forced to flee, for whatever reason, the unit flees at half speed. This spell has no effect on flyers or ethereal creatures.

The swamp disappears at the end of the opposing player's Magic phase.

FATHER OF THE THORN　　Cast on 7+

The Father of the Thorn can be cast on an enemy unit within 24" of the caster, which is not engaged in combat and which is visible to the caster. If successfully cast, thorns and briars shoot from the earth entangling limbs and tearing at flesh.

The spell causes 2D6 Strength 3 hits.

The thorns wither and disappear at the end of the Magic phase.

THE HOWLER WIND
Remains in Play　　Cast on 7+

This spell can be cast upon the Wizard himself. If successfully cast, no shooting with Strength 4 or less can be targeted at units within 12" of the Wizard – even if some models in the unit are more than 12" away. The howling wind engulfs the whole unit if any part of it is within 12" of the caster. This doesn't prevent units from firing through or out of the affected area at targets beyond. In addition, all enemy units within 12" of the Wizard move at half speed due to the effect of the howling wind. Note that this move penalty only applies when actually within the affected area – enemy treat the entire zone as if it were difficult ground. Once cast, the spell lasts until dispelled, the Wizard chooses to end it (which he can do at any time), attempts to cast another spell or is slain.

MASTER OF THE WOOD　　Cast on 7+

This spell can be cast upon an enemy unit that is within 12" of a wood, copse or any other wooded feature on the tabletop which has been identified as such before the game. If there are no such features in range, it can be cast on any enemy unit within 6" of the caster. It cannot be used against a unit that is engaged in close combat. If successfully cast, the unit is battered by the branches of trees if within a wood, or lashed at by roots which erupt from the ground if there is no wood nearby.

This causes D6 Strength 4 hits on the unit, plus a further D6 Strength 4 hits if it is partially or wholly within the wood. This spell does not affect Dryads or Treemen. At the end of the Magic phase, the trees are still again or the roots retract back into the earth.

MASTER OF STONE　　Cast on 8+

This spell can be cast upon an enemy unit that is within 12" of a hill, rocky outcrop, ruins or any area which has been identified as high ground, rocky or ruinous before the game. If there are no such features in range, it can be cast on any enemy unit within 6" of the caster. It cannot be used against a unit that is engaged in close combat. If successfully cast, shards of stone fly against the unit.

The spell causes D6 Strength 5 hits on the unit, plus a further D6 Strength 5 hits if the unit is partially or wholly within the feature.

THE RAIN LORD　　Cast on 9+

This spell can be cast on an enemy unit within 24" and which is visible to the caster. If successfully cast, the target unit is enveloped in rain and gets a soaking.

A soaked unit must roll a 4, 5 or 6 when attempting to shoot because bow strings become damp and useless whilst ropes stretch and don't work properly. A unit using gunpowder, including cannons, must roll a 6 in order to shoot. Dwarf Flame Cannons and any other shooting weapons powered by steam, blackpowder or flame must also roll a 6. If the roll is failed, the affected unit cannot shoot during that Shooting phase. Once affected a unit stays soaked for rest of game – this is not a magical effect, you are wet! A unit can only be soaked once.

THE LORE OF DEATH

Though the Lore of Death, or Amethyst magic, is the most feared of sorceries, not all practitioners are evil or ill-intended. It is the magic of the bygone ages and draws its power deeply from the realm of the dead.

To randomly generate a spell, roll a D6 and consult the chart below. If you roll the same spell twice for the same Wizard, roll again.

D6	Spell	Casting Value
1	Dark Hand of Death	5+
2	Death Dealer	5+
3	Steal Soul	8+
4	Wind of Death	8+
5	Drain Life	10+
6	Doom and Darkness!	12+

DARK HAND OF DEATH — Cast on 5+

This is a *magic missile* with a range of up to 24". If successfully cast, the spell hits its target and causes D6 Strength 4 hits.

DEATH DEALER — Cast on 5+

This spell can be cast on a friendly unit that is engaged in close combat and which is within 24" of the caster. If successfully cast then models which fall casualty can fight back, stabbing at their enemy with their last strength.

The spell lasts for the duration of that turn's Close Combat phase. Fight the combat as normal. Any model in the affected unit which falls casualty during the combat may make one further attack with its basic Strength before it is removed – this is regardless of whether the model has already fought or not. In the case of mounted models, models riding chariots or monsters and so forth, only riders may strike back.

STEAL SOUL — Cast on 8+

This spell can be cast on an enemy model within 12". If successfully cast, the victim's soul is torn and rendered by dark forces and sacrificed to the caster himself.

The enemy model loses 1 Wound. No armour save is allowed. In addition, the casting Wizard gains 1 Wound for the duration of the battle. This spell can be used to increase the caster's Wounds characteristic beyond its normal maximum level, and can be used several times to increase the caster's Wounds even further. At the end of the battle, any stolen Wounds are lost – if the Wizard has no Wounds left once stolen Wounds are removed, he is slain.

The spell cannot affect Undead, Chaos Daemons, and similar units which don't have a soul!

WIND OF DEATH — Cast on 8+

This is a *magic missile* with a range of up to 24". If successfully cast, the spell hits its target and causes 2D6 Strength 4 hits.

DRAIN LIFE — Cast on 10+

If cast successfully each enemy unit within 12" of the Wizard is affected.

Each unit takes D6 Strength 3 hits. No armour saves are allowed against a Drain Life spell. These hits are distributed exactly like hits from shooting.

The spell cannot affect Undead, Chaos Daemons, or buildings and similar models, as they are not truly alive.

DOOM AND DARKNESS!

Lasts one turn+ — Cast on 12+

This spell can be cast upon an enemy unit which is within 24" of and visible to the caster. If successfully cast, the unit is enshrouded by a black cloud of despair.

For the duration of the turn the affected unit will suffer a -3 penalty to any Leadership test (including Break tests) it is required to take. At the start of its following turn, the unit must take and pass a Leadership test (at -3), otherwise it remains affected for the duration of that turn as well. At the end of the affected unit's following turn, the spell ceases to have any effect.

The spell cannot affect Undead targets, Chaos Daemons or unbreakable units. Units immune to psychology are not affected either.

MAGIC ITEMS

Magic items form an important part of the Warhammer game. The Warhammer Armies books describe in detail the many different kinds of magic items which each army can use. Here we shall examine the magic items that are commonly used by all races. In cases of contradiction, the special rule of a magic item takes precedence over normal game rules.

WHO CAN USE MAGIC ITEMS?

Magic items can be carried by characters and, in some cases, by the Standard Bearer of a unit of troops. This is indicated in the army list for each army in the appropriate Warhammer Army book. A character can only have one magic item of each type (weapon, armour, etc) unless otherwise indicated.

No specific magic item can be carried by more than one model in the army, with the exception of scrolls. These are not limited in this respect and several scrolls of the same type can be carried by the same character if you wish.

TYPES OF MAGIC ITEM

For the sake of convenience, we distinguish between the types of magic item in the following way:

MAGIC WEAPONS

By which we mean most commonly swords but also in some cases, axes, maces, spears, bows, crossbows, etc.

A character who has a magic close combat weapon cannot use other close combat weapons – he cannot have a magic sword in one hand and an ordinary sword in the other, for example. You can carry a shield with a magical weapon. No character can carry more than one magic weapon. Magic weapons always ignore any special rules that apply to an ordinary weapon of the same type. All the rules that apply are covered in the description of the weapon.

MAGIC ARMOUR

A character who is not allowed to wear ordinary armour cannot be given magic armour. This includes many kinds of Wizard whose natural magical harmony would be seriously affected by armour. Therefore, Wizards cannot wear magic armour unless specifically mentioned in the description of the item.

If a character wears magical armour, he cannot also wear ordinary armour and, needless to say, he can only wear one set of armour. Magical shields are also counted as magical armour, so you cannot have a suit of magical armour and carry a magical shield unless specifically stated in the description of the magic item.

If a model has a magic shield he is allowed to wear a suit of normal armour. If the model is wearing a suit of magic armour he is allowed to carry a normal shield.

ARCANE ITEMS

Arcane items are items which enhance a Wizard's magical powers in some fashion. Only a Wizard can carry an Arcane item and no character can carry more than one.

Scrolls are a type of Arcane item which contain powerful enchantments that enable Wizards to manipulate the power of magic. They are useful aids to spell casting and to resisting an enemy's spell. Only a Wizard can carry a scroll but, unlike other Arcane items, there is no limit on the number of scrolls a Wizard can carry, other than the total value of magic items he is permitted. Wizards can have one Arcane item as well as carry several scrolls.

As they are expendable items once a scroll is read, it crumbles to dust or its writing fades to nothing. A scroll can therefore only be used once during a whole battle.

TALISMANS

Talismans, charms, amulets and wards are tokens of magical protection. A character cannot have more than one talisman.

BANNERS

Magical banners can only be carried by Standard Bearers as indicated in the army lists in the Warhammer Army book for each army. The only character permitted to carry a magic standard is the army's Battle Standard Bearer, and he can carry only one magical banner.

ENCHANTED ITEMS

Many magic items are unique or belong to limited categories, such as rings. These items are Enchanted items. No general restrictions apply to these, though particular restrictions may apply to individual items. A character cannot have more than one Enchanted item.

MAGIC ITEMS CAPABLE OF CASTING SPELLS

Some magic items have spells that are wrought into their very fabric that can be unleashed by their wielder during the Magic phase. Possessing a Bound Spell item does not make a character a Wizard for the purposes of the rules.

The spell held in a magic item is cast in the player's Magic phase just like other spells, and can be countered in the same way as ordinary spells. Spells cast by magic items succeed automatically – no Power dice are needed.

A spell from a Bound Spell item can be cast once per Magic phase. A character cannot have more than one Bound Spell item. Each Bound Spell item has a Power level included in its description. An opponent must score equal to or greater than this to dispel the spell.

 It was almost unfair, thought Elannion, cleaving his fourteenth or fifteenth Goblin in two. How can these foul creatures hope to stand against a master of battle such as he, especially with the fabled Sword of Sulannar in his hand? He deftly dodged an ungainly swing from the standard bearer of the frantic greenskins, catching the rusting blade with his own glowing sword and snapping it off just above the guard. The Gobbo stared in amazement for a moment, and then fell himself as Elannion's blade cut him down too. The banner wavered, but eager green hands clutched at it to stop it from falling, until Elannion's blade flashed once more and chopped the ragged banner from the staff. As the tattered fabric slumped to the ground the Goblins recoiled, leaving Elannion facing just one of their number – the largest Goblin he had ever seen. Malevolent red eyes glowed under his black hood as the Goblin hissed his hatred at the Elf. 'You', he said, pointing at Elannion. The noble Elf motioned to his followers to stay back. At last he had found an enemy who was perhaps worthy of him. This little fracas would be decided in single combat.

The two warriors circled each other slowly, each sizing up his opponent. Elannion was taller, faster and undoubtedly better dressed, but the Goblin had a certain wiriness and an evil glint in his eye. Elannion darted forward, striking at the Goblin leader before he could react. The Sword of Sulannar slid easily through his filthy robes only to rebound from something lurking beneath. The vicious greenskin grinned broadly and pulled aside the robe to reveal a shimmering coat of fine scale armour that glowed gently with a pale blue light where it had been struck. Elannion narrowed his eyes. Magic, eh? Before he could compose an appropriately heroic remark the Gobbo struck back, stabbing with his own saw-toothed blade. Elannion dodged, but not quickly enough. By the gods this one was fast! But that blow too skimmed off magical armour and Elannion thanked his forefathers for such well enchanted protection. He grinned in turn; they were evenly matched.

Again the Goblin struck only to be parried by Elannion's glimmering blade. A strike back, a parry, then another. The fight grew swifter by the moment and the onlookers forgot their animosity as they strained to follow the frenetic combat before them. Sparks flew as magical blades rebounded from enchanted armour, but neither could gain the upper hand. At last they separated, drawing back towards their followers, panting with the exertion. 'You fight well, for an Elf', hissed the Goblin.

'So do you', replied Elannion. 'For a stunted abomination.'

The Goblin grinned at the insult, calmly pointing a scrawny finger at the Elf. Magical fire leapt from the ring on his outstretched hand, engulfing Elannion in a firestorm of destruction from which nothing could escape.

'Next!'

COMMON MAGIC ITEMS

The following magic items are considered to be common items – which is to say that they are common to all armies in the Warhammer world and not that they are commonplace in any sense. Far from it, even the least potent magic item is a dangerous device, steeped in the fickle powers of sorcery, and is extremely rare. Complete lists of magic items available to each of the different armies are included in the Warhammer Army book for each race.

SWORD OF STRIKING   (+1 To Hit)
30 points (Magic Weapon)

A Sword of Striking is possessed of a keen intelligence that guides its blade to the target. The sword confers a dice bonus of +1 to the character wielding it. For example, where 3 is normally required to score a hit, the character will hit on a 2. However, a dice roll of 1 is always a miss regardless of bonuses – the minimum successful roll to hit is therefore 2.

SWORD OF BATTLE   (+1 Attack)
25 points (Magic Weapon)

A Sword of Battle is forged with potent magic that enables its wielder to employ it with dazzling speed and deadly effect. The blade confers +1 Attack on the character wielding it.

SWORD OF MIGHT   (+1 Strength)
20 points (Magic Weapon)

A Sword of Might is wrought with enchantments that bind within its fabric a great and magical strength. The blade confers +1 Strength upon the character who fights with it.

BITING BLADE   (-1 armour save)
10 points (Magic Weapon)

The Biting Blade is forged with bitter curses that work against the armour of its foes. The blade confers an additional -1 armour save modifier on any blows stuck. This is in addition to any normal armour save modifier for Strength, so a blow struck at Strength 3 or less will have a -1 armour save, a Strength 4 hit has a -2 armour save, Strength 5 has a -3 armour save and so on.

ENCHANTED SHIELD (5+ armour save)
10 points (Magic Armour)

The Enchanted Shield protects its user with powerful magic. The shield confers an armour save of 5+ rather than a mundane shield's armour save of 6+. This can be combined with other magical or mundane armour – for example, light armour + Enchanted Shield = armour save 4+, heavy armour + Enchanted Shield + mounted = armour save 2+.

STAFF OF SORCERY (+1 to dispel)
50 points (Arcane)

A Wizard who has this benefits from the arcane power stored within it. Whenever he dispels a spell, the score required to make a successful dispel is reduced by 1.

POWER STONE   25 points (Arcane)

The Power Stone is imbued with a powerful magical invocation. When it is held out by a Wizard before he casts a spell, the effect is to enhance the efficacy of the magic. A further two dice are added to the Casting roll. Note that using a Power Stone will allow a Wizard to use more Power dice than he is normally permitted. For example, a First Level Wizard may read a Power Stone and thus use four Power dice to cast a spell (2 basic + 2 from a Power Stone). A Power Stone can only be used once – after one use its power is exhausted.

Using a Power Stone will bring any spell in play cast earlier by that Wizard to an end in the same way as casting a new spell by ordinary means.

As with scrolls, Power Stones are not unique items – they are prepared by a Wizard prior to battle and it is quite possible for several Wizards to carry Power Stones, and for a Wizard to carry more than one. However, only one Power Stone can be used to enhance a spell.

Note that a spell cast with a Power Stone can never be cast with Irresistible Force, though it can be Miscast.

DISPEL SCROLL   25 Points (Scroll)

A Dispel Scroll is inscribed with a powerful anti-magical invocation. When it is read out by a Wizard, the effect is to drain away magical power and weaken a spell that has been cast. As soon as a spell has been cast, any Wizard who has a Dispel Scroll can read it. This automatically dispels the cast spell, no dice roll is required.

Reading a Dispel Scroll will bring any spell cast by the Wizard reading it to an end. To put it another way, a Wizard who has a spell in play will automatically cancel it by reading a Dispel Scroll.

As with all scrolls, Dispel Scrolls are not unique items – they are prepared by a Wizard pµrior to battle and it is quite possible for several Wizards to carry Dispel Scrolls, and for a Wizard to carry more than one. However, only one can be used at a time.

Note that a Dispel Scroll will not help if the spell has been cast with Irresistible Force. Any spell that is successfully cast with a result of 12 is irresistible and no Dispel roll is permitted.

TALISMAN OF PROTECTION (6+ Ward Save)
15 points (Talisman)

The Talisman of Protection is a protective charm. This confers upon its wearer a Ward save of 6+.

WAR BANNER (+1 Combat Resolution)
25 points (Banner)

The War Banner carries powerful enchantments that fill all those who fight beneath it with heroic courage and determination. A unit which has a War Banner adds a further +1 to its combat resolution when working out which side has won the combat.

Then chiefs came to Sigmar, to his hold
Let us fight Goblins, let Orcs be fought!
Sigmar, hammer-bearer lead us in war
And the tribes went forth
With iron of the Dwarfs, to do battle
With Goblins and Orcs.
On the plain of battles, beside the mighty Stir
Met they the Goblin horde, eager for slaughter
And the number of Goblins
Was beyond counting.
And the number of Orcs, was as the trees in the forest.
And the number of Trolls,
was more than boulders upon the mountains
And the number of men, was but a few.
And the gods gave the victory, to the men
To the Worlds Edge, the Goblins fled.
But the greater number of them, were dead.

Dwarfs came, from King Kurgan
High King of Dwarfs, whose hall
Is in Karak. A noble messenger
Alaric the Runesmith
From the far Black Mountains
Who braved the Blackfire Pass
Where Goblins unnumbered
And Hobgoblins uncounted
And Black Orcs eager for slaughter
Besieged the Dwarf holds.
Sigmar, hammer-holder
Shall come, and fight beside his friend
Goblins shall not stand between us.
Dwarfs and men.
In Blackfire Pass, men fought the foe.
Cut a swathe through the horde
Met Dwarfs and embraced them
Brothers in battle.
Sigmar Helden Hammer and Kurgan the King.
The Hammer of the Goblins
And the Anvil of the Dwarfs.

WORLD OF
WARHAMMER

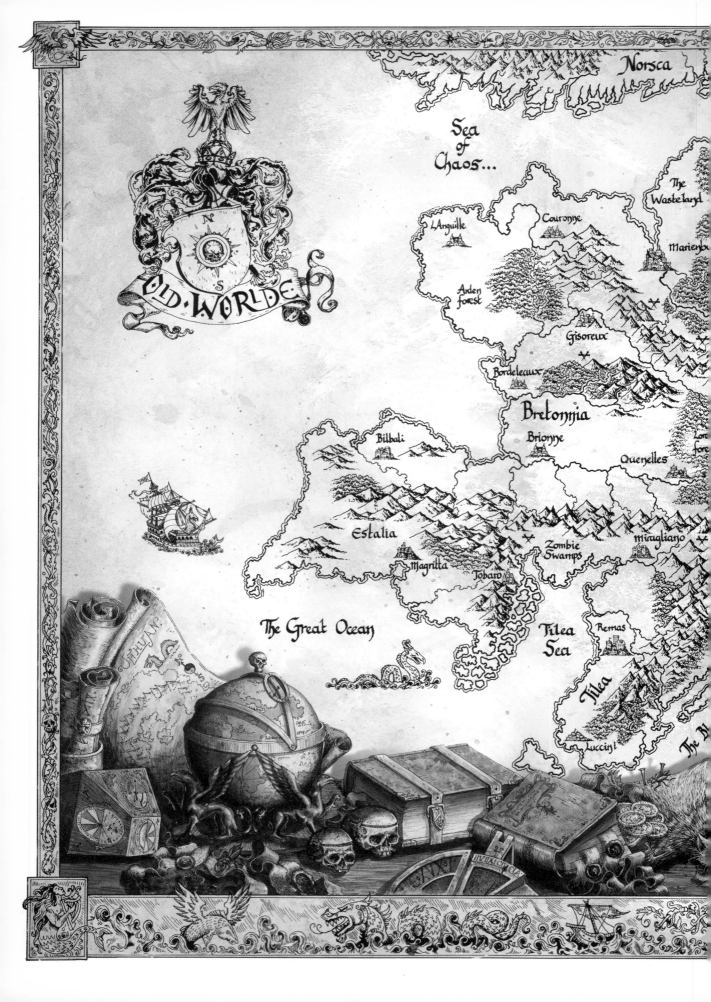

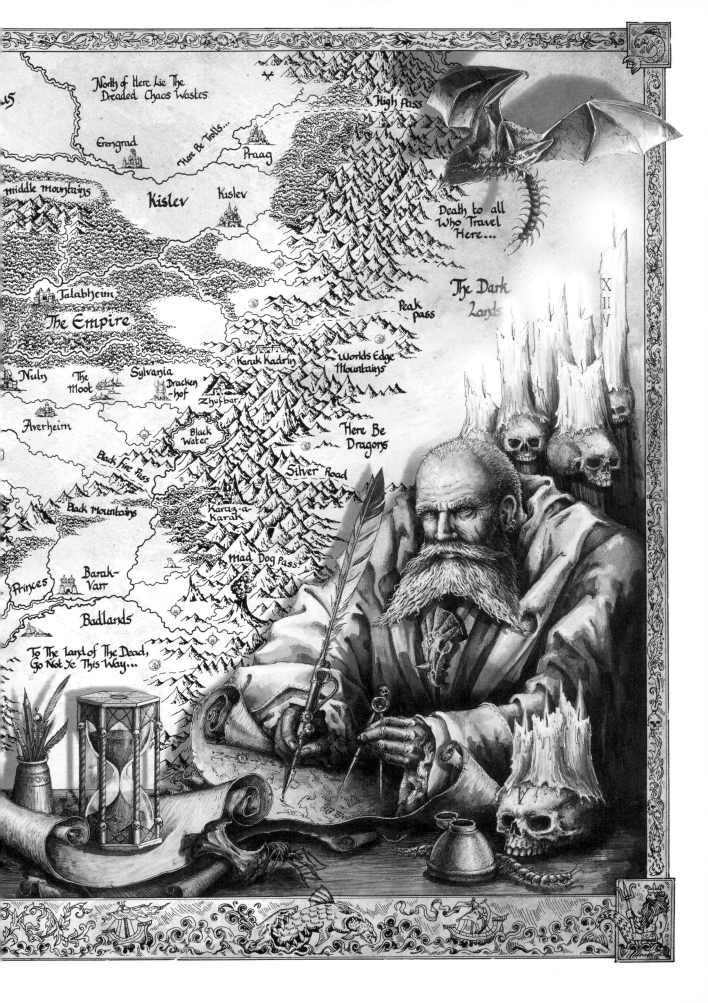

EMPERER · REX · HONORIS · KARL · FRANZ

YE HISTORY OF YE OLD WORLD

as told by the Venerable Hieronymous of Nuln

'Dark and dangerous is the world. A place filled with conflict.'

To his most Imperial Majesty, the Prince of Reikland, the ruler of the holy Empire, sovereign of heights and depths, Karl–Franz I of Altdorf.

According to your most imperial order, I am to compile a manuscript which explains in detail the great realms of the Old World and the wondrous inhabitants of these lands. As Sigmar is my witness I will describe truthfully the lands of the Old World, the southern continents and the New World. I shall also discuss the eastern lands beyond the Worlds Edge Mountains: the great steppes of the east and the mysterious lands of Cathay.

Thus I write under the two moons, Morrslieb and Mannslieb. I write of the days long gone and I write of the days that are yet to come, and those days are the days of Man. We are the inheritors of the twin bounties of wealth and wonderment that the Old World has to offer, if we can defeat the evils that besiege us.

The twin–tailed comet is the symbol of our glorious Empire. It has heralded the birth of many great heroes in the past.

Of the Old World

The Old World is bounded by the immeasurably high Worlds Edge Mountains in the east, by the dark and deep Great Ocean to the west, and by the forbidding Troll Country in the north. To the South lies a broad arm of the Great Ocean and beyond this the shores of the land of Araby.

In ancient times Dwarfs and Elves fought over possession of the Old World and, after many centuries of bitter conflict, retreated into their own lands. In their wake came the Orcs from the east, who infested the trackless forests and wastes and ruined the abandoned cities of the Dwarfs and Elves. Later the tribes of Mankind wandered into the Old World and began to clear the land and dwell there. Incessantly did they fight against the Orcs and out of this long conflict arose the great realms of men, namely the Empire and Bretonnia, Estalia, Tilea and Kislev.

The map I have included prior to these pages was presented as a gift to Emperor Leopold from the Cartographers of Altdorf.

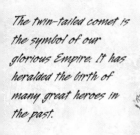

The great Worlds Edge Mountains were once believed to mark the edge of the world. They are home to the last Dwarf Clans, whose scattered strongholds guard the mountain passes.

THE LEGEND OF SIGMAR HELDENHAMMER

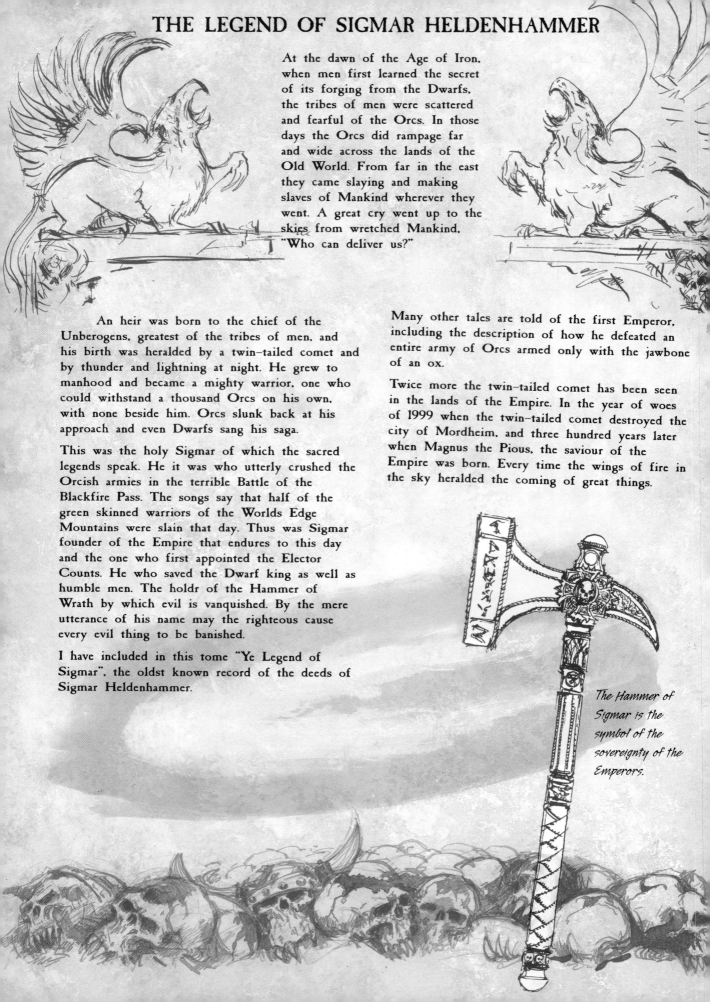

At the dawn of the Age of Iron, when men first learned the secret of its forging from the Dwarfs, the tribes of men were scattered and fearful of the Orcs. In those days the Orcs did rampage far and wide across the lands of the Old World. From far in the east they came slaying and making slaves of Mankind wherever they went. A great cry went up to the skies from wretched Mankind, "Who can deliver us?"

An heir was born to the chief of the Unberogens, greatest of the tribes of men, and his birth was heralded by a twin-tailed comet and by thunder and lightning at night. He grew to manhood and became a mighty warrior, one who could withstand a thousand Orcs on his own, with none beside him. Orcs slunk back at his approach and even Dwarfs sang his saga.

This was the holy Sigmar of which the sacred legends speak. He it was who utterly crushed the Orcish armies in the terrible Battle of the Blackfire Pass. The songs say that half of the green skinned warriors of the Worlds Edge Mountains were slain that day. Thus was Sigmar founder of the Empire that endures to this day and the one who first appointed the Elector Counts. He who saved the Dwarf king as well as humble men. The holdr of the Hammer of Wrath by which evil is vanquished. By the mere utterance of his name may the righteous cause every evil thing to be banished.

I have included in this tome "Ye Legend of Sigmar", the oldst known record of the deeds of Sigmar Heldenhammer.

Many other tales are told of the first Emperor, including the description of how he defeated an entire army of Orcs armed only with the jawbone of an ox.

Twice more the twin-tailed comet has been seen in the lands of the Empire. In the year of woes of 1999 when the twin-tailed comet destroyed the city of Mordheim, and three hundred years later when Magnus the Pious, the saviour of the Empire was born. Every time the wings of fire in the sky heralded the coming of great things.

The Hammer of Sigmar is the symbol of the sovereignty of the Emperors.

OUR HONOURED LAND - THE EMPIRE

Our beautiful empire is the largest, the most powerful nation in all of the Old World. We, the sons of Sigmar, have a right to be proud. For over two millennia the banner of the Griffon has flown over Castle Reikschlosse, proclaiming the might and glory of the Emperors.

Altdorf is the capital of our glorious Empire and the seat of the Emperor. Here all manner of arts and sciences flourish under the patronage of the imperial crown. Here lies the great Shrine of Sigmar and the Engineers' Guildhall, and the spires of the Colleges of Magic rise high above the rooftops of Altdorf. Herein lies the heart of our trade: river barges laden with goods dock and depart here, and our rich markets bustle with traders from as far as Araby.

While Altdorf is second to none in its glory and splendour, our Empire encompasses many other places of beauty and awe besides the capital. The prosperous fields of Reikland stretch around the capital, and farms, estates and villages dot the fields before giving way to the all-encompassing forests of the Empire.

Middenheim rests upon a mountain pedestal, said to have been splintered by the axe of Ulric, the god of winter and wolves.

The griffon is the symbol of the dynasty of Magnus the Pious, often seen in architecture, guarding the gateways and temples.

Nuln is the gem of Reikland situated above the mighty River Reik. Once she was the first city of the Empire and of old the seat of Emperors. Many Dwarf craftsmen came to dwell here and work their forges along the Reik, where great oak barges arrive daily with ore and coals. The great bridge which spans the broad Reik at Nuln is wondrous to behold and the glory and pride of the city. Beyond this there are no more bridges for the river is too wide. Within the boundaries of Nuln stands the Imperial Artillery School, and many universities for the studious amongst the population of Empire. Herein rules the Elector Countess Emmanuelle von Liebewitz, a beauty who is famous for her masked balls and lavish parties, which almost rival the splendour of the Imperial court.

Middenheim, the city of the White Wolf, is built upon a towering crag rising up out of the great forest. It is an impregnable fortress which may only be approached by four roads raised up on arches. Ulric is patron god of this mighty city and his high priest rules alongside the Elector Count of the city. Herein lies the stronghold of the famed order of the ferocious Knights of the White Wolf.

Marienburg, the busy prosperous port which lies at the mouth of the Reik is no longer part of our great Empire. Her wealth is legendary. Here ships from every realm are docked bringing all manner of exotic goods and luxuries. The pride and pretension of the citizens knows no bounds and they claim to be the equal in every way of the Tileans in art and culture.

Talabheim lies also in the midst of the forest in the very heart of the Empire. Here dwell the hardy woodsmen and hunters who keep their axes and bows by the threshold of their cottages. The city itself rests within a rocky bowl whose steep outward sides present wall–like fortifications. Within these natural walls stand the sturdy buildings of Talabheim.

Mordheim, that once great city is no more. Of this place it is wise to say little. Such was the sin of this city that a great thunderbolt from the heavens did raze it to be no more than a bleak ruin. Some say this was the Hammer of Judgement, wielded by Sigmar himself.

Lastly, there is the cursed lands of Sylvania, the most infamous of the provinces. It was here that the dreaded Vampire Counts rose five hundred years ago. These aristocrats of the night sent their hordes of zombies and skeletons to ravage all the lands between the sea and the Worlds Edge Mountains. Only after centuries of war were they defeated at the grim Battle of Hel Fen.

Many of the derelict villages are abodes of Ghoul clans, and travellers are warned from approaching the ruined castles and mansions of Sylvania after dark. Travellers should be wary and avoid the cursed soil of Sylvania if you can. The less said about this desolate and ghastly land, the better. Mannfred von Carstein, the last of the dread Vampire Counts is dead. Long may he rest.

Ostland, snow bound and windswept, marches with Kislev and is the bastion of the Empire against Orc and Chaos alike. Her warriors are well accustomed to war and know little comfort in their great timber fortresses.

The Moot is a fat land, rich in pastures and produces much that is good for the tables of the nobility. It is inhabited by Halflings who are renowned for their greed and craving for good food, rather than their courage.

Solland, the southernmost of our provinces is no more. During the rampages of the Orc Warlord Gorbad Ironclaw Solland was razed and deserted. The Elector Count of Solland fell in battle and his Runefang was lost. After the war the lands of Solland and its few remaining inhabitants were divided between the neighbouring provinces.

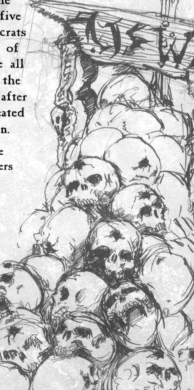

Karl Franz

OF BRETONNIA

Beyond the Grey Mountains lies the kingdom of Bretonnia, inhabited by the descendants of the Bretonni tribe. It is a great kingdom, next only to our great Empire in power and wealth. Indeed they are our chief rivals in trade and war.

The kings of Bretonnia live in the most sumptuous luxury imaginable. Their stables are filled with the finest warhorses, their weapons are encrusted with jewels, and their silk banners glitter with gold.

Yet you should hesitate from mocking a Bretonnian nobleman (to his face, at least), for behind the courtly graces is a warrior born and bred to battle. From a very early age the knights of Bretonnia are taught to bear the traditional arms of a knight, to ride and to endure the hardships of war. There are no greater warriors amongst the race of Man (or at least so say the Bretonnians).

Bretonnia was founded by King Gilles le Breton, whom the Bretonnians hold to be as renowned as Sigmar. He was the first of all knights of Bretonnia, and established their military traditions.

Their kingdom is divided into fourteen great dukedoms, from the fair Couronne in the north to the rugged land of Carcassonne to the south. Each of the powerful dukes commands an army of knights supported by squires, men-at-arms and archers drawn from the ranks of the commoners. This way of fighting, though old-fashioned in our Empire, has proven time and again effective in repelling numerous invading armies.

Each knight of Bretonnia bears his own unique heraldic device on his shield and livery. The Fleur de Lys, or Flower fo the Lily, is the most common of these symbols, signifying a knight's dedication to the Quest for the Grail.

It is the ideal of knighthood which inspires the warriors of Bretonnia. The worship of the Lady of the Lake, their goddess of virtue and honour, is widespread, and sets the code of honour under which the finest of nobility conducts itself in peace and war.

While most of the Bretonnians are rural folk, there are still numerous walled cities: the capital, Couronne, with its marble temples; Parravon, which guards the Axe Bite Pass; Gisoreux, which protects the reaches of the Upper Grismerie river; Quenelles with its chapels and vineyards, and lastly the dreaded city of Moussilon, a squalid ruin which is now a lair of evil creatures. Bordeleaux, L'Anguille and Brionne, the coastal cities of Bretonnia are trading ports and havens for the dreaded war-fleet of Bretonnia, and control much of the wealth of the kingdom.

OF KISLEV

North from the lands of our magnificent Empire the forests give way to great wind–swept plains and dark birch glades. These are the lands of Kislev. For one thousand years this kingdom has endured the attacks of the savage Norse and the incursions of dread Chaos.

During the long winter nights the men of Kislev, known as Gospodars, gather around their log cottages, remembering the glory of the Tzars of old and the might of the Ice Queens of bygone ages. They sing songs of war and dream of happier times, for their own age is filled with much strife. Kislev guards the borderlands of the north against the terrible servants of Chaos. Each year the northern border is harder to defend. Each year the toll of death is greater. But to Kislevites this matters not. North is their home and if they cannot live there, they will die there.

Kislevites are great warriors and magnificent horsemen. They tirelessly patrol the northern border along the forbidding Troll Country, trying to keep the rampaging Chaos warbands in check.

The cities of Kislev are ruled by Tzars and boyars who all owe their fealty to the overlord of Kislev. Tzarina Katarin the Great, the current ruler of all Kislev, is a mighty Sorceress, mistress of the cold winds and ice of the north. She is known for both her beauty and her haughty and cold manners which have earned her the title of Ice Queen of Kislev. So suffused is she with magic that it is said that her flesh is cold to touch and she rules her lands with icy efficiency.

Erengrad is one of the greatest trading ports of the Old World. Here the wares of the north are traded with merchants from Bretonnia, Tilea, Estalia and, of course, our own noble Empire.

The city of Praag has an evil reputation, for during the last Great War against Chaos the city was overrun with the servants of the Ruinous Powers and twisted beyond recognition. After Magnus the Pious defeated the forces of the Dark Gods the city was razed to the ground and rebuilt, but Chaos returned. Travellers tell tales in hushed tones of cries of agony that pierce the night and faces that appear in the walls of buildings to consume the unwary with savage ferocity. The citizens of Praag are forced to burn down and rebuild their homes if they are to retain some small measure of sanity.

The flags of the Pirates of Sartosa carry the grim device of skull and crossbones.

OF TILEA AND ESTALIA

South of the Empire and Bretonnia lie the lands of Tilea and Estalia. Cut–throats and sell–swords to a man, Tileans often offer their services as mercenaries when no wars are waged in their own country. For in this land each city is a separate principality in unfettered rivalry with its neighbours. Every merchant prince looks to himself and his own wealth and seeks only to stab and poison his neighbours, while extending the hand of friendship. In some cities, the citizens, tiring of their own corrupt nobility, overthrew the princes to rule themselves as a republic. Yet even there it is the dagger that rules. Despite this, the Tileans are cultured people, expert in all the arts and master seafarers. Their explorers have discovered many lands.

Mention must be made of Sartosa, which is an island near to Tilea, inhabited entirely by pirates. Though they plague the seas thereabouts, they are a fitting match for the cruel corsairs of Araby and both are much deserving of each other.

Tilean wines fetch high prices throughout the Old World, and their large fleet of merchant vessels ply the seas trading with all nations from the north of Kislev to the scorched lands of Araby. Art, sciences, innovation and music are all strongly supported by the princes of the city states.

Of Estalia, little is to be said for it is a rugged place. Within its few fortified cities live hardy people who make their living with fishing and trade. Jaffar, the Sultan of Araby once invaded that land and nearly conquered it but for the great army of knights which came to drive out his hordes. It is said that the Estalians are very hardy folk, who will slay a man for mistaking them for a Tilean or even greeting them in the Tilean dialect by mistake.

OF THE
LANDS OF ARABY

South of Tilea, past the stormy seas of the Black Gulf, lies the kingdom of Araby. Here the decadent Caliphs and Sultans rule cities made of white stone, and their realms are the vast deserts, oases that glitter like jewels, and mountains inhabited by fierce nomad warriors. Several great cities form a loose coalition, though in effect they are all independent states with their own rulers, traditions and customs.

The Sheikhs, Emirs and Sultans of Copher, Lashiek and Martek live in unimaginable luxury, served by hundreds of slaves who will fulfil their every whim, their harems are filled with voluptuous beauties from across the world and their treasure chambers with all the splendour and wealth of that distant land. Some of these despots are cruel by their nature, ordering beheadings and mutilation of even the pettiest criminals, while others are great rulers and patrons of art and science.

In contrast the nomadic peoples, who are the subjects of the Arabian rulers, do not build permanent settlements, preferring to travel far and wide in the desert. Some ride not upon horses, but on strange and most bad-tempered beasts which never thirst and appear never to drink.

There are many sorcerers in Araby, who can perform strange works of magic. It is said that they can conjure up spirits which they call genies and imprison them in glass bottles. When the bottle is uncorked, the spirit emerges as a vapour and grows to immense size to do the bidding of his master. Other tales speak of Wizards who fly high above the sands on carpets. Believe this if you will.

In the Old World the Arabians are known to be cunning traders and merchants. It is said that an Arabian can trick even a Tilean into a bad bargain, and I know few more crooked traders than the treacherous Tileans.

The most infamous of the Arabians are the merciless pirates of Copher. The ships of the Old World fear few perils of the sea as much as the Corsairs of Araby. The port of Copher holds many sleek and deadly ships which prey the seven seas.

Weapons and armour of the Eastern Kingdom of Cathay brought by the caravans are both bizarre and outlandish.

OF THE SOUTHLANDS

Of the hot jungles of the south I can say little, for few have dared the stormy seas of the south and even fewer have returned from the Dark Continent. The Southlands encompass vast, untouched jungles and snow-capped mountains. The western coast boasts a number of small colonies of Arabian Mmerchants which serve as havens for their ships.

The jungles themselves are said to be impenetrable and trackless, filled with all manner of dangerous animals and monsters. All attempts to explore this hostile, steaming hell have failed. The few survivors talk of the last of the great Dwarf strongholds, surrounded by savage Orcs and Goblins and all manner of other monsters. Other tales speak of a great High Elf fortress which guards the tip of the Southlands and the way to the distant east and the lands of Ind and Cathay. But whatever power holds the Southlands, it is welcome to it. Keep your dark secrets and your cursed treasures!

OF THE DISTANT
KINGDOM OF CATHAY

Past the Worlds Edge Mountains and across the Great Skull Lands, on the other side of the Mountains of Mourn and the vast steppes, begin the uncharted lands. Only a single path travels to the east, known as the Silk Road. It runs through the untamed steppes until its destination, the fabled kingdom of Cathay. The lure of the Silk Road is great to the merchant houses of the Tilea and the Burgomeisters of the Empire, as well as the traders of Araby. But the road is far from safe: roving bandits, steppe nomads, and the vast hordes of Hobgobla-Khan who rule the steppes are an ever-present threat, and one that cannot be taken too lightly. Only one caravan out of ten makes the trip safely.

The travellers that return from Cathay tell tales of great goldn pagodas and the inexhaustible armies of the eastern despots. They bring exotic spices and finest silks, gleaming gold, luxurious porcelain vases and all manner of strange and wonderful items from the Kingdom of the Dragon, glimpses of the mysterious glory of the distant and rich orient.

They also bring tales of jade cites and high temples where mystics probe the movements of the heavenly bodies and the positions of the stars, of the scholars who inscribe every word ever uttered by their divine Emperor. Many strange creatures are said to live in the land of Cathay, from serpentine dragons to gigantic living stone dogs which guard the temples of the multitudinous gods of Cathay.

Records of travellers tell of the thousand, thousand footsoldiers of the Emperor, the mystic brotherhoods of monks who can kill you with a touch of their hand, and the strange monkey warriors living high in the Mountains of Heaven.

Most of these tales are highly fanciful, but certainly the Empire of the Celestial Dragon must be a wondrous and rich place, but until the trade routes to the east are safe it will remain a realm of legend.

THE LAND OF THE DEAD

East of Araby lies a great desert and amongst the dunes rise the necropolises, tomb-cities which are said to be the home for the unquiet dead. In that dread desert, beneath the moon's pale gaze, dead men are said to walk. They haunt the dunes and ruined pyramids in the breathless, windless night.

It is told in my most obscure and ancient scrolls that the Great Necromancer himself, Nagash the Black, ruled here long, long ago, and the land still bears the scars of his clawed hand. Here stand the great pyramids built to be the tombs of the past kings of Nehekhara. These ancient tombs are said to hold untold riches, and yet only few travel to this most desolate of places to face the dangers of the ancient necropoli. Entire armies, commanded by their mummified kings, march under the scorching sun to wage war against the living and each other. My source of these ancient and evil things is the blasphemous tome known as the Liber Mortis, the Book of the Dead, which rests at my desk. Bound as it is by the prayers of the Grand Theogonist and wards of the Light Wizards, I know it cannot corrupt me, but yet still I fear and dare not do more than glimpse at its cursed pages, where long-dead faces leer back at me. I can barely bring myself to touch the human-skinned covers or the pages where the rites of Necromancy and the spells of blood magic are written by the hand of the Great Necromancer. For this book comes from the land of Sylvania, and it once belonged to the foul Vlad von Carstein, the most infamous of all the Vampire Counts, who was defeated by the holy Grand Theogonist Wilhelm at the Siege of Altdorf.

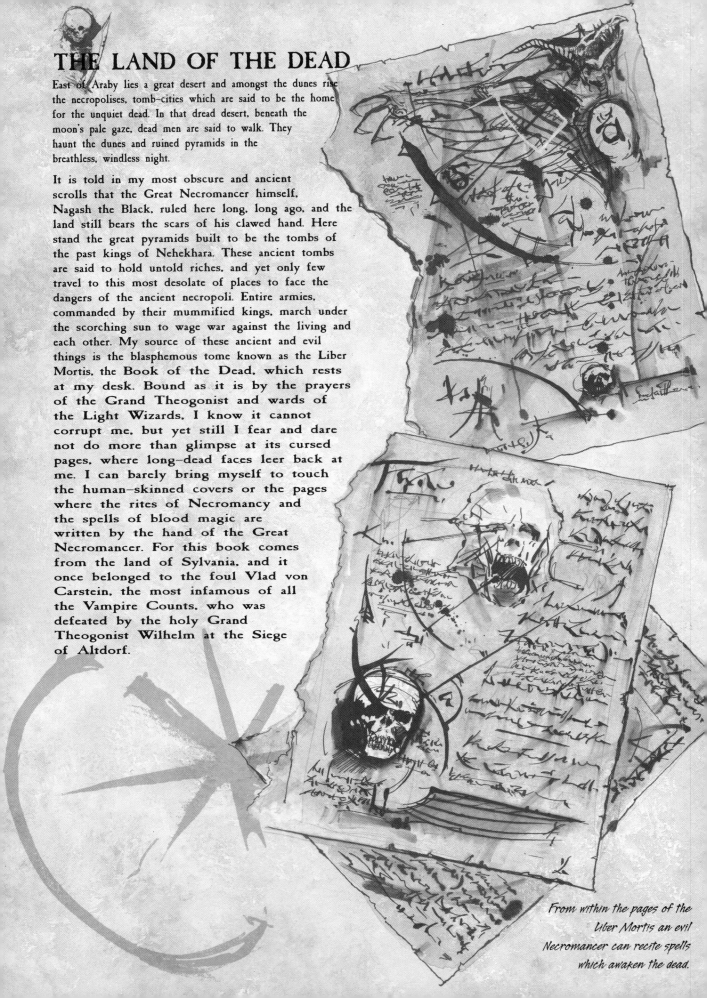

From within the pages of the Liber Mortis an evil Necromancer can recite spells which awaken the dead.

OF DWARFS

Dwarfs are an ancient race, wide of girth, strong of arm, and stubborn of mind. Unless killed in battle, a Dwarf can live to a very great age, as long as 400 years, though the Dwarfs claim that some of their Runesmiths have lived considerably longer. I can scarcely believe these tales, even though it is not in the Dwarf nature to lie.

The mighty Worlds Edge Mountains have been their home since time immemorial. Once, a long time ago, mighty Dwarf strongholds formed an unbroken chain along the mountain range. Great were the halls and vaults hewn out of the mountains, and great was the clamour of Dwarf hammering and song singing echoing in the depths. Now, alas, many of these once great holds resound only to the scampering feet of Goblins.

Dwarfs are the greatest smiths and craftsmen in the world. Not even Elven smiths can match the skill and care of the Dwarfs. It was the Dwarfs who in days past forged the Runefangs, the twelve swords of the Empire, as a payment for Sigmar's help against the Orcs. Today they are the symbols of office and authority of the Elector Counts of the Empire.

Dwarfs are as strong and unbending as stone (and some would say as forgiving) and grim as the mountains they live in. From Karaz-a-Karak, the most ancient of the Dwarf holds, the last High King of the Dwarfs wages a never-ending war against Orcs, Goblins and other evil creatures. Each year Dwarf numbers dwindle. Each year the war becomes more desperate. Each year the enemies of the Dwarfs become more numerous. In my mind the wisdom of continuing this struggle is doubtful, even if its heroism is not. But as long as one of their warriors draws breath, the Dwarfs will not set aside their axes or forget their grudges.

In my youth I travelled to Karaz-a-Karak, the seat of the Dwarf High Kings to study their lore. For seven years I stood behind the door of the Hall of Remembrance to prove my dedication to learn the Dwarf Lore. Finally the locked doors were opened for me, and even then the Dwarf Loremasters were reluctant to part with their knowledge, and only taught me because of the long-standing friendship between the Emperors and the Dwarf Kings.

I studied the Great Book of Grudges and the Book of Remembrance, where the history of the Dwarf race is recorded in the runescript, and the annals of their kings are kept, with each passing day recorded in meticulous detail by dozens of Dwarf scribes.

The Book of Remembrance claims that during the ancient times the mighty Dwarf empire stretched across the entire Worlds Edge Mountains, from the lands of Norsca in the north to the distant Southlands, encompassing dozens of Dwarf Holds. But those days are now long gone, only a memory recited in sagas sung in the few Dwarf halls that still survive. For long before the time of Sigmar, there was a war in the Old World.

Dwarf fought Elf and Elf fought Dwarf. It seems that for an entire age the slaughter continued, and many great battles were fought where both races suffered terribly. The war finally ended when the Dwarf High King defeated the Phoenix King in single battle and the Elves retreated from the Old World.

Huge earthquakes and volcanic eruptions shattered the vaults and chambers of the Dwarf holds and broke the power of the Dwarf empire for all time. Evil creatures from below the bowels of the earth then emerged to challenge the Dwarf supremacy of the mountains, and cast them onto the precipice of extinction where they now fight.

The Great Book of Grudges which is kept in Karaz-a-Karak holds the record of great breaches of faith against the Dwarf people. Its words are written in the blood of kings - so seriously do Dwarfs regard such matters.

OF THE ELVES

Elves are an ancient, fey and rare folk. Some scholars believe that the Elves are immortal, but I believe that it is the cruel fate of all living things to perish, and even these fey creatures die as time passes. But the Elves do live for a very long time indeed. Some of their lords have lived for two millennia, though I hazard a guess that the lifespan of the Elf warrior be until he is slain in battle, which will oft be sooner than his natural death. Can it therefore be any wonder that the Elf wears upon his face such a sorrowful countenance and speaks much of fate and doom?

Physically Elves are tall, slender and elegant creatures with aesthetically beautiful features. Their flowing hair is as fine as flax. Their movements are graceful, and their speed is inhuman. To the eyes of a Man, the Elves appear radiantly beautiful, but the wise should not let appearances fool them, for the Elves are quick to anger and slow to appease. A mortal Man who might by chance cast his eyes upon an Elf maid would think her to be a goddess and would be incapable of any thought but her for the rest of the day. The wise do not judge Elves by their divine appearance alone, but shun these fey and strange creatures, for beneath the beautiful exterior lies an enigmatic and mystic psyche.

The minds of the Elves are every bit as quick and agile as their bodies, but at the same time they are inhuman and strange, their mentality completely alien to a Man. They can concentrate on a single task with terrifying intensity. An Elf can quickly master any skill and far surpasses humans in song, writing, magic, alchemy, architecture or any other fine art. Elves call themselves the First Speakers, and it is true that their gifts of song and speech surpass by far any of the mannish races.

But such mental discipline comes at a price. Elves can lose track of time and the affairs of the world around them, foregoing rest and nourishment. Indeed an Elf may lose himself for weeks, staring intently at a beautiful sculpture or painting, uncaring of the flow of time or events evolving around him. Elves are also aloof, proud, arrogant, and uncaring of 'lesser' races. In their eyes, Men are little better than Orcs, and more often than once Men and Elves have come to blows.

The Elves are divided into several peoples and kindreds. The Great Ones, known as the High Elves, inhabit the great island–continent of Ulthuan which rests in the Great Western Ocean. Their great capital of Lothern in the land of Eataine is the hub of Elven trade, and the port of the mighty Elven armada. From here their fleet plies the waves to dominate trade and explore the world.

Finubar the Seafarer is their ruler, and he is the most cosmopolitan of all the Phoenix Kings. He lifted the ancient bans which decreed that no ship save those of the Elven fleet may ply the seas for three hundred miles around Ulthuan. The city is as far as any non-Elf can go. Human traders can taste the pleasures of the most wondrous city of the world (after our beloved Altdorf, that is) and ply their trade in the bazaars and merchant houses of Lothern. But to try to pass the Emerald Gate is to invite swift and certain death. A ten thousand strong guard keeps vigilance over the city and the citadel of Glittering Tower, the beacon which guides the Elven craft through the straits of Lothern.

Elven craftsmanship is exquisite and wondrous to behold. It is said that often their artefacts have magical powers.

Outside their blessed island, Elves are rare nowadays, and getting rarer. Only in the land of Bretonnia, amongst the hidden glades of the Loren Forest, survives the last kingdom of the Wood Elves in the Old World.

The Wood Elves of Loren are the masters of the bow, and it is said that an Elven marksman can hit an eye of a Goblin in the dark. Many strange tales are told in the land of Bretonnia about the fey Elf Lords of Loren. Troubadours of Couronne sing of a cult of Wardancers, young Elves with lethal acrobatic abilities as well as strange and terrible Beastmasters, Elves who live amongst the wild animals of the forests. Tales also tell of Elves who sing to the trees and plants, shaping them to form houses and make the paths of the forest misdirect intruders. The most fanciful tales speak of Forest Spirits, of giant trees that walk like men, but these are probably mere fables. Few men ever venture to the glades of Loren, and fewer still return. When they do, they are found on the boundaries of the Loren Forest, their bodies broken and strung on the branches of the trees as warnings to trespassers. Bretonnians have learned to fear the 'Fayrie Folk', and leave their woodland kingdom alone.

So Loren rests, shrouded by mists and magic, brooding and forbidding. Be wary traveller, and do not venture to the shadow of Loren. For even if you do not lose your life to an Elven arrow or sword, you might travel for three hundred years amongst the glades, never realising the time that has passed until you return to your home and the years take their toll on you in an eyeblink.

Wood Elves live in very few places besides Loren. The Forest of Shadows and Drakwald Forest are said to hold small Elven communities still. A man should be wary in these places, for many have died by unseen arrows when they have trespassed into the domains of Elves, even without knowing that they had passed their invisible borders.

According to folklore, many towns of Bretonnia are built upon places where Elven cities once stood.

There is said to be a third kindred of the Elves as well, even more sinister than the other two. From across the separating seas come piratical Elf raiders dressed in black, bringing death to the coastal areas with fire and steel. No scholar that I have talked to knows their true origin. Perhaps they live at sea, or come from some other land of the West, past the blessed island of Ulthuan. The Lords of Ulthuan say little of these raiders, but warn us to slay them without mercy. They call these black-garbed Elves the Dark Elves, and hint at some ancient schism amongst the Elves which led to their downfall. It is said that over a millennia ago these Dark Elves sacked the city of Remas in the land of Tilea, razed it to ground and took thousands of prisoners to be carried off to slavery. It is a proof of how the race of Elves is capable of great cruelty and evil despite their fair countenance and apparent civility.

To me the Elven race remains a fascinating, complex and dangerous mystery. But I shall rejoice when they are no more, for then all that remains shall be left for Man. These are the last days of the Elves, and their sun is setting – glorious, blood-red, and ultimately dying.

OF THE LANDS ACROSS THE SEA

Across the Great Western Ocean, south of the bleak lands of the northern shores lies the hot and uncharted land which is called Lustria by the scholars of the Empire. Many fortune-seekers travel there, and, though few return, they bring tales of the steaming-hot jungles and strange inhabitants, of howling dusky warrior-women and of the lizard-men which dwell amongst ruined temple cities of immeasurable antiquity.

I have seen the dissection of one of these corpses and witnessed its strangeness and unwholesome appearance. They appear to be giant lizards of sorts, walking on two feet like men, though they are far taller and have heavy musculature, and their blood is said to be cold and venomous.

Their temples reputedly hold vast riches such that the Emperor equipped an expedition to bring back the wealth of distant Lustria to the Empire where it could be put to good use in the service of his most Imperial Majesty Karl-Franz. That was many years ago and there has since been no word of the fate of this expedition.

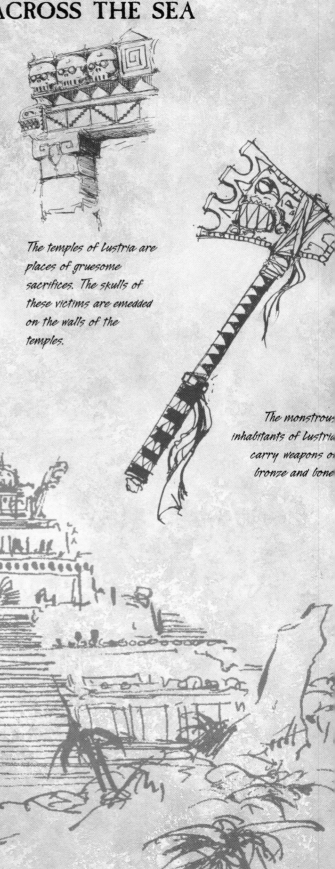

The temples of Lustria are places of gruesome sacrifices. The skulls of these victims are emedded on the walls of the temples.

All manner of strange scaly monsters dwell in the jungles of Lustria; for it is a morass from which but few return who have gone thence. Great are the treasures heaped up in the cities of the lizardmen, to whom gold is commonplace.

The monstrou: inhabitants of Lustria carry weapons of bronze and bone

OF THE ENCROACHMENTS OF DREAD CHAOS AND THE ENEMY WITHIN

Even here in my own chamber, protected by the Templars of Reiksguard and by the prayers of the most pious priests of Lord Sigmar, I shiver with fear when I write of the unspeakable beast, the abomination, the enemy of life, the dread power that men call Chaos.

It is claimed by the foul daemonologists that our world is but one of many, and all of us exist in the world of shadows as well as in the real world we can see. They say that our shadow-selves live in the strange and unfathomable place known as the Realm of Chaos, the shadowy, immaterial abode of daemons. Known also as the Aethyr, the Warp, the Underworld, the Utterdark and by many other names. Here time has no meaning and the events of past, present and future meld into one, chaotic existence. Some debate that this is not one dimension but many, an infinite number of alternative worlds where everything is possible and every variation of human history is played out as decreed at the beginning of time.

North from the borders of Kislev, past the rugged Troll Country, lies the hellish Realm of Chaos where the daemons roam, servants of Entropy and the Long Night. These creatures consist of thoughts alone, and these thoughts are terrible.

The Realm of Chaos is a home to many terrible entities of cosmic power. I tremble as I write down the names of the Four Great Gods of Chaos. I dare not speak their names aloud, for their servants can see and hear anything that is said anywhere, and the wise do not draw the attention of the denizens of the dark to themselves. Therefore I shall write them down and pray for your souls.

There are four vile and loathsome Dark Gods of Chaos – four brothers in darkness. The first of them is Khorne, the great god of War, the Lord of Skulls. He takes many shapes: a gigantic blood-stained hound, a bestial warrior, his hands dripping with blood, a brooding king sitting on a throne of skulls. In his hand is a sword, upon him, brass armour, and he sits on a great mound of skulls which stretches around him eternally. His bellow of rage echoes throughout time and space, and it is he who brings the curse of war to the unhappy world.

Next is Tzeentch, the Great Conspirator, the master of the mutable timestream. He is the Sorcerer of Chaos, and his sphere of influence is change. He is the Ever-changing One, the master of magic, and mutator of Mankind. His followers infiltrate the human society, forever plotting, biding their time, waiting for the moment to rise up against law and order.

Nurgle is the nauseating Lord of Plague. He is described as a vast mountain of rotting and corpulent flesh, ridden with all the diseases of the world. In his physical form Nurgle is a mountain of filth and corruption. But these words scarcely do justice to the true foulness that is Father Nurgle, the lord of physical corruption and disease, morbidness and hopelessness. It is he who unleashes the horrific diseases that take such a terrible toll on the inhabitants of the Old World.

Lastly there is Slaanesh, the keeper of hidden vices and terrible passions, the Lord of Forbidden Pleasures, the decadent Prince of Chaos. Slaanesh is said to be neither man or woman yet both, and that to see the physical perfection of his form is to be damned to love him forever with passionate and undying intensity. His followers and daemons cavort naked with the fallen, driven forth to new and agonising pleasures by his stinging whips.

There are many other lesser powers of Chaos: lesser gods, godlings, daemons and demigods, but only the Four Great Powers are known everywhere in the known world. They are worshipped throughout the world in different guises and names, but always they remain the same, as do their goals

Many mortals serve the daemonic overlords of Chaos. From the north come the black-clad warriors of Chaos, followed by the barbarian tribes that worship the gods of Chaos. These are the enemy without, the dark armies that gather on our borders.

More insidious are the followers of Chaos within. In the lands of men there are reviled and sick heretics who worship the Chaos gods in secret. Despite the efforts of the order of Witch Hunters, their influence grows daily. It grows in secret, and many powerful and influential men secretly throw their lot in with the Ruinous Powers, hoping to gain great power and immortality as their reward. In deep cellars and hidden temples these despicable and insane men perform hideous rites and living sacrifices to appease their dark masters. Each year they are said to be more numerous and powerful.

Many of us believe that we live in the dusk-time of the world. I fear that they might be right. Sigmar forgive me, for these are heretical thoughts, but the shadow of the north has grown so huge that I see little hope for our survival. Sigmar preserve us and deliver us, for our world has grown very dark indeed. Perhaps I have doomed myself by what I have written, but I have sworn to write the truth for scholars who come after me, and warn them of the danger.

OF THE POWER OF MAGIC

Long ago the study of magic was forbidden in the lands of the Old World, and all men and women who saw visions or could perform miraculous deeds were (quite sensibly) burned at the stake. But during the Great War against Chaos, Magnus the Pious, the uniter of the Empire, lifted the ancient ban against sorcery, and established the Colleges of Magic. From that day on the Empire has been served by a corps of Battle Wizards.

The Aethyr, or the Wind of Magic, encompasses eight strands of Magic: that of Fire or Pyromancy, Gold or the Lore of Alchemy, Amber the Wind of Beasts, Light which is the Heavenly lore of Astromancy, the Shadow Wind and the Jade Wind of Life as well as the purple Wind of the Dead. These are the disciplines of sorcery as they are taught in the Colleges of Magic today.

But though many do not know it, all magic originates from the Realm of Chaos. In the furthest north, say the scholars of the Colleges of Magic, stands a colossal gateway to the dimension of nightmares and daemons. From this gaping maw spews forth unnatural winds and mutating dust. This energy coils around the world like an immense serpent, and it is this power that the Wizards employ when they are casting spells.

Those with the gift (or, indeed the curse) of second sight can perceive these eight energies as they emerge from the Northern Wastes, and coil over the world like a serpent strangling its prey. Humans specialise in one of these strands of magic, and there are schools of sorcery which specialise in each of the colours of magic.

The Wizards of the Gold College make many powerful magical artefacts, such as scrolls imbued with enchantment and potions which can heal the sick.

Fierce Wyverns are said to be kin to Dragons. They have serpentine bodies, huge wingspans and their tail ends with an envenomed barb.

OF THE MONSTROUS BEINGS

Many of my grimoires show pictures of frightening beasts. Of Giant Octopi that lurk beneath the waves: of great Kraken which emerge to consume entire ships before sinking back to the dark depths of the ocean. Of the strange Jabberwock, said to eat beautiful maidens. Of the Winged Folk of the southern isles, and the serpentine Wyrms of the East. Of course, a rational scientist such as myself does not believe in things such as these.

But there are other beasts which do exist, as I have seen with my own eyes. The zoo of our most beneficent Emperor here in Altdorf holds many strange and terrible creatures which can be brought to war: Griffons with the bodies of lions and heads of fierce eagles, steaming winged horses called Pegasi, giant snakes brought by the Arabian merchants from the Southlands, Hippogriffs that nest in the crags of the Massif Orcal, great lumbering beasts of Araby known as elephants, and many more.

Dragons are the most ancient of the creatures. Under the Worlds Edge Mountains and stony mounds the Dragons are still said to slumber. Even Kalgalanos the Black, the father of all Dragons is rumoured to have his lair beneath the bowels of the earth, with the mountains as his spine, waiting for the doomsday, when the Dragons will be roused from their slumber, and soar above the clouds once more.

OF ORCS AND GOBLINS

The Orcs and Goblins are the bane of all civilised races. These creatures have hides of greenish hue and are hideous in appearance. Their beady eyes glow red in the dark and their foul fangs protrude from their gaping mouths which utter such grunts as pass among them for language. They converse among themselves as much by blows and cuffs as by words and it is a wonder that they can make or do anything at all. Indeed, their weapons and artefacts are of the crudest kind, yet effective enough to wreak havoc in every land.

Their encampments are squalid in the extreme and, every so often, the tribes gather and migrate in great hordes across the land, waging war which is their greatest delight. Indeed, it is said that Orcs in particular live for war. Goblins, their lesser cousins eagerly follow and serve the Orcs. The names of many tribes are known, such as the Festering Scabs, the Iron Claws, the Red Eyes, and the Broken Tooth, and these tribes are swayed by their Shamans who wield strangely potent magical powers. It is they who invoke their idols and raise up warlords and set the tribes in motion, stirring up the great Wargas or wanderings of which the Kislevites speak.

Orcs are constantly fighting amongst themselves to establish the rule of the strongest. Thus there are endless layers of leaders and warlords, each vying for power. Thus much of their energy is spent fighting amongst themselves. It is claimed there is no Orcish word for 'equal'.

There is no counting the numbers of Orcs and Goblins which infest the barren places of the world and no matter how many are slain, there are always more. Certain other creatures slink and grovel around the Orc encampments such as Trolls, who are foul and ghastly beyond description and the Snotlings who infest the dungheaps in their multitudes.

Do not, however, underestimate the power of the Orcs. For sometimes, when led by a warlord who is inspired by his idols, the horde becomes unstoppable and will cut a swathe through the realms of Men, Dwarfs and even Elves. Great cities have been laid low by the Orcs and many fine things have been overthrown and trodden into dust.

The Orcs are green of skin and strong of stature. They are taller and broader than a man but stooped like an ape of the Southlands. Orcish kind has fangs which are bared and their eyes are set deep beneath a thick brow. When an Orc speaks he utters but few uncouth words, in a deep voice. The Orc has but little intelligence excepting for some glimmer of cunning.

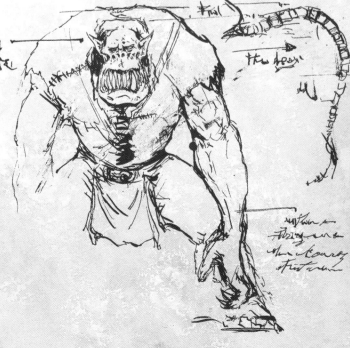

Many strangely-shapen and fanged skulls found in sewers are often claimed to be remains of Skaven, doubtlessly they originally belonged to mutants which infest such places.

The scroll below is said to contain a detailed plan of attack against the fair city of Nuln. The scribe who translated the text has been entrusted to the care of the priestesses of Shallya in the great Altdorf Asylum.

OF THE RATMEN OF THE UNDERWORLD

One of the most persistent legends in the folklore of ignorant and uncouth peasants is that of giant rats who walk on two feet in the manner of men. It is said that their vast empire stretches for untold miles beneath the earth. Allegedly their society is divided into several Great Clans, each ruled by powerful Skaven collectively known as the Lords of Decay. Most of the time they are said to fight amongst themselves like rabid rats, but sometimes they set their bickerings aside and wage war against other inhabitants of the Old World. When the rat-host goes to battle, they muster the innumerable hordes of the lesser Warlord Clans.

There are lunatics and madmen in the Great Altdorf Asylum who claim that they have escaped from the slavery of these rat-men, and others who say that even as we speak they are preparing for a great war against Mankind.

I have never seen such creatures, and as the learned professors of Nuln have shown, irrefutable scientific proof exists that these creatures are but a sham and a hoax. I have included here a parchment which is said to been written by one of these creatures known as Skaven. I have brought it before your Majesty for the sake of completeness, despite my firm belief that it is but a clever forgery.

These Skaven are but a figment of imagination, and there are enough real dangers in this grim world of ours. Let your thoughts concentrate on the tasks at hand and not on babblings of old senile saga poets.

According to these questionable reports, each of the Greater Clans has its own armaments and foul methods to wage war. The clan known as Moulder are powerful Beastmasters and use magical warpstone to breed and mutate ferocious fighting beasts. Clan Eshin are feared assassins and stealthy murderers. It is even rumoured that one of their number assassinated Emperor Mandred. Clan Skryre are known as Warlock Engineers, masters of an insane blend of magic and science. The Clan Pestilens are also known as the Plague Monks. They are disciples of disease and initiates of infection. It is told that their clan holds a great book called Liber Bubonicus which lists all diseases known to man and many unknown besides. As instructed by their god, the Plague Monks are dedicated to spreading pestilence and plague amongst the cities of men.

In the land of Tilea the men of that land tell tales of the great city of Skaven hidden deep in the rotting heart of the Blighted Marches. This city is called Skavenblight (Tileans are not noted for their originality) in the legends. Herein lies the temple of the Horned Rat, the foul Chaos god of Skaven, and here multitudinous millions of the Skaven hordes scuttle, plot, fight and murder, each vying for supremacy. No man has seen this city, and like most I believe it is just a myth, for the Blighted Marches are impenetrable and poisonous, thus giving rise to the legends of the Skaven city.

WARHAMMER ARMIES

The following pages give you an overview of the armies and creatures that inhabit the Warhammer world. The miniatures, superbly painted by the 'Eavy Metal team, will provide you with an insight into the diverse background of each race. We hope that this section inspires you to collect and paint your own armies to add to the rich tapestry that makes up the Warhammer game.

EMPIRE

The armies of the Empire are professional, well-disciplined and led by some of the finest generals in history. Facing attack from every border, the soldiers of the Empire defend humanity against countless invaders. A typical Empire army is based around units of heavily armoured Knights such as the legendary Knights of the White Wolf, or the noble Reiksguard Knights. These elite warriors are supported by regiments of highly trained infantry.

A regiment of Spearmen from the province of Talabheim. Recruited from the local towns and villages, these brave soldiers wear the livery of their Elector Count. Their shields bear the traditional device of the lion, a symbol that is commonly associated with Talabheim.

Battle-hardened and highly trained, Knights form the elite cavalry of the Empire, and are the stalwarts of any Imperial army.

The Free Companies of the Empire Militia are deadly street fighters, perfectly suited to battle in the armies of the Empire. These units band together in times of danger to defend their homes and villages from attack.

The Imperial Artillery School of Nuln trains men in the art of blackpowder weaponry. These brave crews use their expert knowledge of gigantic war machines, such as the Great Cannon or Imperial Mortar, to provide supporting fire for Imperial cavalry and infantry units.

Empire troops wear clothing with the colours of their home province. Variations in a unit's livery to denote its speciality are common practice. Several individual regiments wear their own unique livery.

Talabheim Swordsman

Empire Wizards hone their arts at the College of Magic. They are able to cast deadly spells across the battlefield.

Swordsmen of the Empire are expert fencers and highly skilled at fighting opponents one-on-one. This unit comes from Middenheim, the Empire's second largest city.

Handgunners are state troops and are part of the standing army of the Empire. This regiment from Talabheim has been tirelessly drilled in the use of their dangerous blackpowder weapons.

Master Engineers are experts in the fine craft of blackpowder weapons.

Spearmen form an essential part of an Empire army.

Pistolier regiments comprise young nobles eager to fight for their Emperor but who are not yet experienced or old enough to join the Reiksguard. They are known for their recklessness and hunger for victory.

The backbone of the Empire army is its brave infantry regiments. Swordsmen, Halberdiers and Spearmen are formed together in orderly ranks to defend their homelands, and Handgunners and Archers provide supporting fire to whittle down the advancing foes. At the rear of the army, heavy artillery pounds holes in enemy formations before they even come close to the Empire troops.

ORCS AND GOBLINS

Orcs and Goblins have a vast diversity of troops at their disposal, more so than perhaps any other army. Orcs excel at close combat, and boast some of the toughest warriors in the world. Orc and Savage Orc Boar Boyz are feared for the speed and destructive power of their charges. The mighty Black Orcs march at the front of any assault, using their sheer size and strength to brutal effect against any foe they face. The Goblins, smaller in size than their Orc cousins, use superiority of numbers along with evil cunning to defeat their enemies. With the support of many strange creatures such as the repugnant Trolls or the towering Giants to help them in their unquenchable thirst for battle, an Orc and Goblin horde is a force to be reckoned with.

Fuelled with a potent fungus brew, Night Goblin Fanatics are a menace to every unit on the battlefield, including their own regiments!

Orc Warriors wield huge weapons in battle known as 'choppas'. These great cleavers are far larger and more dangerous than the mere swords and axes of men. The standard of the unit is their tribal totem and is decorated with grisly trophies from previous victories.

Boar Boyz are among the most dangerous warriors in the Orc army. Should an enemy avoid being skewered on the tips of their wicked barbed spears, they then must face being gored to death on the tusks of the massive boars.

Subterranean Night Goblins emerge from their dark network of mountain tunnels and gather into large mobs in battle. Whilst not being the toughest of fighters, their sheer numbers, as well as the Fanatics hidden in their ranks, will often give an opponent cause to stay clear.

Orc Arrer Boyz can fire a hail of arrows into the massed ranks of an approaching army.

Goblin Shamans wield unpredictable, destructive magic powers.

The sight of a Giant looming over the battlefield is enough to strike fear into the hearts of an entire enemy army.

Orc Boar Chariots are often ridden by Big Bosses and Orc Warlords, sweeping away all who stand before them in a furious assault. Together with other war machines, such as the mighty Orc Rock Lobba, or monsters, such as the slow-witted Stone Trolls, the Orc army is a diverse, unpredictable force able to defeat any opponent, as long as they don't end up bickering amongst themselves.

DWARFS

The Dwarfs are an ancient, proud and grim race. Their heavily armoured infantry commands well deserved respect from any enemy who has ever stood against them. Dwarf Warriors are legendarily stubborn in defence of their mountain homelands, and are as equally unrelenting in their assaults. Dwarf artillery is amongst the most potent and destructive machinery in the known world. The legendary Dwarf Engineers have developed many unique and powerful war machines such as Gyrocopters and Flame Cannons. Having no aptitude for magic, the Dwarf army contains no Wizards. Instead they forge magical runes onto their weaponry, putting faith in the power of these symbols to aid them in battle.

Dwarf Rangers guard the mountain passes and trade routes against bandits and raiders. During battle, they fight alongside the other warriors of their stronghold. Dwarf Rangers are skilled in setting traps and pitfalls to hold up the advance of the enemy while the rest of the army prepares for the coming battle.

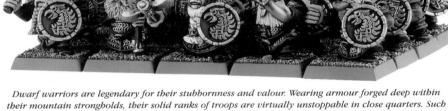

Dwarf warriors are legendary for their stubbornness and valour. Wearing armour forged deep within their mountain strongholds, their solid ranks of troops are virtually unstoppable in close quarters. Such a regiment typically carries ancient axes, some of which have been used by many generations of their kin before them. They fight under a standard depicting one of their venerated ancestors.

Crossbows are the favoured long-range weapons of Dwarf warriors. Many an Orc has died under a hail of bolts from a regiment of Dwarf Crossbowmen.

Longbeards are the most senior Dwarf warriors of their strongholds. They are known for their strength, skill at arms and long memory of any grudges that the Dwarfs have against their enemies. This regiment is from Karak Varn and is famous for never retreating from a battlefield.

SKAVEN

Pouring out from their network of labyrinths that run throughout the Old World, Skaven attack in massive hordes, overwhelming the opposition through sheer force of numbers. In battle their huge regiments are surrounded by unusual war machines, such as the deadly Warpfire Throwers or the Doomwheel. Masters of treachery, Skaven assassins strike deep into the heart of their opposing army.

Plague Censer Bearers spread disease through enemy ranks.

Globadiers carry fragile spheres of lethal warpstone gas to hurl amongst enemy ranks.

A Jezzail team prepares to fire. These are extremely long-range guns firing small pellets of Warpstone, and are used by the Skaven to deadly effect.

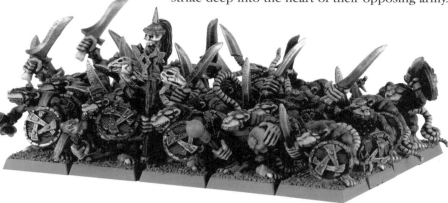

Clanrats form the vast bulk of Skaven hordes that pour forth in times of war. Individual Skaven are vicious but rather cowardly. In huge hordes, however, they turn into an unstoppable mass which overwhelms the opposition through sheer weight of numbers.

Stormvermin are the hand-picked elite troops of the Clanrat masses. They carry the best weapons and wear the best armour. Most Stormvermin are black-furred – the mark of a pure killer.

Rat Ogres are massive mutated monsters, created by the twisted genius of Clan Moulder. They have enough strength to tear apart a fully-armoured knight and their speed and inhuman ferocity makes them a fearsome enemy. With the support of deadly weaponry, such as the Warpfire Thrower which fires a flammable gas mixture into the enemy ranks, the Skaven are an army best kept at a distance by their opponents.

HIGH ELVES

A High Elf army arrayed for battle is an awe-inspiring sight. The citizen-soldier regiments of Spearmen and Archers form deep and disciplined ranks, their mithril armour shining bright in their enemies' eyes. Magnificent High Elf cavalry, such as the Silver Helms and Dragon Princes, hold lances high in preparation to charge. Combined with the firepower of war machines, such as the deadly Repeater Bolt Throwers, many armies are devastated before they even reach the High Elves' front line.

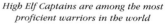

Silver Helms charge into battle.

Ellyrian Reavers hail from the outer Elven kingdoms, and their feats of horsemanship are legendary.

High Elf Captains are among the most proficient warriors in the world

Well practiced in all of the lores of magic, Elven Mages are potent Wizards.

High Elf Spearmen form ranks of silver armoured, highly disciplined warriors. So strong is their determination that they are capable of withstanding even the fearsome charge of a unit of Knights.

WOOD ELVES

Deep within the dense enchanted forest of Loren lie the mystical glades of the Wood Elves. Whilst the Wood Elf armies include formidable spearmen and swift cavalry, it is the skill of the archers that makes up the true strength of their forces. They are renown for their ability to out shoot any enemy. To help them in their battles to protect the forest from invasion, the Wood Elves call upon the aid of the magical beings of the forest: Dryads and mighty Treemen emerge from deep slumber to avenge any intrusion on their realms.

Wood Elves ride wild warhawks into battle, swooping down upon the unprotected flanks of the enemy.

Often wearing protective talisman paint, Wardancers leap and twist, leaving the enemy unable to strike them before delivering a fatal flurry of blows.

Wood Elf Mages use their affinity with nature to cast spells on any intruders in their forest realms

The Glade Guard roam the forest, gathering together whenever danger threatens. Their skill with spears is legendary. Many a foe has fallen before them, regretting the day that they dared trespass into the forest.

◄ *Wood Elf Scouts patrol the edges of Loren, warning of danger long before it nears.*

▲ *Wood Elves can muster formidable armies supported by mighty Treemen and Dryads. Together they guard the forest realm of Loren against invaders who seek to destroy their woodland home.*

CHAOS WARRIORS

Chaos Warriors gather together in bands to ravage and plunder the lands of the Old World, all in the name of their dark gods.

The dark warriors of Chaos descend from the Northern Wastes leaving nothing but carnage and destruction in their trail. These heavily armoured fighters wield cruel and menacing weapons, and there are very few troops who dare stand before the onslaught of these bloodthirsty beings. Leading the advance of a Chaos Warrior army are the mighty Chaos Knights, more than capable of riding down any troops that stand in the path of their charge. Hordes of Chaos Marauders, savage barbarians from the North, join the invaders, as do monstrous Ogres and all manner of vile creatures created by the mutating powers of the Chaos gods.

Chaos Sorcerers conjure their dark magic to cast upon the enemy.

The armour of a Chaos Warrior is carved with runes to give its wearer extra magical protection.

A mighty Chaos Warlord astride a dark Chaos Steed charging into battle is a fearsome sight.

Chaos Knights ride wickedly armoured steeds into combat; there are few foes who can withstand the power of their deadly charge. Chaos Ogres can easily rend a man limb from limb. Confident in their ability to defeat anyone in hand-to-hand combat, Champions of Chaos dare any mortal to fight against them.

DAEMONS

Spawned from the dark magics of the northern lands, Daemons cause terror and dread in the hearts of all mortals. Led by dark Lords and evil Princes, they seek to corrupt Mankind and gain control of the Old World. Khorne's Bloodletters slay for their master, whilst the Daemonettes of Slaanesh entice mortals to their death, a sacrifice to their cruel lord. The powers of Tzeentch twist and warp magic to use against their chosen victims, whilst the followers of Nurgle spread disease and pestilence wherever they pass. It is a brave general indeed that leads his men against a Daemon horde, for they are wholly different from any mortal force, having unworldly magical powers and inhuman strength.

The Bloodthirster, Greater Daemon of Khorne, seeks the skulls of foes rent asunder in the throes of battle, to place on his master's throne.

The Plague Bearer of Nurgle spreads all manner of vile plagues throughout the land.

Spawned from the twisted magic of Tzeentch, the Pink Horror tears its opponents apart in a frenzy of destruction.

A Greater Daemon of Slaanesh, the Keeper of Secrets leads his Daemonettes and Fiends of Slaanesh into battle against their foes. Luring mortals to an eternity of hellish torment, Greater Daemons are among the most powerful creatures that exist.

BEASTMEN

Twisted by the mutating powers of Chaos, Beastmen hunger for slaughter. Venturing forth from the darkest forests to kill and destroy in the name of their foul gods, the horned Gors revel in the spilling of blood. Mighty Minotaur Lords wield gigantic axes as they join the carnage. Wickedly scythed chariots pulled by mighty Tuskgors cut a swathe through the enemy ranks, scattering all before them.

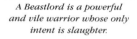

A Beastlord is a powerful and vile warrior whose only intent is slaughter.

Beastman Shaman

This Beastman Battle Standard bears the symbol of the horned skull, a common motif amongst the Beastmen armies.

The largest breed of Beastmen are known as Gors. These are huge and brutal creatures that have an unnatural vitality and hate all Mankind. They gather into great herds and strike out of the dark forests, destroying everything that stands in their path.

A Beastman warherd of the Drakwald Forest. A pack of Chaos Hounds is capable of rending the flesh off even large monsters, whilst the Minotaur is one of the most powerful creatures in the Old World. A unit of them in close combat is easily able to destroy any creatures that they may face.

TOMB KINGS OF
KHEMRI

It is said that more Undead roam the earth than mortals. The dread Tomb Kings of Khemri command a host of mummies and skeletal warriors that serve them in an unholy afterlife. Striking forth from the desert lands of the South, the skeletal host rides forth on ghastly chariots of bone to reclaim the land from the living.

This unit of Skeleton spearmen is led by a mummified Tomb Lord, raised from the dead. With many such regiments guarding numerous ruined temples, the desert lands of Khemri are a desolate and dangerous place for the unwary to seek ancient treasures.

Reanimated to create an unholy war machine, the Skeletal Chariot is both fast and deadly on the battlefield.

VAMPIRE
COUNTS

From the cursed land of Sylvannia come the immortal Vampire Counts, who rise from deep within the vaults of castles and temples that lie in ruins. They seek their prey from amongst their opponents' finest warriors. Commanding hordes of Undead warriors, the Vampire Counts thirst for the warm flesh and blood of the living.

Those mortals that do not fall prey to the Lahmia Vampire's seductive charm soon perish on her blades.

The Undead horde gathers to prepare for battle. Wight Cavalry sit astride their steeds, which faithfully serve them after death. A Vampire Count rides at the head of the army, whilst the Black Coach carries its sinister cargo, almost unstoppable as it rolls into battle. Regiment upon regiment of Undead warriors stalk the land: Ghouls, Skeletons, Zombies and Grave Guard. A ghastly sight to behold, few live to tell of glimpsing an Undead horde.

BRETONNIANS

A Bretonnian Sorceress weaves her magic spells to protect and aid the gallant Knights.

Bretonnia is the land of chivalry and honour. One of the most powerful nations of the Old World, the strength of the royal army of Bretonnia can be summed up in one word: Knights. From the reckless Knights Errant, valiantly seeking to prove their worth in combat, to the noble Grail Knights favoured by the Lady of the Lake, Bretonnian cavalry is unmatched in its martial prowess. With its sturdy barded steeds and the colourful heraldic coats of arms, the Bretonnian army is an imposing sight on a battlefield.

Though Knights form the backbone of Bretonnian armies, the army is nevertheless bulked out by other troops as well. These forces are made up of Commoners armed with bows, spears and halberds, as well as Squires who fight both mounted and on foot.

The noble Grail Knights have fulfilled their quest and so are granted the favours of the Lady of the Lake. They ride into battle without fear and with the experience of many years of combat behind them.

The valiant Knights of the Realm charge to meet the foe. The charge of Bretonnian Knights is powerful enough to cause most enemy units to turn tail and flee from the battle. Should the enemy be able to withstand the lances as they puncture through their ranks then they must face fully armoured Knights trained in martial skills. For a Bretonnian Knight, combat is a daily ritual; though few in number, they are strong of heart.

LIZARDMEN

Lizardmen inhabit the vast jungles of the distant land of Lustria. It is a realm where the mystical Slann hide away deep within their pyramid cities to study secret texts of ancient times. Their armies consist of cohorts of powerful Saurus warriors and masses of darting Skinks. The envenomed arrows and javelins of the Lizardmen drive off those who seek to steal the treasures of the forgotten civilisation. Often travelling to the other continents to take back treasures that rightly belong to their ancestors, the Lizardmen will swiftly punish anybody daring to interfere in their cold-blooded affairs.

This Slann Mage-Priest of Chaqua uses his knowledge of ancient texts to cast very powerful and potent spells.

Fortress-like Stegadons are capable of crushing entire regiments of troops. With giant crossbows mounted on their howdahs, they are dangerous creatures to stand up to.

Skink Warriors fight in huge units. This regiment carries the banner totem of Sotek, the great serpent god. The different spawnings of Skinks and Saurus have different coloured hides and crests.

Saurus Temple Guards protect the sacred Lizardmen temples from plunderers.

A massive Kroxigor; the most powerful of the Lizardmen warriors. Their giant bronze axes can easily crush smaller opponents.

A Saurus regiment marches through the thick tropical jungles of Lustria. Their scales are thick enough to give them a measure of armoured protection, whilst their crude spears are effective enough to scare off any invaders.

DARK ELVES

Dark Elves dwell in the realm of Naggaroth, the Land of Chill, far in the northern part of the New World. From their six menacing fortified cities, they march forth to enslave the free peoples. The bulk of the Dark Elf army is made up of Spearmen and Warriors drawn from amongst the citizens of the Dark Elf cities. Sacrifices of blood are made in the name of the Witch King, and the bodies of slain victims litter the battlefields of the Dark Elf armies. No one is spared the wrath of the Dark Elf army, for mercy is an ideal beyond their understanding.

A Witch Elf uses her menacing blades for combat. Witch Elves bathe in the blood of their victims to gain everlasting youth.

A Corsair is a deadly warrior. Wearing a cloak made from the scales of a Sea Dragon, he is a formidable opponent.

After sacrificing victims in dark rituals, a Dark Elf Sorceress can wield magic with deadly intent.

Dark Elf Spearmen form the core of the Dark Elf army. Disembarking from raiding fleets, they ravage and plunder the Warhammer world in search of slaves to take back to the dark cities of Naggaroth.

Dark Elf armies are fast and deadly due to their warriors being highly trained and well-equipped. In addition to the Repeater Crossbows, who can darken the sky with a hail of bolts, the maniacal Witch Elves work themselves into a frenzy of bloodshed. The Harpies of Clar Karond are able to swoop down and tear apart their foes with massive talons, whilst the Dark Riders quickly ride down any enemies who try to flee.

Then all chiefs made an oath
To stand together, united as men
And a crown was fashioned
By Alaric, runesmith of the Dwarfs
Placed by Ulric, the priest
Upon noble Sigmar's brow.
Henceforth let all men
unite and appoint the greatest
among them to wield the hammer
Then did Sigmar cause to be built
the greatest of halls beside the Reik
The high hall of kings.

SCENARIOS

Scenarios

The Battlefield

SCENARIOS

This section of the book includes some of the many different types of battles that you can fight out using the Warhammer rules.

WHAT IS A SCENARIO?

Imagine you are watching a game of Warhammer as a spectator. Two players line up their armies opposite each other across the wargames table. Then they begin the battle, playing turn by turn until one army has mostly fled or been wiped out. The army with the most troops left is deemed to be the winner. You are observing the game in its simple and typical form. This is in fact, a 'pitched battle' in which both sides have approached the battlefield head on, made camp for the night and formed up their battle lines at dawn, steadily marching in battle array towards each other until they clash. The only strategy in the minds of the Generals is to smash the opposing army in a frontal attack. In reality, this only represents one sort of scenario. There are many others.

In the course of a war or a campaign, many battles will not be 'pitched battles' since a General will try to outwit his opponent in strategy, by leading his army by devious routes or luring him into a trap, for example. This will more often than not lead to one of many possible battle scenarios such as an ambush, flank attack, encirclement or even a siege.

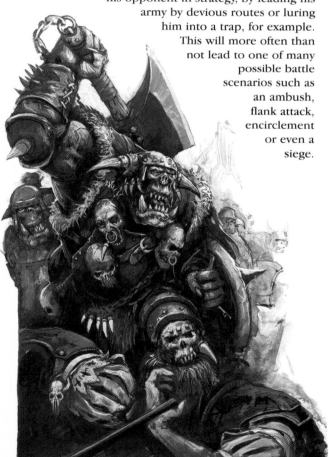

Nor is it likely that the armies would always be equally matched in numbers or fighting strength when they encounter each other.

In this section, various battle scenarios are described. These have been gleaned from the diverse annals and legends of the known world. Each scenario, as the name suggests, sets the scene of a particular battle. These encounters occurred during the course of wars and campaigns which had an influence on the time, the place and the circumstances in which the battle was fought as well as the forces involved. The commanders tried to outmanoeuvre each other with their entire armies during the marches which led up to the final encounters. Some succeeded in bringing their opponent to battle at a disadvantage. Others recklessly or despite every effort, found themselves fighting against the odds. For each side the challenge was that of a real battle: Can we fight our way out of this? Will our strength of numbers and tactical advantages win the day? Can we snatch victory from the jaws of defeat? or if all seems lost: Can we at least die heroically and win a place in legend?

Different scenarios require the players to re-examine their army choices and tactics, and ensure that every game is always different to the last. A player might choose an army which they feel confident can beat any foe in a Pitched Battle, but how would they fare if faced with fighting a Last Stand? It is this variety which constantly tests the generalship of the players, and every battle tells a different story and adds to the history of your army.

CHOOSING A SCENARIO

On the following pages are nine different scenarios, ranging in complexity. For your first few games, we recommend you just play the Pitched Battle scenario until you are confident with most of the Warhammer rules – there's quite a lot to learn without adding extra rules for a scenario!

Once you've got to grips with the basic Warhammer rules you might like to try out some of the other scenarios. The scenarios are presented in order of increasing complexity, so you might like to try scenarios 2 and 3 next.

Scenarios 1 through 5 all use an equal points value, so if you and your opponent have already agreed on the size of the battle to be played, you won't have to decide which scenario to play until you meet up. If you wish, you could randomly generate which of the scenarios you are playing after you have picked your armies – neither player knows exactly what they'll have to do and will need a balanced force to cover every eventuality. To randomly generate one of these scenarios, roll a dice and consult the following table:

Scenario chart

D6	SCENARIO
1-2	Pitched Battle
3	Breakthrough
4	Meeting Engagement
5	Flanking Force
6	Capture

The other battles use uneven points values or have additional restrictions on what to take in your armies and you will need to agree with your opponent beforehand which of these you want to play, as this will affect the size and/or type of army you can choose.

CREATING YOUR OWN SCENARIOS

Making up a scenario to fight isn't as difficult as it might seem at first. Inspiration can come from many places, including military history, films, books or comics. If you follow the same format we have used for our scenarios, filling in the blanks as it were, you'll see that coming up with a little bit of history, deployment rules and victory conditions isn't hard. In fact, some players just play scenarios they've invented themselves, because they know best what armies and terrain they and their opponents have.

The scenarios on the following pages all follow the same format:

BACKGROUND
This part gives an example from the Warhammer world of the type of battle the scenario outlines.

OVERVIEW
Provides a summary of what the armies are trying to achieve.

ARMIES
Details the size and composition of the armies that take part in the scenario. Any restrictions in this section are in addition to the normal rules for choosing an army, unless otherwise stated.

BATTLEFIELD
A map accompanies this short description of the battlefield, along with any special terrain rules used for the scenario.

DEPLOYMENT
This details where and in what order armies are set up.

WHO GOES FIRST?
Have a guess! Yes, this tells you how to determine which player gets the first turn.

LENGTH OF GAME
Here you'll find out how long the battle lasts.

SPECIAL RULES
Any additional rules particular to the scenario will be found in this section.

VICTORY CONDITIONS
This is where you can find out how to be victorious!

HISTORICAL RE-FIGHT
Includes any notes about re-fighting the battle presented in the Background section.

VICTORY POINTS

Many of the scenarios use Victory points to determine who has won the battle. Victory points (sometimes shortened to VPs) are a way of measuring how much damage has been done to the enemy army, as well as other factors such as a better tactical position and morale-boosting endeavours like capturing enemy banners. A player scores Victory points as shown in the Victory Points chart below. Compare the difference between the players' scores and size of the battle on the second chart to determine the result.

VICTORY POINTS CHART

You receive a number of Victory points equal to the points value of each enemy unit either destroyed, fleeing or having fled the table.

For example, a unit worth 400 points is worth 400 Victory points.

Each independent character is counted as a separate unit for this purpose, and characters mounted on monsters are also counted separately from their mount.

Eg, a Hero on a Dragon is slain, but the Dragon is still alive, score Victory points for the Hero only.

You also receive Victory points for each enemy unit reduced to below half its original starting number of models, and Independent models (characters, chariots and monsters) reduced to below half their starting number of wounds.

Do not count this if Victory points have already been scored for the unit being wiped out, as detailed above. Score Victory points equal to half the unit's points value (round up).

Eg, a unit worth 325 points is worth 163 Victory points if reduced to below half strength.

Divide the table into four quarters. Each table quarter that contains at least one of your units with a Unit Strength of 5 or more that is not fleeing, and no enemy units which are not fleeing – 100 Victory points.

Enemy General slain, fleeing or having fled the table – 100 Victory points in addition to Victory points scored for being a destroyed unit.

Each enemy unit Standard captured at the end of the battle – 100 Victory points.

Enemy Battle Standard captured at the end of the battle 100 VPs.

Victory points chart

		SIZE OF BATTLE (POINTS)					
		1-1,999	2,000-2,999	3,000-3,999	4,000-4,999	5,000-5,999	6,000+
VICTORY POINTS DIFFERENCE	0-149	D	D	D	D	D	D
	150-299	MV	D	D	D	D	D
	300-449	SV	MV	D	D	D	D
	450-599	SV	MV	MV	D	D	D
	600-749	M	SV	MV	MV	D	D
	750-899	M	SV	MV	MV	MV	D
	900-1,199	M	SV	SV	MV	MV	D
	1,200-1,499	M	M	SV	MV	MV	MV
	1,500-1,799	M	M	SV	SV	MV	MV
	1,800-2,099	M	M	M	SV	SV	MV
	2,100-2,499	M	M	M	M	SV	SV
	2,500+	M	M	M	M	M	M

D= Draw. Neither side holds the upper hand.

MV= Minor victory. You have won the battle, but only just!

SV= Solid victory. You have decisively defeated the foe. History will remember your endeavours today.

M= Massacre! You have ruthlessly crushed your foes and are a hero of your people!

SCENARIO 1 – BATTLE OF NEBELHEIM

This battle is often held up as an example of a true pitched battle, by scholars of the Empire.

In this battle the army of the Empire, led by Konrad, Elector count of Ostland, engaged a large horde of Orcs, led by Warlord Gorkfang. Knowing that the Orcs would press on regardless of losses and seek to overwhelm the Empire army by force of numbers alone, Konrad chose his ground carefully and devised a cunning plan. Then he deployed his army in the path of the invading Orc horde, forming up his carefully considered battle line in open, rolling terrain that formed a natural arena for the battle. Konrad then deliberately positioned thin lines of missile troops in the centre and big blocks of solid troops on the flanks.

The Orcs approached and seeing the apparently thin and weak centre, went into a headlong and ill-considered advance. Of course Konrad's centre gave way and the

Orcs surged onward oblivious to the approaching doom. It was now time for Konrad, relying on the immense discipline of his men, to close the trap. The massive and resistant Empire formations on both flanks, swung inwards and hammered the Orc army from both sides. It is said that the Orcs were jammed together so closely in the melee that they were unable to use their weapons and so fell readily and in great heaps to the massed halberds of the Ostlanders. Gorkfang, himself fell, and his horde was annihilated. It was a famous victory.

PITCHED BATTLE

Overview: Both armies are fully prepared for battle and their goal is simple – wipe out their enemy and take the field!

Armies: Both armies are chosen using the Warhammer army lists to an agreed points value.

Battlefield: Lay out the terrain in any mutually agreeable manner.

DEPLOYMENT

1. Both players roll a dice, the player who scores highest can choose the side of the table to deploy his forces on.

2. The players roll a dice, the highest scorer may choose whether to start deploying first or second.

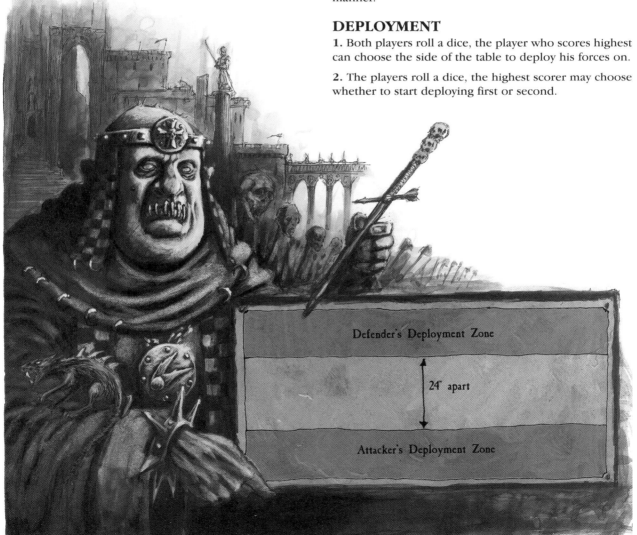

Defender's Deployment Zone

24" apart

Attacker's Deployment Zone

3. Taking it in turns, each player deploys one unit at a time, at least 24" from the opposing deployment zone.

4. All war machines in a player's army are deployed at the same time, though they can be deployed in different parts of the battlefield.

5. Champions are deployed with their unit, all other characters in the army are deployed after all other units, all at the same time.

6. Scouting units are not deployed with the rest of the units. Instead they are placed on the table after all units in both armies have been deployed, as described in the rules for Scouts.

Who goes first? Both players roll a dice, the player who finished their deployment first (not including Scouts) may add +1 to their dice roll. The player who scores highest may choose whether to go first or second (re-roll ties).

Length of game: The game lasts six turns or until one player concedes defeat.

Special rules: There are no special rules in this scenario.

Victory conditions: Unless one player concedes, use the Victory Points chart to determine who the winner of the battle is.

HISTORICAL RE-FIGHT

To re-fight the Battle of Nebelheim, simply use the Pitched Battle scenario as described. Of course, the Empire player cannot rely on his opponent being as reckless as Gorkfang, although he can try to be as cunning as Konrad. The battlefield is best represented by an open plain in the centre with perhaps low hills on the flanks to partially conceal either end of the Empire deployment zone from the approaching enemy.

SCENARIO 2 – THE BATTLE OF THE NECROPOLIS, Imperial Year 2480

Count Schuvaltz, one of the border princes, heard tale of the fabled Land of the Dead which lay across the sea to the south. Most interesting to him was the rumour of great treasures heaped up in the ancient tombs, just waiting to be taken. The Count was badly in need of funds to raise an army and fortify his castle, so he decided to send a small expedition to seek and bring back treasure from the necropolis of Zandri, the pyramids of which were spied by one of his ship's captains, whilst he sailed along the desert coast.

The force which the Count sent was fairly small and is likely to have included mercenaries. Only one survivor returned to tell the tale. They had indeed found tombs, full of golden artefacts, but their desecration had awakened the long dead dwellers of the necropolis. The expedition was attacked by overwhelming forces of skeleton soldiers led by their mummified king, and wiped out. Their bones remained among the sands to slowly bleach in the sun.

BREAKTHROUGH

Overview: In this scenario the attackers must sweep aside their opponents to break through to their objective.

Armies: Both armies are chosen using the Warhammer army lists to an agreed points value. The players have to decide which army will be the attackers and which will be the defenders.

Battlefield: Much of the battlefield is littered with scattered walls (linear obstacles), and the odd ruin or dune (difficult terrain). This serves to reduce some of the lines of advance available to the attacker.

Defender's Deployment Zone

24" apart

Attacker's Deployment Zone

12"

Viktor gazed out over the plain and his heart sank. Countless ranks of warriors were calmly arraying themselves for battle, forming up in regiments, dragging bizarre war engines into position and driving their chariots out to the flanks. They moved with a single will, in complete silence save the clatter of ancient arms and equally ancient bones, for this was an army of the dead.

Gaston caught his sleeve and pointed to the distant temple. Something else was moving there, moving towards them. Something huge, but thankfully unclear in the haze of heat and dust that hung over the scorched land. Somehow Viktor knew he wouldn't be cheered when he got a good look at it. How could it be that only an hour ago he had been running coins through his fingers like washing his hands in a golden stream? All had seemed well, no sign of life anywhere. He smiled bitterly, still no sign of life, just this vast host of skeletal monstrosities between his pitifully small army and the safety of their ships.

There was nothing for it but to act and act quickly. Barking orders to the captains of regiments, Viktor rode along his hastily forming battle line. At least they were a lot faster than the dread horde they faced. With courage and luck they would be able to smash a hole through the enemy and, forming up as a moving square, keep fighting their way to the ships. He had heard better plans in his day, but there was not a great deal of choice.

Good. Everything was ready. Everyone knew their places and the desperation of their plight. There was only one order to give: Charge!

From atop the pyramid the lone deserter watched in awe as the ragged and sunburnt mercenaries surged forward. As they advanced the guile of Viktor's plan was revealed. Instead of charging in a mass, the centre of the mercenary line advanced quickest, the flanks moving in towards the centre to form first an arrowhead that smashed into the Undead line, then a column that pushed its way through. The slothful reactions of the Skeletal host left most of their army without a foe to fight, both flanks staring with empty sockets as their opponents redeployed. For a moment it looked as if the plan might even work, then the advance faltered. Skeletons erupted from the sands before the regiments that had broken through the line, forming new blocking units as fast as the old ones were cut down. Fallen mercenaries clutched their swords once more with dead hands and turned on their former comrades. It was a massacre.

DEPLOYMENT

1. Both players roll a dice, the player who scores highest may choose which side of the table to deploy on.

2. The players roll a dice, the highest scorer may choose whether to start deploying first or second.

3. Taking it in turns, each player deploys one unit at a time, no closer than 24" to the enemy and 12" from the neutral table edges.

4. All war machines are deployed at the same time, though they can be deployed in different parts of the battlefield.

5. Champions are deployed with their unit, all other characters are deployed after all other units, each player deploying their characters all at the same time.

6. Scouting units are not deployed with the rest of the units. Instead they are placed on the table after all units in both armies have been deployed, as described in the rules for Scouts.

Who goes first? Both players roll a dice, the player who finished their deployment first may add +1 to their dice roll. The player who scores highest may choose whether to go first or second (re-roll ties).

Length of game: The game lasts six turns.

Special rules: There are no special rules in this scenario.

Victory conditions: At the end of the battle, each attacking unit in the defender's deployment zone is worth its points value in Victory points. Units that are fleeing, monsters and characters do not count towards this total. No other Victory points are used. The attacker wins if they can score a number of Victory points equal to a third or more of their starting points value (rounding fractions down). For example, a 1,500 points attacking force must have 500 points or more of units in the defender's deployment zone to win.

HISTORICAL RE-FIGHT

The Battle of the Necropolis took place between an attacking Empire force and a Tomb Kings of Khemri army. To represent the soft, shifting sands of the desert, any war machine that tries to move must first roll a 5 or 6 on a D6 or can do nothing that turn.

In addition, attacking troops wearing heavy armour (including Knights) roll 1D6 less than normal for Flee and Pursuit rolls to represent their exhaustion under the blazing sun. In the defenders' deployment zone is the treasure-filled tomb of Prince Anera-kotrak, the objective of the Empire army.

SCENARIO 3 – THE BATTLE OF SWARTZHAFEN, Imperial Year 2050

During the period of the three Emperors the Empire was riven by civil war as rival claimants to the throne fought against each other. At this time Sylvania was in the grip of the Vampire Count Vlad von Carstein, who sought to exploit the situation and make his own bid for power.

As Vlad set his Undead host marching from Sylvania, the Elector Count of Middenheim was preparing to attack the province. The two armies surprised each other, clashing a few miles inside the borders of Sylvania. Even though the Middenheim army was engaging the Undead on very unfavourable ground, among ruins, cairns and the dark forest, the Middenheimers responded more rapidly, fought hard and won the day. Vlad himself was smashed down in battle by the Knights of the White Wolf and disappeared for a year before re-emerging from Sylvania at the head of another Undead army.

MEETING ENGAGEMENT

Overview: In this scenario both armies must deploy from a column of march and engage the enemy.

Armies: Both armies are chosen using the Warhammer Army lists to an agreed points value.

Battlefield: A Meeting Engagement can take place over any terrain you like.

Defender's Deployment Zone

6"   6"

24" apart

Attacker's Deployment Zone

DEPLOYMENT

1. Before the battle the players must write an Order of March, to show where in their column each unit is. All war machines are included as a single unit for these purposes, as are all the characters in the army. Characters are always deployed last.

2. The players roll a dice each, highest scorer is allowed to choose a table edge.

3. Each player rolls a dice and the highest scoring player may decide whether to begin deploying first or second.

4. The players take it in turns to deploy their units, starting with the one at the top of their Order of March and working down. The second and subsequent units must be deployed closer to the neutral table edges than any unit already in play – in effect the army deploys outwards from the first unit.

5. All war machines are written as a single entry on the Order of March, though they can be deployed anywhere on the battlefield within the normal deployment zone.

6. Champions are deployed with their unit. All other characters are deployed after all other units in the army, each player deploying their characters all at the same time. Characters may start the battle within units.

7. Units must be deployed at least 6" from the neutral table edges and 36" from the enemy table edge.

8. Scouting units must be deployed in the same way as other units, except they may be deployed up to 18" from the enemy (they don't have enough time to work their way as far forward as normal).

Who goes first? Both players roll a dice, the player who finished their deployment first may add +1 to their dice roll. The player who scores highest may choose whether to go first or second (re-roll ties).

Length of game: The game lasts six turns.

Special rules: There are no special rules in this scenario.

Victory conditions: At the end of the game, players calculate Victory points using the Victory Points table on p.198.

HISTORICAL RE-FIGHT

To re-fight the historical scenario you would choose armies from the Vampire Counts and Empire army lists. The Empire army must include at least one unit of White Wolves and the Vampire Counts army is led by Vlad von Carstein. If Vlad is slain or flees from the table, the Empire win a decisive victory at the end of the turn. Knights of the White Wolf are immune to *fear* to represent their historic determination and valour on the day.

SCENARIO 4 – THE BATTLE OF THE BURNED BANNER, Imperial Year 1214

The High Elf stronghold of Tol Ista, a treaty port on the west coast of Estalia was besieged by a large warband of marauding Orcs and Goblins. These were the remnants of tribes driven out of Bretonnia and which had taken refuge in the rugged mountains of Estalia, led by Bruza da Big. A desperate attempt to sally out was repulsed and the Orcs captured the Elven banner. The surviving Elves fled back within the walls and were so greatly outnumbered that they prepared to abandon the port and sail away across the sea where the Orcs could not follow. At that moment a message was received from a carrier hawk. This said that an Elven force, led by Prince Ethwar was on its way to relieve the stronghold and was only one day's march away. The

besieged Elves sent back the hawk with another message telling Ethwar that they would hold out for one more day and then abandon the stronghold.

Ethwar pressed on to reach the stronghold, knowing that if he failed to break through the Orcs and Goblins, the garrison would have no option but to abandon it and save the ships and whatever else they could. Carrying aloft the Elf banner, which he had set alight as a burning beacon for his troops to follow, Bruza deployed his army on rising ground behind a stream so as to block the Elven advance, the flanks of the greenskin's position being protected by boggy ground. On the highest point he planted the Elven banner where it could be seen by the besieged and the relieving force as a taunt to Elven pride. Thus the engagement became known as the Battle of the Burned Banner.

The Orcs and Goblins began shooting at the advancing Elves as they struggled to form up a battle line. Ethwar's force was mainly cavalry and being sorely pressed for time, as well as enraged at the sight of the burned banner, recklessly charged the strongly held Orc and Goblin positions. Despite a timely attack along the Orcs' flank by the garrison of Tol Ista, the difficult approaches and massed formations of the Orcs and Goblins took a heavy toll on the Elves until the Elven army eventually recoiled and fled in confusion. As the sun set in the west, the last Elves of Tol Ista put to sea under cover of night and abandoned the stronghold, which was sacked by Bruza da Big the next day.

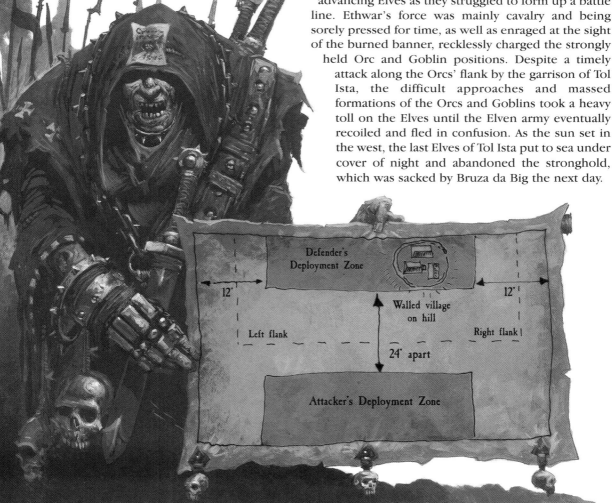

Defender's Deployment Zone

12"

Walled village on hill

12"

Left flank

24" apart

Right flank

Attacker's Deployment Zone

FLANK ATTACK

Overview: In this scenario the attacking force is divided between two armies, each attacking from a different direction. If they coordinate their attack well the defender will be overwhelmed, if they attack piecemeal they will be destroyed one army at a time.

Armies: Both armies are chosen using the Warhammer Army lists to an agreed points value. The players need to decide who is attacking and who is defending.

Battlefield: The defender's deployment zone is centred on an important defensible feature such as a hill or village. Other than this the players should set up the terrain in any mutually agreeable fashion.

DEPLOYMENT

1. Before any deployment, the attacker assigns up to one third of their army (in points) to be the flanking force. Units cannot be split between the two forces. The attacker must also write down whether these are flanking to the left or the right.

2. The players roll a dice each, highest scorer is allowed to choose a table edge.

3. Each player rolls a dice and the highest scorer may decide whether to begin deploying first or second.

4. Taking it in turns, each player deploys one unit at a time, no closer than 24" to the enemy deployment zone. Units can be no closer than 12" to the neutral table edges.

5. All war machines in a player's army are deployed at the same time, though they can be deployed in different parts of the battlefield.

6. Champions are deployed with their unit, all other characters are deployed after all other units in a player's army, all at the same time.

7. Scouting units are not deployed with the rest of the units. Instead they are placed on the table after all units in both armies have been deployed, as described in the rules for Scouts.

Who goes first? Both players roll a dice, the player who finished their deployment first may add +1 to their dice roll. The player who scores highest may choose whether to go first or second (re-roll ties).

Length of game: The game lasts six turns.

Special rules: At the start of the attacker's third turn, they start to roll to see if the flanking force has arrived. On a roll of a 4+ the flanking force turns up. If it does not turn up, roll again at the start of subsequent turns, adding +1 to the dice roll for each roll after the first (they turn up on a 3+ on the fourth turn, and so on).

The units in the flanking force move on from the table edge nominated before the battle, in the opponent's half of the table. Units may not charge on the same turn that they move onto the table, but do not count as starting their move within 8" of the enemy and so may march. You do not have to move all units on at the same time, units that are left off the table can move on in subsequent Movement phases.

Victory Conditions: The standard Victory points are used to determine the winner.

HISTORICAL RE-FIGHT

The Battle of the Burned Banner took place between a High Elf host and an Orc and Goblin horde. A burned banner is placed in the middle of the defender's deployment zone, on a hill. Any attacking unit that is within 18" of the banner *hates* the enemy. At least half the units in the High Elf force must be cavalry and the General must stay with the main force.

SCENARIO 5 – THE BATTLE OF BOGWURST, Imperial Year 1485

Baron Rikhardt succeeded to the Lordship of the Marches of Couronne by dubious and devious means. It was not long before his arch-rival, Count Henry, gathering an army in the Empire, invaded the Marches to oust him from power by force. Henry had secretly plotted with the disaffected Baron Lestanne and was counting on him either refusing to support Rikhardt or joining forces with Henry against him. When Henry's army invaded, Rikhardt gathered his own army and went forth to give battle commanding Lestanne to bring his contingent in support of his Lord. Lestanne took his time and turned up on the flank of the two opposing armies as they drew up their battle lines across a long ridge of dry ground surrounded by bogs. This ridge formed the main highway from the Empire through the marshes into Bretonnia. Neither of the two opposing Lords knew for sure who Lestanne would support. Maybe he would wait and see who prevailed or remain neutral throughout the battle?

Efforts by both sides to prompt Lestanne to show his hand before battle commenced were rebuffed. Exasperated, Baron Rikhardt advanced his army along the ridge and engaged Count Henry's army. The battle raged indecisively until late in the day. When Henry's army managed to advance on a commanding promontory at the height of the ridge, Lestanne decided to commit his forces, joining Count Henry's side. Lestanne advanced to engage Baron Rikhardt's army in the flank. Overwhelmed by force of numbers, Baron Rikhardt's army crumbled. Baron Rikhardt himself was cornered among the bogs and slain while trying to mount up on his warhorse and escape. Count Henry took over the Marches lordship. He rewarded Lestanne, but could never really trust him.

CAPTURE

Overview: In this scenario two forces are attempting to seize control of an important point on the battlefield. The generals do not know how soon they must capture the objective or how long they have to hold on to it, and so must commit themselves fully to the attack from the start.

Armies: Both armies are chosen using the Warhammer Army lists to an agreed points value.

Battlefield: The objective is placed in the middle of the battlefield. This could be a treasure-filled tomb, a keep, village, hill, or anything else you think appropriate to fight over.

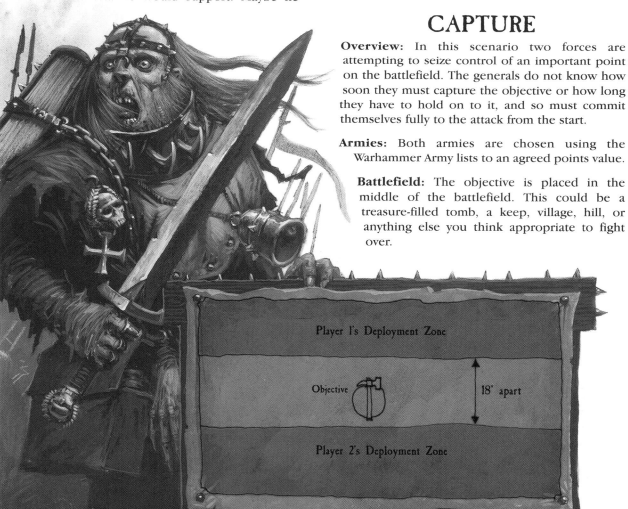

DEPLOYMENT

1. Both players roll a dice, the player who scores highest may choose which side of the table to deploy on.

2. The players roll a dice, the highest scorer may choose whether to start deploying first or second.

3. Taking it in turns, each player deploys one unit at a time, at least 18" from the opposing deployment zone.

4. All war machines in a player's army are deployed at the same time, though they can be deployed in different parts of the battlefield.

5. Champions are deployed with their unit, all other characters in the army are deployed after all other units, all at the same time. Characters may start the battle with units if you wish.

6. Scouting units are not deployed with the rest of the units. Instead they are placed on the table after all

> "I order the execution of the prisoners with extreme prejudice. It is the righteous judgement upon these barbarous wretches."
>
> Baron Rikhardt ordering the execution of Bretonnian prisoners during the Battle of Bogwurst

units in both armies have been deployed, as described in the rules for Scouts.

Who goes first? Both players roll a dice, the player who finished their deployment first may add +1 to their dice roll. The player who scores highest may choose whether to go first or second (re-roll ties).

Length of game: The game lasts for a random length. At the end of the fourth turn roll a dice. On a 2 or more, play a fifth turn. At the end of the fifth turn roll a dice again, on a 3 or more play a sixth turn, etc.

Special rules: There are no additional special rules.

Victory conditions: The army with the unit closest to the objective at the end of the battle wins. Fleeing units, monsters and characters can't capture the objective. If both players have a unit equidistant from the objective, one player wins if their unit is worth more than double the points value of the closest enemy unit to the banner. Otherwise it is a draw.

HISTORICAL RE-FIGHT

This took place between an Empire army and a Bretonnian force. You will also need Lestanne's force, which is equal to one third of the points value of one of the player's armies, chosen from the Bretonnian army list. At the end of the battle, Lestanne's force joins the winner (in the case of a draw, players roll to see who gains control of Lestanne's force) and the players fight for three more turns, at the end of which victory is decided using the normal Victory points rules. Lestanne's army arrives as a flanking force, as in the Flank Attack scenario (randomly generate a neutral table edge for him to arrive on).

SCENARIO 6 - THE BATTLE OF PINE CRAGS, Imperial Year 1350

Grungni Goldfinger led an expedition of Dwarf treasure hunters down from the Grey Mountains into the Forest of Loren, seeking burial mounds to rob. Grungni only had old Dwarf sagas and legends to guide him, which dated back to the days before the War of the Beard. The mounds he was seeking were probably those of the wild heaths which surround the Forest of Loren to the north and west. Grungni's route would thus have to pass through Loren, which had since become the realm of the Wood Elves. The invading force was either unaware of this or recklessly overconfident.

The Dwarfs felled trees and lit fires as they went, which alarmed the Wood Elves dwelling in the forest. When the Dwarfs approached the sacred glades of the Elves, this provoked them to resist. As the invaders advanced along a ravine known to the Wood Elves as the Pine Crags, the Wood Elves, led by Findol, ambushed them.

The Elves attacked the Dwarfs with arrows while remaining concealed in the trees and drew the reckless Dwarfs onwards, while the rest of the Wood Elf force closed in from behind. In these circumstances, the Wood Elves would not need to outnumber the Dwarfs and may even have been a smaller force.

Despite forming a shield-wall, the Dwarfs were unable to fight their way back out of the ravine and were all slain.

AMBUSH

Overview: In this scenario a smaller force takes advantage of surprise and better position to ambush a larger force.

Armies: Both armies are chosen using the Warhammer Army lists. The defender has 50% more points than the attacker (rounding fractions down). Eg, 1,500 points of attackers would face 2,250 points of defenders.

Battlefield: Set up the terrain in an agreed manner.

DEPLOYMENT

1. The defender must set up their army first, in the deployment zone shown on the map. All units must face towards the same table edge. They do not have to deploy their Scouts until the attacker has set up their army.

2. The attacker then deploys their army. At least one third of the attacker's units (not counting Scouts, characters and monsters) must be in each deployment zone.

3. The defender then deploys any Scouts, followed by the attacker deploying their Scouting units.

Who goes first? The attacker goes first.

Length of game: The game lasts for five turns.

Special rules: There are no additional special rules.

Victory conditions: Calculate Victory points for destroyed units and units below half strength. Do not award Victory points for anything else. The player with the highest Victory points total is the winner.

HISTORICAL RE-FIGHT

The battle took place between Dwarfs and Wood Elves, in a ravine with heavily wooded sides. Other than this, the normal scenario rules apply.

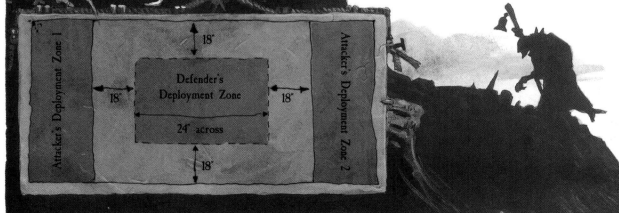

SCENARIO 7 – ELDRETH'S LAST STAND, Imperial Year 1575

It is not usual for a Dwarf army to be in the position of surrounding the enemy on the battlefield. More often than not it is the other way round. In this battle, known only from the Saga of Thurgar Elfhater, which occurred sometime in the last years of the great War of the Beard between Elves and Dwarfs, a Dwarf force managed to corner a much smaller Elf army. This was probably because the Elves had found themselves in mountain terrain which the Dwarfs knew well. The Elves, of whom we know little except that they were led by Eldreth, a very noble, but somewhat reckless commander, had no option but to defend themselves against the Dwarfs in the hope of slaying all of them. With true Dwarf determination and many grudges to be avenged, there could be no chance of surrender and no quarter would be given on either side. According to the saga, the Elves fought on until darkness fell and then those who remained, being few in number, managed to escape from the tired and exhausted Dwarfs, taking their banner and the body of their slain leader with them.

LAST STAND

Overview: In this battle a vastly outmatched defender must sell the lives of his troops as dearly as possible.

Armies: Both armies are chosen using the Warhammer Army lists. The defender has half the points of the attacker. Eg, 2,000 points of attackers would face 1,000 points of defenders.

Battlefield: Set up the terrain in an agreed manner.

DEPLOYMENT

1. The defender must set up their army first, in an 18" square centred on the middle of the table. All of the units must face towards the same table edge. Scouting units must be set up with the rest of the army.

2. The attacker then deploys their army. They may set up anywhere at least 24" from a defending unit. Scouting units may be set up at least 18" from the enemy.

Who goes first? The defender goes first.

Length of game: The game lasts until the defenders are all either dead or fleeing.

Special rules: The defenders are expecting to die and so are immune to *panic*.

Victory conditions: Calculate Victory points for destroyed attacking units and attacking units reduced to below half strength. If the result is more than the starting points value of the defenders, the defenders win, even if they were wiped out. If it is less than half the starting points value of the defenders, then the attackers win. Any other result is a draw.

HISTORICAL RE-FIGHT

Eldreth's Last Stand takes part between a Dwarf army and a High Elf war host. The Dwarfs are attacking, but may not take any blackpowder war engines (bolt throwers and stone throwers only) and may not field Thunderers. Such technology had not been developed by the Dwarfs at the time of the battle. The High Elves may not include any mounted troops or chariots.

Defender's Deployment Zone — 18" square. Attacker deploys 24" away from defending units

SCENARIO 8 – THE FALL OF CHAQUA, Imperial Year c.001

A plague, originating from the Skaven Clan Pestilens had spread throughout Lustria devastating the pyramid cities of the Lizardmen. Many of the cities were deserted or abandoned and the Skaven, advancing in the wake of the plague, occupied the ruins. Shortly before the plague arrived in Chaqua, a heavenly portent in the form of a forked tongue (twin-tailed comet) was observed and a sacred plaque foretelling the rise of the god Sotek to overthrow the ratspawn was discovered. Soon after, the Mage-priests of the city perished and were sealed up in hidden vaults by their faithful Saurus guards. Meanwhile the Skinks migrated from the city taking the sacred plaque and news of the new god with them to bring hope and inspiration among the Lizardmen.

The Saurus of Chaqua, and a few other elements of the army remained to guard the deserted city until the bitter end if need be. Suddenly the Skaven arrived, infiltrating the squalid and deserted Skink barrios and closing in on the central plaza. Eventually they made an assault across the plaza to the temple precinct. Opposing them were the last remaining Lizardmen in Chaqua acting as a rearguard while the tombs of the Mage-priest mummies were sealed and the Skinks escaped. The Saurus defied the Skaven for long enough for the last Skinks to seal up the tomb vaults beneath the pyramid with colossal blocks of the hardest stone.

REAR GUARD

Overview: An outnumbered defendering force must hold off their attackers to gain time for the rest of their army to escape. The longer the defenders hold out, the greater the chance that their comrades will escape.

Armies: Both armies are chosen using the Warhammer Army lists. The defender has half the points of the attacker. Eg, 2,000 points of attackers would face 1,000 points of defenders.

Battlefield: Set up the terrain in an agreed manner.

DEPLOYMENT

1. The defender must set up their army first, in the deployment zone shown on the map. Scouting units may deploy up to 6" outside the deployment zone.

   2. The attacker then deploys their army. They may set up anywhere at least 24" from a defending unit (not including defending Scouts). Scouting units must be set up at least 18" from the enemy.

   Who goes first? The attacker goes first.

   Length of game: The game lasts a random number of turns. At the end of the fifth turn, roll a D6. On a score of 1 the game ends. At the end of the sixth turn roll again, the game end on a score of a 1 or 2, and so on.

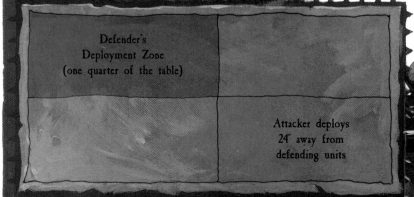

Defender's
Deployment Zone
(one quarter of the table)

Attacker deploys
24" away from
defending units

Orcs and their Goblin kin are our enemies, for they are the defilers of glades and murderers of our folk. Beastmen, the children of Chaos and Long Night are our enemies. They fight us for our right to exist in the woodlands and forests. Skaven of the Underworld are our enemies, for they gnaw the roots of our world and bring pestilence and death to our forests. Dwarfs are our enemies, for they cut down trees to fill their furnaces and to power their infernal machines, and many times they have waged war against us. Kegh-mon, the hairy Humans are our enemies, for they are war-like and greedy, and would drive us from our homes if they could. Many, many of them have turned to worship of the Dark Powers. Halflings are our enemies, for they clear trees away for their fields to crow crops which they then consume with unsatisfiable hunger. They would eat the whole world if they could. Elves of Naggaroth and far-off Ulthuan are our enemies, for they have turned their backs on Isha and Kurnous, and betrayed their Elf heritage.

These are your enemies, child. Know them well and keep your bow and arrow ready.

What a Wood Elf mother told her son.

Special rules: The defenders are expecting to die and so are immune to *panic*.

Victory conditions: For every turn past the fourth turn the game lasts, the attacker must move at least one unit off one of the defender's table edges. Characters and monsters do not count for these purposes. Also, units that flee off these table edges do not count. If the attacker moves fewer units out of play than there were turns over the fourth, the defender wins. Any other result is an attacker victory. Eg, if the game lasts for seven turns (three turns extra), the attacker must have moved three or more units off the table to win.

HISTORICAL RE-FIGHT

This battle is re-fought between the Lizardman defenders and Skaven attackers. The Lizardmen must spend at least a third of their points on Saurus units and characters, while the attackers must spend at least half of their points on units and characters from Clan Pestilens. Due to the plague unleashed by the Skaven, the Lizardmen lose 2D6 points worth of troops at the start of every Skaven turn. The Lizardmen player may choose which models to lose. The defender must lose whole models (they can't lose weapons, for example) and so the defender may well have to lose more than the 2D6 roll indicates.

SCENARIO 9 –
THE SEVEN KNIGHTS, Imperial Year 1123

A Bretonnian troubadour song tells of a heroic battle in which seven gallant knights fought against many times their number of Goblins. The Goblins, led by Ironfang had accomplished the defeat of Baron de Fette's army, which had been caught unawares through recklessness and been ambushed in rugged countryside. Only seven knights survived the battle and were riding back, tired and bleeding, to carry on the fight from behind their own castle walls. Their names are recorded as Louen de Ledarre, Guy le Galant, Jules de Touph, Gaston de Reclasse, Bertrand Lestrong, Gui du Lambert and Evrard de Mellay. As they crossed a bridge and rode through a village, the villagers begged them not to abandon them to the Goblins and appealed to their honour. They pointed to the famous grail chapel which would fall into enemy hands. The honour of the knights, had been stung by defeat and they decided that this was as good a place as any to win it back or die in the attempt. The knights armed themselves with holy relics from the shrine and took up their positions awaiting the onslaught. The Goblins appeared and tried to swarm across the bridge as well as various points along the stream, only to be hurled back by the reckless bravery of the knights, charging into the hordes. By the end of the day, all the brave knights lay dead or dying, but not one Goblin crossed the stream and the village was saved.

SHEER HEROISM!

Overview: A few determined characters set forth to battle an entire army. This is the stuff of legends!

Armies: Both armies are chosen using the Warhammer Army lists. The attacker chooses their army as normal. The defender only chooses from the Characters section of their army list, ignoring all normal restrictions for choosing an army. They may choose twice as many Lords as normally allowed for the size of game being played.

Battlefield: Set up the terrain in an agreed manner.

DEPLOYMENT

1. Both players roll a dice. The player who scores highest may choose which table edge is to be the baseline of their deployment zone.

2. The attacker must set up their army first, in the deployment zone shown below. Scouting units may deploy after the defender.

3. The defender then deploys their army. They may set up anywhere up to 18" from a short table edge.

4. The attacker may set up Scouts as outlined in the Warhammer rules.

Who goes first? The defender goes first.

Length of game: The game lasts for six turns.

Special rules: The defenders are totally dedicated to their cause and are immune to *fear*, *terror* and *panic*.

Victory conditions: At the end of the battle calculate Victory points to see who has won.

HISTORICAL RE-FIGHT

This battle could be fought between seven Bretonnian characters (with no monster mounts) and a 1,500 points army of Goblins (no Orc or Rare units may be chosen). There is a river with a bridge between the armies (the river counts as very difficult terrain). Place several buildings in the Bretonnian deployment zone to represent the village they are defending.

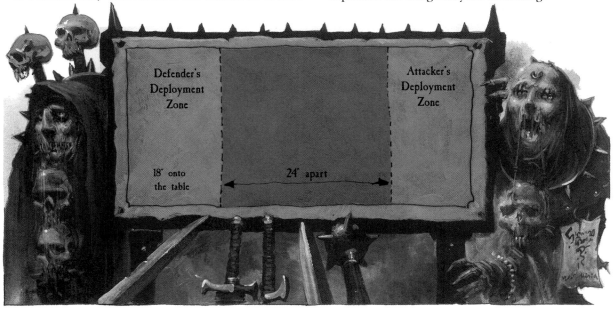

Defender's Deployment Zone

Attacker's Deployment Zone

18" onto the table

24" apart

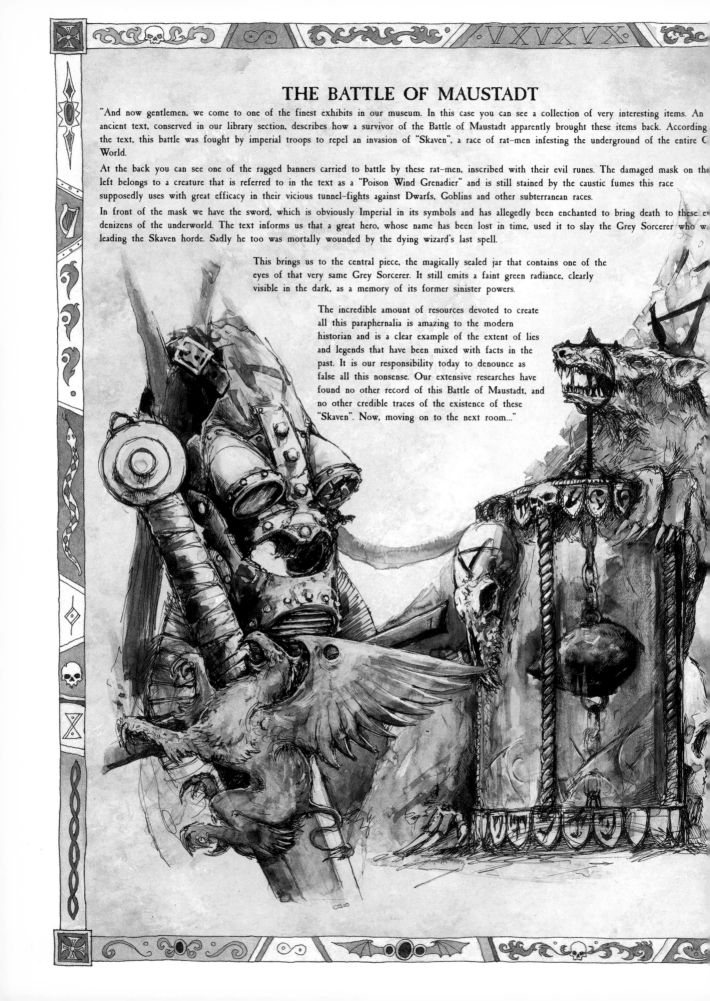

THE BATTLE OF MAUSTADT

"And now gentlemen, we come to one of the finest exhibits in our museum. In this case you can see a collection of very interesting items. An ancient text, conserved in our library section, describes how a survivor of the Battle of Maustadt apparently brought these items back. According to the text, this battle was fought by imperial troops to repel an invasion of "Skaven", a race of rat-men infesting the underground of the entire Old World.

At the back you can see one of the ragged banners carried to battle by these rat-men, inscribed with their evil runes. The damaged mask on the left belongs to a creature that is referred to in the text as a "Poison Wind Grenadier" and is still stained by the caustic fumes this race supposedly uses with great efficacy in their vicious tunnel-fights against Dwarfs, Goblins and other subterranean races.

In front of the mask we have the sword, which is obviously Imperial in its symbols and has allegedly been enchanted to bring death to these evil denizens of the underworld. The text informs us that a great hero, whose name has been lost in time, used it to slay the Grey Sorcerer who was leading the Skaven horde. Sadly he too was mortally wounded by the dying wizard's last spell.

This brings us to the central piece, the magically sealed jar that contains one of the eyes of that very same Grey Sorcerer. It still emits a faint green radiance, clearly visible in the dark, as a memory of its former sinister powers.

The incredible amount of resources devoted to create all this paraphernalia is amazing to the modern historian and is a clear example of the extent of lies and legends that have been mixed with facts in the past. It is our responsibility today to denounce as false all this nonsense. Our extensive researches have found no other record of this Battle of Maustadt, and no other credible traces of the existence of these "Skaven". Now, moving on to the next room..."

THE BATTLEFIELD

To play Warhammer you will need a flat, level playing area to be the battlefield. The most useful dimensions for this are 6'x4'. This is the average size of a wargames battlefield but it can be larger or smaller depending on the size of the room and the table. This size of battlefield provides enough room for a good battle between two players with 2,000 or 3,000 points armies (roughly 100-300 models). Larger areas allow room for larger battles with bigger armies and more players. Smaller areas are better suited to smaller armies.

The simplest way to create the basic battlefield is to drape a green cloth over the floor, a table or a bed. For a desert battlefield use a yellow cloth. Games Workshop stores sells both a green and a desert yellow Battle Mat, which are made of thick plastic sheet and covered with a realistic ground texture. Another alternative is a green army blanket. For a more stable battlefield place plywood, chipboard or MDF sheets on the floor, table or bed and drape the cloth over them. The most convenient way to do this is to use three 4'x2' boards side by side. These can be more easily transported and stored than a single large board. These boards should be thick enough not to sag, a thickness of at least one centimetre is best. If you have no table you can make a temporary wargames table by resting two long timbers (two pieces of wood of dimensions 6'x2"x2" for example) on two trestles, chairs, boxes or the bed or over a small table. Lay the boards on these timbers, etc, but always make sure that whatever you rest them on can bear the weight of the armies and the players leaning on it!

If you are using boards then you can dispense with a cloth if you paint the boards green or cover them with textured paint (paint with sand in it normally used for outdoor walls), cloth, green carpet tiles, flock, or whatever you like to create a realistic ground effect. At this point you are half way to creating modular terrain since all you need to do is add model hills onto one or two of the boards and paint rivers and roads onto them. If you do this you may want to have extra spare boards with certain features on them, or use both sides of the boards so that they can be flipped over (in which case the features on them must be flat to allow the board to rest on the floor or a table).

SCENERY

If the battlefield is just a wide, open flat plain two things will happen during your battles. Firstly, missile troops and war machines will be able to shoot at almost everything in sight because there is no terrain in the way. Secondly, mounted troops will ride about all over the place charging when and where they want.

If you have any other troops in your army, or you would like to try any other tactics, the best thing to do is play on a battlefield which has more varied scenery. If the scenery includes such terrain features as hills, woods, buildings and streams or rivers it will look better, be more realistic and make for much more interesting battles.

Right: By building the board up in layers, see the stepped hill instructions for details, you can create both mountains or gorges.

Above: On this board the terrain has been designed so that the river actually cuts through the edge of the hill.

Left: These two boards have been made so that they combine to create a long straight river. You could also create a curve in the river so that it meanders off a side edge instead.

There are two ways of obtaining a collection of terrain features. One is to buy them ready made from Games Workshop stores and other model shops. The other is to make them yourself. Most players do a bit of both.

Many useful items of scenery can be made quickly and easily using simple techniques and commonly available materials. These are described in detail in the *How to make Wargames Terrain* book available from Games Workshop stores.

The most useful items of terrain that you can have are hills, woods, sections of wall and buildings. A basic collection of scenery might include a couple of hills, enough model trees to make three woods, three 6" long sections of wall, two or three small peasant cottages, a ruined building, a scattering of stones to represent boulders and a couple of sections of river. This would be quite adequate to create many varied battlefields and we have included basic instructions for making these over the next few pages.

These scenic items are placed on the flat plain of the battlefield in various ways to create landscapes. This is the easiest way of creating a different battlefield each time you play. Another method is to mount scenery on large boards, such as the 2'x4' boards (shown opposite) or on 2'x2' square boards.

This advanced method is known as **modular terrain**. It can be used in combination with small, loose items of scenery for maximum variation and is most useful if you want to make larger terrain features which need a big base board to support them. This kind of scenery has the added advantage of being easier to store because it can be stacked away unlike a gaming table or board.

MAKING A STEPPED HILL

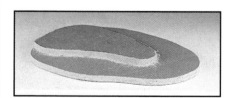

1 The base of this hill forms the first 'step'. The base and the top layer were each made from two sheets of thick card.

2 The hill has been sprayed green and is now ready for the flock to be glued on.

3 The hill has been painted with diluted PVA, and scattered with flock.

MAKING A RIVER

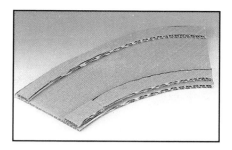

1 Glue together some sections of cardboard as shown above to make the base of the river.

2 Then combine together a mixture of sand, PVA and water to texture the banks of the river with.

3 Apply the PVA/sand mixture to the banks of the river.

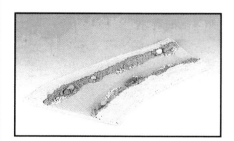

4 The banks of the river are now finished, and once the model is dry it will be ready to be painted.

MAKING A HUT

1 *The basic form of the hut is complete, though no details have been added.*

2 *The finished hut. The walls have been lightly textured with filler before painting and drybrushing.*

MAKING A WOOD

Cut a base for your wood out of polystyrene and then push some trees into it. When you are happy with their positions, glue the trees into place. If you want to add any extra details, such as clumps of grass or small rocks, now is the time to do it. The base can then be painted and flocked as usual.

PLACING SCENERY

Terrain features on the battlefield will have a significant effect on the game. Some features, such as woods and walls, can conceal troops and provide them with cover from shooting. Other features, such as hills, will give a height advantage to troops occupying them, enabling them to see over and shoot at enemy troops or over friendly troops on lower ground. Rivers and similar features can be a barrier to movement and will cause delays to troops trying to cross over them. Buildings not only block lines of sight but also can be defended as strongpoints. Since terrain can have such a drastic influence on the outcome of the battle, and confer great advantages and disadvantages to one side or the other, the placing of terrain needs to be considered very carefully.

There are two approaches to setting up battlefield scenery. One way is to set up the scenery according to an historical scenario such as those described in the Scenarios section. In such scenarios it may be that the terrain did indeed favour one side rather than the other and this is therefore part of the challenge of the scenario.

The other is to place the scenery according to a method which will create roughly the same advantages and disadvantages to both sides. The battlefield does not have to be arranged symmetrically to do this, and several methods which will achieve this effect are as follows:

METHOD 1

One player sets up the scenery on the battlefield. The other player chooses which edge of the table to deploy on. This method is useful when playing at a friend's house since it allows one player to set up the table before his opponent arrives for the game. It also allows him to use whatever terrain he has available. The fact that his opponent could choose either side of the table makes sure that the player setting up the battlefield places the terrain without undue favour to either side.

METHOD 2

The table is divided in half (use a row of dice) and each player sets up the terrain in one half of the table. When this is done, both players roll a dice and the higher scoring player chooses his preferred half of the table in which to deploy. This is suitable for a game at a club where both players arrive at the same time to set up the battlefield. Neither player will know for certain where he is to deploy while setting up the terrain and so will not create an undue advantage or disadvantage for either army. This is also a good method for a limited collection of terrain pieces in that roughly half can be allocated to each side.

METHOD 3

Each player chooses his preferred edge on which to deploy before the scenery is set up. Both players then roll a dice and the highest scoring player has first option to place a terrain feature. The player then rolls on one of the terrain generators on the next few pages to generate a terrain feature. If the feature generated is not available roll again.

He then positions the feature somewhere in his own half of the table. Then it is the other player's turn to generate and place a terrain feature. This continues until either all the features are placed or until one player considers that there is enough terrain on the battlefield and opts not to generate or place a feature in his turn. The other player may then generate and place the last feature.

The battlefield is now deemed complete. This method is suitable for creating a themed battlefield since you can use various generator charts for different regions. It works best with a large and varied collection of terrain pieces. The great advantage of this method is that it is 'tactical' in that players can try to arrange advantageous terrain in their half of the battlefield yet the system does not allow either player to gain an undue advantage.

This method represents the sending out of scouts to look for a good place to deploy before the battle begins.

METHOD 4

Divide the battlefield into 2'x2' squares. Generate (from the terrain generator) or choose one terrain piece for each square and place it in the centre of the square. Players may wish to take it in turns to position features as in Method 3. Then the players roll a dice for the choice of edge on which to deploy their force. Alternatively one player can set up the terrain and the other can choose his preferred edge. This method is suitable for modular terrain in which case each terrain board is positioned until the battlefield is completed. If you are not using modular terrain boards, this method can ensure that terrain features are spaced apart with plenty of open ground and is particularly good for a limited choice of quite large pieces of scenery.

DIMENSIONS OF TERRAIN PIECES

There are two kinds of terrain pieces; **areas** and **linear** features. Areas include all such things as woods, hills, marshes, villages, scatters of boulders, lakes and anything which can be represented by a single terrain piece or a group of small pieces placed within a defined area. Linear features are such things as walls, hedges, fences, streams, rivers, roads, ditches, ravines, gullies and anything which is several times longer than it is wide or made up of several sections laid end to end.

In the terrain generator charts which follow, areas are all assumed to be no greater than 12" across at their widest point. So, a wood or hill can be 12" in diameter or 12"x6" for example. Anything larger than this counts as two terrain items of the same type joined together, or in other words a double feature. In this way a wood could be a single piece which is 12" in diameter, or made up of three clumps of trees arranged so that together they are not more than 12" across.

All linear features are assumed to be in sections and each section is assumed to be no more than 12" long and no more than 6" wide. Any section longer or wider than this is assumed to be two sections joined together or in other words a double section.

When, for example, a section of river is generated, This can be placed from one edge to another across a corner of the table. If a subsequent section is generated, this is added to the first section to lengthen the river.

These simple guidelines for the dimensions of terrain features will help to make it easy to place scenery generated from the charts. If an item is rolled again,

> All men dream, but not equally. Those who dream by night in the dusty recesses of their minds wake in the day to find that it was vanity; but the dreamers of the day are dangerous men. Their dreams are dreams of hope, of improvement, of change. Amongst these are rise the damnable followers of Chaos.
>
> From the Lectures of Grand Theogonist Volkmar

you can replace a small area feature with a double one instead of re-rolling on the chart.

Also it will help in the planning and design of terrain features, since you can cut out the required shapes for area and linear features from coloured felt or cloth or build base boards of these dimensions on which to make model terrain. So, for example, your terrain collection might include a box full of loose model trees and several pieces of green felt up to roughly 12" in diameter and from them you will have what you need to create several woods.

The height and slope of hills should allow troops to be placed on them while making it clear whether the hill is flat topped and whether troops can see or shoot over others on lower ground. You could, as a rule of thumb, declare that if a model falls over when placed on a slope, that slope is a steep slope! Similarly, if a model is pointing his bow at the back of another model, he is probably not high enough to shoot over him! Simple hills with stepped slopes help to clarify things, but hills which have carefully made gentle slopes on which models can be placed are more realistic.

With area features such as woods and villages it is a good idea to leave open spaces within the feature in which to place models. This will make it easier to actually place models in the terrain feature to show that it is occupied. As a rule of thumb, you could declare that features which force models to be spread apart like skirmishers are difficult ground. Similarly, if you have to shift the odd tree or boulder aside to move a regiment through, then the feature is probably difficult ground.

THE REALMS OF MEN
BRETONNIA, THE EMPIRE & TILEA

This terrain generator represents the green lands of the Old World such as Bretonnia, the Empire, Tilea and neighbouring lands. Large partsare inhabited and cultivated by men. Even larger areas are covered in forests, marshes and sparsely settled highlands. Battles tend to be fought along major routes, near river crossings, towns and settlements. The open, cultivated nature of much of the terrain favours pitched battles between large armies.

To generate an item of scenery roll 2D6. You may re-roll duplicate rolls or if you wish, add to an existing feature. All features are assumed to be no larger than 12" in diameter if described as an area or 12" long if a section.

2D6	Result
2	**A river or lake** Choose either a section of river, or area of open water representing a lake. A river must be placed so that it flows onto the battlefield from one side and out from either the same or another side. It may not extend over more than half the length of the table unless your opponent agrees. The river cannot be crossed anywhere along its length except at a ford or bridge and should always include at least one somewhere along its length. If it extends over more than half the table length it should include two crossing places, one of which is chosen and placed by the opposing player. A lake is impossible to cross.
3	**A stream** Choose a section of stream. It is counted as difficult terrain and must enter and leave at a table edge. It may have a single bridge or ford along its length if you wish.
4	**A marsh** An area of water and reeds counting as difficult terrain.
5	**Field boundaries** Up to three sections of fences, hedges or walls arranged touching each other in a line or as three sides of a field. Fences, hedges or walls are obstacles which provide cover.
6	**A wood** An area represented by model trees. Woods are difficult terrain and provide cover.
7	**Low hill or wood** Choose either a low hill or wood.

2D6	Result
8	**A low hill** This is an area of high ground sloping gently on all sides. The top of the hill may be almost flat.
9	**A peasant farmstead** This is an area bordered on all sides by fences with a peasant cottage in the middle or aligned along one edge. This basically creates a model farmyard. There should be at least one gateway on one side. The entire area of the farm is difficult ground, due to the fences, mud, dung, ditches and loose chickens. The fences are treated as obstacles.
10	**A village** An area containing two or more buildings arranged in a group represents a village. There may be fences between the buildings or around the edges of the area. There should be a road running through the village from one side to another. The road is open ground, but the rest of the village is difficult ground. The fences are treated as obstacles.
11	**A ruin** A ruined building, stone circle or ancient burial mound. This is represented by an area of tumbled ruins, or large boulders protruding from the ground or arranged in a circle. Ruins are difficult ground,
12	**A large building** A single substantial building, such as a castle, temple, watchtower or mill which is on its own or surrounded by a stone wall marking the limits of the area. If so there should be a gateway into the area. Surrounding walls are obstacles, but open spaces within the area are open ground.

BADLANDS, DARK LANDS, BORDER PRINCES AND SIMILAR WILDERNESS REGIONS

This terrain generator chart represents the barren lands of the Old World such as the Badlands, the Dark Lands, the realms of the Border Princes and similar wilderness regions. These lands are infested with Orcs, Goblins, Trolls and other hostile creatures and are sparsely inhabited by men, if at all. Much of the land is no more than desolate steppe broken by areas of tangled scrub and rocky uplands. The overall colour of the landscape is a dusty brown, with patches of green pasture here and there. Battles tend to be fought along the trade routes, near river crossings and wherever there are Orc and Goblin tribes. The vast desolation of the terrain favours fast moving mounted hordes and small, slow moving infantry armies are very often surrounded and destroyed.

To generate an item of scenery roll 2D6. You may re-roll duplicate rolls or if you wish, add to an existing feature. All features are assumed to be no larger than 12" in diameter if described as an area or 12" long if a section.

2D6 Result

2 Crag
A huge outcrop of craggy rock. The slopes are more or less sheer cliffs and impassable. Only flying beasts such as eagles or harpies might be able to find a perch on a few ledges.

3 A shallow river
A section of shallow river which is difficult ground. The river must enter and leave at a table edge and cannot extend over more than half of the table length without your opponent's consent. The river must have at least one ford. If the river extends over more than half the table length it must include two crossing places, one of which is chosen and positioned by the opposing player.

4 Fen
This is an area of water and reeds with the odd gnarled tree here and there. This is difficult ground.

5 Cairn
A huge pile of boulders, probably marking the burial place of a formidable Orc warrior. It is treated as impassable terrain.

6 Scrub
An area of tangled scrub, thorn bushes and stunted trees probably mingled with boulders. Scrub is difficult ground and provides cover.

2D6 Result

7 Hill or scrub
Choose either a hill or scrub.

8 Hill
A low hill with gently sloping sides. The top is also gently sloping or flat. There may be boulders, rocks or cliffs on one side making it difficult terrain or impassable on that side. In this region, long low ridges are common.

9 Boulders
An area strewn with boulders. This is difficult ground and provides hard cover.

10 Ruin
A ruined building, such as a ruined tower or stronghold. This is basically an area surrounded by a ruined stone wall. The wall is an obstacle but should have gaps on all sides. Within the area there may be the higher walls of a ruined fortification.

11 Ravine
A section of ravine or gully. This has rocky edges and a boulder-strewn floor and so is difficult terrain.

12 Rocky ridge
A steep hill which is longer than it is wide and rises up to a definite craggy ridge. The slopes are steep and rocky, and strewn with boulders, scree or scrub. Some slopes may be sheer cliffs. This is very difficult terrain.

THE CHAOS WASTES

This chart represents the Chaos Wastes, which are cold, desolate and extremely perilous. This region suffers extremes of temperature as well as the polluting effects of chaos. Only a few savage tribes of men which worship Chaos can live here. Even Orcs and Goblins shun this place although Trolls don't seem to mind it. The overall appearance of the landscape is a kind of dark ash colour. Battles tend to be fought near to the strongholds, tombs and idols of the Chaos Warlords that somehow manage to survive here. The extremely rugged and hostile nature of the terrain favours small bands of hard and predatory warriors.

To generate an item of scenery roll 2D6. You may re-roll duplicate rolls or if you wish, add to an existing feature. All features are assumed to be no larger than 12" in diameter if described as an area or 12" long if described as a section.

2D6	Result
2	**Foetid mere**
	This is an area of stagnant water with gnarled trees protruding from it, rotten corpses floating in it and a cloud of flies buzzing over it. It is treated as impassable.
3	**A lava flow**
	A section of lava flow. This is basically a river of slow flowing lava descending from some distant volcano. The steaming crust conceals molten rock beneath. It is impassable.
4	**Heap of bones**
	A vast heap of bones, among them may be skeletons of huge monsters. This is difficult ground.
5	**Rocky ridge**
	A steep hill which is longer than it is wide and which rises up to a definite craggy ridge. The slopes are steep, rocky and strewn with boulders, scree or maybe even scrub. Some of the slopes may be sheer cliffs. The foot of the cliff may have caves in which Trolls or other creatures make their lairs. This is treated as very difficult terrain.
6	**A gnarled wood**
	A gnarled wood is made up of old dead gnarled trees lacking any leaves. It is difficult ground and provides cover due to the size of the trunks. A nice place for harpies!

2D6	Result
7	**Gnarled wood or plateau**
	Choose either a gnarled wood or plateau.
8	**Plateau**
	This is a low, flat-topped hill of bare, weathered rock. The sides of the plateau are either steep slopes or sheer cliffs and so will be difficult ground or impassable.
9	**Malignant marsh**
	A vile, stagnant, foul-smelling marsh surrounded by tangled scrub. This is very difficult ground.
10	**Chaos monolith**
	A colossal standing stone on its own or surmounting a cairn of boulders, decorated with skulls and other debris, or surrounded by a circle of boulders.
11	**Cairn**
	This is a huge mound of boulders or an area of smaller cairns. A cairn might be the burial mound of a warrior or even an entire army, marking the site of a battle or even a place where treasure has been hidden. Cairns are difficult ground.
12	**A sorcerer's tower**
	A tall eerie stone tower. This may be ruined or intact. It may or may not have an entrance.

ULTHUAN & NAGGAROTH

This terrain generator chart represents the mysterious Elven landscapes of Ulthuan and Naggaroth. Strange as it may seem, the majestic scenery of Ulthuan has its counterpart in the awesome landscape of Naggaroth. The differences between the terrain reflect the differences between the Elves that dwell there; one is the dark and evil side of the other. Whereas a forest in Ulthuan is in perpetual spring, with lofty trees and sunlit glades, its counterpart in Naggaroth is dark and brooding, with equally tall pine trees twisted into menacing shapes and hidden in shadow. While the mountains of Ulthuan shine like silver in the sun, those of Naggaroth are dark purple, like volcanic glass or meteoric iron. Elves are a dwindling race and settlement in both regions is sparse, being mainly concentrated in the ancient cities. Buildings in the landscape are as likely to be shrines or tombs as houses. Battles tend to occur most often along the coasts and in the vicinity of the great cities. The indented and mountainous nature of the terrain favours small forces which attempt to block the advance of larger armies and also treacherous ambushes and surprise raids by land or sea.

To generate an item of scenery roll 2D6. You may re-roll duplicate rolls or if you wish, add to an existing feature. All features are assumed to be no larger than 12" in diameter if described as an area or 12" long if described as a section.

2D6   Result

2   Inlet of the sea

A long, narrow area of water extending into the battlefield from the table edge. It must be put along one edge of the table. Sand and boulders define the edges of the water and the inlet is assumed to be shallow water. Troops may wade across but count it as very difficult terrain.

3   Chasm

A chasm is a deep, steep sided gorge. It cannot be crossed anywhere along its length except at a bridge. A chasm must be placed so that it enters the battlefield from one side. It can taper to an end in the battlefield if you wish. It may not extend over more than half the length of the table unless your opponent agrees that it may do so. If it extends over more than half the length of the table it must include a bridge, chosen and positioned by the opposing player.

4   Rocky peak

A steep hill rising to a rocky peak. It may have cliffs on one or more sides, treated as impassable. The rest of the peak is very difficult ground. A great place for eagles and Dragons!

5   Ancient wall

A section of ancient stone wall, now in ruins, but still an obstacle and providing cover. Such walls marked the boundaries of the great estates of the Elven nobles of former times.

6   Deep forest

An area of very tall trees. These may be deciduous or coniferous trees in Ulthuan, and tend to have light green or even golden foliage. In Naggaroth the forests consist of tall, dark pine trees with dark green, almost blue, foliage. Ulthuan's forests are difficult ground and Naggaroth's forests are very difficult ground.

2D6   Result

7   Hill or deep forest

Choose either a hill or a forest.

8   Hill

This will be either a low, gently sloping hill of Ulthuan or a high hill of Naggaroth with steep rocky slopes. The top of the low hill of Ulthuan can be almost flat while the high hill of Naggaroth will be rugged and rise up into jagged peaks. The hills of Naggaroth are difficult ground.

9   Monolith

This is a single large monolith or an area of several smaller monoliths. These magical inscribed stones channel energy around Ulthuan. In Naggaroth, similar stones exist but have a much more sinister purpose connected with the debased rites of the Dark Elves.

10   Watchtower

A lone watchtower. Usually this will be quite tall and slender and will have a cunningly concealed or protected entrance. The top is usually covered with a tapering tiled roof.

11   Secluded shrine

A shrine to one of the Elven deities. Both High Elf and Dark Elf shrines exhibit the age-old features of Elven architecture. These include high arched portals, domes, spires and circular or triangular plans. High Elf shrines are built from white shining stone while dark purple or red hued stone is favoured in Naggaroth.

12   Elven hall

It is quite rare to find an Elven hall located out in the countryside. Only the most hidden and secluded places are favoured in these days of strife. In ancient times they were a more common feature of the countryside. The hall is long and narrow with a high pitched roof.

THE DWARF REALMS
THE WORLDS EDGE MOUNTAINS, GREY MOUNTAINS AND SIMILAR MOUNTAINOUS REGIONS

This terrain generator chart represents the high mountain ranges of the Old World and especially the Dwarf realms. These regions are very sparsely inhabited, and then only by Dwarfs, Goblins and Trolls, although Skaven may dwell deep beneath. Dwarf settlements are concentrated in strongholds but there are isolated mining settlements, trading posts and other workings. Often these are old abandoned ruins of former times. Most of the landscape is inhospitable mountain peaks and densely forested lower slopes and much of this terrain is impassable in winter. Battles tend to be fought along the major passes through which the trade routes go. The Dwarf strongholds are near to these passes and even the Orc and Goblin hideouts are within raiding distance. The nature of the terrain tends to result in pitched battles or ambushes in the passes.

To generate an item of scenery roll 2D6. You may re-roll duplicate rolls or if you wish, add to an existing feature. All features are assumed to be no larger than 12" in diameter if described as an area or 12" long if described as a section.

2D6	Result
2	**Chasm**
	A chasm is a deep, steep sided gorge. It cannot be crossed anywhere along its length except at a bridge. A chasm must be placed so that it enters the battlefield from one side. It can taper to an end in the battlefield if you wish. A chasm may not extend over more than half the length of the table unless your opponent agrees (in which case it must have a bridge positioned by your opponent).
3	**Raging torrent**
	A section of fast flowing mountain stream, cascading between boulders. The torrent must enter and leave at a table edge. It can only be crossed at narrow points where troops can jump across or step from one boulder to another, or by a bridge (and is therefore impassable except at these points). There must be at least one bridge or crossing point (represented by a mass of boulders or stepping stones). If the stream extends over more than half the table length it must include two crossing places, one of which is chosen and positioned by the opposing player.
4	**Boulders**
	An area of big boulders which have tumbled down from the mountains. This is difficult ground and hard cover.
5	**Rocky peak**
	A very steep hill which rises up to a rocky peak. It may have cliffs on one or more sides. The peak is difficult ground and the cliffs are impassable.

2D6	Result
6	**Pine forest**
	A dense forest of fir trees. Can be on a hill with rocky slopes and boulders among the trees. This is difficult ground and provides cover.
7	**Peak or pine forest**
	Choose either a peak or a forest.
8	**Rocky ridge**
	A long, narrow steep sided hill with a jagged rocky ridge running along its summit. Any sides may be impassable cliffs. It is difficult ground.
9	**Scree**
	Area of loose rocks treated as difficult ground.
10	**Watchtower**
	A stone watchtower. May be ruined or intact.
11	**Dwarf mines**
	This is made up of a mineshaft and some shacks (between two and four is enough). It may be surrounded by a stone wall, but will have at least one gate. There may be a stack of empty beer barrels within the enclosure. Alternatively, this could be a row of cave dwellings with walls as outworks, a tiny stronghold with boulder ramparts or a row of rock tombs.
12	**Tarn**
	A small, round mountain lake that is impassable. Monsters probably lurk within it.

THE DESERTS OF KHEMRI AND ARABY

This terrain generator represents the parched deserts of Araby and Khemri and similar landscapes. Apart from a few cities clinging to the coasts, these regions are uninhabited except by a few nomads and the Undead. The land of Khemri, which was once cultivated and populated by teeming multitudes, is now a desolation, its ruined cities buried under the sand. In the vast necropoli lurk the Undead servants and armies of the Tomb Kings. The landscape is a barren sea of sand, a monotonous yellow-brown, scorched by the merciless sun. Battles tend to be fought along the caravan routes and in the vicinity of the ancient necropolis, not only because these attract adventurers and tomb robbers, but also because of the Tomb Kings who awaken from time to time to do battle among themselves. The nature of the terrain is well suited to pitched battles between enormous, fast moving armies.

To generate an item of scenery roll 2D6. You may re-roll duplicate rolls or if you wish, add to an existing feature. All features are assumed to be no larger than 12" in diameter if described as an area or 12" long if a section.

2D6 Result

2 A deep ravine
This must be placed so it enters from one side of the table. It can taper to an end on the battlefield but may not extend over more than half the table's length unless your opponent agrees. It has rocky sides, maybe even sheer cliffs, and the bottom is strewn with boulders. It is very difficult ground

3 A wadi
This is a dry riverbed filled with sand instead of water. Only rarely, perhaps once every hundred years will it rain enough to make a trickle of water run along the wadi which soon evaporates. The wadi must enter and leave at a table edge. It is difficult ground.

4 Boulders
A scattering of boulders and loose rocks, possibly even fallen statues or rubble from tombs. Treated as difficult ground and hard cover.

5 A jebel
This is a rugged desert hill of bare weathered rock. It is difficult ground, and may have cliffs on one or more sides. The cliffs are impossible to move over and act as a barrier to movement. The top may be almost flat or rise up into eerie crags sculpted by the wind blown sand.

6 A sand dune
These are gently sloping hills made up of wind blown sand. The deep sand will slow troops down and so sand dunes are difficult terrain.

2D6 Result

7 Jebel or sand dune
Choose either a jebel or a sand dune.

8 A palm grove or scrub
A palm grove or scrub, which can be thorn bushes or cacti, is difficult ground and provides cover.

9 A ruin
A ruin half buried by sand which could be an adobe house, a temple, tomb, pyramid, or a watchtower. A wall may surround the area and it will have at least one gateway.

10 Group of buildings
A group of several buildings (between two and four is enough). This could be a few mud brick hovels, a nomad tent encampment or a necropolis made up of several small tombs or pyramids. For any subsequent rolls simply add another tomb or tent or a short section of mud wall.

11 Oasis
A roughly circular pool of deep water, surrounded by palm trees and boulders. The pool of water is impossible to cross. For any subsequent rolls simply add another palm tree.

12 Quicksand
Any models entering this area suffer 2D6 casualties each turn that they are in it. The models are assumed to be swallowed up.

LUSTRIA AND THE SOUTHLANDS

This terrain generator chart represents the dense jungles of Lustria and the Southlands. These regions are the domain of the Lizardmen. Their cities and temples are well hidden in the midst of the vast trackless jungle and are very difficult to find. Apart from a few areas of open cactus scrub or scrubby upland, the landscape is covered in dense vegetation and swamp. The only way to travel through it is to hack your way in or go up one of the wide rivers into the interior. The paved causeways of the Lizardmen extend for only a short distance from their cities. Battles tend to be fought on the coast, where invaders first encounter the Lizardmen or each other, or in the vicinity of the Lizardmen temple cities, which attract adventurers seeking gold and magical artefacts. The dense, hostile nature of the terrain tends to result in ambushes and running battles and occasionally pitched battles in the streets and plazas of the temple cities.

To generate an item of scenery roll 2D6. You may re-roll duplicate rolls or if you wish, add to an existing feature. All features are assumed to be no larger than 12" in diameter if described as an area or 12" long if a section.

2D6 Result

2 A crag

A rocky crag is difficult ground, and may have steep impassable cliffs on one or more sides. Instead of cliffs the crag may have dense vegetation on one or more slopes. The top may be a flat plateau.

3 A shallow river

This can be crossed anywhere but is treated as difficult ground. The river must enter and leave at a table edge and cannot extend over more than half of the table length without your opponent's consent. The edges of the river are lined with mangroves and thickets of reeds providing cover.

4 Scatter of boulders

An area of large boulders embedded in vegetation. This is difficult ground and provides cover.

5 Tangled scrub

An area covered in bushes and small stunted thorn threes, possibly tall cactus, bamboo or pampas grass. Treat as difficult ground.

6 Swamp

An area of shallow water full of mangrove trees or similar tropical plants. It is very difficult ground and impassable to war machines.

2D6 Result

7 Dense jungle

An area of dense, tangled jungle with the trees and vegetation so closely spaced that it is impossible for any troops other than skirmishers on foot to pass through or hide among them. It is very difficult ground, and provides cover.

8 Tall rainforest trees

A clump of tall trees counting as difficult ground and cover. These block any line of sight from any level.

9 A hill

A low hill with gentle slopes, entirely covered with scrub vegetation, counting as difficult ground and cover.

10 Overgrown temple or shrine

A ruined temple or colossal fallen idols overgrown with vegetation. The temple may rise up in steps and can be used tactically as a hill, providing high ground and a vantage point for shooting.

11 Grass huts

A group of several grass or wicker huts (between two and four is enough). A fence of stakes may surround the area and if so it must have a gateway.

12 Lagoon

An area of open shallow water remaining after the torrential monsoon and seasonal floods. It is probably infested with alligators and piranha fish. It counts as very difficult ground. Any troops in it suffer 2D6 Strength 3 hits each turn from the vicious creatures who lurk in the water.

In the bygone ages, an ancient civilisation rose up in the land of Nehekhara, which is the old name for the Land of the Dead. No one knows what it means, it is in the lost tongue of the first human civilisation. The name is still used in Arabia as Nehekhariya. Indeed the primitive nomadic ancestors of the Arabians, known to the people of Nehekhara simply as 'desert dwellers' were frequently conquered and enslaved by the kings of Nehekhara and so the name became engraved into their legends.

The land of Nehekhara was really the flat, fertile plain of the great river Mortis, known anciently as Mortish. This mighty river flows from the mountains of the east, known nowadays as the Worlds Edge Mountains, to the sea, dividing into a delta of enormous extent. Here, the earliest human tribes learned the arts of farming by means of irrigation, writing in hieroglyphic signs and living in cities made of mud brick buildings. Only the inscrutable mage priests of Lustria are likely to have any idea when, why or how this happened. As the centuries passed, two powerful city states dominated the plains of Nehekhara. Both of these realms were wealthy and flourishing, with an abundance of manpower, agricultural produce and a wide ranging trading network. These two kingdoms were Zandri, located in the Delta and Numas (anciently known as Numash) far upstream within sight of the mountains.

Each of these realms was ruled by a king, supported by a priesthood and nobility. Each raised a strong army from among his subjects. In those remote times, the kings were really just war-leaders and the civilisation of Nehekhara had yet to reach its cultural zenith. Apart from regular forays against the desert dwellers, in reprisals for coming out of the desert to steal flocks, the kings of Zandri and Numas had no one to fight except each other, so they did this with great enthusiasm.

Settra was the first king to unite both Zandri and Numas under his rule as sole monarch. It is not known to which dynasty he belonged, if any. He began his career as a prince, and was probably entrusted with command of an army. He may even have come from some minor settlement. According to his own inscriptions, the gods of the desert prophesied his rise to power. Whatever the circumstances, he was undoubtedly a mighty warrior and great conqueror, probably the greatest, apart from Alkhadizzar, his remote successor.

Settra conquered both Zandri and Numas thereby uniting the entire river valley of Nehekhara and binding it into a single kingdom. Soon after, he decided to build a completely new capital city at the point where the delta met the upper river valley, the border of the two former kingdoms. This marked his unification of the land and demonstrated his sovereignty over both regions. The city was to be his residence, where his great palace and eventually his magnificent tomb, would be built. It would also be the mightiest fortress in the land, where his vast army would be marshalled, ready to crush any rebellion and hold down his numerous subjects. this city was called Khemri. It is not known what the name means or whether it is the name of the village which was expanded into a city on the king's orders. This city rapidly grew to become the greatest city in Nehekhara and for a time, during Settra's long reign, the entire land of Nehekhara was renamed Khemri, to satisfy the vanity of the king.

Long did noble Sigmar reign
Among his people and Orcs
Dare not trespass into his realm.
To each chief and each tribe
Did Sigmar, the wise, appoint his lands
And did he appoint Alaric the Dwarf
To forge, with all his skill,
Twelve swords, one for each chief.
And holy Sigmar bade each to wield it
In justice for his people
And to pledge to fight one for another
In undying unity.
Thus did every chief's hall
Become a stronghold in the realm of men.

APPENDIX

Campaigns
Preparing for Battle
Skirmish
Rules of Siege
Preparing for a Siege
Rules Commentary
Special Rules
Scale & Measurement

APPENDIX ONE – WARHAMMER CAMPAIGNS

Fighting one-off battles is all well and good, but at some point or other any serious Warhammer player will consider fighting a campaign. A campaign is the name we give to a series of battles linked together by a story and by the forces fighting it. Battles are not fought in isolation and a campaign reflects this, linking the games you play together to create an enthralling and exciting narrative that will make the games you play much more compelling. As well as providing a reason and 'context' for your battles, in a campaign the result of each battle that you fight will have an effect on future battles; if you suffer an ignominious defeat you will be at some disadvantage in the next battle, while a victory will result in some kind of advantage. Fighting a campaign like this can be a very satisfying experience but is not without its pitfalls, so we've put together this section to describe how to run a campaign, based on methods that have proved successful for the authors. It is by no means exhaustive, but should act as a good starting point for players who want to bring their games to a new level.

STARTING A CAMPAIGN

Most experienced Warhammer players belong to a regular gaming group, either a formal club or an informal group of friends who routinely get together to fight battles. There are many advantages to forming an association with other players. For example, you can pool your resources to buy scenery or pay for the hire of rooms. Players can swap troops amongst themselves, and newcomers can come along and learn the skills of generalship, painting and scenery making.

However, one of the most entertaining group activities is to organise a campaign or league. There are many different ways to run a campaign, ranging from simply linking games together with an ongoing story (usually called a 'narrative campaign'), through to complex map-based campaigns. What follows is a description of the different ways you can approach running a campaign, to give you some idea of the different options available. After this, we've provided a full set of example rules that will allow you to run a simple campaign. Unlike the rules in the rest of this book, the campaign rules really are just an example of one way to run a campaign, and you should feel free to dive in and change them as you see fit for your own campaign. To be honest, being able to tailor the rules to suit your own style of play is one of the really great benefits of running a campaign.

LEAGUES

The simplest form of campaign, and one that is well suited to large clubs or gaming groups, is to run a league. In a league the players fight battles as they would normally, but score points depending on how well they do. For example, a win might be worth three points, a draw worth two points and a loss one point. The players' total points are tracked by the league's moderator and the current 'standings' can be posted up when players meet to play games so that everyone can see how well they are doing. You might want to include extra information on the standing sheet, like a player's average score, the number of battles he's fought, and so on.

It's possible to expand on this basic idea and add in some of the trappings of a 'proper' campaign. For example, you might say that a General who wins a battle can add +1 to his Leadership in the next battle he fights, or a unit that captures a Standard is allowed to re-roll a set of dice rolls in its next game. However, the main advantage of a league is that it is easy to run, so if you want to add in much more detail than this to your league you should instead consider running one of the other types of campaign described below.

NARRATIVE CAMPAIGNS

A narrative campaign is a series of battles linked together by a story. This story is often created by an independent referee who can introduce special scenarios, victory conditions, strange events, extra rules and so forth. The campaign continues like this until the narrative suggests an ending.

For example, many years ago one of the authors ran a narrative campaign based on an Orc invasion of the Empire. The first game took place near the border, as an Empire army attempted to stop the Orcs before they penetrated too far into Empire territory.

The Empire army was decisively defeated and the referee decided that the second game would be about a small Empire force defending a vital bridge in order to slow down the Orc army's progress long enough for a new Empire army to be gathered together. A number of special rules and special pieces of terrain were used in this scenario to represent the unique situation. It was also a good example of an 'unbalanced game'. The Empire army was horribly outnumbered, and couldn't hope to win the scenario in the sense of defeating the Orc army.

This didn't matter, however, as the Empire army's objective was only to slow the Orcs down, not to destroy them. The result was an interesting game that was very different from a normal run-of-the-mill battle. You'll be happy to learn that the Orcs were slowed down long enough for a large Empire army to be gathered to confront the Orc horde, setting up a large multi-player battle as the next 'episode' in the campaign.

The Battle for Tor's Gate
(Week 4 – The final battle)

1st: James (Dwarfs) – 12 pts
2nd: Michael (Empire) – 10 pts
3rd: Douglas (Slaanesh Chaos) – 9 pts
4th: Darren (Tzeentch Chaos) – 7 pts
5th: Terri C (Dark Elves) – 5 pts
6th: Nathan (Bretonnian) – 4 pts

This week's battles

James vs. Darren   Michael vs. Terri
Douglas vs. Nathan

Special Addition
Coming to your aid (or wanting to be part of your glorious victory) your force is about to be joined by a warrior (Hero). Roll a D6 at the start of each of your turns. On a 4+ he arrives.

Example of a league standing sheet

In some cases, the result of a battle may suggest that one side or the other has a number of different options as to what to do next. For example, a victorious army might be within striking distance of two or more of its objectives, or a defending army might have to decide whether to counter-attack at once or wait for reinforcements. Considering such circumstances, rather than the referee deciding arbitrarily what to do next, the players could decide what happens. What the players opt for will alter the course of the campaign so that their strategic decisions, in combination with the results of the battles fought, will decide the outcome of the campaign.

Of course, a referee isn't essential in a narrative campaign – the players can discuss the various options and decide on the course of their actions between themselves. Alternately the players can take it in turn to devise the scenarios, with the referee running any scenarios that they create. The only important thing to remember is that a narrative campaign, more than any other type of campaign, is about more than just winning games – it's an exciting story where the results of your battles help decide the outcome.

LADDER CAMPAIGN

In this type of campaign the players agree to play a pre-set series of battles, with each battle affecting the outcome of later battles. Unlike narrative campaigns, which let each battle's outcome drive the story, the links within a ladder campaign are predetermined, so you don't need a referee.

A good example of a ladder campaign was 'The Grudge of Drong', a campaign pack published by Games Workshop some years ago. The campaign consisted of three preliminary battles which led up to an all-out, death or glory final conflict. The first three battles were relatively small actions with up to 1,500 points a side. The final battle involved massed armies of 3,000 points or more. However, the results of the earlier battles restricted what you could include in your army. For example, if the Dwarfs won the first battle (the Battle of Grudge Pass) they could take over a set of mines and have as many war machines in the final battle as they liked; if they lost

they could only have a single war machine. The result of the second battle affected the number of runes they could use, and so on.

TREE CAMPAIGN

A more elaborate form of ladder campaign is known as a tree campaign. This campaign needs a set of pre-written scenarios and a flow diagram which is used to determine what scenarios are played. Each time a battle is fought, the diagram tells you which scenario to play next by following the correct path. The longer the campaign goes on, the larger the diagram will need to be. In the tree campaign example shown above, which uses the scenarios presented in the Scenarios section of this rulebook, there are only two battles to fight and winning or losing determines whether your army achieves a major victory in the campaign or is crushed by your foes.

In more involved campaigns you could also include paths on the diagram which loop back, or sub-plots that branch off of the main tree. You can also allow winning or losing certain scenarios to have a permanent effect on an army as well as determining the next scenario that is played. For example, winning a battle might allow an army to use a unique magic item you've created for the campaign in all its future battles. The amount of variation depends only on the campaign's background and your imagination.

MAP CAMPAIGNS

A map-based campaign uses a map (well who'd have thought it!). This shows the extent of each player's empire and the territories that they control. The map can also be used to regulate movement and show the location of each player's army and characters.

The campaign rules that follow are an example of the first type of map-based campaign, where the map is used to simply show how large each player's empire is and what territories he controls. Refer to the rules to find out how this type of campaign works.

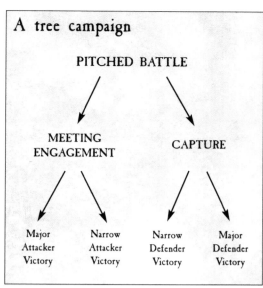

A tree campaign

PITCHED BATTLE → MEETING ENGAGEMENT, CAPTURE

MEETING ENGAGEMENT → Major Attacker Victory, Narrow Attacker Victory

CAPTURE → Narrow Defender Victory, Major Defender Victory

In the second type of map-based campaign, the location of each player's army is shown on the map. This is somewhat more easily said than done, as a campaign usually lasts for weeks, if not months, and the map will need to be permanently set up during this period. One solution is to mount the map on a cork board and use map pins to show the location of the armies, or use Blu-Tak to stick counters onto the map. There are campaign turns between battles, in which the players move their armies around the map. When armies move into each other on the map a battle is fought to determine the outcome of the encounter.

Map campaigns like this often include special rules to cover things such as scouts, supply, raising new troops, assassins, revolts and all kinds of other events. Often, this side of the campaign turns into a game in its own right and actually fighting battles on the tabletop becomes secondary to outmanoeuvring your opponent on the campaign map.

Sadly, while map-based campaigns like these offer the greatest number of possibilities in terms of what can be done, in the author's experience they very rarely work in practice unless they are played by a small group of very dedicated players. The reason is that in order for the campaign to work it is vital that any battles which result from movement on the map are fought out promptly, as otherwise the campaign will bog down waiting for the result of a certain battle.

The other problem is that a cunning General will do his best to make sure that when he fights a battle he has ensured that the odds are well in his favour and that he heavily outnumbers his opponent. This can result in very lop-sided games that are not all that much fun to play; what's more, once you've lost one battle things tend to 'steam-roller' and it becomes increasingly difficult to win future battles. For these reasons, it helps to keep map-based campaigns quite small and with limited objectives. It also helps to have a 'campaign umpire' who can force the players to fight their battles in time for the next campaign turn, and impose forfeits on players that do not. However, the best asset such a campaign can have is very dedicated players, who will play their battles before the next campaign turn and won't drop out when things start going against them.

RUNNING A CAMPAIGN

You don't have to have an umpire or controller to run a campaign, but most players would agree that things go better if a person is nominated as overall umpire. The umpire can interpret the rules and improvise new ones, keep the players informed about forthcoming battles and invent special events, spread rumours and generally keep the campaign going. An umpire can be one of the players, or he can be someone who devotes all of his time to running the campaign and does not play himself. Another option is for different players to take it in turns to be umpire, sharing the burden equally.

The most useful thing that an umpire can do is publish a regular campaign newsletter in which battles fought over the previous weeks are summarised, the defeated are mocked, players are listed and their achievements recorded. Victorious players can place notices of their success and ridicule their enemies. The newsletter can also be used to announce local events and special games.

The opportunity to play God is probably as much fun as actually fighting the battles, and an imaginative umpire can make a big contribution to a campaign. He can also ensure that players don't deliberately avoid fighting enemies

whom they fear will beat them, and can impose penalties on players that fail to show up for games. The umpire can also draw the campaign to a close once the players start to lose interest or one player gains ascendancy. All campaigns, even the very best, come to an end at some point, and it's generally better to make sure this happens sooner rather than later. Leave your players eager for more so that they join up for the next campaign with alacrity!

Finally, bear in mind that a campaign is not wholly fair or perfectly balanced. They aren't, and aren't meant to be. Part of the challenge of a campaign is to fight a battle against the odds – after all, if you lose such a battle it doesn't mean much, while if you win, the glory is greatly enhanced! In any case, a good umpire will be able to even things out without displaying blatant favouritism.

THE BORDER PRINCES

The rules that follow will allow a group of players to fight a simple map-based campaign set in the Border Princes. The Border Princes is a wild territory that lies to the south of the Empire. It has no single ruler, but is instead made up of many petty princedoms each with its own ruler. In truth, many of the 'rulers' are little better than brigands who make a living by extorting tolls from the travellers that pass through their territory, and by raiding and stealing from their neighbours. Many of the Border Princes kingdoms are very short-lived, but there are always new adventurers ready to try and carve themselves out a princedom, exercising what authority they can by sheer force of arms. The Border Princes thus forms a perfect place to set a campaign, as it allows pretty much any army to exist side by side in the same area.

As noted above, this is a map-based campaign. The map is used mainly to show what territories each player controls within their kingdom and is not used to regulate movement or show the location of the players' armies. Instead, each player in the campaign is allowed to arrange battles in pretty much the same manner that they would arrange a normal one-off battle. The difference is that the forces a player can use in his army may be restricted by the territories that he

controls, while the outcome of the battle may affect the political situation and determine who controls certain territories on the map. This system allows those taking part to play each other as and when they wish, without obligation to play a set number of games or against any particular opponents. We've found that this very loose format is a great advantage when playing a campaign, as it makes it possible for players to participate on an occasional basis.

GETTING STARTED

In order to start the campaign you'll need at least four players, but the more the merrier! Once you've got your players together you need to create a map (or you could use the one on the opposite page!). You'll see that each player has their own 'princedom' shown on the map, and that each princedom is subdivided into three territories and a capital. Coastal areas, mountain ranges and areas of wilderness have been added to the map between and around the princedoms. This makes it look attractive, though they have no direct effect on play. The map and the princedoms marked upon it can be of pretty much any size, just so long as the territories within each princedom include enough space to add the important territorial features that are within them (more of which next).

Once you have made up a map with a princedom for each player, it's time to determine what important territorial features he controls. These territorial features represent settlements, geographical features and other resources which constitute the player's empire. These territories are generated randomly from the Territory chart on page 237. As noted earlier, each player also gets a capital, which is in effect a fourth territorial feature already marked on the map. The more territories a player controls, the bigger and better his army will be, and the more varied the types of troops he can field.

The players take it in turn to pick one feature and randomly generate two more. They then mark the territories on the map of their princedom (each territory can have only one feature). We've found it best to mark the features in pencil and then for one player (preferably the most artistically gifted!) to update the map so that all the features are represented in a pleasing manner. The illustration shows our map once the features have been generated and added to it. Notice that in some cases the features 'spill' outside the territory. This is purely decorative and has no effect on play, but it does mean that you don't get odd things like roads or rivers that don't lead anywhere! We've also added names to the important features on the map.

CAMPAIGN ARMIES

Before the campaign begins, the participating players need to agree a suitable points value for their armies. This is the base or starter value of all armies in the campaign and a player may field a larger army by conquering more territories. A reasonable starting value is 1,500 points, although you might wish to start with 1,000 points if players do not already have large established armies, or 2,000 points if all the participants are veteran players with large armies.

Each time players fight a battle they choose an army to the agreed points total, modified by the territories which they control, as described later on. Forces are chosen afresh for each battle, although a player must stick to the same race each time – Orcs, High

Elves, Bretonnians, etc. The armies are chosen from the appropriate army list with the additional limitations described as follows. The players may agree additional limitations if they wish.

ARMY LIMITATIONS

The number and type of troops which a player can field is restricted by the territories that they control. Because of this, the limitations of what can be included in the army lists are **not** used. To begin with, each player is restricted in his choices for his army as follows:

Characters: Each army is allowed one character, representing the player himself. This character may be of any type allowed to the army. Otherwise the army may not include characters unless the player controls a territory that allows them to be used.

Special troops: The army may have two units of special troops. Additional special units may only be included if the player controls the appropriate territories.

Rare troops: The army may have one unit of Rare troops. Additional Rare units may only be included if the player controls the appropriate territories.

Skirmishers: A player's army may not include troops that can skirmish unless the player's territories include mountains or forests; the people from such territories provide the bulk of skirmishing troops.

War machines: The army may have one war machine. Additional war machines may only be included if the player controls the appropriate territories.

Monsters: The army may have one monster. Additional monsters may only be included if the player controls the appropriate territories.

Magic items: The player's army may have up to three magic items with a points value of no greater than 100 points in total. Any additional magic items may only be included if the player controls the appropriate territories.

THE CAPITAL

Each player's princedom includes a capital. It is the capital which allows the player to use the special units, rare units, war machines, monsters and magic items noted above. If it is ever lost then none of these things may be used unless the player controls other territories that allow him to use them.

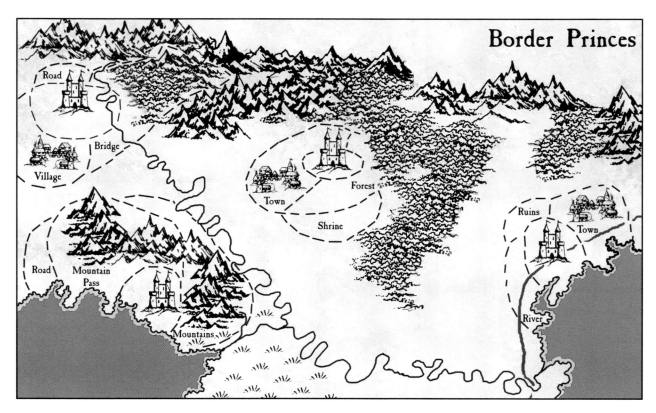

Border Princes

TO WAR, TO WAR!

Players are free to fight each other as they wish, representing encounters along their common borders, intrusions into their rival's territory, chance encounters in the wilderness and other minor conflicts. These clashes don't result in the loss of territory but can have other consequences, and can lead to an outright war of conquest.

Before the battle, roll on the Scenario table on page 197 to determine the scenario that will be used for the battle. Note that this stage is not optional; in a campaign not all battles are even head-to-head fights and the Scenario table represents this fact. You are now ready to begin fighting the battle.

Each player uses his entire army for the battle, even though their points value may be different because the players hold different territories.

Terrain can be set up for the game in any mutually agreed manner.

Fight the battle using the rules for the scenario being played. The winner of the battle may choose to 'steal' the benefits of one of his opponent's territories and use them in his next battle. The loser must forgo all benefits of that territory in his next battle. The winner may not choose to steal the benefits of the loser's capital unless this is the only territory left.

For example, Rick wins a battle against Tuomas and chooses to steal the benefits from Tuomas's mine territory. This means that Rick counts as having a mine in his next battle, while Tuomas does not. The effect of stealing the benefits of a territory in this way only counts for the next battle. The territory does not permanently change hands.

WARS OF CONQUEST

Every time you fight against another player you will score **Grudge points** against them. These represent the simmering anger generated by a conflict, which can cause it to escalate into a full-scale invasion! The number generated depends on the outcome; the winner of a battle receives one Grudge point, and the loser gets two. In a draw, both players get two points. Keep track of the Grudge points you have against each opposing player.

When you fight a battle against an opponent that you have Grudge points against, you can try to escalate the battle. Roll a D6 and compare the number rolled to the amount of Grudge points that you have against this opponent. If you roll equal to or under the number of Grudge points you have the battle escalates. If you roll higher the battle is fought normally. In either case, all the Grudge points you have against this opponent are reduced to zero after the attempt to escalate the conflict.

If the conflict escalates then it becomes a war of conquest. The battle is fought using the normal rules, but if the player who escalated the conflict wins, instead of stealing the benefits of a territory for one battle, he is allowed to conquer a territory and add it to his empire. Denote a captured territory on the campaign map with a suitable marker. A player's capital can only be captured if it is the last territory they control.

It is possible for both players in a battle to escalate the conflict. If both do this the winner is allowed to take a territory from the loser.

WINNING THE CAMPAIGN

It is entirely up to the players to set a limit on how long the campaign lasts. A campaign could go on indefinitely, but it is often better to end it once a player has established a dominant position. In this way a winner can be declared and a new campaign started.

Saying that the winner is the first to conquer three territories, or get so strong that the other players refuse to fight him, is a good method for your first campaign. By then you'll have developed your own ideas about how to 'improve' this campaign system, and will probably be thinking about adding in new rules for things such as spies, assassins, ambassadors, etc. The possibilities really are endless.

Territory Chart (D66)

Each player picks one territory from this chart then randomly generates two more. To randomly generate a territory roll two ordinary D6s one after the other. The first roll represents 'tens' and the second 'units' to give you a score between 11 and 66. This method of rolling dice is referred to as a 'D66 roll'.

D66   **Result**

11-12   **Wizard's Tower**
For each wizard's tower you control your army may include one extra Wizard. The Wizard may not be a Wizard Lord but can be of any other type allowed in your army.

13-14   **Sacred Grove**
For each sacred grove you control your army may include one extra Rare unit.

15   **Shrine**
For each shrine you control your army may include one Battle Standard Bearer. An army may never have more than one Battle Standard no matter how many shrines it controls.

16   **Temple**
For each temple you control your army may include one extra Wizard Lord.

21-32   **Village**
For each village you control your army may include one extra Special unit.

33-34   **Town**
For each town you control your army may include one extra character. The character may not be a Lord but can be of any other type.

35-43   **Road**
If you control a road you are able to move troops more quickly to meet your enemy. To represent this add 25 points to your army for each road under your control.

44-46   **River**
The land near a river is very rich and provides frequent and bountiful harvests. To represent this add 25 points to your army for each river you control.

51-52   **Bridge**
If you control a bridge then you are able to move troops more quickly to meet your enemy, while the rich soil makes perfect farmland. To represent this add 50 points to your army for each bridge you control.

53   **Silver Mine**
For each silver mine you control you may take one magic item worth 50 points.

54   **Gold Mine**
For each gold mine you control you may take one magic item worth 100 points.

55   **Mountain Pass**
If you control a pass you are able to move troops through to reach your enemy. To represent this add 75 points to your army for each pass you control.

56   **Mountains**
If you control a mountain your army may include up to two extra monsters. In addition roll a D6. On a roll of '6' the mountain includes a gold mine (see above).

61-65   **Forest**
If you control a forest your army has sufficient supplies of wood to build two extra war machines.

66   **Ruins**
You may take one magic item worth 3D6x10 points. It is retained by your forces and its value is added to the points value of your army. The magic item can be given to any character in the normal way at the start of a battle. If the character carrying the item is lost then the item is captured by the opposing side, who may use it in future battles just as if they had discovered it themselves.

APPENDIX TWO – PREPARING FOR BATTLE

It is quite possible to play a game of Warhammer with an army that consists of every model you own, regardless of race or quantity! However, as I'm sure will be immediately apparent, such a game wouldn't be very satisfying and is unlikely to be very fair. It would also be missing the point. Warhammer is about collecting an army of one of the races of the Warhammer world and bringing it to battle against an equally matched opponent.

In order to ensure that games are as fair as we can make them, every model is ascribed a **points value** which reflects its value in the game as closely as possible. Of course, some players will naturally tend to do better with certain types of troops, so those types may be more effective under their command.

Similarly, some types of troops will perform better in certain kinds of terrain or against specific opponents. For example, a huge, monstrous Dragon isn't going to be worried if it finds itself confronted by a horde of tiny Goblins because the Goblins are just too small and weedy to stand much chance of hurting it – in such a situation the Goblins are literally worth almost nothing!

Bearing all of this in mind, it is obviously impossible for points values to reflect the absolute value of every model in every circumstance. Instead, a model's points value is a useful compromise which should be viewed as representing its fighting ability in the circumstances of a typical battle.

THE ARMY POINTS VALUE

When Warhammer players arrange a game it is usual to fix a points value total for each side – typically 2,000 points or 3,000 points for a really big game. Of course, there is no limit on the size of the armies. You can fight a game with 500 points a side, 1,000, 10,000 or 10 million points and anything in between! For practical purposes, however, 2,000 or 3,000 points is usually regarded as just about right for a game that will last over an evening or the best part of an afternoon. Games of up to 3,000 points can be accommodated on a table of about 4' x 6-8' (120cm x 180-240cm) whilst larger games will usually require more time and a larger playing area.

The lists of points values for all the different troop types, including machines, monsters, characters, and magic items are given in complete detail in the Warhammer Armies books. Each book covers the army of one race and includes an army list that explains which troops the army is allowed, along with their points values. So, for example, we have one book which covers the High Elves, and others for the

Empire, Skaven, Orcs & Goblins, and so forth. The lists are far too exhaustive to give here in their complete form, but to give you an idea we have included some details of army composition and points values in the examples that follow.

UNIT POINTS VALUES

Units are usually made up of a number of models of the same type. It therefore follows that a unit of, say, ten models each of, let us assume, 9 points is worth a total of 10 x 9 = 90 points. It is quite usual to refer to a unit in terms of its value, so you might hear players talk of 'a 140 point unit of Orc warriors', '150 points of High Elf archers', or some such expression. As most practically sized units are likely to be between 100 and 300 points, it can be assumed that a 2,000 point army would have about ten units.

However, this doesn't allow for character models. Once points have been allocated for these important pieces the typical 2,000 point army is more likely to have about seven units in total, of which some might be a single piece such as a chariot or war machine.

Obviously this varies; we need only consider the matter here insofar as it gives a fair idea of what's meant by a 2,000 point army.

THE ORC ARMY

Orcs are one of the most dangerous of the monstrous races that inhabit the Warhammer world; they are also one of the most popular armies amongst Warhammer players. The 'Orc' army actually encompasses many different creatures of which Orcs are but one type, so we often refer to the army as 'Orcs & Goblins' or 'greenskins'. We are going to use one type of Orc army as an example of how a player might put together such a varied army. The same considerations also apply no matter what army you choose.

If you want to collect an Orc army then you will need the separate Orcs & Goblins Army book. This contains extra games rules, more magic spells and items, and extensive painting and collecting tips, as well as the all important army list.

The army list is used to choose an army before each battle. Obviously, you will need to assemble a collection of models from which you can choose the exact force for a particular battle. Needless to say, most players prefer to build a collection around a typical 2,000 or 3,000 point army, but it's always a good idea to have a few extra models to give you some additional choice.

Before we start to look at the details of how to choose a force for a battle, it is worth pointing out that most players will cheerfully buy and paint a handful of models before deciding to commit to collecting a whole army. There's no point in buying hundreds of Orcs only to discover that you really can't abide painting green! So, whatever army you fancy the look of, buy a few samples first and see how you get on painting them. It doesn't matter if you dabble with several races before settling on the one you like best, it is far more important to choose the army that is right for you.

THE ARMY LIST

As well as providing points costs for different models, the army list also divides the army into its constituent units. For example, the Orc army list includes Orc Boyz, Goblins, Orc Boar Boyz and Snotlings... amongst others. For each of these units, the list defines the weapons the unit has and any optional upgrades it can include.

The list also places certain restrictions on the availability of some models. It would plainly be ridiculous for an army to consist entirely of fire-breathing Dragons, thundering cannons or Giants, to give just three examples. The army lists are designed to restrict the player's choice of units and characters so that the resulting force is reasonably balanced and will make for an enjoyable and fair game.

HOW THE LISTS ARE ORGANISED

The Warhammer Army books that go with this rulebook are entirely new. The army lists they contain are quite different in detail to earlier versions published for previous editions of this game. It is therefore worth explaining how these work for the benefit of veteran and beginner players alike.

The army lists in each of the Army books are divided into four basic sections: characters, core troops, special troops and rare troops.

Characters represent individual character models. In the case of the Orcs these are the most able, brutal and successful individuals in your army. Amongst them are included extraordinary leaders such as Big Bosses and sorcerous Shamans.

Core troops represent the most common warriors in the army. These usually form the bulk of the army and will often bear the brunt of the fighting. Every army has to include at least some core units.

Special troops are the best of the army's warriors, as well as certain war machines or chariots. These are available in limited numbers.

Rare troops are so called because they are scarce compared to ordinary warriors. This category includes uncommon monsters, unusual war machines and unique units of extraordinary troops.

In as far as it is practical, you will find that the core troops, the ones you will need most of, are available in the form of plastic kits. This enables you to build up a force of core troops relatively cheaply. Special and rare troops are available only as metal models, but their individual fighting worth is greater than that of core troops so fewer are needed to match a specific points value. Rare troops include many of the especially large, spectacular and effective pieces. In the case of the Orc army this category includes Giants, for example. Such models are relatively expensive and require expert assembly and painting, as is reflected by their high points value and status as rare troops.

SELECTING THE ARMY

Unless players have elected to fight a scenario that requires otherwise, games are played to an agreed points value for each army. If players agree to a 2,000 points game, this means that each player can spend up to 2,000 points on his army. He cannot spend more points but he may spend less. Sometimes, it's impossible to spend all the points, so a typical 2,000 point army might contain 1,998 or 1,999 points. This doesn't matter! The army is still a 2,000 point army for the purpose of determining the characters and units available.

SELECTING CHARACTERS

Character models are divided into two categories – the best and the rest! In the case of Orcs these are Warlords (the best) and Big Bosses (the rest). The maximum number of characters an army can contain is determined by its agreed points size as shown on the example chart below. Bear in mind that this is only an example chart – the actual chart for each specific army may well vary in detail.

| | Maximum number of | | |
Army Value	Characters	Lords	Heroes
Less than 2,000	3	1	3
2,000 or more	4	1	4
3,000 or more	6	2	6
4,000 or more	8	3	8
Each +1,000	+2	+1	+2

So, in this case, a 1,500 point army could include a maximum of three characters, of which up to all three could be Heroes and no more than one can be a Lord. In a 3,500 points army there can be a maximum of six characters with up to two Lords. The army doesn't have to include the maximum number of characters and doesn't have to include Lords at all.

SELECTING TROOPS

Troops are divided into three categories. The number of each type available depends upon the agreed points value of the army in the same way as for characters. As with the Character chart, the Troop chart below is an example, the chart for each army may well be different.

| | UNITS | | |
Army Value	Core	Special	Rare
Less than 2,000	2+	0-3	0-1
2,000 or more	3+	0-4	0-2
3,000 or more	4+	0-5	0-3
4,000 or more	5+	0-6	0-4
Each +1,000	+1	+0-1	+0

As you can see every army has to include a minimum number of core troop units. The bigger the army is, the more core units it needs to include. More core units can be included if desired. In the case of special and rare troops the number of units is restricted to a maximum in each case.

The number of models a unit can (or must) include is also indicated in each army list. Core troops must be of a specified minimum size consistent with the idea that these are numerous troops. For example, in the Orc army a Night Goblin unit must be at least 20 models strong, whilst an Orc Boyz unit must have at least ten models. Special units usually have smaller minimum sizes, for example, five models in the case of Orc Boar Boyz.

SELECTING OPTIONS

The army list for each army includes options and upgrades for characters and units of troops. All of these cost extra points to reflect the increased worth of the character or troops.

For example, characters can carry extra weapons or extra armour. They might ride some kind of mount, a boar in the case of Orcs, or they might ride in a chariot or on a monster.

In the case of characters that are also Wizards (Shamans in the Orc army) they can also increase their magic level at additional cost. Characters can also carry magic items to a predetermined total points value, and the more powerful the character the greater the total points value of magic items he can carry.

Units of troops can also be given extra weapons or armour. In the case of units all the models are given the same options automatically, so the total cost will vary depending on the size of the unit. In addition some troops have unique options depending on their type. For example, one unit of Orc Boyz can be chosen to represent 'Big 'Uns' – the best warriors in the tribe with improved characteristic values.

In most cases a unit of troops can also have individuals upgraded to represent a Champion (called Bosses in an Orc army), Standard Bearer or Musician. Champions have superior characteristics and cost extra points as you would expect.

TWO SAMPLE ARMIES

ORC ARMY

CHARACTER (HERO)

	M	WS	BS	S	T	W	I	A	Ld	
1 Orc Big Boss	4	5	3	4	5	2	3	3	8	89 points

Save: Light armour confers 6+ save; Talisman of Protection gives user 6+ Ward save
Note: Additional choppa +1A

CORE UNITS

	M	WS	BS	S	T	W	I	A	Ld	
16 Orc Boyz with bows	4	3	3	3	4	1	2	1	7	128 points

Note: Choppas and bows

	M	WS	BS	S	T	W	I	A	Ld	
16 Orc Boyz	4	3	3	3	4	1	2	1	7	127 points

Save: Light armour confers 6+ save
Notes: Additional choppa; Standard +1 to combat resolution; Musician +1 to Leadership tests to rally

SPECIAL UNIT

	M	WS	BS	S	T	W	I	A	Ld	
1 Orc Boar Chariot	–	–	–	5	5	4	–	–	–	80 points
2 Orc Crew	–	3	3	3	–	–	2	1	7	
Boar	7	3	–	3	–	–	3	1	–	

Save: 4+
Note: Crew have spears and choppas

Total: 424 points

EMPIRE ARMY

CHARACTER (HERO)

	M	WS	BS	S	T	W	I	A	Ld	
Captain	4	5	5	4	4	2	5	3	8	72 points
Warhorse	3	3	0	3	3	1	3	1	5	

Save: Barding, heavy armour, shield and being mounted confers 2+ save
Notes: Lance +2S when charging; hand weapon

CORE UNITS

	M	WS	BS	S	T	W	I	A	Ld	
8 Hand Gunners	4	3	3	3	3	1	3	1	7	64 points

Notes: Hand weapon; Hand gun

	M	WS	BS	S	T	W	I	A	Ld	
8 Hand Gunners	4	3	3	3	3	1	3	1	7	64 points

Notes: Hand weapon; Hand gun

	M	WS	BS	S	T	W	I	A	Ld	
16 Spearmen	4	3	3	3	3	1	3	1	7	111 points

Save: Light armour confers 6+ save
Notes: Hand weapon; Spear (second rank may fight except when charging)

SPECIAL UNIT

	M	WS	BS	S	T	W	I	A	Ld	
1 Cannon	–	–	–	–	7	3	–	–	–	100 points
3 Crew	4	3	3	3	3	1	3	1	7	

Note: Hand weapons

Total: 411 points

APPENDIX THREE – WARHAMMER SKIRMISH

Sometimes you might not have time to play a full-scale battle, or perhaps your armies are not yet completely painted. In such situations the rules given below will allow you to play games using small skirmish forces.

The Skirmish rules allow you to play battles between small forces of a dozen or so models. When you start playing you can decide who has the first turn, what scenery to use, etc, by using the core Warhammer rules or by agreeing with your opponent first.

All Warhammer rules apply in a skirmish game apart from the exceptions and modifications given below.

Mordheim: City of the Damned (available from Games Workshop's Mail Order and stores) provides a complete set of rules for skirmish battles set in the Warhammer world.

The skirmish force

The following rules work best with modest forces, say 100-250 points per side. Such forces should include very few, if any, magic items or Wizards (who should be limited to Level 1). You should choose one character from your army list to act as leader. A Hero level character will make a fine leader for the skirmish force and rules for leaders are explained below. Otherwise, feel free to choose any troops that suit the scenario you're playing, ignoring the limitations of core, special and rare units.

The biggest difference between Warhammer and the Warhammer skirmish game is that in a skirmish game each model forms a unit on its own, rather than several models being formed into units in ranks.

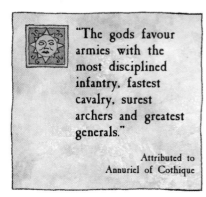

"The gods favour armies with the most disciplined infantry, fastest cavalry, surest archers and greatest generals."

Attributed to
Annuriel of Cothique

Skirmish scenarios

Skirmish games are far more entertaining if you come up with a scenario which supplies a reason for the battle. This could simply be a border skirmish, two scouting forces meeting each other, a local militia defending their village from raiders, or an expedition to rob the tomb of an Undead king. Feel free to come up with scenarios for your own battles.

PHASES

To keep track of who is doing what and when, each turn is split into four phases. This is called the **Turn Sequence**.

Turn sequence

1. Recovery
During the Recovery phase you may attempt to rally individuals who have lost their nerve and recover models who have been *knocked down* or *stunned*.

2. Movement
During the Movement phase you may move the warriors of your force according to the rules given in the Movement section.

3. Magic
In the Magic phase any Wizards in your force may use spells.

4. Shooting
In the Shooting phase you may shoot with any appropriate weapons as described in the rules for shooting.

5. Close combat
During the Close Combat phase all models in close combat may fight. Note that both sides fight in the Close Combat phase, regardless of whose turn it is.

RECOVERY PHASE

During the Recovery phase you may attempt to rally any of your models that have lost their nerve. To take a Rally test, roll 2D6. If the score is equal to or less than the model's Leadership, the model stops fleeing and has rallied; turn it to face in any direction you wish. The model cannot move or shoot for the rest of the turn, but models able to do so can cast spells. If it fails the dice roll, the model continues to flee towards the closest table edge.

Note that a model cannot rally if the closest model to him is an enemy model (fleeing, *stunned*, *knocked down* and hidden models are not taken into consideration for this).

During the Recovery phase, warriors in your force who have been *stunned* become *knocked down* and warriors who have been *knocked down* may stand up (see the Injuries section).

MOVEMENT PHASE

During the Movement phase models are moved in the following order:

1. Charge!
If you want a model in your force to charge at an enemy model and attack it in close combat then you must do this at the start of the Movement phase before moving any of your other models.

When you charge a model, declare to your opponent that it is doing so and indicate which of his models it is attacking.

2. Compulsory moves
Sometimes a model is forced to move in a certain way and this is called a *compulsory move*. For example, a fighter whose nerve breaks must run away from his enemies and take cover.

Make all of your models' compulsory moves before finishing any remaining movement.

3. Remaining moves
Once you have moved your chargers and made any compulsory moves that are needed, you may move the rest of your warriors as you see fit.

Moving
During their Movement phase, models can move up to their Movement rate in any direction. They may move up and down ladders and stairs and over low obstacles such as barrels and boxes.

In normal circumstances, models are not obliged to move their full distance, and don't have to move at all if you do not want them to. Any exceptions are explained later on and invariably involve either charging or compulsory moves.

Running

The Movement value represents how far a warrior can move whilst going at a fairly rapid rate, allowing him time to aim and shoot a weapon and to observe what is going on around him. If you wish, a model may move much quicker than this – he can run! A running warrior can move at double speed (for example, 8" rather than 4"). Note that running is not the same as charging as it does not allow your model to engage the enemy in close combat.

A model can only run if there are no enemy models within 8" at the start of the turn (fleeing, *stunned*, *knocked down* and hidden models do not count). Check this distance after any charges have been declared. If there are any enemies within 8" at the start of the turn, the model will prepare to fight instead and so is unable to run. The running model can move closer than 8" to an enemy as it moves.

Any model that runs loses its chance to shoot during that turn. He is concentrating on running and is not prepared to fight, having sheathed or shouldered his weapons. You should declare that models are running as they move, as this will remind both players that the model is unable to shoot that turn. Running models can cast spells as normal.

Charge!

If you want a model to engage the enemy in close combat then you must make a special move called a *charge*. Without measuring the distance, declare that your model is charging and indicate which enemy model he is going to attack. You can charge any opposing model if you can draw an unobstructed line from your model to the target. If your warrior wants to charge an enemy model within 4" that he can't see (eg, it is behind a corner) but has not been declared as hidden, he must pass an Initiative test to detect it. If he fails the roll, your model may not charge this turn, but can move his normal distance, shoot and cast spells.

A charge is like a running move and is performed at double the model's Movement rate, but ends with the attacker moving by the most direct route into base contact with an enemy model. Once their bases are touching they are engaged in close combat.

Models are also considered to be in close combat even when separated by a low wall or obstacle, where it is impossible for bases to physically touch because the obstacle is in the way.

A model may charge any model within its charge range as long as there is no enemy model who is not in combat within 2" of the charge route (see diagram). It will undoubtedly be intercepted if it tries to run past the enemy.

In this situation, move the intercepting model into the charge path and the charging model then engages the intercepting model instead of his original target. The charging model still counts as charging when determining the strike order, weapon bonuses, etc.

Sometimes a charging warrior may not reach the enemy because you have miscalculated the distance. If this happens, move your warrior his normal Move distance towards the enemy. This is called a *failed charge*. The model cannot shoot in the same turn in which he failed a charge, but he can cast spells as normal.

Models cannot be moved into close combat except by charging – any move that brings a warrior into close combat is a charge by definition.

Charging more than one opponent

If you can move your warrior into base contact with more than one enemy model with its charge move, it can charge them both. This might be inadvisable as it will then be fighting two enemies at once!

Hiding

The Hiding rule represents warriors concealing themselves in a way that our unmoving and dramatically posed models cannot. A hiding warrior keeps as still as possible, just peeking out of cover.

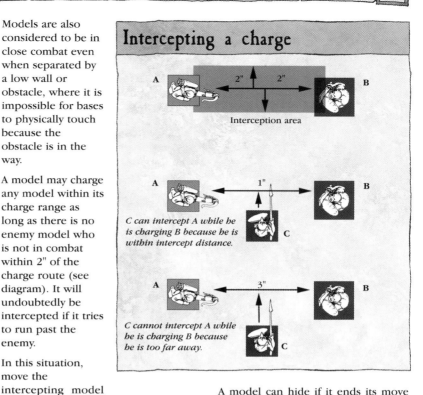

Intercepting a charge

C can intercept A while he is charging B because he is within intercept distance.

C cannot intercept A while he is charging B because he is too far away.

A model can hide if it ends its move behind a low wall, a column or in a similar position where it could reasonably conceal himself. The player must declare that the warrior is hiding and place a counter (such as a coin, dice, etc) beside the model for it to count as being hidden.

A model that runs, flees, is *stunned* or charges cannot hide that turn. His sudden burst of speed prevents it.

A model may stay hidden over several turns, so long as he stays behind a wall or similar feature. He may even move around provided that he stays hidden while doing so. If an enemy moves so that he can see the hidden warrior, the model is no longer hidden and the counter is removed. When hidden, a warrior cannot be seen, shot at or charged.

When hiding, a model cannot shoot or cast spells without giving away its position. If a hidden model shoots, or moves so that he can be seen, he is no longer hidden and can be shot at.

A model may not hide if he is too close to an enemy model – he will be seen or heard no matter how well concealed. Enemy warriors will always see, hear or otherwise detect hidden foes within their Initiative value in inches. So a warrior whose Initiative value is 3 will automatically spot all hidden enemies within 3".

Climbing

Ruined buildings, etc, do not always have stairs or ladders, so your warriors will have to climb to reach higher ground.

Any model (except animals!) can climb up or down fences, walls, etc. He must be touching what he wants to climb at the start of his Movement phase. He may climb up to his total movement in a single Movement phase (but cannot run while he is climbing). Any remaining movement can be used as normal. If the height is more than the model's normal move, he cannot climb the wall.

To climb, a model must first take an Initiative test. If he fails the test whilst climbing up, he cannot move that turn. If he fails the test while he is climbing down, he falls from where he started his descent (see the Falling section).

Jumping down

Your warrior may jump down from high places such as walkways and balconies at any time during his Movement phase (to a maximum height of 6"). Take an Initiative test for every full 2" he jumps down. If he fails any of the tests, the model falls from the point where he jumped, takes damage (see Falling) and may not move any more during the Movement phase. If successful, the model can continue his movement as normal (jumping down does not use up any of the model's Movement allowance).

Diving charge

You may charge any enemy troops that are below a balcony or overhang, etc, that your model is on. If an enemy model is within 2" of the place where your warrior lands, he may make a diving charge against that model. Take an Initiative test for each full 2" of height the model jumped down, up to a maximum of 6", like a normal jump. If he fails any of them, your model has fallen and suffers damage, may not move any more during the Movement phase and cannot charge the enemy. If he succeeds, the model gains a +1 Strength bonus and +1 to hit bonus but only during the following Close Combat phase.

Jumping over gaps

Models may jump over gaps (up to a maximum of 3") and streets, (eg, from the roof of one building to another).

Deduct the distance jumped from the model's movement but remember that you cannot measure the distance before your model jumps. If your model does not have enough movement to jump the distance, it automatically falls. If your model is able to cover the distance, it must pass an Initiative test first or will fall. A model is able to jump over a gap and still fire a missile weapon if it is not running. It may also jump as part of its charge or running move.

Warriors knocked down or stunned

If a warrior is *knocked down* or *stunned* (see the Injury section on page 245) within 1" of the edge of a roof or building, there is a chance that it will slip and fall off.

Take an Initiative test. If the model is unfortunate enough to fail the test, it falls over the edge to the ground and suffers damage.

Falling

A model that falls takes D3 hits at a Strength equal to the height in inches that it fell (eg, if the model fell 4", it would take D3 hits at Strength 4). No armour saves apply. Falling will not cause critical hits (see the Close Combat section for the Critical hits rules).

A model that falls may not move any further or hide during that turn, even if it is not hurt.

MAGIC PHASE

During the Magic phase, Wizards can cast spells as detailed in the Magic section. For the purposes of spells which target units, all enemy models that are within 2" of each other are considered to be a single unit, and can all be affected by spells which target units.

Jumping down

The Orc runs/charges from the top of a building, jumping down during the move. It moves 3" to reach the edge, then jumps down and has to see whether it can safely make it to the ground. As it has to jump down 5", it must pass two Initiative tests to avoid taking D3 S5 hits. If it fails it will stop its move at the bottom of the wall (if it is not taken out of action). If it passes both tests, it can continue its run/charge and move the remaining 7".

SHOOTING PHASE

Apart from the following exceptions, all the normal rules governing shooting in Warhammer apply:

During your force's Shooting phase each of your warriors may shoot once with one of his weapons. This means that he can fire a bow, shoot with a crossbow, or hurl a throwing knife, for example.

Work through the models one at a time. Pick which warrior is going to shoot, nominate his target, work out whether he hits the enemy and, if he does, any wounds or injuries that are caused. Then continue with the next shooter. You can take shots in any order you wish. Be sure to remember or note down which models have already shot.

Who can shoot

Each model can shoot once during the Shooting phase, so long as the model can see a target and assuming that it has a suitable weapon to shoot with.

The model may not fire in the following circumstances: if it is engaged in close combat, has run or failed a charge in the Movement phase, has rallied this turn or is *stunned* or *knocked down*.

To shoot at a target, a model must be able to see it, and the only way to check this is to stoop over the tabletop for a model's eye view.

Models can see all around themselves (ie, 360°), and they may be turned freely to face in any direction before firing. Note that turning on the spot does not count as moving.

Closest target

Your model must shoot at the closest enemy because he represents the most immediate threat and therefore the most obvious target. However, he may shoot at a more distant target if it is easier to hit or if closer models are *stunned* or *knocked down* (see the diagram below).

For example, a closer target may be hard to hit because it is in cover, whilst a more distant target might be in the open and therefore an easier shot.

Your model can shoot at models that are fleeing, *knocked down* or *stunned*, but he can choose to ignore them, because they do not represent an immediate threat. It is better to shoot the closest standing enemy model instead.

Note that your model may not shoot at models engaged in close combat, as the risk of hitting his comrades is too great.

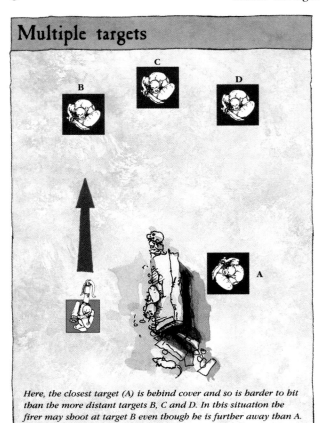

Multiple targets

Here, the closest target (A) is behind cover and so is harder to hit than the more distant targets B, C and D. In this situation the firer may shoot at target B even though he is further away than A.

Shooting from an elevated position

A model situated in an elevated position (ie, anything that is more than 2" above the table surface, such as an upper floor of a building) may freely pick any target he can see and

shoot at it. The exception to this rule is that if there are enemies in the same building and in line of sight of the shooter, he must shoot at these, as they present a more immediate threat.

CLOSE COMBAT

Apart from the following exceptions, close combat follows the same rules in the main rules section:

Who can fight

Models whose bases are touching are engaged in close combat. This can only happen once a warrior has charged his enemy, as models are otherwise not allowed to move into contact.

All close quarter fighting is worked out in the Close Combat phase. Regardless of whose turn it is, all models in close combat will fight. A warrior can fight against enemies to his side, front, or rear. In reality the fighters are constantly moving, dodging, and weaving as they struggle to kill their adversaries.

Models fighting in close combat do not shoot in the Shooting phase. They are far too busy fighting for their lives. Any very close range shots they are able to make using pistols are treated like close combat weapon attacks (see the Weapons & Armour section).

Which models fight?

A model can fight if its base is

touching the base of an enemy model. Even models attacked from the side or rear can fight normally.

If a warrior is touching more than one enemy, he can choose which to attack. If he has more than 1 Attack, he can divide them in any way the player wishes, so long as he makes this clear before rolling to hit.

Hitting the enemy

To determine whether hits are scored, roll a D6 for each model fighting. If a model has more than 1 Attack roll a D6 for each Attack.

The dice roll needed to score a hit on your enemy depends upon the Weapon Skills of the attacker and the foe. Compare the Weapon Skill of the attacker with that of his opponent and consult the To Hit chart on page 69 to find the minimum D6 score needed to hit.

Critical hits

If you roll a 6 when rolling to wound (only in close combat and shooting) you will cause a **critical hit**, which counts as 2 hits with no armour save. In addition, if the attacker normally needs 6s to wound his target, he cannot cause a critical hit. His opponent is simply too tough to suffer a serious injury at the hands of such a puny creature!

Each warrior may only cause one critical hit during each Close Combat phase (see the Close Combat section for more details), so if he has several attacks, the first 6 rolled to wound causes a critical hit.

Injuries

Most warriors have a Wounds characteristic of 1, but some have a value of 2 or more. If the target has more than 1 Wound then deduct 1 from his total each time he suffers a wound. Make a note on his roster sheet. So long as the model has at least 1 wound remaining he may continue to fight.

As soon as a fighter's wounds are reduced to 0, roll to determine the extent of his injuries. The player who inflicted the wound rolls a D6 for the wound that reduced the model to no wounds and for every wound the model receives after that. If a model suffers several wounds in one turn, roll once for each of them and apply the highest result.

Injury table

D6	Result
1-2	**Knocked down**

The force of the blow knocks the warrior down. Place the model face up to show that he has been *knocked down*.

3-4	**Stunned**

The target falls to the ground where he lies wounded and barely conscious. Turn the model face down to show that he has been *stunned*.

5-6	**Out of action**

The target has been badly hurt and falls to the ground unconscious. He takes no further part in the game and is immediately removed from the battle.

Knocked down

A warrior who has been *knocked down* falls to the ground either because of a jarring blow, because he has slipped, or because he has thrown himself to the ground to avoid injury. Turn the model face up to show that he has been knocked down.

Knocked down models may crawl 2" during the Movement phase, but may not fight in close combat, shoot or cast spells.

If he is in base-to-base contact with an enemy, a knocked down model can crawl 2" away only if the enemy is engaged in close combat with another opponent, otherwise he has to stay where he is. In combat, he cannot strike back and the enemy will have a good chance of putting him *out of action*.

A warrior who has been knocked down may stand up at the start of his next turn. In that turn he may move at half rate, shoot and cast spells, though he cannot charge or run. If he is engaged in close combat, he may not move away and will automatically strike last, irrespective of weapons or Initiative. After this turn, the fighter moves and fights normally, even though he has no wounds left. If the model takes any further wounds, then roll for injury once more, exactly as if the model had just sustained its last wound.

Stunned

When a warrior is *stunned*, he is either badly injured or temporarily knocked out. Turn the model face down to show that he has been stunned. A fighter who is stunned may do nothing at all. The player may turn the model face up in the next Recovery phase, and the warrior is then treated as *knocked down*.

Out of action

A warrior who is *out of action* is also out of the game. Remove the model from the tabletop. It's impossible to tell at this point whether the warrior is alive or dead, but for game purposes it makes no difference to the result of the game.

Breaking from combat

A warrior who *panics* whilst fighting in close combat will break off and make a run for it, as described in the Psychology section.

When a fighter breaks from combat he simply turns and runs. His opponents automatically hit the warrior as he breaks, each inflicting 1 hit which is worked out immediately.

Note that warriors cannot choose to leave a fight voluntarily.

All alone

Being outnumbered and alone is a nerve-racking situation for any warrior.

If your warrior is fighting alone against two or more opponents, and there are no friendly models within 6" (*knocked down*, *stunned* or fleeing friends do not count), he must make a test at the end of his Close Combat phase. The test is taken against the model's Leadership on 2D6.

If the warrior scores equal to or under his Leadership then his nerve holds.

If the score is greater than his Leadership, the warrior breaks from combat and runs. Each one of his opponents may make one automatic hit against him as he turns to run. If the model survives, he runs 2D6" directly away from his enemies.

At the start of each of his turns, the warrior must take another Leadership test. If he passes, he stops but can do nothing else during his own turn except cast spells. If he fails or is charged, he runs 2D6" towards the nearest table edge, avoiding any enemy models. If he reaches the table edge before he has managed to recover his nerves, he is removed from combat.

If a warrior is charged while he is fleeing, the charger is moved into base contact as normal, but the fleeing warrior will then run a further 2D6" towards the table edge, before any blows can be struck.

Leaders

A warrior within 6" of his leader may use his leader's Leadership value when taking Leadership tests. This represents the leader's ability to encourage his warriors and push them beyond normal limits.

A leader cannot confer this bonus if he is *knocked down*, *stunned* or fleeing himself. The sight of your leader running for cover is obviously far from encouraging!

The Rout test

A player must make a Rout test at the start of each of his turns if a quarter (25%) or more of his force is *out of action*. For example, in a force that has 12 warriors, a test is needed if three or more are *out of action*. Even forces that are normally immune to psychology (such as Undead) must make Rout tests.

If the Rout test is failed, the force automatically loses the fight. The game ends immediately and surviving warriors retreat from the area. A failed Rout test is the most common way in which a fight ends.

To take a Rout test roll 2D6. If the score is equal to or less than the force leader's Leadership value, the player has passed the test and may continue to fight.

If the force's leader is *out of action* or *stunned*, then the player may not use his Leadership to take the test. Instead, use the highest Leadership characteristic amongst any remaining fighters who are not *stunned* or *out of action*.

"Remember men, we are fighting for this lady's honour; which is probably more than she ever did!"

Unknown Bretonnian Knight

APPENDIX FOUR – RULES OF SIEGE

This section explains the basic rules you need for fighting siege battles in and around a castle. If you are new to Warhammer, we suggest that you familiarise yourself with the basic game first before trying to fight a siege. As you will notice, there are quite a few rules for sieges and for this reason we suggest that you read the following section carefully.

Anatomy of a castle

In the Warhammer world, kings, barons, dukes and lords spend many years and vast fortunes building impregnable fortresses. The variation between the fortifications of different races is almost endless, but all have some things in common. There are three main parts that make up a castle: the **walls**, the **towers** and the **gate**.

Walls

Solidly built of stone or brick, walls form the main body of any castle or fortress. In a game of Warhammer, the walls require a rampart that is roughly 50mm (2") wide. With a rampart of this size you will have enough room to line up two rows of troops against each other, and larger models such as Trolls will be able to fit on as well.

A length of wall between two towers is called a *wall section*. Each section is considered to be a separate target for the purposes of the rules. Very long walls will obviously consist of more than one section.

Wall sections are taken to be roughly 12" (30cm) long. Fortunately most model castles are made of conveniently sized pieces. Games Workshop produces a castle which has exactly the right dimensions for playing siege battles.

Any troops on the walls count as being in hard cover as detailed earlier in this rulebook, so any missile fire against troops on the ramparts suffers a -2 to hit penalty.

Troops on a wall must be placed in single file, which will leave enough room for the attackers to be placed on the wall as well. Note that this is a very important rule! You may place as many models as you wish on the walls as long as they are in a single file. Place any defenders on the wall so that there is roughly a 1" gap between them and the battlements. Any troops assaulting the walls will be placed in this gap facing the defenders.

Towers

Towers are the strongest point of a castle. They can be easily defended even if the walls of the castle have been demolished and, because they command a view over the entire tabletop, they make ideal positions for archers and war machines.

You can place as many models on a tower as you wish within the limitations of the space available. Models that are going on top of the tower can simply be placed there, but if troops are going inside the tower (to shoot from windows for example) it is more practical to remove the models from the table and make a note of how many there are and where they are shooting from. You can fit as many models inside the tower as you can place on top.

A single war machine along with its crew occupies the entire top level of the tower. Note that you cannot move war machines if they are on the top level of a tower, except to turn them to face the direction in which they are going to fire. Troops occupying towers can shoot in any direction, either over the ramparts or through arrow slits.

Troops on the top level of a tower are vulnerable to missile fire, but they do receive the benefit of being in hard cover because they are protected by the ramparts and so are -2 to hit with missiles. Troops inside a tower are safe from harm except, obviously, if the entire tower collapses.

Gates

In many ways, gates are the weakest part of any fortification. Although they are normally made of iron, wood or steel and guarded by massive bastions, it is still much easier to break through a gate then it is to batter down the walls of a fortress. To combat this, most gates are flanked by two towers and guarded by the best troops available to the fortress commander.

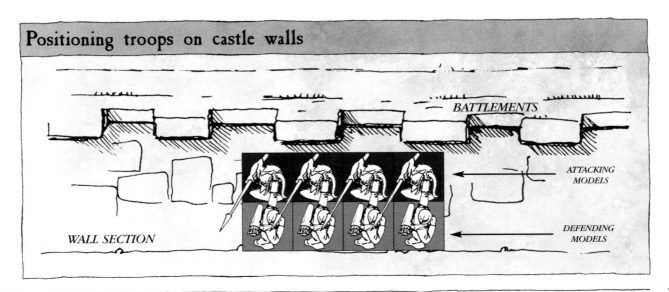

Positioning troops on castle walls

BATTLEMENTS

ATTACKING MODELS

DEFENDING MODELS

WALL SECTION

At least two models are needed to open or close the fortress gates from the inside. This can be done in their Movement phase, and the models opening or closing the gate suffer no penalties for their movement. Gates cannot be opened from the outside. Your force must break in!

Moving through a gate

A single unit of any size can move through a gateway in its Movement phase with no reduction to its movement. The unit doesn't need to change formation as it is presumed that it pours through the gate and reforms on the other side.

It is not uncommon for the front of a unit to end up on one side of the gate and the back of the unit to be on the other. This is fine. Place the part of the unit that has passed through the gate on the far side and leave the part that is still to pass through on the other. As long as the ranks on both sides are in contact with the gate, this is perfectly acceptable. Depending upon the size of the gate, some larger models, such as Giants and Dragons, may be too large to pass through the gate so they will obviously not be able to get into the fortress that way!

Courtyard

The courtyard is the area that is contained by the fortress walls. All the normal Warhammer rules apply for models who are in the courtyard. Models may move onto the walls and towers from the courtyard (this will be explained later). Any troops in the courtyard can move freely up to the towers and ramparts, provided these are not held by the enemy.

Movement

Models defending a castle are organised into units just as they would be in a normal Warhammer battle. In theory, a unit in a siege battle can be as large or as small as you like, but you will find that between five and twelve models is the most convenient size.

All troops (including the besiegers) can adopt a skirmish formation when deployed on the ramparts or towers to aid with movement. The rules for skirmishing are repeated here for your convenience. Some exceptions to the normal skirmish rules will apply, as noted below.

Skirmish formation

If you decide to deploy your troops as skirmishers, the models are placed up to 2" apart. Should the unit be split up as a result of casualties, or individuals have become divided from it for some reason, the player must rectify this situation during his next Movement phase.

Shooting at troops in skirmish formation

There are no penalties for shooting at troops in skirmish formation who are on the ramparts or towers. Being in skirmish formation merely enables troops to move around the castle with relative ease.

Movement on the walls and ramparts

When moving onto fortress ramparts or inside towers, simply follow the normal Warhammer rules for movement. Remember that there is

room for only one rank of troops on each wall section, so if the rampart is already completely occupied, there will be no room for any extra models. However, a unit may pass another unit during the Movement phase as long as all the troops who are on the wall end the phase in single file. Troops can freely move from a castle tower or a wall section to any adjacent wall section or castle tower if they have enough movement left available to them.

March moves

The proximity of the enemy does not affect march moves on ramparts or towers in any way.

Movement onto the ramparts or a tower from the courtyard

A unit may move from the courtyard to the ramparts or onto a tower during its Movement phase if it can move into base contact with the wall or tower.

Models in the unit are placed anywhere within the tower or along the rampart that the player wishes. If there is insufficient room to move all the models in the unit onto the rampart or tower, the rest of them are left in the courtyard in base contact with the tower or wall, and are still considered to be part of their unit. They must be moved onto the rampart or tower as soon as there is sufficient room.

No large creatures, such as Trolls or Ogres, may enter a tower, though they may move onto the rampart. Cavalry cannot move onto a tower or rampart for obvious reasons!

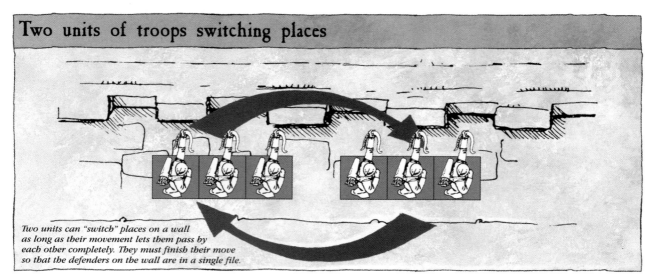

Two units of troops switching places

Two units can "switch" places on a wall as long as their movement lets them pass by each other completely. They must finish their move so that the defenders on the wall are in a single file.

Movement from the walls and towers into the courtyard

Units may also move from walls or a tower to the courtyard in a single Movement phase, and they may be placed in any formation normally allowed to them. Moving from the ramparts or from a tower into the courtyard costs half the movement of a unit. Measure any remaining movement from the base of the wall or tower. If there is insufficient room in the courtyard for all the models (because of enemy troops, for example), then any models that do not fit must be left on the ramparts or the tower. Note that no models may move from the ramparts to the courtyard if any models in the unit are engaged in close combat.

Movement outside the castle and in the courtyard

Movement outside the fortress and in the courtyard is done exactly as described earlier in this rulebook. Note that troops outside a castle may march even if there are enemies within 8" of them, as long as these enemies are on the ramparts, towers or on the other side of a wall.

Assaulting the walls

It is a brave commander that orders his troops to assault the ramparts of a castle! The majority of his men will be killed by incoming enemy fire, boiling oil and rocks poured down the walls. Fighting for control of the ramparts is a bloody affair, where the lives of brave warriors are lost by the score.

Despite this, many generals of the Warhammer world enjoy these bloody spectacles. These commanders are always eager to sacrifice troops in order to witness a magnificent battle. Bretonnian dukes in particular are always keen to launch their stalwart men-at-arms against castle walls. Any survivors are, of course, eligible to be Knights Errant! The following rules apply when assaulting the ramparts.

Charges

Troops may declare their charges against a castle as if it were an enemy model. They may move up to double their normal movement to reach a wall section, tower or gate. If they can reach the wall and are equipped with ladders, grappling hooks or ropes, or are in a siege tower, they may assault the ramparts in the Close Combat

phase. Otherwise they can make close combat attacks against the castle itself as explained later.

Charge reactions

Troops defending walls can declare normal charge reactions, and can use boiling oil and rocks in a stand & shoot reaction, unless the chargers are using a siege tower. The defenders can, still use normal missile weapons, such as bows, etc, against a charge from a siege tower. The defenders may also choose the Man the Walls! charge reaction.

Means of assault

Generally speaking, attackers may use ladders, grappling hooks and siege towers to assault walls. Note that towers are too high to be assaulted with these.

Ladders

As soon as a unit is within base contact of a wall, it may erect any ladders it has. This does not reduce its movement in any way, and the troops may assault the rampart during the same turn. Towers are too high to be assaulted with ladders.

One model per ladder may move onto the ramparts at the start of the Close Combat phase. These models are placed directly above the point where they were on the ground. You may choose any model from the unit to scale the ladder. This allows powerful characters to attempt to take the ramparts, where an ordinary trooper might fail. If the

rampart onto which the models move is occupied by the enemy, these models are now in close combat. The defenders will strike first (even if using double-handed weapons) and have the advantage of the defended obstacle bonus, meaning that attackers only hit them on natural 6s. This makes assaulting walls very difficult indeed! Note that these penalties apply each turn unless the attacking model manages to seize the ramparts.

Grappling hooks

Once a model with a grappling hook is in base contact with the wall he may throw the grappling hook. This is done automatically as soon as the model moves into base contact with the wall. This does not reduce his movement in any way, and he can assault the ramparts during the same turn.

A model equipped with a grappling hook and rope may climb up onto the ramparts. Any model climbing a rope is placed on the rampart at the end of their Move phase. This model is then placed directly above the point where he was when he was on the ground.

If the wall is occupied by the enemy, then they are now in close combat. Models defending the wall strike first (even if they are using double-handed weapons) and have the advantage of the defended obstacle bonus, ie, the attacker hits them only on natural 6s. Note that these penalties apply each turn unless the attacking model manages to seize the ramparts.

Siege towers

Once a siege tower is in base contact with a castle, any troops from the regiment pushing it can assault the walls. Up to two models can attack the ramparts from a siege tower at any time. Place these models on the drawbridge of the siege tower. The player can choose which models from the unit pushing the tower can assault the walls. This allows the best fighters a chance to clear the ramparts for their comrades.

The siege tower negates all benefits that the defender normally enjoys, so chargers can strike first and suffer no penalties to their to hit rolls, for example. This makes siege towers extremely useful in an assault!

After the initial turn when the siege tower charged in, the attacker may replace any casualties in the normal way, so there will always be two models assaulting the wall from the tower. These models can be freely chosen from the unit.

Man the walls!

Models defending the walls against an assault may make a special Man the Walls! charge reaction. This reaction allows any unengaged models defending the ramparts to move up to 2" towards the enemy after the enemy has assaulted the walls and placed its models on the ramparts. This movement is done out of the normal movement sequence, immediately before the Close Combat phase. This rule represents the defenders throwing their forces against the enemy's assault. The troops may also use rocks or cauldrons of boiling oil (though not in assaults by siege towers).

Seizing the ramparts

The attacker is deemed to have seized the castle ramparts as soon as his troops win a round of close combat against the defenders. The attacker can now move the whole of his unit, space permitting, onto the ramparts to fight against any defenders they wish, suffering no to hit penalties and striking first as if they were charging.

Undefended ramparts

If a wall has no defenders at all, any unit with ladders, grappling hooks or siege towers may move as many models onto the ramparts during its Movement phase as it is physically possible to fit in single file.

Break tests on assaulting the ramparts

When fighting on towers or ramparts Break tests are taken on the unmodified Leadership of the unit. Ranks and standards have no effect on the test, so it is the side who suffered the most wounds in a combat who has to take the Break test. The only thing that affects a unit's Leadership in a Break test is the higher Leadership of the character leading them, or their General being within 12". Note that the number of wounds caused in close combat will not modify the Leadership score.

These rules apply for all fighting on the ramparts and towers, including assaults by siege towers, troops scaling the walls with ladders, etc.

Note that troops (such as Skeletons) who suffer extra casualties due to losing rounds of combat also lose one model for every wound they lost the combat by.

If both sides suffer the same number of casualties, then the combat is a draw and no tests are taken by either side. No other factors, such as Musicians, affect the result. As the chances of a regiment breaking are less than usual, battles inside castles tend to last longer. This makes assaults bloody and dangerous affairs – just as they are in real life.

A unit that is charged in the courtyard while it still has models on the ramparts or inside a tower may not claim a bonus for any extra ranks. The unit is considered to be too disorganised to take advantage of this rule.

Pursuit

Troops assaulting the walls with siege towers, ladders or grappling hooks who are broken in close combat flee directly away from the castle along with the rest of their regiment. This is worked out exactly like a normal flee move, ie, the unit moves 2D6" away from the castle. Note that the defenders of the wall may not pursue in this case.

Manning the walls

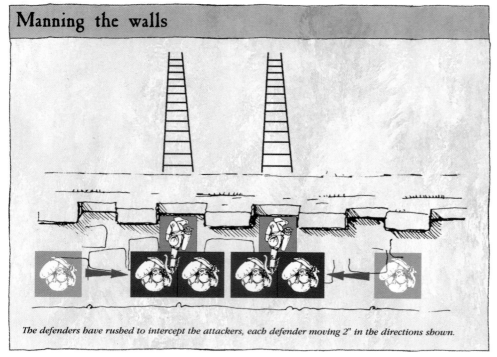

The defenders have rushed to intercept the attackers, each defender moving 2" in the directions shown.

For any other fighting on the ramparts, roll the flee and pursuit moves as normal. If the pursuer beats the score of the fleeing troops, the fleeing troops are destroyed. Simply remove the casualties and leave the pursuers in their place – they catch up with the fleeing troops and hack them down where they stand. If the fleeing troops manage to beat the score of the pursuers, they may move into the courtyard (remember that fleeing into a courtyard costs them half their movement) or into any adjacent wall section or tower. Do not move the pursuers. If there is nowhere for the troops to flee to then the broken units are automatically destroyed.

Fighting in the courtyard or outside the fortress

When troops are on ground level, the usual Warhammer rules apply. As you can see, it is very important for the attacker to demolish the walls as he will be able to use the bonuses he gains from his superior numbers, extra ranks and standards. The defenders will stand little or no chance under such circumstances!

Charging from the courtyard onto a tower or rampart

Troops in the courtyard may charge enemies on the ramparts or in a tower as long as they can see them and can move into base contact.

Work out the charges as you would in a normal game of Warhammer. If the enemies on the wall or tower are unengaged they may claim the defended obstacle bonus (attackers need 6s to hit) as they are defending the doors of the towers or stairs up to the ramparts. In the case of towers, up to two models per side may fight across a door. If the enemy models are already engaged, then the chargers may attack them normally. Place the models on the flank of the troops they wish to attack.

Note that you may not charge troops on walls if there is not enough room for them to move into. The walls are already far too crammed with fighting men.

Charging from the ramparts or a tower into the courtyard

Any units on the ramparts or a tower may charge any enemies they can see

in the courtyard. Work out the charges as you would in a normal Warhammer game, remember though that moving from the ramparts to the courtyard costs a unit half its movement. Measure the distance of the movement from the base of the wall. The charging unit may assume any formation it wishes, as long as it fits into the courtyard. If the charged unit elects to flee, they move 2D6" away from the chargers as normal, and the charging unit is placed in the courtyard as if it had moved there normally (see above).

Attacking a castle

Some races of the Warhammer world build their castles from materials other than stone. Wood Elf forts are living structures with huge trees making up the walls and their branches serving as the battlements. In the darkness of the Realm of Chaos, the strongholds of the arrogant champions of the Dark Gods

are made from metals such as bronze and brass, or even more exotic materials like glass or smoke. Beastmen carve their crude forts from stone to protect their holy herdstones and Dwarfs hew their strongholds from the very bones of the earth, constructing their battlements and ramparts on top of towering mountain cliffs. No matter what material the fortress is made out of, the following rules apply:

Shooting at the towers, walls and gates

Each tower, gate and wall section counts as an individual target for any enemy attacks, be they shooting, magic, or physical blows. Note that each gateway is situated in a wall section and these are separate targets.

All hits against towers, gates and walls are resolved by using the Damage charts on page 254.

To find out what damage the attack has caused, simply roll the number of wounds/hits the attack causes and add the Strength of the attack to the result. Consult the Damage chart for the appropriate section of castle to find what result the attack will have. As you will see, only very powerful attacks have a chance of damaging the castle.

For example: A cannonball from an Empire Great Cannon hits a tower. To see how much damage it does, the player rolls a D6 (the number of wounds that the attack normally causes) and adds the Strength of the attack, which is 10 in this case. He then consults the Tower Damage chart.

If the castle is hit by a stone thrower or some similar weapon, the castle and any troops that are under the template are automatically hit if the central hole covers any part of the castle. If the central hole does not cover the castle but other parts of the template do, the castle is hit on a D6 roll of 4+.

In the case of a unit armed with missile troops, count only one hit which the unit causes (the one with the highest Strength).

Shooting at the gates

All the normal rules for walls are also applied to the wall section that contains the gateway. Note that if the wall section where the gate is situated is destroyed, the gateway is also demolished.

You can only shoot at the gate itself with cannons and other weapons that have a flat trajectory. Randomise any shots aimed at the gate between the gate and the wall.

D6	Result
1-4	Hits the wall
5-6	Hits the gate

Cannons

A cannonball is fired over a fairly flat trajectory, unlike a stone thrower's rock which has a more curved trajectory. Because of this, cannonballs will, strangely enough, tend to smash into tall obstacles like castles rather than fly over them! It is, after all, quite difficult to miss a castle.

To represent this, cannons (including organ guns, but not earthshaker cannons or mortars) will always automatically hit castle walls (provided they have sufficient range). The shooter must still roll the Artillery dice to see whether a misfire has occurred.

Cannons may also pack in an extra charge of powder in an attempt to knock the fortress walls down quicker. This gives the cannon +1 to the damage it causes, but there is a risk involved. Stuffing a cannon full of black powder is extremely

dangerous. To represent this, the shooter must roll the Artillery dice twice each time he attempts to shoot to determine whether a misfire has occurred.

Attacking the castle in close combat

Generally speaking, the walls, gates and towers of a castle are far too massive and solid for ordinary troops to knock down, but there are exceptions. Some exceedingly powerful models may be able to knock down castle walls, etc, due to their sheer brutality and awesome strength. Greater Daemons, Dragons and Giants, for example, are so big and powerful that they pose a serious threat to even a well-constructed fortress.

Models may make one attack (and one attack only, regardless of the number of attacks they normally have) against a wall, tower or gateway in each Close Combat phase. Not surprisingly, any part of the castle will be hit automatically. The model must, of course, be in base contact with its target. Note that chariots may not attack castle walls, towers or gates, as they would undoubtedly be smashed to smithereens. The same also applies to Skaven Doomwheels and Screaming Bells.

Determine damage normally, ie, roll the number of hits/wounds the attack causes (normally this will be 1), consult the appropriate Damage chart, and apply the given result. Any bonuses from magic weapons apply.

In general, close combat attacks are not powerful enough to tear down walls or shake towers, but they are useful for breaking down gates and attacking structures already weakened by earlier bombardments.

CASTLES AND SPELLS

Castles cannot be damaged by spells – they are normally, though, protected by defensive spells, prayers, runes, and their massive size! Generally speaking, spells are best targeted at troops defending the walls.

DAMAGE CHARTS

You will notice that most of the results on these charts will cause modifiers to further dice rolls. These can be marked in some way, such as by placing a piece of cotton wool or loose rubble by the affected section to represent the damage. Note that any modifiers on the tables below are cumulative! This is the only way to destroy a castle, by building up the damage gradually until the walls collapse, towers topple and the gates are broken.

WALL DAMAGE CHART

2D6	Effect
2-12	**No effect.**
13-14	**Shaken.** Add +1 to any further rolls on this chart.
15-16	**Severely Shaken.** Troops on this section of the wall cannot shoot during their next turn on a D6 roll of 4+. Roll separately for each unit. Add +1 to any further rolls.
17-18	**Rampart Destroyed.** Any unit on this section of the wall suffers D6 S4 hits. Any troops which are on this section of the wall are no longer in hard cover. Add +1 to any further rolls. If you roll this result again there is no further effect apart from the cumulative +1 modifier.
19	**Breach!** The attack rips a massive hole in the wall. Add +1 to any further rolls that are made on this chart. If you roll this result again there is no further effect apart from the cumulative +1 modifier.
20+	**Collapse!** Wall collapses. Any troops on the wall take a single S5 hit. All troops that are within 4" take 1 S3 hit. The rubble counts as a defended obstacle and hard cover.

TOWER DAMAGE CHART

2D6	Effect
2-12	**No effect.**
13-14	**Shaken.** Add +1 to further rolls on this chart.
15-16	**Severely shaken.** Any troops in the tower may not shoot on a D6 roll of 4+ during their next turn. Roll separately for each unit. Add +1 to any further rolls
17-18	**Rampart Destroyed.** Any models on the top of the tower suffer D6 S4 hits. Any troops at the top of the tower are no longer in hard cover. Add +1 to any further rolls. If you roll this result again there is no further effect apart from the cumulative +1 modifier.
19	**Partial Collapse.** Any troops in the tower must roll under their Initiative or suffer a S5 hit. Add +1 to any further rolls. If you roll this result again there is no further effect apart from cumulative +1 modifier.
20+	**Collapse!** Roll a D6: **1-3** The tower partially collapses as above. In addition all troops within 4" of the tower suffer 1 S3 hit. **4-6** The entire tower collapses! All troops inside suffer 1 S5 hit. All models within 4" suffer 1 S3 hit. The ruined tower counts as hard cover and a defended obstacle.

GATE DAMAGE CHART

If the gates are made of metal, apply a -1 modifier to any results.

2D6	Effect
2-10	**No effect.** The gate survives the attack and does not budge.
11-12	**Crack!** The gate splinters. Add +1 to further rolls on this chart.
13-14	**Crunch!** The gate groans under the pressure. Add +2 to any further rolls that are made on this chart.
15	**Gate Broken.** The way to the fortress is free. However, some pieces of the gate remain, so troops can only move through at half speed. You can attack the gate again in the next Close Combat phase to destroy it completely, in which case add +3 to the dice roll, along with any other bonuses accumulated.
16+	**Crush!** The gate is utterly destroyed. The way to the fortress is now open!

PREPARING YOUR ARMY FOR A SIEGE

Choosing your force

When you are choosing an army for a siege battle simply choose a force from the relevant army list that is of an appropriate points value for each scenario. However, there are some extra restrictions that will apply to the choices from your army list and any scenario you are playing will clearly tell you these.

To choose an army for a siege game, refer to the Siege scenario on page 259-260 and to the relevant Warhammer Army book for your army. Note that you must always follow the normal quotas for army selection and any restrictions given in the Army book will still apply.

Siege equipment

Siege equipment is a very important part of any siege battle. Both the attacker and defender are allowed to use a number of new items in a siege, which are described below. You may spend any amount of points on siege equipment when taking part in a siege.

Siege equipment is divided between equipment for the besieged force and equipment for the besieging force. Note that you may not have more than one of the following pieces of equipment in a unit: siege towers, log rams and battering rams. You cannot have a log ram and a battering ram in the same unit.

EQUIPMENT OF THE BESIEGED FORCE

REINFORCED GATE

As any fortress commander will tell you, the weakest part of a fortress is its gate. For this reason many races will build their gates from the strongest and most enduring materials available to them. This can include replacing wooden gates with iron ones, building several gates within the gateway, or constructing a portcullis. You can represent this with suitable modelling or simply tell your opponent before battle commences that the gate is reinforced.

If the fortress gate is reinforced, a -1 penalty on the Damage chart applies. So, to get a Crash! result and smash your way into the castle, you would need to get a total of 17+ on a reinforced gate instead of 16+.

Points cost: 20 points

BOILING OIL

One of the most effective ways of deterring persistent attackers from scaling fortress walls is to drop nasty and unpleasant things onto them.

Boiling oil scalds unprotected flesh, soaks through armour and clothing and causes excruciating wounds. It is also sticky, smelly and extremely painful. In other words, it's the perfect way to deter attackers from taking your fortress.

As well as oil, the different races in Warhammer use molten bronze, boiling blood, alchemical fire and even oxtail soup! Of course, during the long history of sieges many other things have also been used, such as hot water, lime, heated sand and lead.

Cauldrons and units

You may only buy one cauldron per infantry unit you have in your army. One cauldron has enough boiling oil to last for the duration of the entire battle.

Cauldrons can be moved around the ramparts at half the normal speed of the regiment moving it. The unit may not move a cauldron and pour the boiling oil down the wall during the same turn.

If a unit panics and flees they will abandon the cauldron, which is assumed to be knocked over in the process. In this case, remove the cauldron model.

Using boiling oil

This can be used in the Shooting phase just like any other missile weapon. You can declare a stand & shoot reaction with boiling oil against troops climbing up using ladders or ropes.

Models that are defending a wall section or tower may pour boiling oil over their enemies in their own turn provided that they are not engaged in close combat.

It requires two unengaged models to use the cauldron of boiling oil, and they may not use any other missile weapons during the same Shooting phase.

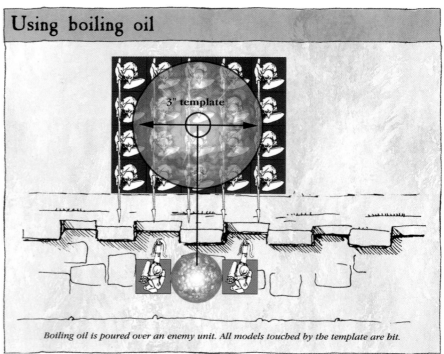

Using boiling oil

Boiling oil is poured over an enemy unit. All models touched by the template are hit.

To use boiling oil take the circular 3" template and position it directly below the cauldron and in front of the wall as shown in the diagram on page 254. Any model whose base even touches the template is hit. No rolls to hit are needed. As the cauldron uses a template, the characters can be saved by a successful "Look out, Sir!" roll.

All models hit suffer a S5 hit with no armour save possible. Against boiling oil, molten metal, etc, the crew of a battering ram receive a 4+ special save, as the mantlet of a battering ram has been specifically designed against such attacks. Boiling oil can only be used every other turn – it takes time to heat and fill a cauldron!

Points cost: 25 points per cauldron.

Some races have created other, even more unpleasant things to use to repel besiegers. All the rules for boiling oil apply with the following exceptions:

Boiling Blood

Dark Elves have a particularly nasty way of repelling attackers. Using slaves and captives as donors, the Naggarothi fill their cauldrons with blood mixed with corrosive poisons.

These are then heated up, laced with even more poison and poured down the fortress walls.

Troops that suffer casualties from boiling blood must make an immediate Panic test.

Boiling Blood: 30 points per cauldron. Dark Elves only.

Molten Metal

Dwarfs and Chaos Dwarfs use molten bronze, hot lead and other heavy metals instead of oil, as their mountain homes are rich with metal ore, whilst oil is hard to come by. Any molten metal uses exactly the same rules as boiling oil, except that its hits are resolved with a Strength of 6.

Molten Metal: 30 points per cauldron. Dwarfs and Chaos Dwarfs only.

Alchemical Fire

High Elves have perfected an arcane formula for an extremely lethal substance called Deathfire, or *Ielthan* in the Elven tongue. It is Strength 5, causes D3 wounds and inflicts double damage on flammable creatures.

Alchemical Fire: 30 points per cauldron. High Elves only.

ROCKS

Rocks are stones small enough for men to pick up and throw. They may be thrown singly, or a whole basket can be tipped onto the attackers. More technically advanced races use machines to drop huge boulders onto their attackers.

Models defending a wall section or tower can drop rocks in their own turn if not engaged in close combat. Rocks are thrown during the Shooting phase and can be used instead of any other missile weapons a model might have. Use the model's basic BS without any modifiers for range. Any enemy unit with models in base contact with the same section of wall or tower may be targeted.

Note that rocks can be used in a Man the Walls! reaction against enemies charging up ladders and ropes. A rock hits with Strength 4, causes 1 wound and has the standard -1 save modifier.

If you are choosing to arm a unit with rocks then all the models in the unit must be equipped with them, otherwise you cannot include any rocks in that unit at all.

Points cost: 1 point per model.

EQUIPMENT OF THE BESIEGING FORCE

RAMS

LOG RAMS

Log rams are massive tree trunks used to knock down castle gates. Easy to make and use, the log ram is the ideal weapon for the besieging General on a tight budget.

Log rams in units

At least four man-sized models are needed to carry a log ram. Large creatures, such as Ogres, count as two man-sized creatures. You may only buy one log ram for each infantry unit in your army. Units with log rams move as normal, so they may march, wheel and turn, etc.

A unit carrying a log ram may charge against a gate, wall or a tower, and make a single attack during each Close Combat phase. The Strength of the attack is equal to the number of models in the regiment carrying the ram, up to a maximum of 8. Log rams cause D6 wounds per attack. Only one ram at a time may attack a gate.

A regiment carrying a log ram fights normally in close combat, although a log ram cannot be used in mêlées at all. A unit can abandon it at any time it wishes (if the troops manage to break down the gate for example). Put the ram on the ground or remove the model.

Position the log ram at the front of the unit, in the centre of it, or as centrally as you can (see the diagram). Any number of models are permitted in the regiment carrying the ram, although at least four are needed to carry the ram. The regiment still counts its rank bonus as normal.

Psychology

A unit with a log ram will abandon it if they flee because of *panic*, *terror*, a failed Break test, etc. Leave the log ram where the unit

failed its test. Another regiment may pick up the abandoned ram by moving into base contact with it. Place the ram in the middle of the unit as normal.

A unit which is subject to *stupidity* may not carry a log ram.

Points cost: 10 points for each log ram.

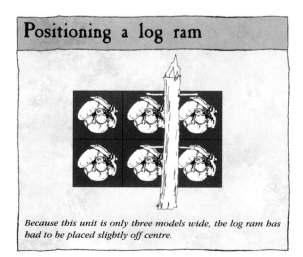

Positioning a log ram

Because this unit is only three models wide, the log ram has had to be placed slightly off centre.

Positioning a battering ram

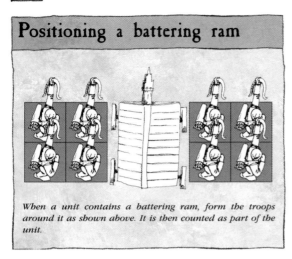

When a unit contains a battering ram, form the troops around it as shown above. It is then counted as part of the unit.

BATTERING RAMS

This is a larger version of the log ram, with the log suspended on a wheeled frame. It is ideal for breaking down fortress gates and is covered with a wooden roof to give protection against arrows and other nasties the enemy might pour down the walls. The heads of battering rams are often made to resemble ferocious creatures such as bulls, wolves or Dragons.

The same rules apply to battering rams as to log rams, with the following exceptions:

Battering rams in units

A battering ram is positioned in a unit as shown above. Any number of models are permitted in the unit pushing a battering ram, although at least six models are needed to move it. The unit still counts its rank bonus as normal. Due to the weight of the ram, any unit pushing it suffers a -1 Movement penalty.

Shooting

The battering ram's mantlet has been specifically designed to provide protection for the unit from things such as crossbow bolts, arrows, dropped missiles, etc. All missile fire targetted against a unit that is using a battering ram is randomised using the following table. This represents the troops huddling behind the mantlet.

D6	Result
1-2	Battering ram
3-6	Unit

A battering ram has the following profile, and it can be attacked in close combat.

	M	WS	BS	S	T	W	I	A	Ld
Profile	As crew	–	–	6-8	7	5	–	–	–

Points cost: 50 points for each battering ram.

LADDERS

Ladders are used by all the Warhammer races. They are handy for stealing apples, little paint jobs and scaling fortress walls. Scaling ladders are equipped with hooks on the top and spikes at the bottom to wedge them firmly in place.

Ladders are used for assaulting the walls. See the rules on page 250.

Carrying ladders

A regiment can carry any number of ladders. Troops carrying them may move at full speed unless there are less than four models carrying the ladder, in which case they move at half speed. At least two models are required to carry a ladder, so, if the unit suffers casualties, it must abandon any ladders it is incapable of carrying. Place the ladders on the ground at the spot where they were abandoned.

The unit may also drop ladders voluntarily, usually doing this to abandon ladders that are slowing the regiment down.

Units subject to *stupidity* may not carry ladders, and no large creatures, such as Ogres, may use them to assault the walls. Skirmishing units may not carry ladders.

If a unit carrying a ladder flees for any reason (failed Break tests, *panic*, etc) they have to abandon the ladder at the point where they fled. Any unit may pick up the ladder simply by moving any model into contact with it.

Points cost: 5 points per ladder.

GRAPPLING HOOKS

Grappling hooks with ropes are used by every race in the Warhammer world. They consist of a metal hook with a rope attached, often wound with steel cord to prevent it from being cut whilst the attacker is climbing up.

Skirmishers, such as Skaven Gutter Runners, have made great use of grappling hooks in the past. The hooks are particularly suitable for smaller regiments for whom heavy and clumsy ladders would be impractical.

Carrying grappling hooks

Any infantry model that can skirmish may carry a grappling hook and rope. All models are restricted to one hook and rope each. This does not affect their movement in any way.

Scaling walls

Only one model may climb up the rope to the battlements per grappling hook. This makes them less useful for big regiments, but small units of elite troops will find hooks and ropes ideal. See the special rules for assaulting ramparts for details.

You must equip all the models in a unit with grappling hooks; you cannot choose to provide only part of the unit with them. Only units that can skirmish may buy grappling hooks and ropes.

Points cost: 1 point per grappling hook and rope.

MANTLETS

Mantlets are wooden barriers, about the height of a man, which are often used by besiegers to shield them from missile fire.

By and large, mantlets are too cumbersome to be used by marching armies, so they are not available in standard Warhammer games where two armies move rapidly over large distances. They are, however, used extensively in siege warfare and are excellent for giving cover to archers so that they can pin down any missile troops on fortress walls.

Only infantry units that are equipped with missile weapons may use mantlets. You must buy them for all the models in a unit; you cannot choose to give them to part of a unit.

Moving with mantlets

Troops carrying mantlets may not march, charge or move-and-fire. However, mantlets may be deployed 2D6" closer to the castle than any other troops. This represents the ability of troops to advance closer with mantlets because enemy fire is ineffective against them at long range. This can allow archers to get relatively close to the castle at the start of the battle.

Troops do not abandon mantlets voluntarily (wisely putting their safety above other things), but if they flee for some reason (such as when they have failed a Panic or Break test) the mantlets are thrown aside and abandoned. Remove the mantlets from the table.

Shooting

Troops protected by a mantlet are considered to be in hard cover and are -2 to hit with missile weapons. Note that troops may not claim the defended obstacle bonus when fighting from behind a mantlet.

Points cost: 1 point per model in the regiment.

SIEGE TOWERS

Siege towers are the most effective way of assaulting the walls of a castle. The siege tower itself gives protection against enemy missile fire while it approaches the castle, and saves the troops from the dangerous prospect of assaulting the walls with ladders.

Siege towers, constructed by almost all races in the Warhammer world, are extremely common. They are often made of wood, though some armies use more exotic materials: Undead siege towers are grisly constructions made of bones and evil spells, Chaos Dwarfs build their siege towers with a reinforced chassis of bronze and the Wood Elves bring to the battlefield wondrous living trees bristling with warriors to assault enemy castles. Whatever the appearance of a siege tower, the following rules apply:

Siege towers and troops

Any infantry regiment with at least ten models can have one siege tower. Up to eight models in the regiment may be placed on the siege tower itself, ready to assault the walls. The rest are placed behind and around the tower pushing it. Troops on the siege tower can use their missile weapons in the Shooting phase as normal, but do not count towards the total number of models needed to push the tower.

Movement

The unit pushing the tower is placed on and around it to show their efforts at pushing and dragging it forward. Note that a unit pushing a siege tower can never have a rank bonus as it is considered to be far too disorganised to fight effectively in close combat. If the tower's unit becomes engaged in a mêlée, only troops in base contact with an enemy model may fight.

After deployment, but before the beginning of the battle, the tower may move 2D6" towards the castle. This represents how easy it is for a siege tower to advance under a hail of missiles compared to the difficulty faced by normal troops.

The siege tower moves at the same speed as the regiment pushing it (4" for Men, for example). Siege towers may never be moved at march speed, but they can make an assault against the walls at double speed. The tower may not turn or wheel, it always moves straight forward.

The minimum number of crew needed to move a siege tower at full speed is ten. If a unit of ten or less models pushing the tower takes any casualties, the tower's movement is reduced by -1" for each casualty suffered. If the unit pushing the tower suffers enough casualties to reduce it to six or less models, the siege tower cannot be moved at all.

For example, ten Men may push a siege tower up to 4" per turn. Nine Men who are pushing the tower can move it up to 3" per turn, etc. If there are less than seven Men left, the siege tower cannot move at all.

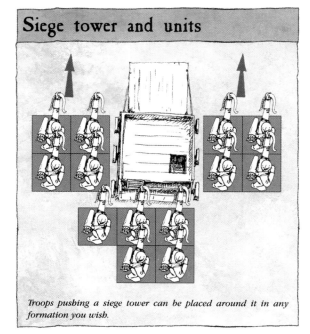

Siege tower and units

Troops pushing a siege tower can be placed around it in any formation you wish.

Attacking the siege tower

Models in base contact with the siege tower may attack it if they wish. Any close combat attacks against the tower hit automatically. Resolve damage as normal.

Shooting

Because the siege tower is so much larger than the unit that is surrounding it, it can be singled out as a target by troops firing missile weapons. The siege tower and any models on board are considered to be a single target when working out missile fire. Any troops shooting at the tower also gain the standard +1 bonus for shooting at a large target. Randomise any hits according to the following chart.

D6	Result
1-2	Crew
3-6	Siege tower

If the tower is destroyed all models on board must roll under their Initiative or suffer 1 S5 hit. Survivors should be placed where the siege tower was destroyed. These troops and the unit that was pushing the siege tower may now reform into any formation they like.

War machines and the siege tower

When you are firing at the siege tower with a weapon or making an attack that uses a template, it is possible to hit the tower and the crew depending on where the template is placed. Position the template normally. Each part of the crew and the tower is treated as a separate target. Weapons such as cannons and bolt throwers will only strike the siege tower itself.

Flee and pursuit

If the unit pushing a siege tower flees, then the tower will be abandoned until another unit turns up to push it. A unit that is pushing a siege tower may never pursue, even if it consists of frenzied troops such as Witch Elves.

Assault

The siege tower always charges at double the speed of the troops pushing it, though it may be slowed by the effect of casualties as explained earlier. This represents the impetus and effort of the unit pushing the siege tower once they are close to the fortress.

During the turn that you get a siege tower into base contact with the castle, you may attack the ramparts. Up to two models per turn may attack from the tower. Note that if there were no troops aboard the tower when it came into contact with the wall, you must spend one turn moving models up the tower's ladders before you can attack.

Troops attacking from a siege tower suffer no penalties when attacking troops occupying walls. They may also charge the defenders in the same turn in which the tower came into contact with the wall, and will strike first as normal. The defenders may still stand & shoot or Man the Walls!, but cannot use boiling oil or rocks. In subsequent turns, you can bring extra models into battle if you suffer casualties, but neither side counts as charging. You can move any models from the unit pushing the siege tower.

Points cost: 100 pts per siege tower.

You may have a maximum of one siege tower per 1,000 points of the value of your army.

	M	WS	BS	S	T	W	I	A	Ld
Profile	*	0	–	–	7	4	1	–	–

* Same as the crew pushing the tower.

SIEGE EQUIPMENT

Purchasing siege equipment

In a siege, both the besiegers and the besieged may spend up to any amount of the army's points value on siege engines. These are chosen from the list below.

Using siege equipment

Siege engines can be used in the Siege scenario.

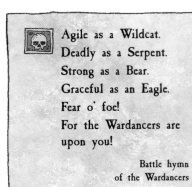

Agile as a Wildcat.
Deadly as a Serpent.
Strong as a Bear.
Graceful as an Eagle.
Fear o' foe!
For the Wardancers are upon you!

Battle hymn of the Wardancers

BESIEGING PLAYER'S EQUIPMENT

Siege Tower . . . . 100 pts
Any infantry regiment that consists of at least ten models in the besieger's army can have one siege tower. You may have a maximum of one siege tower per 1,000 points, eg, a 3,000 points army could have a maximum of 3.

Battering Ram . . . . 50 pts
Any infantry regiment in the besieger's army can include a single battering ram.

Log Ram . . . . 10 pts
Any infantry regiment in the besieger's army can have one log ram.

Ladders . . . . 5 pts
All infantry regiments, apart from any skirmishers, in the besieger's army can have any amount of ladders.

Grappling Hooks . . . 1 pt per model
Any skirmishing infantry regiment in the besieger's army can be equipped with grappling hooks.

Mantlets . . . . 1 pt per model
Any infantry units armed with missile weapons, in the besieger's army, can be equipped with mantlets.

BESIEGED PLAYER'S EQUIPMENT

Rocks . . . . 1 pt per model
Any infantry regiment that is in the besieged army may be equipped with rocks.

Boiling Oil . . . . . 25 pts per cauldron
Any infantry regiment in the besieged army can have one cauldron.

Reinforced Gate . . . . 20 pts
The defender may buy a reinforced gate for his castle.

WARHAMMER SCENARIO – SIEGE

Fighting the scenario

This scenario is a fight to the death between the defenders of the fortress and their attackers. This battle will decide the fate of the fortress once and for all. The besieger has mustered all his available forces for this final attempt and the defender will have to repel them or die.

Objectives

The besieger's objective is to knock down the fortress walls, slay all the defenders and conquer the fortress. The besieged player's objective is to hold the fortress at any cost, and repulse the assault. He must survive long enough to receive any reinforcements, or drive away the attackers.

The battlefield

The battlefield consists of the castle walls, towers and gateway, and the surrounding countryside.

Terrain

The map below shows one possible way to lay out the castle for a siege. The besieging player may then use the terrain charts on pages 222-228 to generate up to three extra pieces of terrain for the battle. These may be set up anywhere on the table, more than 24" from the fortress walls (leaving an open killing ground around the castle).

On the map you will see a typical layout for a 1,500 point force of besieged troops. Add an additional tower and section of wall for each full 500 extra points worth of besieged troops.

The forces

Each player refers to his force selection in order to choose models for this game. These tell you how many points you can use and which troop types are allowed.

Special rules

The scenario is played using the Warhammer rules with the following exceptions:

Castle. All the rules for attacking a castle apply. See the Rules of Siege section for details.

Siege Equipment. Both sides are allowed to buy siege equipment as explained in the Rules of Siege section in this book.

Special Deployment. Any troops with special deployment rules such as Wood Elf Scouts may not use them in this scenario.

Deployment

The besiegers are deployed first. They may be deployed anywhere on the battlefield no closer than 24" to any part of the castle. The defending force is deployed afterwards anywhere in the fortress.

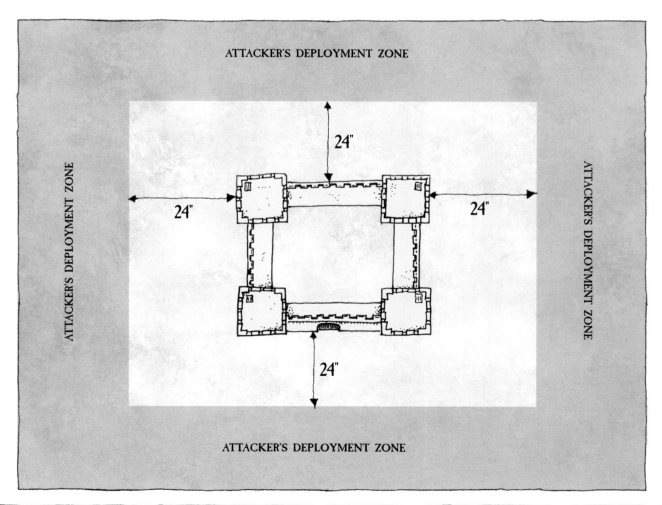

Who has the first turn?

The defenders have the first turn.

How long does the scenario last?

The scenario lasts for seven turns. If the fortress is not captured within that time, the assault will fail.

Victory or defeat

If either side is completely wiped out, then their opponents win by default.

Otherwise, the area within the fortress walls should be divided into four equally sized zones (see the map on the previous page). Note that the towers and walls are not included in this area.

To control one of these zones, a player must have a unit of at least 5 models in the zone. If both players have at least one unit of 5 models in the same zone, then neither player controls the zone. Note that flying troops do not count towards the victory conditions as they cannot take the fortress by themselves.

The player who controls the most zones at the end of the game is the winner. If both sides have the same amount, the game is a draw.

Assault force

The assault force consists of twice as many points as the besieged force, thus the force can be of any size.

We recommend using 3,000 points of besiegers. Use the Warhammer Army book for the appropriate race to choose an army from.

Note that if your army has no infantry available from its Core choices, you may replace one of the Core units with any infantry unit from the Special category.

Siege equipment

You may freely purchase any siege equipment allowed for the besieging force. See the Rules of Siege section for details.

Defenders

The defenders of the besieged fortress number half the points value of the besieging force.

We recommend using 1,500 points of defenders against 3,000 points of attackers. Use the Warhammer Army book for the appropriate race to choose an army from.

Note that if your army has no infantry available from its Core choices, you may replace one of the Core units with any infantry unit from the Special category.

Siege equipment

You may freely purchase any siege equipment allowed to the besieged force. See the Rules of Siege section for details.

Fill the moat with the corpses of your comrades. Trample on their broken carcasses to reach the ramparts. Bring down the walls with the weight of the dead.

Arbaal the Undefeated to the Warriors of Chaos during the Siege of Praag.

APPENDIX FIVE – ACCIDENTAL CHARGES

In the hurly-burly of combat you sometimes need to charge across the front of one enemy unit to reach another. Normally the only problem this gives you is the fact that you can end up with your flank exposed to an enemy charge in the following turn. However, sometimes your unit ends up touching, or very nearly touching, another enemy unit with its side. It is obviously wrong to ignore this second unit when it comes to working out the combat, but what happens? Do they get a charge reaction such as stand & shoot?

In Fig. 1, unit X is free to declare a charge on unit A as it can clearly see it and it is within the charge arc.

In Fig. 2a, the cavalry charge in (remembering to bring as many models into contact as possible) and realign themselves on the target. This brings them within a fraction of an inch of the front of a rather surprised unit B.

From the point of view of unit B the enemy's charge goes thundering past their noses, but instead of disappearing into the distance, the unfortunate foe halts with their exposed flank a mere sword's length away. It's too good an opportunity to miss! Unit B can't believe its luck and charges into contact.

Note that unit B does not get a charge reaction in this case but does count as charging and all the normal rules apply.

In the subsequent mêlée both units X and B count as charging so fight in Initiative order. Unit A strikes after the chargers as usual.

Note that this extra move only applies if a charging unit ends up within 1" of the front of an enemy unit, ie, somewhere they could be charged by it.

Fig. 2b shows that sometimes you can follow the letter (if not the spirit) of the rules and bring the maximum number of models in while still staying over 1" away from unit B. In this case the cavalry charge in and the combat proceeds as usual. Unit B has to hope the combat remains where it is so they can charge the cavalry's flank in the following turn.

Note that as you aren't allowed to measure before you declare a charge it is extremely difficult to do this deliberately (and rightly so as it is almost as bad as the evil clipping!).

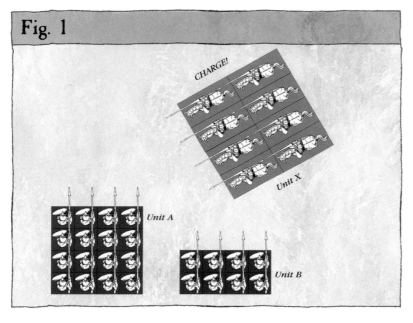

Fig. 1

CHARGE!

Unit X

Unit A

Unit B

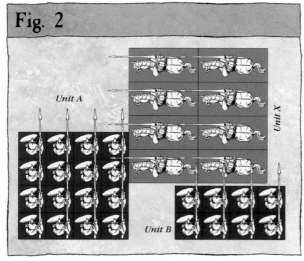

Fig. 2

Unit A

Unit X

Unit B

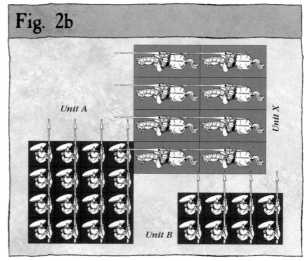

Fig. 2b

Unit A

Unit X

Unit B

APPENDIX SIX – RULES COMMENTARY

This following pages offer some observations on the game rules. These notes have been placed here at the back of the book so that the rules themselves could be kept reasonably concise. Amongst the commentaries are some further rules which we have found to be useful occasionally.

Changing formations (page 49)

Units can add to or reduce the depth of their formation by a single rank at a penalty of half their Movement rate, or by two ranks if they remain stationary. A rear rank still counts as a rank even if it only contains one model, although no close combat benefit is conferred unless it contains at least four models.

The units in Fig. 1 are each deployed in two ranks, although only the third unit has sufficient rear rankers to earn a combat resolution bonus because the rank has four models.

In Fig. 2, there is a unit of 15 models arranged in three ranks, and the same unit redeployed into two and four ranks. In both cases the centre front model remains in place (the ideal position for the unit's champion) whilst the length of the line is reduced or expanded as evenly as possible about this centre point.

Often, as in this case, you will have to decide whether to move models from the left or right side as the number of models in the line shifts from odd to even, but you must still try to keep the centre front rank model as close to the centre as possible.

The easiest way to reduce a rank is to remove an entire rank from the unit's formation, and then rearrange the models evenly to the each side.

When adding a rank remove a file from one end of the formation and line it up at the back, then, if there is sufficient room, remove the file from the other side of the formation and line it up – and so on until there is no room left to rearrange a whole file.

When adding or reducing ranks you must be careful to ensure that there is room for the models to fit into their new formation.

The formation change is not permitted if space is blocked by other models or impassable terrain or buildings, if the edges of a line should creep into difficult terrain the unit does not already occupy, or if models must move over an obstacle.

Fig. 1

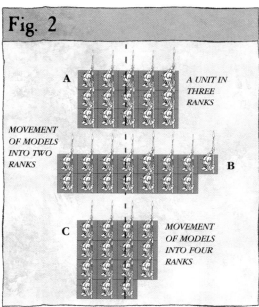

Fig. 2

A — A UNIT IN THREE RANKS

MOVEMENT OF MODELS INTO TWO RANKS

B

MOVEMENT OF MODELS INTO FOUR RANKS

C

Turning & the incomplete rank

The last rank of a unit is very often incomplete and if the units decide to turn 90° or 180°, it can cause a problem on the final formation. The best thing to do is to turn the models in the complete ranks first and then remove the incomplete rank and move its models to the back of the new formation, forming new ranks if necessary (Fig. 3). In extreme situations (long lines of missile troops mostly) this can look a bit bizarre, but on the whole this is a simple principle and helps in keeping the game tidy.

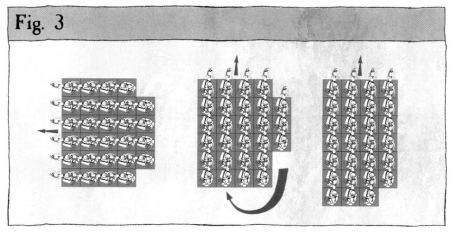

Fig. 3

Close combat & the incomplete rank

Models in the incomplete rank must normally be kept as close to the centre as possible.

If the unit is charged in the flank, the models in the incomplete rank are moved in contact with the enemy and fight normally (Fig. 4).

If the unit is charged in the rear, some enemy models might end up not in base contact with the enemy because of the width of the incomplete rank's models (Fig. 5 shows an extreme case). In this situation, models can attack the enemies in front of them even if not physically in base-to-base contact. In reality the chargers would not have stopped one metre away from the enemy and would have moved in, finishing their charge.

Fast cavalry formations

Fast cavalry can perform great feats of speed and manoeuvre, being able to reform once as they move, even when marching! This enables a unit in a column to deploy to its left and right in a single line as shown.

The first thing to note is that the unit has deployed as equally as possible around the front model. It would deploy about the middle model in the front if the unit were formed into a wider column. Units changing their frontage rapidly in this way always do so about the centre front model. This applies equally to units forming a column from a line, or otherwise adding or reducing ranks to lengthen or shorten a line (see Fig. 6)

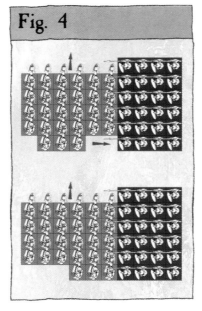

Fig. 4

Fig. 5

Models who are considered to be in base contact can attack each other.

The second thing to note is that the models at the rear of the column have actually moved a long way! The longer the column the further they move. This is not a problem in itself – fast cavalry are supposed to be fast and manoeuvrable after all – but it can become a problem if the column is very long, say 20 models for example.

For this reason, when deploying from a column into a line, models must be within their Movement distance of the position they want to occupy in the front rank. Models may not move further than their Movement distance in order for the unit to redeploy, so the frontage of the unit will be reduced as a result.

The third point is that models moving from the rear of the column might find their most direct path blocked by difficult terrain, obstacles or other troops. In this case models must be able to trace a clear path to their new position without having to cross the difficult terrain/obstacle/troops, and they may not travel further than their Movement rate to do so. Fig. 7 shows how this happens when a column rides past and behind an enemy unit, then deploys into a line.

As a general rule, if models at the rear of a formation cannot trace a path to their intended position without moving into difficult terrain, crossing an obstacle, or moving through other troops then the unit cannot redeploy as intended.

Fig. 6

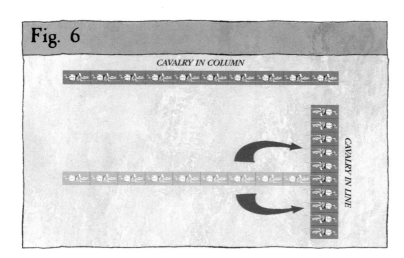

CAVALRY IN COLUMN

CAVALRY IN LINE

Fig. 7

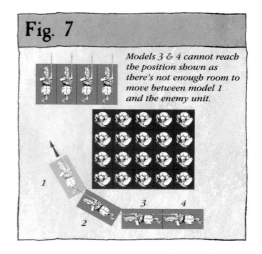

Models 3 & 4 cannot reach the position shown as there's not enough room to move between model 1 and the enemy unit.

Awkward charges

Firstly, in the case of an awkward charge, a charging unit must be able to see its enemy. That is to say, the enemy unit must lie within the 90° arc of vision of at least one model in the unit.

Players are not permitted to measure to their intended target when they declare a charge. A player must use his judgement when declaring a charge, because if the target is too far away he will only be permitted to make a normal move and also loses any opportunity he might otherwise have to shoot with missile weapons. On the whole, a failed charge is bad news for the would be charger; not only might he suffer unnecessary stand & shoot hits but he will be vulnerable to an enemy charge in the next turn.

When he declares a charge a player must be reasonably sure that his unit will reach his target. A player cannot attempt to gain an advantage by declaring a charge if it is immediately obvious his unit cannot reach its target. In most cases this will be disadvantageous, but it is possible that an advantage might be gained in some situations. Where it is blindingly obvious a unit would be unable to reach its target a player is not permitted to declare a charge.

Moving chargers is perfectly straightforward in most cases. However, a battle being what it is, fought over infinitely variable terrain and subject to the strangest of circumstances, charging can sometimes degenerate into a tangle of units scattered all over the countryside. If players bear in mind the following principles they should be able to sort out even the most complex situations.

A charging unit can wheel at any point of its move in order to bring as many of its models in frontal base contact with the enemy as possible. A wheel that reduces the number of models that would otherwise fight is not allowed.

Apart from this one wheel, no other manoeuvres are allowed in a charge. Units cannot wheel again, nor may they turn or change their formation.

Once the charging unit has touched its opponent the combat is committed and it only remains to align the antagonists where the charge has been made at an angle. Bear in mind what is really happening. The two units have clashed and some warriors in advance of the rest have struck the enemy first, but the rest will pile in beside them and gradually both sides come together into a wave that ebbs and flows as the troops fight.

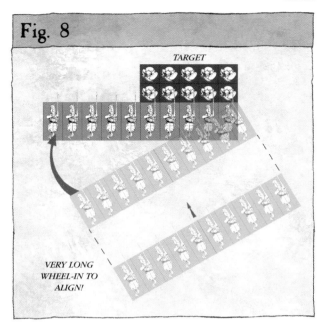

Fig. 8

TARGET

VERY LONG WHEEL-IN TO ALIGN!

For the purposes of the game we simply move the combatants against each other so that a battleline is formed, and for convenience it is easier to move the chargers. Therefore, the charging unit is aligned to its target, but in situations where it would be more convenient (eg, if impassable terrain is in the way) it is entirely possible to move the charged unit to align it with the charger.

This extra 'wheel in' happens automatically and can result in some models moving further than their normal charge distance (see Fig. 8). On the whole this isn't worth worrying about.

Generosity

Having laid down some harsh guidelines about overlong and impeded charges it's only proper to point out that winning because your opponent has misjudged a charge by a fraction of an inch is no victory at all!

Players are encouraged to play in a spirit of cooperation, and should be prepared to allow some slight repositioning of units rather than spoil a good game. If in doubt be generous… or roll a dice to decide where things are very close.

'Clipping'

Some players have been known to exploit the rules by intentionally clipping a corner of the target unit in order to have just a few models fighting and thus gaining some kind of unfair advantage. Situations like this are unrealistic and should be avoided whenever possible by applying a bit of common sense.

Unfortunately sometimes 'clipping' is completely unavoidable. This can happen when the units are far apart, exactly at the maximum charge distance of the chargers (Fig. 1). This situation will make it impossible for the chargers to wheel, because any wheel would mean that they fail the charge. Therefore they will have to charge directly forward. Funnily enough, a very similar situation can occur when the units are too close and the charging unit cannot physically wheel enough to bring the maximum number of models in combat (Fig. 2).

In these extreme situations you have to live with the clipping and continue with the game. Feel free

to agree with your opponent upon any gentlemanly solution which could avoid situations like the ones in Fig.1 and Fig.2. You could choose to allow a diagonal charge, to allow the chargers some extra movement to wheel and bring more models into contact with the enemy, or slide the chargers sideways to bring more models in to the fight. All these systems are not technically allowed by the letter of the rules, but if both players agree to use any of them, the game will benefit in realism and fun (you get to roll lots more dice as well).

Only fools claim to understand Chaos, for by definition Chaos is inhuman and incomprehensible. The mortal sages and mystics who dare to debate upon the nature of Chaos succeed only in attracting the attention of the creatures of Chaos. Many wise men have been carried alive and screaming to the charnel houses of the Realm of Chaos, there to writhe in eternal debate with the daemons of Torment.

Some of them have claimed that Chaos, in its eternal diversity, has spawned an infinite number of gods. Others say that all the apparently different gods are no more than different aspects and manifestations of one supreme being: The Great Unnameable One, The Abomination, The Unspeakable Beast, The Chaos Undivided.

But the true nature of Chaos is beyond any comprehension. No mere mortal can ever hope to understand these matters, and the wise do not puzzle too deeply over Chaos gods, or try to fathom their wars, rivalries and bickerings.

The important thing to understand when you come across these sorts of situation is that clipping is an evil and a very wrong thing to do and every effort should be made to avoid it!

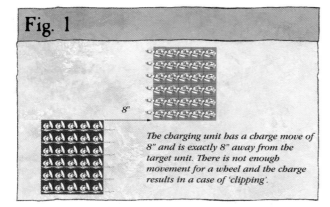

Fig. 1

The charging unit has a charge move of 8" and is exactly 8" away from the target unit. There is not enough movement for a wheel and the charge results in a case of 'clipping'.

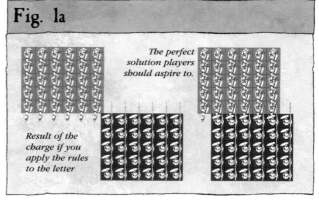

Fig. 1a

The perfect solution players should aspire to.

Result of the charge if you apply the rules to the letter

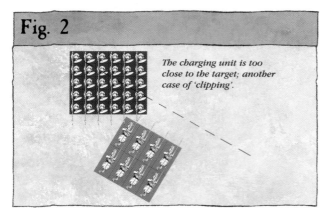

Fig. 2

The charging unit is too close to the target; another case of 'clipping'.

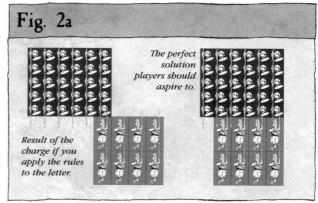

Fig. 2a

The perfect solution players should aspire to.

Result of the charge if you apply the rules to the letter.

Multiple targets

It often happens that two or more units are lined up together, so that a charge against one will result in others becoming involved. Consider the situation in Fig.1 below.

Here a charge against the left hand unit will inevitably bring the other unit into combat. In a case like this the charging player should declare his charge against whichever unit he intends to bring most models to bear against. However, because it is inevitable that other units will be brought into the combat they are also allowed to make a normal charge response – ie, a unit can flee, stand & shoot or hold even if it is not the target of the charge, if it is inevitable it will become engaged in the combat.

Of course, units will never line up exactly. It is inevitable that a charge will reach one unit before the other if only by a fraction of an inch. So, where do you draw the line? If a unit is a fraction of an inch behind one to its side, does it avoid combat or is it drawn into the fighting?

The best way to deal with this is to stop the charge as soon as it hits any unit then align the charge to the unit as normal. If the process of alignment carries you into further enemy units then those units become drawn into the combat and the whole lot are aligned into a battleline in order to bring as many models into combat as possible. In these cases it is often necessary to move all the units, chargers and targets, in order to form a convincing battleline. Units hit

during realignment have the usual options for charged troops: they can flee, hold or stand & shoot.

It can happen that a unit finds itself just out of combat because it is fractionally further away than one lined next to it, or at a slight angle compared to the chargers.

In reality the chargers would not simply stop and form a neat line whilst their enemy are so close. Therefore, the chargers are automatically moved into contact if they are within 1" of the second enemy unit and assuming the chargers have enough move left to reach them. Either move the enemy unit into position, as this is usually easiest, or shuffle all the units together until a battleline is formed.

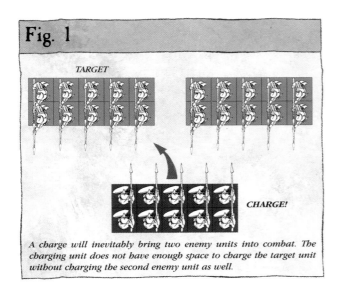

Fig. 1

A charge will inevitably bring two enemy units into combat. The charging unit does not have enough space to charge the target unit without charging the second enemy unit as well.

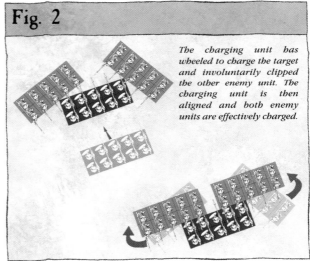

Fig. 2

The charging unit has wheeled to charge the target and involuntarily clipped the other enemy unit. The charging unit is then aligned and both enemy units are effectively charged.

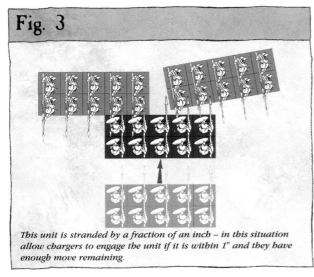

Fig. 3

This unit is stranded by a fraction of an inch – in this situation allow chargers to engage the unit if it is within 1" and they have enough move remaining.

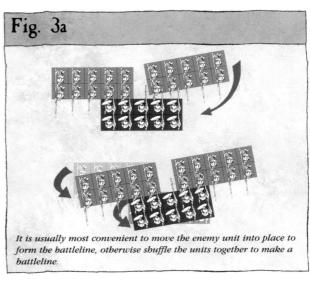

Fig. 3a

It is usually most convenient to move the enemy unit into place to form the battleline, otherwise shuffle the units together to make a battleline.

Multiple charges

When two or more units are charging an enemy unit, the player moving them must divide evenly the frontage of the target unit between the charging units (Fig.1). Also keep in mind that you cannot shuffle around the charging units so that their charges cross in order to bring in the strongest unit (Fig. 2).

Remember, the spirit of the game is the best guideline to follow, so try to do something that 'looks right' and is realistic, as opposed to trying to stretch the rules to create a weird situation which looks obviously wrong (like the infamous 'clipping') and gains some unfair advantage to one player.

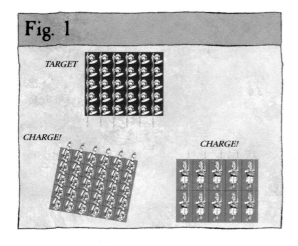

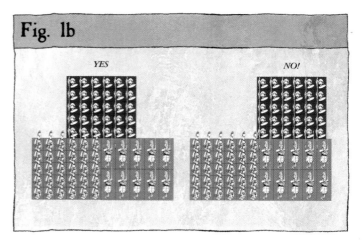

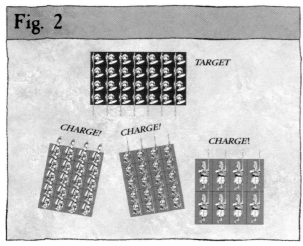

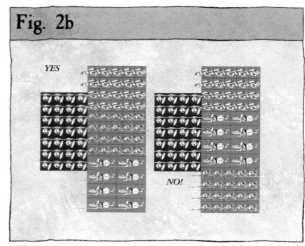

Skirmishers charging other skirmishers

When a skirmishing unit charges another skirmishing unit, take the model of the charging unit which is closest to the charged unit and move it into base contact with the closest model in the charged unit. (Fig. 3)

Then, move all the models which can reach into a fighting line, lining them up with the first model moved. Other charging models that do not have enough movement to line up on the fighting line will form up behind it, as usual for skirmishers charging (Fig. 4)

Now the charged unit will form up as normal for a unit of skirmishers charged by an enemy unit. (Fig. 5)

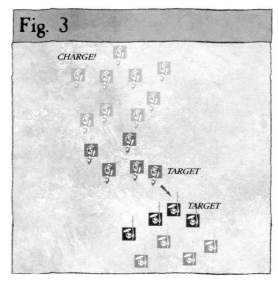

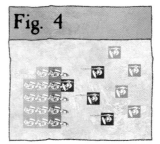

APPENDIX SEVEN – SPECIAL RULES

This section summarises the most common special rules that are used in Warhammer. We have compiled these for the convenience of experienced players to act as a 'memory jogger' during heated games. In all cases the main rules are definitive, and you should refer to the full rules description to solve any disputes.

Skirmishers

1) Skirmishing models in a unit deploy 1" apart from one another.

2) Skirmishers can move at double their Movement rate in any direction they want and suffer no penalties for moving through difficult terrain or crossing obstacles. If skirmishers move at double pace they may not shoot.

3) Skirmishers can shoot and charge within a 360º arc. They do not block line of sight for other members of their own unit but do block the line of sight of other units.

4) Missile fire targeted at skirmishers suffers a -1 to hit penalty.

5) Skirmishers may charge an enemy unit visible to at least one of its members. Models are moved individually towards their target and arranged into a fighting line. Models unable to reach the enemy are formed up behind the models in the fighting line.

6) If skirmishers are charged, the enemy is halted once it reaches the closest skirmisher. The skirmishers now form up as described above.

7) Skirmishers receive no combat bonuses for extra ranks and do not negate an enemy unit's rank bonuses if they charge them in the flank or rear.

8) A character on foot may join a skirmishing unit.

Fast Cavalry

1) If they are not charging, a unit of fast cavalry may reform at any point in its Movement phase with no penalties to its Move distance. Even with this free reform no model may move further than its maximum Movement distance.

2) Fast cavalry units may fire in any direction and can also shoot while marching. Line of sight rules still apply for stand & shoot reactions, etc.

3) If fast cavalry choose flee as a charge reaction, they rally automatically in their next rally phase and may reform facing any direction.

4) A mounted character may join a fast cavalry unit but does not benefit from the special shooting rules.

Flying models

1) Flying units operate as skirmishers and obey all the rules that apply to skirmishing troops.

2) Flying models may fly up to 20" in any direction. Line of sight rules still apply when declaring charges and shooting.

3) Flying models may move along the ground using their Movement rate and all the normal rules governing movement apply. A flyer may either fly or move on the ground, but cannot combine both in a single turn.

4) Flying models may ignore movement penalties for changing direction, overflying scenery or crossing obstacles. They may also freely overfly other models, including enemy units. Flying models may not move, land or take off from within a wood or any terrain feature that the players consider would not allow it.

5) A flyer may declare a charge against an enemy within its 20" move as normal. This aerial move is never doubled during the charge and the charged unit has all the usual charge response options. Note that flyers do cause *panic* if they charge a unit in the flank or rear that is already engaged in close combat.

6) Flyer opponents in close combat never gain the Higher Ground combat bonus and never gain the advantage of fighting from behind a defended obstacle.

7) Flyers always pursue and flee 3D6" unless they are forced to do so on the ground in which case their Movement value will be used to work out how far they move.

Standard Bearers and Musicians

Standard Bearers and Musicians must be placed in a unit's front rank and fight exactly as other members of the unit. When removing casualties it is permissible to remove another model in preference to the Standard Bearer.

1) A unit that includes a Standard Bearer may add +1 to its combat result.

2) If a unit pursues a broken enemy that flees from combat it automatically captures the unit's Standard regardless of whether they catch the unit or not.

3) A fleeing unit with a Musician gains +1 Ld bonus on any attempt to rally (up to a maximum of 10).

4) If a close combat is a draw and one side has a Musician and the other does not, the side with the Musician wins the combat by 1 point. If both sides have a Musician then the combat is still a draw.

Scouts

1) Scouts are set up after both armies have deployed. They can set up anywhere on the table, but must be out of sight of the enemy and no closer to him than 10".

2) If both armies have Scouts then roll a D6. The player with the higher score may choose to deploy his own Scouts before or after his opponent.

Immune to psychology

Units immune to psychology never need test for psychology such as *fear*, *terror* or *frenzy* and they may never choose flee as a charge response. Break tests still apply as normal.

Unbreakable

Unbreakable units never need to take Break tests and are also immune to psychology such as *fear*, *terror* or *frenzy*. They may never choose flee as a charge response.

Scaly skin

Scaly skin may be combined with regular armour to improve a model's saving throw. Scaly skin counts as an armour save and can be modified by weapons with a high strength.

Killing blow

If a model with the Killing Blow skill rolls a 6 when rolling to wound he automatically slays his opponent. Only Ward saves can be used to counter this ability.

This skill may only be used against roughly man-sized opponents.

Regeneration

Every wound suffered by a creature that can regenerate may be recovered on a 4+. Only one attempt per wound may be made. Combat results are worked out after any regeneration. Wounds that are caused by fire cannot be regenerated once the regenerating creature is wounded.

Magic resistance (1-3)

The number of dice in the brackets indicates how many extra dice you may roll when attempting to dispel any magic directed against the magically resistant creature.

Poisoned attacks

Poisoned attacks will cause a wound automatically on a model if a natural 6 is scored when rolling to hit. Armour saves are taken as normal.

Unliving troop types are immune to poison attacks.

Breath weapons

Creatures that utilise a breath weapon may use it during the Shooting phase. The Flame template is placed over the target unit with the narrow end at the creature's head.

Only models that are completely under the template are hit. Work out the effects of the breath weapon as described in the relevant creature's section.

Characters affected are eligible for 'Look out, Sir!' rolls when within a unit.

This weapon cannot be used as a stand & shoot reaction.

Flammable

Creatures that are flammable take double the normal number of wounds caused by flaming attacks. Take armour saves before doubling the wounds.

APPENDIX EIGHT – SEQUENCE OF PLAY

This section of the book summarises the sequence of play and basic rules for Warhammer. In all cases the text in the main rules is definitive.

TURN SEQUENCE (p.42)

1. Start of the turn
2. Movement
3. Magic
4. Shooting
5. Close combat

1. START OF THE TURN

Take any tests required such as Panic, Terror or Stupidity.

2. MOVEMENT

1. Declare charges
2. Rally fleeing troops
3. Compulsory moves
4. Move chargers
5. Remaining moves

Declare charges (p.44)

Indicate which units are charging and nominate the enemy unit which they are going to charge. Take Panic tests for any units that are in close combat that will be charged in the flank or rear. Opponent decides charge responses.

Charge responses (p.45)

Stand & shoot

If the attackers begin their charge more than half their charge move away they may be fired upon by troops armed with missile weapons. Should this cause the chargers to take and fail a Panic test they will flee in the Compulsory Movement phase.

Hold

The unit stands fast and braces itself ready to be charged. This is the usual reaction of troops who are either not armed with missile weapons or are too close to the enemy to be able to use them.

Flee

Models are moved immediately 2D6" away from the enemy if their Movement is 6" or less, 3D6" if their Movement is more than 6".

Rally fleeing troops (p.75)

Troops that fled in a previous turn can be rallied by rolling less than or equal to the unit's Leadership characteristic on 2D6. A unit must have at least 25% of its original number of models surviving to rally. Rallied troops may not move or shoot this turn but may adopt any formation facing the enemy. Rallied characters may cast spells as normal.

Compulsory moves (p.45)

Compulsory movement is done after charges have been declared, but before any movement. Units subject to compulsory movement, such as those forced to flee or under the effects of frenzy or stupidity, must be moved now.

Fleeing troops move either 2D6" or 3D6" depending on their Movement characteristic, ignoring penalties for obstacles and difficult ground but moving around impassable terrain. Frenzied troops move their normal charge distance if they are within range of their target. Otherwise they may move as normal. Stupid troops half their Movement if they fail their Leadership test.

Move chargers (p.52)

Chargers make a double move towards the target unit and must bring as many models into combat as possible. Chargers may not turn or change formation, but can wheel to bring more models into contact with the enemy. However, the unit need not do so if this means that it would not reach its target. Once a unit reaches the enemy it halts and is aligned with its opponent to form a neat battle line. This alignment

move is free. If a charging unit's target has fled but is still within charge range it is destroyed.

Failed charges

If the target unit flees out of reach or the charge move is too short, the charge has failed. Move the charging unit its normal movement unless another unit is also within range in which case the charge may be redirected against this new target. A charge may only be redirected once. Units which fail to complete a charge may not shoot although a wizard is free to cast spells as normal.

Remaining moves (p.49)

Any remaining units may now move up to their maximum move distance. Units may move in a straight line or may manoeuvre. There are four types of manoeuvre:

Wheel

Units can pivot around one corner. Measure the distance travelled from the outside model. A unit may wheel several times in a turn as long as it has enough movement. A unit may wheel once in a charge to bring more models into combat.

Turn

A unit that is not charging or marching may turn 90° or 180° by surrendering a quarter of its move. Note that each individual model turns in place; the unit as a whole does not move. Leaders, Standard Bearers and Musicians are then moved to the unit's new front rank.

Change formation

A unit may increase or decrease the number of ranks it is deployed in by one at a cost of half its move. It may increase or decrease its ranks by two if it does not move at all.

Reform

If it is not in close combat a unit may reform into as many ranks as it wishes and facing in any direction it wishes. If a unit reforms it cannot move at all and may not shoot in the Shooting phase, but Wizards are free to cast spells as normal.

Marching (p.54)

A unit can march if there are no unbroken enemy models within 8" at the start of the Movement phase. It can, however, move to within 8" of enemy units during its march. A marching unit moves at twice its Movement characteristic and the only manoeuvre it may attempt is the wheel; it can neither change formation nor turn. It may not move through difficult terrain or cross obstacles and must stop if it reaches such features. A unit which is marching cannot shoot in the Shooting phase, but Wizards are free to cast spells as normal.

3. MAGIC (p.134)

1. Calculate Power and Dispel dice
2. Cast spells
3. Attempt to dispell
4. Spell succeeds or fails
5. Cast again. Repeat steps 2 - 4
6. Dispel any spells in play

Generate power and dispel dice (p.135)

Power Dice

The player whose turn it is generates two Power dice plus a number of extra dice depending on the number and level of Wizards in his army. This is summarised as follows:

Basic number of dice:	2 dice
For each Level 1 Wizard:	+1 dice
For each Level 2 Wizard:	+2 dice
For each Level 3 Wizard:	+3 dice
For each Level 4 Wizard:	+4 dice

Fleeing or dead Wizards do not generate Power dice.

Add any bonus dice provided by magic items, spells, etc.

Dispel dice

The opposing player generates two Dispel dice (four in the case of a Dwarf army) plus a number of extra dice depending on the number and level of Wizards, Runesmiths or Runelords in his army. This is summarised as follows:

Each Runesmith or Runelord: +1 dice

For each Level 1 Wizard: +1 dice

For each Level 2 Wizard: +1 dice

For each Level 3 Wizard: +2 dice

For each Level 4 Wizard: +2 dice

Fleeing or dead Wizards do not generate Dispel dice.

Add any bonus dice provided by magic items, spells, etc.

Cast spells (p.136)

A Wizard may attempt to cast each of his spells once. Nominate which spell is to be cast and the target of the spell. Roll as many Power dice as you wish up to the maximum allowed by the Wizard's level. If you roll equal or better than the spell's casting value the spell is cast. Expended dice are removed from the casting player's pile whether the spell was cast or not. A roll of 1 or 2 is always a failure, regardless of modifiers.

Maximum Power dice rolled for a single spell

Level 1 Wizard: 2 dice

Level 2 Wizard: 3 dice

Level 3 Wizard: 4 dice

Level 4 Wizard: 5 dice

Miscasts

Rolling two or more 1's means the spell has been miscast. The Wizard must roll 2D6 on the Miscast table.

Irresistible Force

Rolling two or more 6's means the spell has been cast with Irresistible Force. It is cast successfully and cannot be dispelled by the opposing player. If two 6's and two 1's are rolled, the spell fails and the Wizard must roll 2D6 on the Miscast table.

Attempt to dispel (p.137)

The opposing player may make one attempt to dispel the enemy's spell irrespective of which unit it was cast on. Roll as many Dispel dice as you wish up to the maximum number you have. If you wish to use any magic items to boost the dispel you must declare this before rolling the dice. If the number rolled is equal to or greater than the score rolled by the casting player, then the spell is dispelled. If two or more 1's are rolled then the dispel fails automatically regardless of the actual score rolled.

Spell succeeds or fails

Apply the effects of the spell as described in the Magic section.

Cast again

If you have more spells to cast and any Power dice left, you may cast again.

Dispel spells in play

Once all spells have been cast, both players may attempt to dispel any spell cast in a previous turn. The opposing player may attempt to do so first. To dispel a spell already in play the dice only have to equal or beat the casting value of the spell. The casting player may then attempt to dispel spells in play counting any remaining Power dice as Dispel dice and following the above procedure. Spells originally cast with Irresistible Force can be dispelled as normal.

4. SHOOTING (p.58)

1. Declare target
2. Measure range
3. Roll to hit
4. Roll to wound
5. Take armour saves
6. Remove casualties
7. Take any Panic tests

Declare target

A model armed with a missile weapon may choose any enemy unit as a target if it lies within the model's 90° fire arc and the line of sight is not blocked by intervening models or terrain. Hedges and walls block line of sight but a model placed directly behind such features may shoot over them and may in turn be shot at. It is possible to target models which are within 2" of the edge of woods or similar terrain but no further. Only models in the front rank of the unit may fire their missile weapons unless the unit is positioned on a hill, in which case up to two ranks may fire. You must shoot first with all weapons that require the range to be guessed.

Measure range

Measure the range to the target. Determine whether targets are in long or short range. Up to and including half the maximum range of the weapon is short range. Long range is between half and the maximum range of weapon. If targets are out of range the shots miss automatically.

Roll to hit

Consult the following table to find the score required on a D6 to hit the target. A dice roll of 1 is always a miss regardless of modifiers.

Firer's BS:	1	2	3	4	5	6	7	8	9	10
D6 Score:	6	5	4	3	2	1	0	-1	-2	-3

To hit modifiers

+1 Shooting at large target

-1 Shooting while moving

-1 Shooting at a charging enemy

-1 Shooting at long range

-1 Shooting at a single character or or skirmishers

-1 Target is behind soft cover

-2 Target is behind hard cover

Soft Cover	Hard Cover
Hedges	Rocks / Rubble
Woodlands	Walls
Bushes	Wooden palisades
Fences / Railings	Buildings
High Grass	Trenches

7+ to hit

If to hit modifiers result in a required score of 7 or more, consult the table below to work out the dice rolls needed to score a hit.

Score needed to hit	Dice rolls needed
7	6 then 4, 5 or 6
8	6 then 5 or 6
9	6 then 6
10	Impossible!

Roll to wound

Cross reference the Strength of the weapon versus the target's Toughness value on the To Wound table on the next page to discover the minimum score required on a D6 to cause a wound.

Take armour saves

Roll a D6 for each wound caused. If the score is equal to or greater than the model's saving throw then the wound has been saved. A roll of 1 always fails.

Armour

Unarmoured	No Save
Light armour	6+
Heavy armour	5+
Shield	+1
Barding	+1
Mounted	+1

Armour save modifiers

Armour saves are modified by the Strength of the attacking weapon. This is summarised on the table below.

Strength of hit	Save modifier
3 or less	None
4	-1
5	-2
6	-3
7	-4
8	-5
9	-6
10	-7

Ward Saves

Ward saves are unmodified by Strength and allow a model a save even when one would not normally be allowed.

A model can have an armour save and a Ward save, but only one Ward save may be taken per wound.

Remove casualties

Remove all casualties from shooting from the rear, or roughly equally from the sides if the unit has only one rank.

Multiple wound casualties

Where models in a unit have more than 1 wound each, remove complete models where possible and note any extra wounds suffered by the unit.

Take any panic tests

If a unit takes 25% or more casualties from shooting it must immediately take a Panic test.

5. CLOSE COMBAT (p.66)

1. Fight Combats
2. Calculate Combat Results
3. Break Tests
4. Panic Tests
5. Flee!
6. Pursue
7. Redress Ranks

Fight combats

Resolve combats one at a time. The player whose turn it is will determine the order of the combats. Models can fight each other if their bases are touching.

Order of combat

Charging units strike first. Otherwise, models strike in order of Initiative. In cases where Initiative scores are the same, the side that won the previous combat round strikes first. If neither side won the previous combat round, roll a D6 and the player scoring highest strikes first.

Roll to hit

Check on the To Hit table on the next page to find the score needed on a D6 to hit. Cavalry models use the rider's Weapon Skill. For ridden monsters, both rider and mount use their own Weapon Skill. A roll of a 1 always misses and a 6 always hits regardless of the relative Weapon Skills.

Defended obstacles

Models behind or in defended obstacles can only be hit on a roll of a 6, regardless of relative Weapon Skills. Once attackers win a round of combat, further combat rounds are fought as normal.

TO HIT CHART

	Opponent's Weapon Skill									
Attacker's Weapon Skill	1	2	3	4	5	6	7	8	9	10
1	4	4	5	5	5	5	5	5	5	5
2	3	4	4	4	5	5	5	5	5	5
3	3	3	4	4	4	4	5	5	5	5
4	3	3	3	4	4	4	4	4	5	5
5	3	3	3	3	4	4	4	4	4	4
6	3	3	3	3	4	4	4	4	4	4
7	3	3	3	3	3	3	4	4	4	4
8	3	3	3	3	3	3	3	4	4	4
9	3	3	3	3	3	3	3	3	4	4
10	3	3	3	3	3	3	3	3	3	4

Roll to damage

Cross reference the attacker's Strength versus the defender's Toughness value on the To Wound table on the opposite page to find the score required on a D6 to cause a wound.

Take armour saves

Roll a D6 for each wound that is caused. If the score is equal to or greater than the model's saving throw then the wound has been saved. A roll of 1 is always a failure regardless of a model's armour save. Saving throw modifiers for Strength apply. See the Shooting section earlier for modifiers.

Remove casualties

Remove casualties from rear ranks but place them behind the unit in order to make calculating the combat results easier. If more wounds are caused than there are models fighting in the combat, excess casualties are removed as normal.

Combat results (p.71)

Add up the number of wounds caused by each side in the combat,
remembering to count those caused to multiple wound creatures not removed as casualties and ignoring those saved by armour or Ward saves. Add any modifiers that apply from the table below. The side with the higher score has won the combat.

Combat resolution bonuses

+1 per rank after the first, to a maximum of +3

+1 If the unit outnumbers the enemy

+1 Standard bearer in front rank

+1 Unit occupies higher ground

+1 Flank attack. If both flanks are engaged the modifier will still only be +1.

+2 Rear attack. Combined with a flank attack, this gives a +3 bonus.

+1 Overkill. A challenger who kills his opponent and inflicts more wounds than the enemy has adds +1 to the combat result score for each excess wound caused.

Losers take Break test

The losing unit in a combat rolls 2D6 and adds the difference between the
combat results. If the score is greater than the unit's Leadership value the unit has broken and will flee once all remaining combats have been resolved.

Panic tests

All units within 6" of a friendly unit that has broken or been destroyed must take an immediate Panic test. This is done after all Break test have been taken, but before fleeing troops are moved.

Flee! (p.74)

Fleeing troops move directly away from the largest enemy unit involved in the combat. If the unit normally moves 6" or less it flees 2D6". If it normally moves more than 6" it flees 3D6". Fleeing units ignore movement penalties for difficult ground and obstacles, but must move around impassable terrain.

Pursuit (p.75)

Victorious units will pursue fleeing troops 2D6" if their normal movement is 6" or less, 3D6" if their normal movement is greater than 6". If this

score is equal to or greater than the score rolled by the unit it is pursuing, the fleeing unit is destroyed. If pursuers do not move far enough to catch the fleeing unit then they move the distance indicated and no further casualties are caused. Pursuers ignore movement penalties for difficult ground and obstacles, but must move around impassable terrain in exactly the same way as fleeing troops.

Pursuers always move their full pursuit distance towards fleeing troops unless this carries them into a fresh enemy unit in which case the pursuit counts as a new charge and is resolved in the following turn. The pursuers count as charging and receive all the appropriate benefits as if they had charged that turn. If the fresh enemy unit causes *fear* or *terror* the pursuing unit does not need to take a Ld test in order to charge them. In subsequent turns the effects of *fear* and *terror* apply as normal.

Restraining pursuit

A unit may restrain its pursuit by rolling equal to or less than its Leadership value on 2D6. You must declare that you are attempting to do so before the dice are rolled to see how far fleeing troops run.

Units that are fighting from a building or other defended position can automatically restrain a pursuit without having to test against their Leadership.

Pursuit off table

A unit that pursues its enemy off the table returns to the same point as where it left in its next turn. It may not charge, but can otherwise move and fight as normal. Wizards may cast spells normally. The unit counts as having moved for the purposes of shooting.

Redress the ranks (p.76)

Formations are now tidied up ready for the next phase. Fleeing units may not redress their ranks.

Units that have won their combat can, if they wish, expand their frontage or lap around the enemy unit they are in contact with.

The overrun rule (p.78)

If a unit slays all its opponents in the first round of combat it may make an Overrun move if it wishes. This will be either 2D6" or 3D6" depending on the unit's Movement value, exactly like flee and pursuit.

If this carries the unit into a fresh enemy unit it counts as a new charge and is resolved in the following turn. The Overrunning unit counts as charging and receives all the appropriate benefits as if they had charged that turn.

A charged unit may only respond to the charge by holding, it may not stand & shoot or flee. If the fresh enemy unit causes *fear* or *terror* the pursuing unit does not need to take a Leadership test in order to charge them. In subsequent turns the effects of *fear* and *terror* apply as normal.

Assuming that the Overrunning unit doesn't encounter any fresh enemy, it moves the distance indicated by the dice roll and is then free to act as normal in its next turn.

WOUND CHART

		1	2	3	4	5	6	7	8	9	10
	1	4	5	6	6	N	N	N	N	N	N
	2	3	4	5	6	6	N	N	N	N	N
	3	2	3	4	5	6	6	N	N	N	N
	4	2	2	3	4	5	6	6	N	N	N
	5	2	2	2	3	4	5	6	6	N	N
	6	2	2	2	2	3	4	5	6	6	N
	7	2	2	2	2	2	3	4	5	6	6
	8	2	2	2	2	2	2	3	4	5	6
	9	2	2	2	2	2	2	2	3	4	5
	10	2	2	2	2	2	2	2	2	3	4

Target's Toughness (columns), Weapon's Strength (rows)

BLAST MARKERS AND FLAME TEMPLATE

To use these templates simply photocopy them, stick them to a piece of scrap card (old cereal packets are ideal) and cut them out.

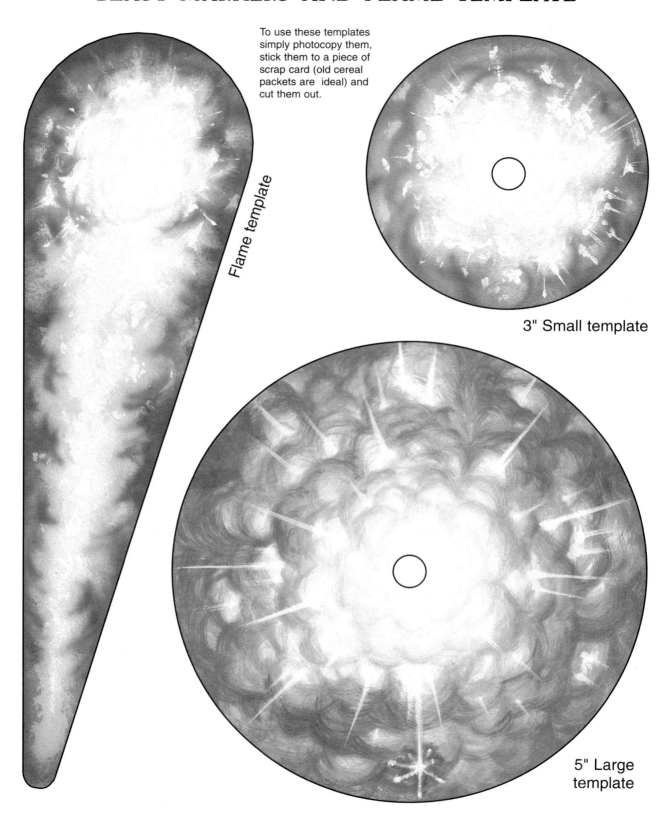

Flame template

3" Small template

5" Large template

Warhammer Glossary

Armour Save

Many models have an armour save. Roll equal to or above the number indicated for a model's save to prevent damage. An armour save can be modified by a variety of factors, such as the attacker's Strength.

Break Test

If your unit loses a combat it must take a Break test. Roll 2D6 and compare the score with your unit's Leadership value, modified by the difference in Combat Results. If you roll over this number, your unit flees.

Cavalry

Models riding creatures with only 1 Wound (such as horses, giant wolves and war boars) are called cavalry. Both rider and mount are considered to be a single model and both are removed from play when the rider loses his last Wound. Attacks are all resolved against the rider only. A calvary model adds +1 to its armour save due to the extra protection offered by the steed.

Champion

Champions are a special type of character who must always be with a unit. Champions must be placed in the front rank of the unit that they are with.

Character

Characters are represented by individual models, which fight as units in their own right. Characters can join units if required. Characters with the ability to cast spells are called Wizards.

Characteristic Profile

Every model in the game is described in terms of its characteristic profile. This profile describes how the creature fights and reacts in the Warhammer world.

Charge Reaction

If a unit is charged it must declare a charge reaction, either Hold, Flee or Stand & Shoot. (see p.45)

Combat Result

The result of a close combat. To calculate the Combat Result add up the number of unsaved wounds you inflicted upon your enemy and apply all of your Combat Result modifiers such as rank bonuses and standards. Your opponent does the same. The unit with the lowest score is the loser and has to take a Break test.

Compulsory Move

A compulsory move is a move that a unit must make whether or not the controlling player wishes to. An example of a compulsory move is the random movement of a Night Goblin Fanatic.

D6

A six-sided dice is referred to in Warhammer as a D6.

Dispel Dice

The amount of dice you have available to dispel magic. You get two basic Dispel dice plus +1 for each 1st or 2nd Level Wizard and +2 for each 3rd or 4th Level Wizard in your army.

Fast Cavalry

Fast Cavalry are a special type of unit and are described on p.117 of the rulebook.

Front, Flank and Rear

The diagram below shows a unit's front, flank and rear.

Flee!

If a unit is forced to flee then you need to see how far it moves. Roll 3D6 if the unit's Movement characteristic is greater than 6", otherwise roll 2D6. The total score on the dice is how far the fleeing unit will move in inches.

Irresistible Force

If you roll two or more 6s when casting a spell, the spell is cast with Irresistible Force. The spell is automatically cast and cannot be dispelled.

Line of Sight

What a particular model can see and therefore charge or shoot at, is normally measured within a 90° arc projected from the front of the model.

Terrain plays an important part in determining line of sight and is discussed in greater depth on p.59 of the rulebook.

Magic items

Magic items are powerful artefacts which confer special powers, bonuses and advantages to models who are carrying them.

Only characters carry magic items (apart from magic banners, which can be carried by certain units).

Manoeuvre

This is the method by which a unit changes direction or changes its formation. Manoeuvring is described further on p.49.

March Move

A march move is double a unit's normal Movement rate. Units that are 8" or closer to an enemy unit may not march move.

Marching units may not perform any manoeuvers, other than wheeling, and may not enter difficult terrain.

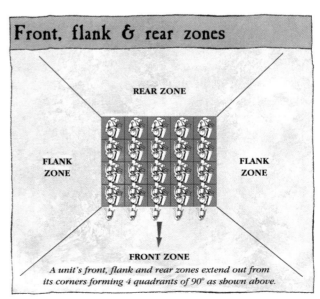

Front, flank & rear zones

REAR ZONE

FLANK ZONE

FLANK ZONE

FRONT ZONE

A unit's front, flank and rear zones extend out from its corners forming 4 quadrants of 90° as shown above.

Miscast

If you roll two or more 1s when casting a spell, a Miscast occurs. The spell is not cast and you have to roll on the Miscast Table to determine what happens to the Wizard who miscast the spell.

Model

Each individual playing piece in a game of Warhammer is defined as a model.

Panic

There are many circumstances in a game of Warhammer that can cause a unit to *panic*. These are listed on p.80 of the rulebook. To make a Panic test roll 2D6. If the total rolled is less than or equal to the Leadership value of the unit forced to make the test, the unit is fine. If the total rolled is greater than the Leadership value of the unit, the Panic test is failed and the unit must flee in the same way as if it had failed a Break test

Power Dice

The amount of dice you have available to cast magic. You get two basic Power dice plus +1 for each level of magic you have in your army.

Pursuit

If a unit flees due to a failed Break test then the winning unit may attempt to pursue. Roll 3D6 if the unit's Movement

characteristic is greater than 6", otherwise roll 2D6. If the total rolled is equal to or greater than the Movement rolled for the fleeing unit then the fleeing unit is caught and destroyed. If the total rolled is less than the fleeing unit's Movement then the fleeing unit remains in play. Whether the fleeing unit is destroyed or not, move the pursuing unit the distance indicated on the dice in inches.

Rally

A unit that is fleeing can attempt to rally in its Movement phase. Roll 2D6 and if the total is equal to or less than the Leadership value of the fleeing unit, it rallies. This means that it stops fleeing and reforms instead. A unit must have at least 25% of its original number of models to attempt to rally.

Rank Bonus

A modifier to the Combat Result. For each rank of four or more models after the first rank you may add +1 to your Combat Result, up to a maximum of +3. The rank bonus is calculated before combat begins.

Re-roll

In some situations the rules allow you a re-roll dice. To re-roll, pick up the number of dice you ORIGINALLY rolled and roll them again. (ie, if you re-roll 2D6 you must roll both dice again not just one of them). The second score counts with a re-roll even if it means a worse result than the first, and no single dice roll can be re-rolled more than once, regardless of the source of the re-roll.

Steed

A steed is any ridden creature which has only 1 Wound.

Turn

Games of Warhammer are split up into turns, with each turn being split into several distinct phases called the

turn sequence. One player takes a complete turn and then his opponent does the same.

Turn Sequence

Turns are split up into a series of steps that are played through in a certain order. This is called the turn sequence. The turn sequence for Warhammer is: Start of Turn, Movement, Magic, Shooting and Close Combat.

Unit

Units are groups of one or more models that fight together on the Warhammer battlefield. Normally all the models in a unit must be in base-to-base contact. Different types of models, such as infantry, cavalry or war machines, make up different type of units. These different unit types are explained on p.40.

Unit Strength

Unit Strength is used to compare the relative impact value of different troops types. Most models have a Unit Strength of 1, but some have more. Cavalry models have a Unit Strength of 2, Ogres and Trolls have 3, and so on.

Ward Save

This is a special type of save. Roll equal to or above the number indicated for a model's save to prevent that model taking damage. This roll is NOT modified by any factors. A Ward save can even stop attacks which do not allow any armour saves.

Weapon

A weapon is what a model uses to attack its enemies. A model may have several different weapons. However, only one of them can be used at any one time (unless a model is armed with two hand weapons). The table on p.93 lists all of the weapon types used in the game together with the effects that that weapon has.

Wizard

A Wizard is a special type of character who has magical powers. The number of Wizards in your army dictates how many Dispel dice and Power dice you get. The Magic section, beginning on p.134 of the rulebook, contains details of how to use Wizards in the Warhammer game.

Notes on scale and measurement

Metric measurements

Warhammer utilises traditional imperial measurements of feet and inches, but it is perfectly possible, if less convenient, to play the game in centimetres should players prefer to do so.

Rather than attempt to translate distances into their metric equivalents, we recommend that players simply double all distances and measure in centimetres. So 12" becomes 24cm, 4" becomes 8cm and so on. This has the effect of slightly reducing the Movement distances and ranges compared to a game played in inches, but this is tolerable and can even be regarded as advantageous in that it allows a game to be played in a slightly smaller area. Randomly generated distances can also be accommodated easily using this method, simply by doubling the scores rolled.

Scale

In Warhammer each model represents a single warrior, monster, machine or whatever, whilst an inch on the tabletop is equivalent to about five feet in real life – the same as the scale height of the models themselves.

Players might correctly point out that in the real world a bowman can shoot an arrow well over 200 yards rather than the paltry 40 yards or so represented by the weapon's maximum Warhammer range of 24". The reason is that we have reduced all measured distances to produce a playable tabletop game. The game's designers reduced distances roughly in the proportion of 1" equals 10 yards, so a bow with a range of 24" is judged to have an effective range of 240 yards. The alternative is to allow the bow a range of 144" and fight all battles in a car park!

A similar observation could be made about the number of models comprising a regiment of troops. It would be impractical though not actually impossible to field regiments comprising hundreds of models, so battles are represented using fewer troops than a literalist might demand. The ten or twenty models in a game unit stand for a regiment of several hundred troops, and for this reason regiments manoeuvre and react as if they were larger formations. As both sides field regiments reduced in size, the relative values are preserved and the results amount to the same thing. To put it another way, if 10 Elves can beat 10 Goblins then 100 Elves can beat 100 Goblins just as convincingly!

Time

Players sometimes ask how long a time is represented by a single turn of play. Does a turn last for hours or does it represent a few minutes? Warhammer has been designed as a game, so events which might realistically last for hours have been compacted into a shorter time though with the same overall results.

A real battle might last for most of a day, whilst a Warhammer game will typically last for 5 or 6 turns on each side. We presume that these 5 or 6 turns represent the passage of about the same number of hours or perhaps slightly longer.

Of course, in reality a warrior can shoot more than 5 or 6 times in that many hours, he can move much further, and so forth. However, we compact events together and cut out all the time spent in inactivity. In a real battle troops stand idle for much of the time, only moving into action when required, and then expending much of their energy all at once.

If you like, think of a Warhammer turn as a short period of activity together with longer periods of idleness, waiting for orders, resting, and so forth. Similarly, just as one model stands for many, so an arrow or crossbow bolt might be thought of as representing a whole shower of missiles fired by shooters who have limited supplies of missiles, and who would soon become tired by repeated firing.

On house rules

Most gamers like to make up their own rules, to invent characters, and perhaps even design their own scenarios. Traditionally, when players reinterpret or modify the game rules, or add new rules of their own, these are referred to as 'house rules' – literally the rules played when gaming at that person's house. When you go round to a fellow enthusiast's home it is only fair to play to his house rules. After all, he is supplying the tea and biccies.

Warhammer lends itself to adaption very well and players should feel free to change, remove, or add to the rules if they wish. For example, why not stage an attack on a Dwarf miners' mule train – you'd have to make up rules for mules and wagons, possibly allowing time for loading up the train with gold, and decide how the loss of their gold affects the miners. As is well known 'gold fever' can have very profound effects on Dwarfs and turn them into unstoppable maniacs!

Obviously it's possible to imagine many ways of representing such a scenario, or any situation, from a raid into underground catacombs to sieges, street riots, bank robberies and bar room brawls.

I know of experienced and very confident players who go even further, changing some of the basic rules themselves to suit their own style of play. And why not indeed! Warhammer is supposed to be a broad set of game rules that hardened veterans can adapt, change or add to as they please.

The only disadvantage of making up your own house rules is that you will have to revert to the normal rules when playing other gamers, or if you're taking part in a formal competition where a common standard is required.

EMPIRE

	M	WS	BS	S	T	W	I	A	Ld	Pts
General	4	6	5	4	4	3	6	4	9	80
Wizard Lord	4	3	3	3	4	3	3	1	8	175
Captain	4	5	5	4	4	2	5	3	8	50
Battle Wizard	4	3	3	3	4	2	3	1	7	60
Halberdier	4	3	3	3	3	1	3	1	7	6
Spearman	4	3	3	3	3	1	3	1	7	6
Swordsman	4	4	3	3	3	1	4	1	7	7
Hand Gunner	4	3	3	3	3	1	3	1	7	8
Crossbowman	4	3	3	3	3	1	3	1	7	8
Archer	4	3	3	3	3	1	3	1	7	8
Knight	4	4	3	4	3	1	3	1	8	25
Pistolier	4	3	3	3	3	1	3	1	7	17
Flagellant	4	2	2	4	4	1	3	2	10	11

ORCS & GOBLINS

	M	WS	BS	S	T	W	I	A	Ld	Pts
Black Orc Warboss	4	7	3	5	5	3	4	4	9	135
Orc Warboss	4	6	3	4	5	3	4	4	9	110
Orc Great Shaman	4	3	3	4	4	3	2	1	8	180
Savage Orc Warboss	4	6	3	4	5	3	4	4	9	125
Sav Orc Gt Shaman	4	3	3	4	4	3	2	1	8	190
Goblin Warboss	4	5	3	4	4	3	4	4	8	65
Goblin Great Shaman	4	2	3	3	4	3	2	1	7	155
Night Gob Warboss	4	5	3	4	4	3	5	4	7	55
Nt Gob Gt Shaman	4	2	3	3	4	3	3	1	6	145
Wyvern	4	5	0	6	5	5	3	3	5	–

	M	WS	BS	S	T	W	I	A	Ld	Pts
Black Orc Big Boss	4	6	3	5	5	2	3	3	8	80
Orc Big Boss	4	5	3	4	5	2	3	3	8	65
Orc Shaman	4	3	3	3	4	2	2	1	7	65
Savage Orc Big Boss	4	5	3	4	5	2	3	3	8	75
Savage Orc Shaman	4	3	3	3	4	2	2	1	7	67
Goblin Big Boss	4	4	3	4	4	2	3	3	7	35
Goblin Shaman	4	2	3	3	3	2	2	1	6	55
Night Gob Big Boss	4	4	3	4	4	2	4	3	6	30
Night Gob Shaman	4	2	3	3	3	2	3	1	5	50

	M	WS	BS	S	T	W	I	A	Ld	Pts
Orc Boy	4	3	3	3	4	1	2	1	7	5
Big'Un	4	4	3	4	4	1	2	1	7	7
Savage Boy	4	3	3	3	4	1	2	1	7	7
Goblin	4	2	3	3	3	1	2	1	6	4
Night Goblin	4	2	3	3	3	1	3	1	5	4
Snotlings	4	2	2	2	3	3	3	3	4	20
Black Orc	4	4	3	4	4	1	2	1	8	10

	M	WS	BS	S	T	W	I	A	Ld	Pts
Boar Chariot	–	–	–	5	5	4	–	–	–	80
Orc Boy	4	3	3	3	4	1	2	1	7	–
Boar	7	3	0	3	4	1	3	1	3	–
Wolf Chariot	–	–	–	5	4	3	–	–	–	60
Goblin	–	2	3	3	–	–	2	1	6	–
Wolf	9	3	–	3	–	–	4	1	–	–

	M	WS	BS	S	T	W	I	A	Ld	Pts
Pump Wagon	2D6	–	–	4	4	3	–	–	–	40
Snotlings	4	2	2	2	2	3	3	3	4	–

	M	WS	BS	S	T	W	I	A	Ld	Pts
Troll	6	3	1	5	4	3	1	3	4	50
Ogre	6	3	2	4	4	3	2	3	7	35
Giant	6	3	3	6	5	6	3	Special	6	200

DWARFS

	M	WS	BS	S	T	W	I	A	Ld	Pts
Dwarf Lord	3	7	4	4	5	3	4	4	10	150
Runelord	3	6	4	4	5	3	4	3	10	140
Thane	3	6	4	4	4	2	3	3	10	60
Runesmith	3	5	4	4	4	2	3	2	9	75
Warrior	3	4	3	3	4	1	2	1	9	7
Miner	3	4	3	3	4	1	2	1	9	10
Thunderer	3	4	3	3	4	1	2	1	9	12
Troll Slayer	3	4	3	3	4	1	2	1	9	9
Giant Slayer	3	5	3	4	4	1	2	2	9	50
Dragon Slayer	3	6	3	4	4	2	3	3	10	90
Daemon Slayer	3	7	3	4	5	3	4	4	10	140
Longbeard	3	5	3	4	4	1	2	1	9	11
Hammerer	3	5	3	4	4	1	2	1	9	11
Iron Breaker	3	5	3	4	4	1	2	1	9	13

HIGH ELVES

	M	WS	BS	S	T	W	I	A	Ld	Pts
Elf Prince	5	7	6	4	4	3	8	4	10	130
Archmage	5	4	4	3	4	3	5	1	9	165
Pegasus	8	3	0	4	4	3	4	2	7	–
Griffon	6	5	0	5	5	4	5	4	8	–
Great Eagle	2	5	0	4	4	3	4	2	8	–
Unicorn	9	5	0	4	4	1	6	2	10	–
Dragon	6	6	0	6	6	6	3	5	8	–
Commander	5	6	6	4	3	2	7	3	9	60
Mage	5	4	4	3	3	2	5	1	8	85
Spearman	5	4	4	3	3	1	5	1	8	10
Archer	5	4	4	3	3	1	5	1	8	12
Seaguard	5	4	4	3	3	1	5	1	8	15
Phoenix Guard	5	5	4	3	3	1	6	1	8	11
Swordmaster	5	5	4	3	3	1	6	1	8	12
White Lion	5	5	4	3	3	1	5	1	8	15
Handmaiden	5	5	5	3	3	1	5	1	8	18
Shadow Warrior	5	4	4	3	3	1	5	1	8	15
Ellyrian Reaver	5	4	4	3	3	1	5	1	8	17
Silver Helm	5	4	4	3	3	1	6	1	8	18
Dragon Prince	5	5	4	3	3	1	6	1	9	25

	M	WS	BS	S	T	W	I	A	Ld	Pts
Tiranoc Chariot	–	–	–	5	4	4	–	–	–	80
Crew	–	5	4	3	–	–	5	1	8	–
Elven Steed	9	3	–	3	–	–	4	1	–	–

DARK ELVES

	M	WS	BS	S	T	W	I	A	Ld	Pts
Dark Lord	5	7	6	4	4	3	8	4	10	130
Sorcerer Lord	5	4	4	3	4	3	5	1	9	165
Dark Pegasus	8	3	0	4	4	3	4	2	7	–
Black Dragon	6	6	0	6	6	6	3	5	8	–
Dark Elf Hero	5	6	6	4	3	2	7	3	9	60
Witch Elf Hero	5	6	6	4	3	2	7	3	9	70
Assassin	6	9	9	4	3	2	10	3	10	100
Sorcerer	5	4	4	3	3	2	5	1	8	85
Warrior	5	4	4	3	3	1	5	1	8	7
City Guard	5	4	4	3	3	1	5	1	8	9
Corsair	5	4	4	3	3	1	5	1	8	10
Scout	5	4	4	3	3	1	5	1	8	14
Witch Elf	5	4	4	3	3	1	5	1	8	12
Harpy	4	3	0	4	4	1	2	1	6	12
Executioner	5	4	4	3	3	1	5	1	8	13
Black Guard	5	5	4	3	3	1	6	1	8	11
Dark Rider	5	4	4	3	3	1	5	1	8	17
Cold One Knight	5	5	4	3	3	1	6	1	8	28

VAMPIRE COUNTS

	M	WS	BS	S	T	W	I	A	Ld	Pts
Vampire Lord	6	7	4	5	5	4	8	5	10	250
Vampire Count	6	6	4	5	5	3	7	4	9	180
Necromancer Lord	4	3	3	3	4	3	3	1	8	140
Zombie Dragon	6	3	0	6	6	6	1	4	8	–
Manticore	6	5	0	6	5	4	3	4	7	–
Winged Nightmare	8	4	0	5	5	3	3	2	5	–

	M	WS	BS	S	T	W	I	A	Ld	Pts
Vampire Thrall	6	5	3	4	4	2	6	3	8	75
Wight Lord	4	4	3	4	4	2	3	3	8	60
Necromancer	4	3	3	3	3	2	3	1	7	65
Skeleton	4	2	2	3	3	1	2	1	5	7
Zombie	4	2	2	3	3	1	1	1	5	5
Ghoul	4	2	2	3	4	1	3	2	5	9
Bat Swarms	1	3	0	2	2	5	1	5	10	50
Dire Wolf	9	3	0	4	3	1	2	1	3	10
Grave Guard	4	3	2	3	4	1	3	1	8	10
Wight Cavalry	4	3	3	3	4	1	3	1	8	24
Vampire Bat	1	3	0	4	4	1	3	2	5	20
Spirit Host	6	2	0	3	3	4	2	4	5	90

SKAVEN

	M	WS	BS	S	T	W	I	A	Ld	Pts
Warlord	5	6	6	4	4	3	7	4	7	90
Grey Seer	5	3	3	3	4	3	4	1	6	205
Vermin Lord	8	8	0	6	6	6	10	6	10	475
Chieftain	5	5	5	4	4	2	6	3	6	95
Warlock Engineer	5	3	3	3	3	2	4	1	5	60
Plague Priest	5	5	3	4	5	2	6	3	6	70
Clanrat	5	3	3	3	3	1	4	1	5	5
Stormvermin	5	4	3	4	3	1	4	1	5	8
Warpfire Team	5	3	3	3	3	1	4	1	5	70
Globadier	5	3	3	3	3	1	4	1	5	25
Packmaster	6	3	3	3	3	1	4	1	6	8
Giant Rat	6	2	0	3	3	1	4	1	4	3
Rat Swarm	6	3	0	2	2	5	1	5	10	50
Plague Monk	5	3	3	3	4	1	4	1	5	8
Skavenslave	5	2	2	3	3	1	4	1	4	3
Gutter Runner	6	4	4	4	3	1	5	1	7	14
Rat Ogre	6	3	0	5	4	3	4	3	4	40
Censer Bearer	5	3	3	4	4	1	4	1	5	18

CHAOS WARRIORS

	M	WS	BS	S	T	W	I	A	Ld	Pts
Chaos Lord	4	8	3	5	5	3	8	5	9	170
Sorcerer Lord	4	5	3	4	4	3	5	1	9	190
Exalted Champion	4	7	3	5	4	3	7	4	9	120
Chaos Dragon	6	6	0	6	6	6	3	6	8	–
Chimera	6	5	0	6	5	5	4	5	8	–
Aspiring Champion	4	6	3	4	4	2	6	4	9	70
Sorcerer	4	5	3	4	4	2	5	1	8	70
Chieftain	4	5	3	4	4	2	5	3	8	50
Chaos Steed	8	3	0	4	3	1	3	1	5	–
Chaos Warrior	4	5	3	4	4	1	5	1	8	11
Marauder	4	4	3	3	3	1	4	1	7	5
Chaos Knight	4	5	3	4	4	1	5	2	9	36
Chaos Hound	6	4	0	4	4	1	4	2	5	12
Chaos Spawn	2D6	3	0	4	4	3	3	D6	10	50
Dragon Ogre	6	4	0	5	5	4	2	3	8	75

	M	WS	BS	S	T	W	I	A	Ld	Pts
Marauder Chariot	–	–	–	5	4	4	–	–	–	80
Marauder	–	4	–	3	–	–	4	1	7	–
C Warrior Chariot	–	–	–	5	5	4	–	–	–	100
Chaos Warrior	–	5	–	4	–	–	5	1	8	–
Chaos Steed	8	3	–	4	–	–	3	1	–	–

BEASTMEN

	M	WS	BS	S	T	W	I	A	Ld	Pts
Beastlord	4	7	3	4	5	3	6	4	9	100
Shaman Lord	4	4	3	4	4	3	3	1	8	190
Chieftain	4	6	3	4	5	2	5	3	8	80
Shaman	4	4	3	3	4	2	3	1	7	80
Gor	4	4	3	3	4	1	3	1	7	6
Ungor	4	3	3	3	4	1	3	1	6	3
Bestigor	4	5	3	4	4	1	3	1	7	11
Minotaur	6	4	3	4	4	3	4	3	9	45

	M	WS	BS	S	T	W	I	A	Ld	Pts
Chariot	–	–	–	5	5	4	–	–	–	70
Gor	–	4	3	3	–	–	3	1	7	–
Tuskgor	7	3	–	4	–	–	2	1	–	–

Unit Size: One chariot with two Gor crew, pulled by two Tuskgors.

BRETONNIANS

	M	WS	BS	S	T	W	I	A	Ld	Pts
General	4	6	3	4	4	3	6	4	9	100
Wizard Lord	4	3	3	3	4	3	3	1	8	175
Hippogriff	6	5	0	5	5	4	5	4	8	–
Pegasus	8	3	0	4	4	3	4	2	7	–
Unicorn	9	5	0	4	4	1	6	2	10	–
Hero	4	5	5	4	4	2	5	3	8	70
Wizard	4	3	3	3	3	2	3	1	7	60
Pegasus	8	3	0	4	4	3	4	2	7	–
Knight Errant	4	3	3	3	3	1	3	1	7	21
Knight of Realm	4	4	3	4	3	1	3	1	8	25
Questing Knight	4	4	3	4	3	1	4	1	8	27
Grail Knight	4	5	3	4	3	1	4	1	9	31
Warhorse	8	3	0	3	3	1	3	1	5	–
Man-at-arms	4	3	3	3	3	1	3	1	7	3
Bowman	4	3	3	3	3	1	3	1	7	8
Squire	4	3	3	3	3	1	3	1	7	4

WOOD ELVES

	M	WS	BS	S	T	W	I	A	Ld	Pts
Elf Lord	5	7	6	4	4	3	8	4	10	130
Mage Lord	5	4	4	3	3	3	5	1	9	140
Elven Steed	9	3	0	3	3	1	4	1	5	–
Forest Dragon	6	6	0	6	6	6	3	5	8	–
Great Eagle	2	5	0	4	4	3	4	2	8	–
Unicorn	9	5	0	4	4	1	6	2	10	–
Hero	5	5	5	4	3	2	6	3	9	60
Mage	5	4	4	3	3	2	5	1	8	65
Glade Guard	5	4	4	3	3	1	5	1	8	8
Archer	5	4	4	3	3	1	5	1	8	11
Dryad	5	4	3	4	4	2	4	2	8	35
Scout	5	4	4	3	3	1	5	1	8	14
Wardancer	5	5	4	3	3	1	6	1	8	20
Glade Rider	5	4	4	3	3	1	6	1	8	18
Treeman	6	5	0	5	6	5	2	4	9	220
Waywatcher	5	4	4	3	3	1	6	1	8	20

LIZARDMEN

	M	WS	BS	S	T	W	I	A	Ld	Pts
Slann Lord	4	5	3	5	6	8	4	6	10	350
Slann Mage-Priest	4	4	3	4	5	6	3	4	9	200
Saurus Hero	4	5	0	5	5	2	3	4	9	100
Skink Hero	6	4	4	4	3	2	5	3	7	65
Skink Shaman	6	2	3	3	3	2	4	1	6	65
Cold One	8	3	0	4	4	1	1	1	3	–
Saurus Warrior	4	3	0	4	4	1	1	2	8	15
Temple Guard	4	4	0	4	4	1	2	2	8	18
Skink Warrior	6	2	3	3	2	1	4	1	6	4
Kroxigor	6	3	0	5	4	3	1	3	9	65
Salamander	6	3	3	4	4	3	2	3	6	90
Lizard Swarm	4	3	0	2	2	5	1	5	10	50
Serpent Swarm	3	3	0	2	2	5	1	5	10	50
Terradon	2	3	0	4	4	1	2	1	3	–
Stegadon	6	2	–	5	6	6	2	4	–	220

Designer's Notes
(Or 'How did this book come into being')

"Imagination is more important than Knowledge."

Albert Einstein

Welcome to the sixth edition of Warhammer! If you are a newcomer, I am sure you can tell that Warhammer is a game which requires a great deal from its players. After all, you must collect and paint your army, learn the rules, prepare a gaming table and scenery and find opponents. This however is what makes the game so fascinating – it is a challenge as well as a pleasurable way to spend time. You can also be rest assured that Games Workshop will happily answer any queries you might have about games, secenery, painting and modelling.

A game of this size is a massive undertaking. It took almost two years to design, develop, playtest, illustrate, edit and lay out the book you now hold. A massive number of people took part in making this game a reality. Editors, artists, miniatures designers, writers, graphic designers, miniatures painters, computer operators, cleaners, Pixie Experts… Thanking all the people who deserve to be credited here is an impossible task! However, you all know who you are – my thanks go to you.

If you are a veteran gamer, you will notice that this book includes many improvements and additional material. For example, Warhammer includes rules for playing many different types of games, from tiny skirmishes and bitter sieges to massive open battles. The Scenarios section includes further ideas and developments, allowing you to play highly unusual and tactically challenging games. It is my hope that this material will inspire players to develop their own scenarios, armies, house rules and additions to the game.

One important thing to remember is that this rulebook is a source for ideas and provides a framework for playing fantasy games. Warhammer was never meant to be a game where the rules become more important than the enjoyment of the players. Having said that, we made it our mission to make the Warhammer rules as playable, clear and free of loopholes as possible. With this in mind we developed it in association with gaming enthusiasts and fans. From gruelling playtest sessions to endless commentary on the finer points of the rules, the games designers have been able to tailor the game to suite the taste of the people who play it. I'd like this trend to continue in the future, and the range of the forthcoming Warhammer Army books is being developed with advice from expert players.

Please feel free to write in and tell what you would like to see in the future, and if you are feeling particularly enthusiastic, why not write some articles yourself? Many Warhammer players have become regular contributors to White Dwarf.

I hope that you'll enjoy playing Warhammer.

Thomas

PLAYER:

RACE:

ARMY:

TOTAL POINTS:

GENERAL: **PTS:**

	M	WS	BS	S	T	W	I	A	Ld	Sv
HERO										
MOUNT										

WEAPONS & ARMOUR:

MAGIC ITEMS:

SPECIAL RULES:

CHARACTER: **PTS:**

	M	WS	BS	S	T	W	I	A	Ld	Sv
HERO										
MOUNT										

WEAPONS & ARMOUR:

MAGIC ITEMS:

SPECIAL RULES:

CHARACTER: **PTS:**

	M	WS	BS	S	T	W	I	A	Ld	Sv
HERO										
MOUNT										

WEAPONS & ARMOUR:

MAGIC ITEMS:

SPECIAL RULES:

CHARACTER: **PTS:**

	M	WS	BS	S	T	W	I	A	Ld	Sv
HERO										
MOUNT										

WEAPONS & ARMOUR:

MAGIC ITEMS:

SPECIAL RULES:

MAGIC SPELLS

WIZARD	LEVEL	SPELLS

WAR MACHINES

UNIT	M	WS	BS	S	T	W	I	A	Ld	Sv	TYPE	EQUIPMENT	SPECIAL RULES	PTS
MACHINE														
CREW														
MACHINE														
CREW														

TROOPS

Unit	M	WS	BS	S	T	W	I	A	Ld	Sv	Type	Equipment	Special Rules	Pts
TROOPER														
LEADER														
TROOPER														
LEADER														
TROOPER														
LEADER														
TROOPER														
LEADER														
TROOPER														
LEADER														
TROOPER														
LEADER														

CAVALRY

Unit	M	WS	BS	S	T	W	I	A	Ld	Sv	Type	Equipment	Special Rules	Pts
TROOPER														
MOUNT														
TROOPER														
MOUNT														
TROOPER														
MOUNT														
TROOPER														
MOUNT														
TROOPER														
MOUNT														
TROOPER														
MOUNT														

CHARIOT

Unit	M	WS	BS	S	T	W	I	A	Ld	Sv	Type	Equipment	Special Rules	Pts

Then did noble Sigmar set aside his crown
My beard is long, and peace reigns in the land
The gods call me to attend their mighty hall.
It is time to appoint the greatest among you
My chiefs, to reign after me.
And this hammer which I hold,
I shall return to the place of its forging
To the safe keeping of the Dwarfs
Unto King Kurgan's hall, that he may
In time of trouble, give it to he that is worthy
Now I take this road alone
To Karaz of the Dwarfs.
And thus did holy Sigmar, mighty warrior
Greatest of men, wise ruler
Pass into legend, not to be seen
Until the time when he returns
Hammer held in hand
To bring victory to mankind.
By the sign of the two-tailed sky dragon

AND FINALLY...

If you are new to Warhammer, you might be feeling a little overwhelmed right now. Collecting and painting spectacular armies of model miniatures and fighting tabletop battles with them is an intensely rewarding hobby, but it can be difficult to know where to start. Well, don't worry, because you're not alone. Far from it, there are Games Workshop enthusiasts all over the world. One of the best ways to meet other Warhammer players and get advice is to visit a Games Workshop retail store. Our stores aren't just shops, they are staffed by commited hobbyists who are only too happy to help demonstrate painting and modelling tips, tactics and lots of other helpful stuff. They also run special workshops and gaming events. You can find your nearest store by writing to the addresses shown below, or telephoning the numbers given. There's lots of information on our website, including hobby projects, tips and advice, and of course, all the latest releases. There's even an online store so you can expand your armies from the comfort of your own home.

www.games-workshop.com

£5 UK

$9.99 US

$14.99 CDN

A $15

Mail Order Starter Pack!

Fill in the form below and send it, along with your cheque or postal order (for UK and Australia please make payable to Games Workshop Ltd. For USA and Canada please make payable to Games Workshop). This offer includes free postage and packing. Alternatively, phone your order through to the relevant telephone number.

USA
Games Workshop Mail Order
6721 Baymeadow Drive,
Glen Burnie,
MD 21060-6401, USA
Tel: 1-800-394-4263

CANADA
Games Workshop Mail Order
1645 Bonhill Road, Units 9-11
Mississauga, Ontario,
Canada, L5T 1R3
Telephone 1-888-498-7655

UK
Games Workshop Mail Order
Willow Road, Lenton,
Nottingham, NG7 2WS.
Tel: 0115 91 40000.

AUSTRALIA
Games Workshop Mail Order
P.O. Box 576,
Ingleburn. N.S.W 1890
Australia Telephone: (02) 98296111

We'll send you the following items for a special offer price: 3 x Citadel miniatures, 7 x 4ml Citadel Colour paints (red, black, green, white, yellow, blue and Boltgun Metal), a Citadel paint brush, a World of Hobby Games brochure and a paint guide. Offer applies for a limited period while stocks last. Follow the instructions on the form overleaf and we'll return the special offer through the post plus loads more exciting Games Workshop information. Miniatures may vary subject to availability.

Mail Order Starter Pack!

Name:_____

Address:

_____

_____ Postcode/Zip:_____

Method of Payment and amount (tick relevant boxes):

Credit Card ☐ /Switch ☐ No: _____

Card issue No: _____

Expiry Date: ____/___

Cheque ☐   Postal Order ☐

£5 (if you live in the UK) $9.99 USA (if you live in the US)

$14.99 CAN (if you live in Canada) A$15 (if you live in Australia)

White Dwarf is the essential magazine for anyone interested in the Games Workshop hobby. Each issue contains articles, rules supplements, painting and collecting information and a whole lot more. Visit your local Games Workshop stockist or phone our Mail Order hotlines to reserve your copy now.

UK Mail Order hotline: 0115 91 40000,
USA Mail Order hotline: 1-800-394-4263,
CDN Mail Order hotline: 1-888-498-7655,
AUS Mail Order hotline: (02) 98296111